Civil Rights
and
Liberties

Principles of Interpretation

ANDREA L. BONNICKSEN
Eastern Illinois University

Mayfield Publishing Company

TO MY PARENTS

Esther M. Bonnicksen
and
Arnold E. Bonnicksen

Copyright © 1982 by Mayfield Publishing Company
First edition 1982

Library of Congress Catalog Card Number: 81-81279
International Standard Book Number: 0-87484-476-2

Manufactured in the United States of America
Mayfield Publishing Company
285 Hamilton Avenue, Palo Alto, California 94301

Sponsoring editor: Chuck Murphy
Managing editor: Judith Ziajka
Manuscript editor: Kathleen MacDougall
Designer: Nancy Sears
Cover illustration: Geoffrey Moss
Compositor: TechGraphics
Production manager: Michelle Hogan
Printer and binder: George Banta Company

Contents ‖

ACKNOWLEDGMENTS

I wish to thank Charles H. Sheldon of Washington State University for his helpful and encouraging comments on this manuscript, especially in its early stages. I also wish to thank Tom Tharp and Bruce Scism for their useful suggestions on the penultimate draft of the manuscript and Marie Tipsord and Karen Huebner for their help in editing the book.

Introduction ‖

Most of our civil rights and liberties are contained in the first ten amendments to the Constitution. Others are found in the text of the Constitution and still others in the amendments added since ratification of the Bill of Rights in 1791. The Constitution defines our freedoms in cursory language, thus leaving it to the courts to flesh out the document's skeletal guarantees. The cases that make their way through the courts each year provide fertile occasion for constitutional interpretation. Few novelists could compete with these cases in their range, variety, and sometimes bizarre protagonists and story lines. Consider the case of one McDowell, a purse-snatcher put on probation after his third offense and ordered to wear tap shoes every time he left his house in order to warn purse-toting women of his approach.[1] McDowell appealed the requirement, claiming that it violated his Eighth Amendment right to be free from "cruel and unusual punishments." The tap shoes, he argued, were akin to wearing a badge proclaiming "I am a thief;" they also kept him from football and other normal activities.

Another case involved a Colorado-based religious sect known as the Yhwhhoshua Assembly; the sect opposed hospitals, unemployment insurance, neckties, haircuts, and many other appurtenances of modern society. Soon after its founding by Laycher Gonzales, the sect came into conflict with the state over the issue of drivers' licenses. Under Colorado law drivers were required to have a photograph of themselves on their licenses, but the Yhwhhoshua Assembly, which also opposed all drawings, paintings, and photographs, went to court claiming the law violated the First Amendment rights of its members.[2]

A third case sent a young Oklahoman to court over his inability to buy beer.[3] Under Oklahoma law a man had to wait until he was twenty-one to buy beer; but women, who, the legislators assumed, were less likely than men to drink and drive, were allowed to buy beer at eighteen. One Mr. Boren argued that the law unfairly discriminated against men and violated the Fourteenth Amendment equal protection clause.

The source of civil liberties cases is inexhaustible and no two disputes are exactly alike. The one element that does underlie all litigation, however, is the presence of a conflict between two parties. In civil liberties an individual or group feels the government has violated one or more constitutional guarantees and so goes to court, calling upon judges as arbiters to weigh the conflicting interests and decide which should predominate in the balance. At root a judge's decision is individual and personal. Yet it is not made on a blank slate. Judges draw upon two centuries of judicial interpretation and an even older body of English common law to ferret out biases and weights in existing constitutional law. In short, the balance is tilted at the outset and judges approach each case with a more or less systematic set of principles. The aim of this book is to apprise the reader of these principles so that he or she too may approach unresolved civil liberties issues with something less than a blank slate.

The observer first hearing of McDowell and his tap shoes or Laycher Gonzales's grievance may feel an instant marshalling of sympathies: "But of course tap shoes are cruel and unusual" or "Certainly a religious sect should be exempt from a law intruding on its beliefs." While one's elemental feeling is important, spontaneous reactions are incomplete and not altogether satisfying. The serious observer of civil liberties will want to approach new controversies with more substantive forewarning about how judges will approach the issue and what the authoritative ruling is likely to be. This book identifies clues to watch for in cases so that the observer can position new conflicts and can understand the background from which judges will approach an issue. The book does not promise prediction—no court watcher has developed formulas for predicting judicial outcomes—but it does give the reader enough information on court doctrine to approach controversial cases with foresight. Personal opinion based on emotional reaction is one thing, but opinion grounded on doctrine is a preferable way to review the issues arising each year in the area of civil rights and liberties.

TWO THEMES

This book develops two themes, each based on the supposition that judges approach civil liberties issues with more or less systematic ground rules. The first theme is that the Supreme Court Justices watch some free-doms more carefully than others. As a result their decisions, taken as a whole, have created gradations *among* the guarantees in the Bill of Rights. It is important to understand that these gradations exist because the Justices have devised specially strict tests for reviewing laws that intrude on highly valued freedoms such as the First Amendment liberties. These tests are weighted in favor of the liberty and against the law. They give an immediate clue about the likely outcome of the case and affect how the judges will approach the issue at hand.

A second theme is that the Court's decisions have created gradations *within* the individual guarantees in the Bill of Rights. As interpreted, each guarantee is multidimensional and open to patterned application depending on which facet of the right is at issue. To illustrate, "free press" appears at first glance to be a monolithic liberty, but as interpreted by the Court it is actually tripartite. Over the decades the Court has developed different free press principles for each of the major media that make up the press. Thus, free press means one thing when the written press is at stake, something different when motion pictures are involved, and yet something different for broadcasting. The Court has created a similar gradation for Fourteenth Amendment equal protection. It greatly distrusts laws that classify on the basis of race but is less concerned with laws that fall heavily on poor people, gays, or linguistic minorities. Thus, the Justices will quickly strike down a law segregating public swimming pools by race but will uphold a rule expelling homosexuals from the mili-tary. These differential rulings are not necessarily inconsistent; instead they show a distinct gradation within the broad concept of "equal protection of the laws." The guarantee means one thing when racial classifications are at issue, another when other classifications are involved.

CHAPTER-BY-CHAPTER ORGANIZATION

The book starts off in Chapter 1 with a review of the process of constitu-tional interpretation. Because the book reviews the many legal principles of civil rights and liberties, it is forced only to highlight the historical evolution of each. But, as one student of constitutional law has written, "[o]ur legal rules are subjected to a ceaseless process of reevaluation and inner modification, sometimes of erosion, sometimes of accretion. The name by which a rule is known may remain unchanged for decades, but meanwhile its content may, by almost imperceptible steps, have been materially changed."[4] In order to ensure that the reader be exposed at least once to the rich bases of legal doctrine, Chapter 1 uses one principle, the exclusionary rule, and the case most visibly linked to it, *Mapp v. Ohio*,[5] to review the main forces influencing the Supreme Court as it shapes legal doctrine. The principles covered in subsequent chapters do not receive similarly detailed treatment, but they too are a product of the forces outlined in Chapter 1.

Each remaining chapter is devoted to a particular guarantee in the amendments to the Constitution. Chapter 2 focuses on First Amendment freedom of speech. It reviews the tests that make free speech a preferred freedom within the Bill of Rights and then shows gradations of this freedom. As it turns out, the Court values some expression less highly than others. In fact, it finds some expression so lacking in social utility that it excludes the utterances from First Amendment "speech" altogether. Chapter 3 focuses on First Amendment free press and shows how the doctrine varies according to the medium in question. This feature of Court doctrine is especially problematic given the steady blurring of the media used by the press. Today all-movie channels such as Home Box Office, Showtime, and Movie Channel bridge the gap between motion pictures (normally seen in the theaters) and broadcasting (normally seen in the home). Cable television frees broadcasting from its reliance on a scarce public resource—the electromagnetic spectrum—and brings it closer to the print media, which relies on freely available resources. These and other technological changes call into question gradations in doctrine that the Court feels are necessary in light of differences in the media themselves.

Chapter 4 turns to another First Amendment liberty—freedom of religion—which is guaranteed by the free exercise clause and the establishment clause. The relationship between the two clauses is Janus-like and the Court is continually under pressure to reconcile the contradictory tug each exerts on the other. Analysis of Court doctrine hints that the Court favors one over the other when the two conflict, thereby creating a loose but identifiable gradation within the system of free religion.

Chapter 5 moves to the Fourteenth Amendment and its equal protection clause. Congress added this guarantee against arbitrary government classifications after the Civil War but, interpreted narrowly by the Supreme Court, equal protection lay dormant for nearly a century. Beginning in the 1940s, however, at the hands of a different Court and in a new social context, the Justices engineered equal protection to its present status as a veritable giant in the area of civil rights, using it to strike down hundreds of racially discriminatory laws. The chapter underscores the varying clout of the equal protection clause, pointing out how the guarantee is powerful for attacking racial discrimination, less effective for sexual discrimination, and least powerful for contesting laws that classify on the basis of age, occupation, or economic status. This gradation calls into question equal protection's usefulness as a tool for ensuring the rights of women, the handicapped, prisoners, and other groups newly testing their political strength.

Chapter 6 examines the due process clause, which is found both in the Fifth Amendment (guiding the federal government) and the Fourteenth Amendment (directing the states). Due process has many uses, one of which is to serve as a conduit through which the Court "adds" new rights to the Constitution. The Constitution is a living document, not a stagnant parchment, and some rights rest in its spirit rather than its literal words. One frequently asserted right that is nowhere found in the Constitution but that has constitutional status nonetheless is the right to privacy. Chapter 6 uses privacy as a case study to illustrate constitutional expansion, the special role of due process within that growth, and thereby the high status of due process within the amendments to the Constitution.

Chapter 7 discusses four amendments—the Fourth, Fifth, Sixth, and Eighth—in a review of the procedural rights of criminal defendants and others deprived of their liberty in some way by the state. Here again extant doctrine shows the Court valuing some guarantees more highly than others. For example, the Court has dramatically stretched the Sixth Amendment right to counsel to cover stages in the criminal process that both precede and follow the trial itself, but it has declined to confer the same high status to other procedural rights and has kept the range of their coverage narrow. In view of the large number of procedural guarantees in the Constitution, the volume of criminal law cases is prodigious. It is a fortunate counterbalance to the detail of Chapter 7 that many of the stranger protagonists and more intriguing plots in civil liberties cases emerge from the annals of criminal procedure. Here Mr. McDowell and his tap shoes join with a motley assortment of other criminal defendants to challenge the Court to put order on a fundamental question in civil liberties—What protections must the state offer before depriving its subjects of their basic freedoms?

NOTES

1. *People v. McDowell,* 130 Cal. Rptr. 839 (1976).
2. See *The New York Times,* October 21, 1979, p. 52.
3. *Craig v. Boren,* 429 U.S. 190 (1976).
4. Lewis Mayers, *The American Legal System* (New York: Harper and Row, 1964), p. 348.
5. 367 U.S. 643 (1961).

CHAPTER ONE

Constitutional Interpretation: A Case Study

Justice Robert Jackson once said, "There is no such thing as an achieved liberty; like electricity, there can be no substantial storage and it must be generated as it is enjoyed or the lights go out."[1] Later he pursued the same point, saying that liberty "is something never established for the future, but something which each age must provide for itself."[2] To a great degree the definition of our rights and liberties rests with the Supreme Court. As the Justices have developed and generated the nuances of our constitutional liberties, they have transformed the Bill of Rights from a flat surface to an undulating landscape with distinct inter- and intra-liberty gradations. It is the purpose of this chapter to unveil some of the things that influence how judges, and particularly the Supreme Court Justices, interpret the Constitution. The method is first to outline the key elements of judicial reasoning and then to illustrate with a case study based on the evolution of a Fourth Amendment rule of law. The goal is to help explain some of the inconsistencies and contradictions within our rights and liberties as interpreted by judges. The Bill of Rights is a rocky terrain. How did it get to be that way? In large part it is because each interpretation is a product of a different time and different set of judicial influences. As the judiciary seeks to even out doctrinal

1

inconsistencies in sometimes inelegant ways, one must keep in mind that no one guaranteed that the continual generation of liberties mentioned by Justice Jackson would reach us flawlessly and without trouble.

ELEMENTS OF JUDICIAL REASONING

The things that influence judges are so numerous that courses on the judicial process are now standard fare in pre-law curricula. Increasingly, students of the judicial mind experiment with correlational analysis, small-group observation, content analysis, and other techniques to uncover systematic patterns in judicial deliberation that help explain and predict how judges will act as they entertain the appeals reaching them every year. No matter how sophisticated the empirical methods of analysis, however, there is always a part of judicial reasoning that defies explication. Chief Justice Hughes was well aware of this when, at seventy-seven, he advised the newly appointed Justice William O. Douglas: "Justice Douglas, you must remember one thing. At the constitutional level where we work, 90 percent of any decision is emotional. The rational part of us supplies the reasons for supporting our predilections."[3] Thus, judicial reasoning is the product of subjective as well as objective reasoning, of freely admitted as well as secretive bias, and of recognized as well as latent influences.

The key elements of judicial reasoning may be grouped into four categories: the legal norm of precedent; the social and political milieu; internal group dynamics; and the personal preferences of individual judges. Arranging these factors into a simple model that puts relative weights on each, we put the legal norm of precedent at the center and the other factors at the periphery (see Figure 1.1). This suggests that judges enter their chambers with a predisposition to base their decisions on precedent but that external pressures, the dynamics of the court, and personal predilections chip away at this predisposition.

Precedent involves a respect for tradition. It "consists of an official doiing over again under similar circumstances substantially what has been done by him or his predecessors before."[4] It cautions jurists to "stand by decisions and not to disturb settled matters"[5] and is based on the principle of *stare decisis*, which means "let the decision stand." Judges are educated in the skills of heeding precedent because formal legal training encourages students to seek out precedent. The few lawyers who go on to become judges thus face informal pressures to follow precedent when deciding cases. All judges are policymakers who make authoritative decisions having the weight of law. But when judges veer

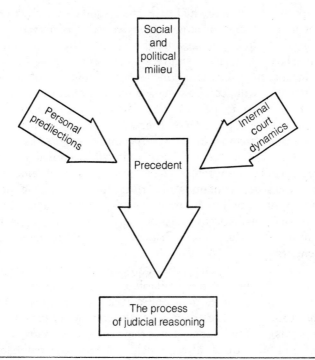

FIGURE 1.1
KEY ELEMENTS IN THE PROCESS OF JUDICIAL
REASONING

too far from precedent, they provoke controversy. The community expects only small policy changes from judges; it does not tolerate dramatic deviations from precedent that produce dramatically new policy.

It makes sense to put precedent at the center of a model of judicial reasoning because that is where precedent is *supposed* to be. The modus operandi of our system of jurisprudence is the incremental development of legal principles. Precedent lies at the heart of this process. But it is only an imperfect guide that counsels rather than dictates. Among other things, it is limited by the perplexing diversity of cases. Strictly speaking, *stare decisis* can hold only if the facts of a present case exactly match the facts of some previous case.[6] But such precision does not occur in practice. Even if lawyers essentially pose the same questions in two different cases, they will speak for unique historical settings and sets of protagonists. It may not be much, but *something* will be different in each new case.

The potpourri of individual cases means judges must actively build precedent much as ancient stonemasons constructed city fortresses by painstakingly sculpting stones until they fit together. Judges will distinguish the current case from preceding cases in order to define a new twist in the law, they will ignore one line of law in favor of another, and in rare cases they will actually reverse a line of precedent.[7] This is all to say that there is no one precedent but there are many intersecting and sometimes conflicting precedents. Precedent is not a grandiose pillar of isolated doctrine; it comes in many forms and strengths. As one student notes, there is no single "correct" answer in constitutional interpretation but rather "two, three, or ten."[8] The Constitution, in the eloquent prose of Justice Cardozo, contains "not rules for the passing hour, but principles for an expanding future."[9] The document's vague and general provisions—its "magnificent indefiniteness"[10]—allow judges to retire interpretations developed in one historical era that are inappropriate in the present era.

By recognizing that there are many correct answers, the question then becomes, "Which of the available correct answers will the court select—and why?" If more than one correct answer exists, "the court always has to select."[11] Precedent lies at the core of our model of judicial decision-making because judges enter their chambers *predisposed* to use precedent. But other things affect which of the precedents the judge will choose and why. It is to a review of these other influences on decision-making that we now turn.

External pressures are one category of influences on judicial decision-making. An important external pressure is the political milieu. A classic example is the Court's "switch in time" of 1937. Attending to President Roosevelt's threat to add two members to the Court so that a newly composed Court would uphold Roosevelt's proposed anti-Depression program, the Justices in 1937 stopped their active scrutiny of economic legislation and let one of Roosevelt's projects pass constitutional review. A similar attentiveness to public opinion occurred in the 1950s when the Court handed down some unusually restrictive free speech decisions—probably with the time's anti-Communist fervor in mind. Another external pressure comes from social mores. Consider what Justice Bradley said in an 1873 concurring opinion in a decision upholding a law that forbade women from practicing law in Illinois: "The natural and proper timidity and delicacy which belongs to the female sex evidently unfits it for many of the occupations of civil life. . . . The paramount destiny and mission of woman are to fulfill the noble and benign offices of wife and mother."[12] No Justice would dare make that claim today. The judicial reaction to sex-based laws in the

1980s is a far cry from the judicial reaction of the 1870s in large part because society's notions of what is "natural" and "proper" for women have changed dramatically over the last century. External cues also reach the Justices through legal research published in law journals and cited by lawyers who argue their cases before the Court. The Court's decision in 1972 striking down the death penalty as then applied illustrates the attention Justices pay to empirical data gathered by scholars.[13] Noting that racial minorities were executed in disproportionate numbers, the Court concluded that the death penalty arbitrarily discriminated against minorities and could not stand under the Constitution.

A second set of forces affecting decision-making is the internal dynamism of the court. An uncertain judge may vote simply as his or her brethren vote. Or, a judge may vote as he or she does simply because he or she is in the position to cast the swing vote. At the Supreme Court level, the Chief Justice's power to assign the writing of Court opinions may also affect how a Justice votes; the implied promise that he can write the majority opinion may be enough to move an uncertain Justice to the majority position.[14] These and other small-group dynamics are hard to measure, but one may safely guess that they influence the reasoning behind a decision even if not the decision itself.

A third set of variables involves the predilections of individual Justices. No matter how persuasive the data spread before him, no matter how loud the public opinion, no matter how strong the precedent, a Justice may reason in quixotic ways. Students of the judicial mind do their best to quantify personal preferences of judges. A common method is correlational research in which key background factors of judges are combined with data on how people with these backgrounds usually act in order to predict how judges with X characteristic will be likely to vote on an issue in a given case. To illustrate, consider the work of one researcher, who found that Democratic judges were more likely than Republican judges to vote on the side of labor unions when unions and corporations conflict.[15] Of course, this method is limited, as President Eisenhower found after appointing Republican Earl Warren as Chief Justice of the Supreme Court. "The biggest mistake I made as President," he later mused as he pondered the liberal ways of his supposedly conservative appointee.

The complex judicial mind does much to sabotage efforts to generalize about judicial reasoning. Even the Justices themselves reveal perplexity about the bases for their decisions. Said Justice Stewart in admitting he had no set definition of obscenity: "I know it when I see it." Here the judge himself realized he had no clear "rational" basis for his decision. Or, consider a quirk in the decisions of Justice Black. Black was an "absolutist" who interpreted the First Amendment to say that the state could pass *no* laws interfering with free speech. Yet Black upheld restrictions on symbolic speech such as picketing. Students were unsure how to explain this apparent inconsistency but Justice Douglas suggested a possible explanation in his memoirs. It seems that after Black was nominated to be Supreme Court Justice in 1937 word of his past membership in the Ku Klux Klan came to light and, as part of the controversy that followed, protesters picketed Black's house. It was Justice Douglas's opinion that the resulting trauma to Black and his family "colored his [Black's] decisions in all subsequent cases involving picketing, mass demonstrations, and protest marches."[16] It is possible Justice Black himself was not aware of the subconscious reasons for his impatience with picketing.

To identify variables that affect judicial reasoning is to open up a potentially limitless task. Although intriguing, the topic will be dealt with only briefly in this book, the main purpose of which is to describe the outcome of judicial reasoning rather than the process through which judicial interpretations came to be made. The model presented here puts precedent at the core of judicial reasoning, suggesting that it is the central force around which the other variables revolve. The model represents a middle position between two extreme models of judicial reasoning. It rejects the idea that judges are like automatons who, in slot-machine fashion, dispassionately pick precedent as the basis for their decisions. Likewise, it rejects the idea that judges are guided solely by their own predilections. Instead, it suggests that judges do seek precedent and do use it to justify their decisions. But *which* precedent they choose depends upon the idiosyncracies of the judges as well as external and internal factors. Hence, two Justices may arrive at completely different conclusions while each sticks to the spirit of judicial self-restraint. There are always loose and unconnected ends. Part of the fascination of civil liberties is to watch new Justices and new Courts attempt to take disjointed lines of law and transform them into creative legal principles. Our rights and liberties are not tidily defined, but it is important to understand that the process arbitrating them is not neat either.

In the following section, we use a case study to illustrate this model in action. The study is based upon an interpretation the Court gave the Fourth Amendment—an interpretation that made a legal principle known as the "exclusionary rule" a part of the meaning of that amendment. It is the story of the rise and fall of this principle; it is a story that places precedent at its core. It traces the Court's building of precedent to reach a particularly sweeping decision in the 1961 case of *Mapp v. Ohio*[17] and then traces ways in which the Court has since undermined the exclusionary rule. Particularly in the post-*Mapp* decisions, one can see the way other variables erode the drawing power of precedent.

THE *MAPP V. OHIO* CASE

The Fourth Amendment bars the government from carrying out "unreasonable searches and seizures":

> The right of the people to be secure in their persons, houses, papers, and effects, against unreasonable searches and seizures, shall not be violated, and no warrants shall issue, but upon probable cause, supported by oath or affirmation, and particularly describing the place to be searched, and the persons or things to be seized.

The amendment is sparely written; it does not define "unreasonable" or "search" or "seizure" nor does it say what will happen if the state carries out an unreasonable search and then tries to introduce the evidence in court. The amendment's cryptic wording leaves it up to judges to put meaning into it. One way they have done this is by pairing a principle known as the "exclusionary rule" with the amendment's sweep. The exclusionary rule holds that evidence seized in violation of the Fourth Amendment is inadmissible in court. It is a deterrent meant to prod police into obeying the Fourth Amendment by telling them that the evidence they seize improperly is useless.

The exclusionary rule was unknown a century ago, but today it is the "supreme law of the land,"[18] held by the Court to be "part and parcel" of the Fourth Amendment and binding on both state and federal authorities. The Court escorted the rule from oblivion to constitutional status gradually in a series of decisions capped by the 1961 case of *Mapp v. Ohio*, which dramatically brought state courts under the command of the exclusionary rule. In the years since *Mapp* the Court has had second thoughts about the rule and has contracted its sweep. Thus, with hindsight, we see that *Mapp* was a pivotal case in that the Court expanded the rule in the pre-*Mapp* years but has limited it in the post-*Mapp* decades. Experience, new data on the rule's effectiveness, new Justices, and the passage of time have put the Fourth Amendment on a curvilinear course. The exclusionary rule's jagged pilgrimage can be used to illustrate the varied principles at work in the Court's interpretation of the Constitution.

The facts of *Mapp v. Ohio* are colorful, originating with a chance event one afternoon in May 1967 that made Dollree Mapp, a Cleveland woman living on the fringes of the boxing world, an unwitting—and probably unwilling—participant in American jurisprudence. Privy to a tip that Ms. Mapp was harboring a criminal suspect in her home and also owned gambling paraphernalia, three city police officers went to Mapp's house on May 23 and rang the doorbell. Mapp looked out her window and asked the police what they wanted. They refused to answer, whereupon Mapp called her attorney who advised her not to let the officers in unless they had a search warrant.

The officers staked out Mapp's home and "laid siege" on it for two hours until they were joined by four more officers and Mapp's attorney. The attorney asked to see the warrant; the officers said they did have a warrant but refused to show it to the attorney. Instead, they forced their way into the house, breaking a glass door in the process, and found Ms. Mapp standing on the staircase. Mapp snatched the alleged warrant, stuffed it in her dress, and in the melee that followed she was manhandled, handcuffed to an officer, taken to her bedroom, and pushed onto the bed. Officers then searched the house, down to such unlikely items as a suitcase, photograph album, and personal papers. They did not find the fugitive nor did they find gambling paraphernalia.[19] What they did find were sexually explicit pamphlets, photographs, and a pencil doodle in a trunk in the basement. The officers arrested Mapp for possession of obscene materials and she was later convicted of this crime.[20]

Mapp had ample grounds for claiming that the police violated her Fourth Amendment right to be free from unreasonable searches and seizures. Courts may disagree on the nuances of an unreasonable search and seizure, but they do agree that a search is unreasonable if officers have time to secure a search warrant but do not. When Mapp appealed her conviction, then, she argued among other things that her conviction should be reversed because it was based on evidence illegally seized by police.[21] Mapp gained a victory of sorts when the Supreme Court of Ohio agreed that the doodle and photographs had been seized illegally. The judges flatly expressed doubt that a bona fide warrant ever existed; they noted that the alleged warrant simply disappeared after the officer retrieved it from Mapp's dress, was never recorded in police ledgers, and was not introduced as evidence in the trial. If no warrant existed, then the search had taken place in violation of the Fourth Amendment of the U. S. Constitution and of Ohio law.[22] Mapp's victory was only symbolic, however, because the Ohio court went on to uphold her conviction. In the judges' way of thinking, the Fourth Amendment forbade unreasonable searches but did not exclude the fruits of unreasonable searches from a criminal trial.

However quixotic the judges' decision might seem, it was perfectly in accord with existing law at that time. When Mapp made her unexpected entrance into the courthouse corridors, the question of what to do with illegally seized evidence was in a state of disarray. Consider that fifty-one criminal justice systems operate in this country—one for the federal government and one for each state. In 1961 the exclusionary rule had only partially made its way into the national system of criminal justice. At the turn of the century the Supreme Court had said that the exclusionary rule must apply in federal courts when the evidence had been illegally seized by federal agents.[23] Then in the 1950s it had said that the rule must apply in state courts when the evidence had been seized illegally by federal agents.[24] Finally, in 1960 it held that the rule must apply in federal courts when state officers had illegally seized evidence.[25] One part of the quadrangle was left to be filled: the Court had not yet extended the exclusionary rule to state courts when state officers were involved. It was Ms. Mapp's misfortune that her case fell into this remaining category. Twenty-six states had taken it upon themselves to apply the exclusionary rule in their courts but twenty-four relied on other methods to enforce the Fourth Amendment. Ohio was among these twenty-four; so this explains why the Ohio Supreme Court made light of the fact that Mapp had been convicted on the basis of illegally seized drawings and photographs.

Mapp next appealed to the U. S. Supreme Court, arguing in part that her conviction ought to be overturned because it was based on improperly seized evidence. Mapp's lawyers were farsighted enough to base the appeal on other grounds as well; they knew that the decade before the Court had explicitly said the states need not be bound by the exclusionary rule.[26] The Court's earlier decision made it unlikely the Justices would reverse their position that each state should decide for itself whether to adopt the rule. Thus, Mapp based her challenge primarily on the anti-obscenity law under which she was convicted. She had no inkling the Court would pick up on her procedural claim and use her appeal as a forum for reversing the position it had taken a decade before—and so would hold that the rule must apply to state courts where state officials were involved. As it turned out, Mapp's case became *Mapp v. Ohio*, a landmark decision that gave the exclusionary rule universal application in the United States, made the rule part and parcel of the Fourth Amendment, and thus elevated the rule to constitutional status. *Mapp v. Ohio* amounted to what one journalist called "the most significant limitation ever imposed on state criminal procedure by the Supreme Court in a single decision."[27] We may infer that Dollree Mapp was delighted with the decision inasmuch as it framed a new liberty and gave her the first chance to savor it. The decision was a menacing one to the twenty-four states that had not adopted the rule, however, because it left officials fearing that criminals would go free as police and trial judges found themselves strapped by the demands of a "reasonable" search and seizure.

Mapp v. Ohio is worthy of special study for several reasons. First, it was a decision meant to resolve a very real and very practical problem. Before *Mapp*, police in many states had no true incentive for obeying the Fourth Amendment. Two of the more common methods of encouraging police to conduct reasonable searches were ineffective. One was stationhouse censure, in which officers with a history of slipshod or brutal searches could expect reprimand from their superiors. The other was a lawsuit filed by the victim of an illegal search. In practice, neither effectively deterred sloppy or heavy-handed searches; officers were rarely penalized within their stations and very few victims sued. Among other things, victims were usually in jail and could not conduct a decent lawsuit, they did not have the money or will for a court battle, they wanted to forget the entire episode if they were found not guilty, and they knew it was unlikely their suit would be successful. The theory behind the exclusionary rule is that officers will conduct legal searches so that the evidence they seize will be admitted into court.

Second, *Mapp* illustrates constitutional interpretation of the sort that enlarges the Constitution's meaning. *Mapp v. Ohio* put an extra twist to the meaning of the Fourth Amendment by saying that the amendment not only forbids unreasonable searches and seizures but also contains a way of enforcing this command. Third, the decision was unusual in that it represented a reversal of a previous Court position. To understand the basis for this decision, we will first look at the case law preceding *Mapp*. We will see that even though *Mapp* was a landmark decision that surprised many people, it did have a foundation in precedent and was not a "revolutionary" decision. Later we will see how the Court is now building post-*Mapp* case law in a way that forewarns a decrease in the scope of the exclusionary rule.

EVOLUTION OF A DOCTRINE: PRE-*MAPP* CASE LAW

Six cases relate directly to *Mapp v. Ohio* and show how the Court subtly builds a doctrine while at the same time essentially adhering to preceding case law. Each buttressed the exclusionary rule and gave the majority Justices in *Mapp* a line of precedent to tap in the 1961 decision itself. These cases are *Boyd v. United States* (1886),[28] *Weeks v. United States*

(1914),[29] *Wolf v. Colorado* (1949) (in part),[30] *Rochin v. California* (1952),[31] *Rea v. United States* (1956),[32] and *Elkins v. United States* (1960).[33] Several other cases relate indirectly and show how a separate line of law interacts with the central line to produce a new legal interpretation.

Beginning with the six direct antecedents of *Mapp v. Ohio*, we see a variety of protagonists, including a dealer in glass, a lottery enthusiast, an abortionist, and a drug user, all of whom were, as was Dollree Mapp, convicted of a crime on the basis of illegally seized evidence. The saga begins with *Boyd v. United States*, a decision handed down in 1886. The facts of *Boyd* are not particularly gripping, involving as they do a sheet of plate glass seized by customs officials, and the decision itself is not especially noteworthy. What is important about *Boyd* is what the Court said in passing as it struck down part of the customs law. In a passage known as "dicta" (that part of a written opinion tangential to the central argument and not crucial to it), the Court added a new meaning to the Constitution by saying that the Fourth and Fifth Amendments "run almost into each other." The Fourth Amendment, we know, forbids unreasonable searches and seizures. The Fifth Amendment's self-incrimination clause makes it unconstitutional for a person to be compelled to be a witness against himself or herself. In *Boyd* the Court opined that when the government improperly seizes someone's property and then uses the fruits of that seizure in court, it runs headlong into the Fifth Amendment by forcing the defendant to be a witness against himself or herself. The Court did not go so far as to say the Constitution forbids the introduction of illegally seized evidence in court, but it did let it be known that it thought the practice was constitutionally shaky.

It took a lottery ticket seller to provide the occasion two decades later for the Court to transform its *Boyd* dicta to official Court doctrine. The case, *Weeks v. United States*, involved a man arrested for using the mails to send lottery tickets and coupons in violation of federal law. Federal agents seized incriminating evidence without a search warrant and a federal judge admitted it in court. The man, Mr. Weeks, was convicted and his appeal eventually reached the Supreme Court. Citing *Boyd*, Mr. Weeks claimed that the warrantless search violated his Fourth Amendment rights and the admission of the fruits of that search violated his Fifth Amendment rights against coerced testimony. In an unanimous vote the Court agreed, thereby marking the "birth" of the exclusionary rule as a constitutional doctrine. In its majority opinion, the Court noted that the exclusionary rule gave meaning to the Fourth Amendment and its absence left the amendment a cipher that "might as well be stricken from the Constitution."[34] Weeks's case involved federal officials and federal courts, however, and the Court made it clear that its decision said nothing about whether the exclusionary rule bound state officials and state courts.

Three decades later the Court addressed this question in the 1949 case of *Wolf v. Colorado*. Here Colorado's authorities had reason to believe that a physician, one Dr. Wolf, had been performing illegal abortions. They went to his office without a search warrant and took his appointment book. The prosecutor later introduced the book in court and used it to convict the doctor of violating the state anti-abortion statute. Dr. Wolf appealed, arguing that the exclusionary rule ought to apply in state courts as well as in federal courts. To entertain this claim the Court looked at two separate lines of law. One was the precedent of *Boyd* and *Weeks*, which said that the exclusionary rule was essential to the Fourth Amendment, at least when federal officials and courts were involved. But *Wolf* involved state courts and state police; in order to apply the rule here the Court would have to take a leap. To understand why, consider the second line of precedent to which the Court looked. It involves what is known as the "incorporation" of the Bill of Rights and dates back to 1833 and the case of *Barron v. Baltimore*.[35]

Barron v. Baltimore is one of the more important cases handed down by the Supreme Court. It involved one Mr. Barron, whose wharf was left useless after the city of Baltimore paved its streets in such a way that gravel from diverted streams settled in his property. Barron claimed that he was entitled to payment as provided for in the Fifth Amendment's guarantee that the government cannot take private property without compensating the owner. The question before the Court concerned just *who* was required by the Fifth Amendment to compensate property owners. Up to that time it had been assumed that the Fifth Amendment, along with the others in the Bill of Rights, applied only to the federal government. But here was Barron, asking that the State (or more precisely, the city of Baltimore) should come under the dictate of the Fifth Amendment too. The Supreme Court rejected Barron's claim, however, holding that the Bill of Rights applies only to the federal government. It was up to the states to ensure free speech, freedom from unreasonable searches, and other civil rights and liberties for their citizens either through statute or state constitutions. In the Court's eyes, the founding fathers framed the Constitution as a document for the federal government. State governments were untouched unless specifically mentioned in that document.

The ruling of *Barron v. Baltimore* went largely unquestioned until Congress added the Fourteenth Amendment to the Constitution in 1868. That amendment specifically limited the state governments and said in part that "No *State* shall . . . deprive any person of life, liberty, or property, without due process of law. . . ."[36] It mirrored the words of the Fifth Amendment, which warned the *federal* government not to deprive any person of "life, liberty, or property, without due process of law. . . ."[37] The identical words raised the question of whether the Fourteenth Amendment's framers intended "life, liberty, or property" to encompass all the rights in the Bill of Rights, that is, to act as a conduit through which the state governments would be brought within the dictates of the first ten amendments. This idea is known as the "incorporation" (also called "nationalization") of the Bill of Rights, and it suggests that the Fourteenth Amendment due process clause "incorporates" or absorbs some or all of the provisions in the Bill of Rights and makes them binding on the states.

A look at the debates surrounding the framing of the Fourteenth Amendment reveals some evidence that the members of Congress did intend the amendment's due process clause to incorporate the Bill of Rights,[38] but the more compelling evidence shows otherwise. The Supreme Court, at any rate, rejected the incorporation argument. In 1884, 1900, and 1908, it held that neither indictment by a grand jury (Fifth Amendment),[39] trial by jury in criminal cases (Sixth Amendment),[40] nor the guarantee against compulsory self-incrimination (Fifth Amendment)[41] applied to the states via the due process clause of the Fourteenth Amendment.

In 1925 the Court indicated it was changing its mind about incorporation. By this year new Justices had joined the bench and state governments had posed new threats to freedom of speech by passing restrictive laws in the aftermath of World War I. Free speech was an especially valuable liberty; should the Court sit idly by when states passed laws that would not withstand constitutional muster if passed by the federal government? In the 1925 case of *Gitlow v. New York*,[42] the Court in dicta made a weighty declaration:

> For present purposes we may and do assume that freedom of speech and of the press—which are protected by the First Amendment from abridgment by Congress—are among the fundamental personal rights and "liberties" protected by the due process clause of the Fourteenth Amendment from impairment by the States. . . .[43]

Commentators today treat the *Gitlow* decision as the first incorporation case, one in which the Court applied First Amendment freedom of speech to the state governments.[44] Apparently the Court saw *Gitlow* as an incorporation case too because it next incorporated First

Amendment press, religion, and assembly[45] in decisions which opened the possibility that other amendments might also apply to the states via the due process clause.[46] What the Court needed now was a "test" or formula for determining which guarantees were to be incorporated. It bequeathed this test in the 1937 case of *Palko v. Connecticut*, in which it said it would incorporate other provisions if they were "of the very essence of a scheme of ordered liberty."[47] It left unclear which guarantees, other than those in the First Amendment, met this test.[48]

We return now to Dr. Wolf's appeal and see that to persuade the Court to bring the states under the control of the Fourth Amendment Wolf had to argue successfully that the protection against unreasonable searches and seizures was "of the very essence of a scheme of ordered liberty." Thus, the Court had to look at its incorporation precedent as well as its exclusionary rule precedent to reach a decision. As it turned out, the Court in *Wolf v. Colorado* handed down a bifurcated decision. On the one hand, in what will be called *Wolf A* for the purposes of this chapter, the Court expanded upon *Boyd* and *Weeks* and incorporated the Fourth Amendment's guarantee against unreasonable searches and seizures. Noting that a citizen's privacy is "basic to a free society" and is "therefore implicit in the 'concept of ordered liberty'," the Court held that the Fourth Amendment, with its power to protect a citizen's privacy "against arbitrary intrusion by the police," is "enforceable against the States, through the Due Process Clause." But this holding gave little solace to Dr. Wolf because in what will be called here *Wolf B*, the Court declined to treat the exclusionary rule as part of the Fourth Amendment and thus did not "incorporate" the rule along with the Fourth Amendment.

The *Wolf B* decision reflected the Court's concern for preserving our federal form of government. The Court noted that at the time fewer than one-half of the states used the exclusionary rule to enforce compliance with the Fourth Amendment. This meant that over one-half of the states used some other method. Who was to say that the exclusionary rule was the single best deterrent of unreasonable searches? Might it not be better to let the states experiment as they saw fit and perhaps come up with a more effective deterrent in the process? The Justices concluded that it would be unwise to impose the rule on all the states; to do so would quash a healthy experimentation,[49] and it had long been a tradition in American politics to encourage diversity among state policies. The same judicial distaste for imposing national standards also explains the Court's reluctance to incorporate other guarantees in the Bill of Rights.

After *Wolf v. Colorado* the Court's composition changed and, as it turned out, the Justices built upon the *Boyd-Weeks-Wolf A* line of law and gradually expanded the exclusionary rule's application. In the 1952 case of *Rochin v. California*,[50] the Court barred from a state court evidence seized by state police in a truly shocking manner. The case involved one Antonio Rochin, a luckless Californian who ran afoul of three deputy sheriffs. Armed with a tip that Rochin sold narcotics, the deputies burst into his house and found him sitting on his bed with his wife. Seeing two capsules on a bedside stand, the deputies asked, "Whose stuff is this?" whereupon Rochin promptly swallowed the capsules. The deputies then "jumped on" the flailing Rochin, handcuffed him, and took him to the hospital where they forcibly pumped his stomach to recover the capsules. Tests showed the capsules contained morphine and the state used them to convict Rochin of illegal possession of drugs. Reviewing Rochin's appeal, the Supreme Court unanimously concluded that the deputies breached the limits of reasonableness.[51] Their conduct offended "canons of decency and fairness" and patently violated due process of law. It did more than "offend some fastidious squeamishness or private sentimentalism about combatting crime too energetically." It "shocked the conscience," and Fourteenth Amendment due process forbade evidence seized in such a search from being admitted in a criminal trial.[52]

Next, the Court frustrated a circumlocutory practice that had arisen because the exclusionary rule applied in federal but not state jurisdictions. In what was known as the "silver platter doctrine," officers in one jurisdiction (state or federal) seized evidence illegally and handed it over to authorities in the other jurisdiction (federal or state) for use in criminal proceedings. Although technically permissible, this practice undermined the exclusionary rule in federal courts by creating an incentive for unlawful searches and seizures. In the 1956 case of *Rea v. United States*, the Court forbade federal officers from turning over illegally seized evidence to the states[53] and, in the 1960 case of *Elkins v. United States*, the Court forbade the introduction in federal courts of evidence seized illegally by state officers.[54]

CULMINATION OF PRECEDENT: *MAPP V. OHIO*

By the time Dollree Mapp's appeal reached the Supreme Court in 1961 the Justices had built a line of precedent made up of *Boyd*, *Weeks*, *Wolf A*, *Rochin*, *Rea*, and *Elkins* that they could tap to support a universal application of the exclusionary rule. On the other hand, Justices not believing the exclusionary rule should apply to the states could construe these cases differently or tap other precedents, most notably *Wolf B* and previous decisions in which the Court had declined to incorporate one or the other provisions in the Bill of Rights. As is always the case in constitutional interpretation, the Justices could hope for no single "correct" answer but instead had to select among several possible answers.[55]

The majority of the Justices in *Mapp v. Ohio* looked to *Boyd*, *Weeks*, *Wolf A*, *Rochin*, *Rea*, and *Elkins* to support their holding that "all evidence obtained by searches and seizures in violation of the Constitution is, by that same authority, inadmissible in a state court." Speaking for five members of the Court, Justice Clark referred to *Boyd v. United States* to point out the constitutional basis of the exclusionary rule.[56] Singly the Fourth and Fifth Amendments guarantee the individual's security; together they create a formidable defense of privacy. For the state to introduce illegally seized evidence in court is "tantamount to coerced testimony" and violates the privacy established by the Fourth and Fifth Amendments and guaranteed to state citizens via *Wolf A*. Next Justice Clark had the task of explaining the Court's reversal of *Wolf B*. He did this first by citing *Rochin*, *Rea*, and *Elkins* to show that other precedents now superseded *Wolf B*. Then he pointed out the changes in law enforcement between 1949, when the Court decided *Wolf*, and 1961, when Mapp's appeal reached the Court. In 1949 only one-third of the states used the exclusionary rule so the Court logically could encourage the states to experiment with different methods of securing compliance with the Fourth Amendment. By 1961, however, a growing number of states had adopted the exclusionary rule, thereby indicating the rule's efficacy and making the call for experimentation less compelling.[57] In his opinion Justice Clark also expressed discomfort at the ease with which law enforcement personnel flouted the Fourth Amendment in defiance of *Wolf A* and noted that "[n]othing can destroy a government more quickly than its failure to observe its own laws. . . ." Finally, he made a telling comment about judicial reasoning when he noted that Mapp's holding "is not only the logical dictate of prior cases, but it also makes *very good sense*."[58] Never far from the marshalling of precedent and pertinent facts, "intuition," "informed guess," and "good sense" are key features of judicial reasoning.[59]

Three Justices dissented in *Mapp*, largely because they saw the case as an inappropriate one in which to apply the exclusionary rule to the states. *Mapp* was primarily a First Amendment case.[60] Police arrested Dollree Mapp for possessing obscene material and her pivotal point on appeal was that Ohio's obscenity law violated her freedom of expression. Mapp raised the question of illegally seized evidence only secondarily and the ACLU mentioned it almost as an afterthought in the written brief it submitted to the Court. When one of the Justices asked Mapp's attorney during oral argument whether he urged the Court to reverse *Wolf B*, the attorney "expressly disavowed any such purpose."[61] The dissenting Justices thus made clear their displeasure that the Court handed down an important decision on criminal procedure in a context precluding an open weighing of the merits of the exclusionary rule. Justice Harlan charged the majority Justices with "simply '[reaching] out' to overrule *Wolf*." Noting that the Court had heard numerous appeals involving illegally seized evidence during the past three terms, he wondered why the Court chose *Mapp* over these more appropriate cases.

Justice Clark did attempt to justify ruling on the Fourth rather than First Amendment issue in *Mapp*,[62] but with hindsight we can point to an unspoken reason the Court chose *Mapp* as a forum for expanding the exclusionary rule. In the decade following *Mapp* the Court exhibited great activism in criminal procedure[63] and showed its partiality to setting national standards in criminal adjudication. This is evident by the flurry of incorporation cases that followed *Mapp* and became the Warren Court's legacy (see Table 1.1).[64] If the Justices were predisposed to extend the exclusionary rule, then *Mapp* provided a suitable context. Presumably the Court would want to hand down such a ruling in a case involving a *clearly* unreasonable search and a minor crime. *Mapp v. Ohio* was such a case because the officers' rough treatment of Dollree Mapp and their inability to produce a search warrant made their actions

TABLE 1.1
CASES NATIONALIZING MAJOR PROVISIONS OF
THE FIRST EIGHT AMENDMENTS AFTER
MAPP V. OHIO

Case	Amendment	Provision
Mapp v. Ohio (1961)	4	Search and seizure
Robinson v. California (1962)	8	Cruel and unusual punishment
Gideon v. Wainwright (1963)	6	Right to counsel
Malloy v. Hogan (1964)	5	Self-incrimination
Pointer v. Texas (1965)	6	Confrontation of witnesses
Klopfer v. North Carolina (1967)	6	Speedy trial
Washington v. Texas (1967)	6	Compulsory process for obtaining witnesses
Duncan v. Louisiana (1968)	6	Trial by jury in serious crimes
Benton v. Maryland (1969)	5	Double jeopardy

SOURCE: Table prepared with the aid of Milton C. Cummings, Jr., and David Wise, *Democracy Under Pressure* (New York: Harcourt Brace Jovanovich, 1974), p. 123.

plainly unreasonable and because Mapp's crime of possessing obscene materials in a basement trunk was inconsequential. It is not inconceivable that the Court acted on this opportunity when it arose, knowing that any public hostility to its decision would be less than if it were to hand down the same ruling in a case involving arguably reasonable police acts and a heinous crime.

Apart from the supporting precedent, which was *Mapp*'s strong point, the decision as a whole was weak, amounting to "one of the untidiest decisions in which the modern Court has announced a salient constitutional doctrine."[65] The arguments were imprecisely thought out, the case for and against the exclusionary rule not fully aired due to the fact that no one expected search and seizure to be the pivotal issue, and the Court was closely divided by a 5 to 3 vote. Perhaps if these conditions had been different, *Mapp* would not have fallen victim to the assault that followed.

DEVOLUTION OF A DOCTRINE: POST-*MAPP* CASE LAW

One commentator said of the exclusionary rule at the time of *Mapp*: "The rule had run its full course. Initially conceived by way of dictum in 1886, the rule had become the supreme law of the land three-quarters of a century later."[66] Unforeseen by the commentator, however, has been the post-*Mapp* snubbing that amounts to a "slow strangulation"[67] of the exclusionary rule. The Court's unhappiness with the rule in general and *Mapp* in particular relates, first, to the burden *Mapp* imposed on state procedure.[68] Twenty-four of the fifty states did not abide by the exclusionary rule in 1961 so the decision "required a complete change in the outlook and practices of state and local police."[69] Until 1961 police in these twenty-four states gathered evidence in a variety of ways with little regard for the legality or ethics of the methods and habitually failed to obtain search warrants.[70] State officials feared that *Mapp* would cause administrative entanglements as police overburdened courts with requests for search warrants. They also feared *Mapp*'s concern over the legality of search techniques would stymie criminal prosecution.[71] For the most part these fears have been unrealized, but *Mapp* did launch what one observer called an "avalanche"[72] and another a "great torrent"[73] of search and seizure appeals. At the time of *Mapp* no one was really sure just what a legal search and seizure was and jurists have defined it on a case-by-case basis. Writing fifteen years after *Mapp*, one observer noted that the number of Fourth Amendment decisions reported in the United States Code Annotated ballooned after *Mapp*, occupying 683 pages in a sample volume.[74]

Second, legal commentary shifted from a positive tone before *Mapp* to a more sour tone after.[75] Until *Mapp* the Court and legal community simply assumed the exclusionary rule deterred unlawful searches and seizures. But the Court's lament in *Mapp* that it had no evidence to test this assumption prompted legal scholars, whose interest in empirical inquiry was coincidentally growing anyway, systematically to investigate the rule's alleged merits. The findings have been equivocal.[76] Even though this equivocation is partly caused by the efforts of scholars to devise appropriate research designs, the failure of scholars clearly to demonstrate the rule's supposed benefits bodes ill for a doctrine that had few enthusiastic supporters to begin with. The Burger Court's lengthy references to these ambivalent findings in at least one post-*Mapp* decision indicate the Justices are aware of and probably influenced by the rule's muddled record.[77]

Third, the Court has changed composition since 1961. Today only two of the Justices who participated in *Mapp*, William J. Brennan, Jr., and Potter Stewart, remain on the Court. President Nixon appointed four of the new Justices with the avowed intent of introducing less active Justices to the high bench,[78] and the Burger Court has indeed retreated from some of the national standards the Warren Court imposed on state criminal procedure.[79] The public greeted some of the Warren Court's decisions with hostility (the fact that they coincided with the "crime wave" of the 1960s did little to quell public anger), so the Burger Court comfortably has been able to disavow some of its predecessor's decisions without fear of public backlash. The Warren–Burger Court transition seems to support one observer's comment that the area of criminal procedure is the "most susceptible to swings of the pendulum after a change of [Court] personnel" in part because it is the area "of the Supreme Court's work that is most prone to emotional reaction."[80]

For these reasons, the exclusionary rule has met with an unsympathetic Court in the post-*Mapp* years. The decision itself, the public and scholarly reaction to it, and the Court's changing composition have created a new perspective from which the Justices approach the rule. Now, rather than lauding it, the Justices are explicitly critical. Some, including the Chief Justice, call the rule a dastardly policy that has "imprisoned" the legal community, exacted a "monstrous price,"[81] and amounts to a "Draconian, discredited device in its present absolutionist form."[82] "[The] exclusionary rule has been operative long enough to demonstrate its flaws," writes Chief Justice Burger. "The time has come

to modify its reach. . . ."[83] It is still too early to tell whether the Court will directly attack the rule by reversing past decisions or simply launch an indirect attack by refusing to hear appeals based on alleged violations of the rule and by strategically construing certain features of criminal procedure.[84] In either case the Court is now building up an anti-exclusionary rule reservoir that will allow it to attack the rule with the benefit of precedent if it decides to reverse any of the principles established in the *Boyd-Weeks-Wolf A-Rochin-Rea-Elkins-Mapp* line of law.

First, the Court's post-*Mapp* dicta about the exclusionary rule is decidedly negative. Although not critical to the case at bar, dicta form a reserve that a future Court can tap as it justifies its decisions. For example, in its *Mapp* opinion the Court elevated to official doctrine the dicta of *Boyd v. United States* pairing the Fourth and Fifth Amendments. Also, the Court refers in its incorporation decisions to the dicta of *Gitlow v. New York* that bound the states to protect First Amendment free speech. Because dicta are elastic, with no rigid demarcations between them and a decision's essence,[85] the Court can steer today's negative dicta (about the exclusionary rule, for example) to a more central place in future decisions.

Second, the Court has lent a new interpretation to *Mapp* by denying the exclusionary rule its constitutional status.[86] Whereas in *Mapp* Justice Clark pointed out the rule's constitutional origin, the Burger Court now calls the rule a "*judicially created* remedy designed to safeguard Fourth Amendment rights generally through its deterrent effect *rather than* a personal constitutional right of the party aggrieved."[87]

Third, the Court has refused to expand the scope of the rule. In *United States v. Calandra* (1974)[88] the Court declined to extend the rule to grand jury proceedings, and in *United States v. Janis* (1976)[89] it refused to extend the rule to federal *civil* proceedings when state officials had seized evidence illegally but in good faith. These decisions allow the Court to show its displeasure with the rule without reversing past rulings. They also make up a bridge that helps the Court disengage itself gradually from the rule, in keeping with the norm of judicial incrementalism.

Fourth, the Court has cut into the rule's enforcement. Until recently, state prisoners who claimed they were convicted on the basis of illegally seized evidence could petition federal courts to review the constitutionality of their convictions. In *Stone v. Powell* (1976), however, the Court blocked this avenue of appeal by ruling that state prisoners given "an opportunity for full and fair litigation of a Fourth Amendment claim" in state courts could not seek relief in federal courts.[90]

The Court has based its post-*Mapp* decisions on experience rather than precedent. Calling experience "the 'most dependable' of all teachers,"[91] the Court in *Calandra*, *Janis*, and *Stone* has set the rule in a cost–benefit framework by asking whether experience shows the rule's benefits outweight its costs. So far it sees the rule's costs, but not its benefits, as clear and demonstrable. Justice Powell described three supposed costs in *Stone v. Powell*. First, the rule bars pertinent evidence from trials and thereby makes criminal convictions harder to obtain. Second, the exclusionary rule has subtly transformed the nature and purpose of the criminal trial. By focusing attention on the technical procedures of search and seizure, argues Justice Powell, the rule upstages the trial's real function, which is to decide a defendant's guilt or innocence. Third, Justice Powell fears the disproportionate concern with procedure the rule creates will ultimately "generat[e] disrespect for the law and the administration of justice" and thereby injure the judicial process.[92] Given this perspective, along with the Court's concern over the inability of scholars clearly to demonstrate that the rule actually does deter illegal searches and seizures, the Justices assume only grudgingly that the rule "works" in enforcing the Fourth Amendment in criminal cases. However, the Court refuses to assume the rule works in the grand jury (*Calandra*) or in civil proceedings (*Janis*). Noting that to extend the rule to these other contexts would produce only "speculative and undoubtedly minimal" benefits, the Court refuses to extend its reach.[93]

It may not be completely fair to use *Mapp* and the exclusionary rule to illustrate the influences on judicial reasoning in that both are entwined in search and seizure, one of the murkiest areas of constitutional law. However, the Court's struggle to develop a working and practical exclusionary rule policy does show the interplay of precedent, experience, common sense, personal philosophies, public reaction, and other forces affecting judicial decisions. The central role of precedent is reaffirmed in Table 1.2, which summarizes selected cases touching upon the exclusionary rule, and Figure 1.2, which presents these cases in graphic form. One can see from Table 1.2 and Figure 1.2 that the Court has supported and criticized the rule gradually, in two great waves, rather than sporadically.

Justice Douglas once said that "happily, all constitutional questions are always open."[94] Happily or not, the exclusionary rule remains an incompletely resolved issue. Table 1.2 shows that litigants have already challenged the admissibility of illegally seized evidence in assorted situations. One can expect more of these diverse appeals. However, recent Court decisions lead one to predict the Court will not expand the exclusionary rule's reach unless it is persuaded that doing so clearly will deter Fourth Amendment violations.

TABLE 1.2
EXCLUSIONARY RULE PRECEDENTS:
SELECTED CASES

Situations in which the Court expanded the rule's scope	Situations in which the Court declined to expand its scope
Weeks v. United States (1914) Evidence seized illegally by federal officials is to be excluded from criminal trials.	*Burdeau v. McDowell* (1921) The federal exclusionary rule applies only to evidence seized by government officials, not to evidence seized by private persons.
Wolf v. Colorado (1949)—*[Wolf A]* Evidence seized illegally by state officials violates the Fourth Amendment as it applies to the states via the Fourteenth Amendment.	*Wolf v. Colorado* (1949)—*[Wolf B]* The exclusionary rule is not mandatory when state officials and state courts are involved.
Rochin v. California (1952) Evidence seized by state officials in a manner that shocks the conscience cannot be admitted in state courts.	*Walder v. United States* (1954) Illegally seized evidence may be introduced in a trial to impeach the credibility of a witness.
Rea v. United States (1956) Evidence seized illegally by federal officials cannot be turned over to state officials for use in a state criminal trial.	*Linkletter v. Walker* (1965) *Mapp v. Ohio* is not to be applied retroactively; to do so would not serve the stated purpose of deterrence of illegal searches and seizures.
Elkins v. United States (1960) Evidence seized illegally by state officials cannot be turned over to federal officials for use in a federal criminal trial.	*Alderman v. United States* (1969) The exclusionary rule does not apply to a person such as a co-defendant who is not directly the victim of the unlawful search.

SUMMARY

The exclusionary rule establishes a liberty, or a freedom of the individual from governmental actions. It arises from a judicial interpretation of the Fourth Amendment that says the amendment's bar against unreasonable searches and seizures is meaningless if officials are free to introduce in court evidence seized in violation of it. The scope of this liberty has fluctuated markedly over the last half-century. Its sojourn is not unique in that time and the differing needs and experience of each generation cause the Court's interpretation of all rights and liberties to expand and contract.

TABLE 1.2 continued

Situations in which the Court expanded the rule's scope	Situations in which the Court declined to expand its scope
Mapp v. Ohio (1961) Evidence seized illegally by state officials cannot be admitted in state courts (overturns *Wolf B*). *One 1958 Plymouth Sedan v. Pennsylvania* (1965) The exclusionary rule applies in "quasi-criminal" proceedings, such as forfeiture proceedings.	*Harris v. New York* (1971) Illegally seized evidence may be used to impeach the credibility of the defendant who voluntarily testifies at his or her own trial even though the same evidence cannot be introduced as part of the government's "case in chief." *United States v. Calandra* (1974) The exclusionary rule does not apply in federal grand jury proceedings. *United States v. Janis* (1976) The exclusionary rule does not apply to civil proceedings when the evidence was seized illegally in one jurisdiction and handed over to the other jurisdiction. *Stone v. Powell* (1976) State prisoners, when given an opportunity for appeal of a Fourth Amendment claim in state courts, may not seek a writ of federal habeas corpus on the ground that the evidence used to convict them was illegally seized.

This chapter uses the exclusionary rule and the case intimately associated with it, *Mapp v. Ohio*, to illustrate judicial interpretation of the broadly outlined rights and liberties in the Bill of Rights. It is a process that juxtaposes tightly reasoned logic with reliance on "common sense" and isolated precedents. It is a process in which Justices criticize their brethren's rationale and then use a similar rationale to justify their own position. It is a process with a steady undercurrent of subjectivity — but how can it be otherwise when the Constitution's words are vague, abstruse, and defy simple translation? As Anthony Amsterdam remarked, "The work of giving concrete and contemporary meaning to

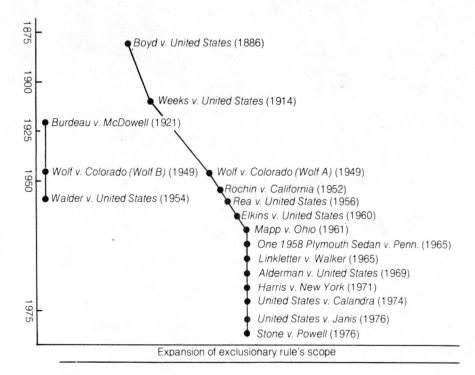

FIGURE 1.2
SELECTED CASES IN THE HISTORICAL
DEVELOPMENT OF THE EXCLUSIONARY RULE:
EARLY EXPANSION AND LATER PLATEAU

that brief, vague, general unilluminating text written nearly two centuries ago is inescapably judgmental."[95]

Precedent helps limit the breadth of subjectivity. Legal training and the nature of the legal process predispose judges to base their decisions on preceding case law. But precedent gives only partial answers to legal issues, and normally more than one possible line of precedent exists for any one question. Thus, judges are influenced by more than an array of precedents. They also review the experience different jurisdictions have with a rule of law, the range of legal commentary, and the various "publics" interested in the outcome of a case. By selectively choosing from these influences, judges construct a rationale for their decisions. A judge's personal philosophy determines which of the precedents and experiences he or she will select. When, for example, Justice Clark argues that public disrespect of the judicial process comes from the *absence* of the exclusionary rule and Justice Powell claims disrespect comes from the rule's *presence*, we have reached a point of individual differences beyond which further explication becomes difficult.

Supreme Court Justices do not participate in the same kind of open decision-making that allows us to examine the legislative or the executive mind. As a result certain "loose ends" cannot be explained and do not tidily fit into a model of judicial decision-making. For example, the image of impartiality surrounding the Court prevents it from publicly acknowledging some of the things that affect its decisions.[96] It is conceivable that the Court rooted *Mapp* in its distrust of state police, but it could never reveal this publicly. The remainder of this book discusses other legal doctrines that are also the outcome of the interplay between reasonably stable precedent and such numerous if less certain influences on judicial decision-making as secrecy in deliberation, individual differences, and inevitable compromises.

Questions for Thought

1. The exclusionary rule is only one of many concepts associated with Fourth Amendment search and seizure. Others include the stop and frisk doctrine of *Terry v. Ohio*, 392 U.S. 1 (1968) and the plain view doctrine of *Harris v. United States*, 390 U.S. 234 (1968). These too can be dissected as was the exclusionary rule. Take a Fourth Amendment concept and a landmark case associated with it and reconstruct the pillar or pillars of precedent upon which the Court built its decision in that case. How strong a part did precedent play in the majority opinion? What other elements of judicial reasoning are revealed in the majority opinion? Upon what bases did dissenting Justices, if any, reach their decisions? Did they find different lines of precedent to cite in their written opinions? Did they cite the same cases but put a different interpretation on them?

2. The Court is always building new lines of precedent, as the post-*Mapp* decisions illustrate. Such construction is not limited to the Supreme Court, however, and many lower courts share in the task through their decisions in the numerous cases reaching them each year. Using West's regional reporters, *American Jurisprudence,* or *U.S. Law Week* as a guide to lower court decisions, note how lower courts have responded to the Supreme Court's decision in *Mapp v. Ohio* or the key decision investigated in Question 1 above. Comment on the variety of questions raised by litigants in these cases. Have the lower court decisions as a whole supported the Supreme Court's ruling? Or have they tended to undermine it?

3. Select a Supreme Court Justice in whom you are interested. Find ten or so opinions (majority, concurring or dissenting) he has written in the civil liberties

area. Does he have a noticeable style of judicial reasoning, that is, does he pay special attention to precedent? the intentions of the framers of the Constitution? social data? emotion? Select a second Justice and study several of his written opinions. How does his style differ from that of the first Justice?

4. Justice Brandeis, concurring in *Ashwander v. TVA*, 297 U.S. 288, 346-348 (1936), offered several rules of judicial self-restraint that, if followed, would limit judicial "policy-making." One rule is that the Court will not "anticipate a question of constitutional law in advance of the necessity of deciding it," another is that the Court will not "formulate a rule of constitutional law broader than is required by the precise facts to which it is to be applied." Generally speaking, a Justice who follows these rules carefully is what President Nixon called a "strict constructionist." Look at written opinions of one of the supposedly strict constructionists appointed by President Nixon (Chief Justice Burger, Justice Blackmun, Justice Rehnquist, Justice Powell). Using the pertinent *Ashwander* rules as a guide, ask just how much of a strict constructionist the Justice turned out to be. Also, as you read other Court opinions in connection with the chapters ahead, ask which of the *Ashwander* rules are still favored by the Court today. Which are cited often? Have other rules of self-restraint been added to the Court's lexicon since 1936?

NOTES

1. M. Frances McNamara, comp., *2,000 Famous Legal Quotations* (Rochester, N.Y.: Aqueduct Books, 1967), p. 402.

2. Robert H. Jackson, *The Supreme Court in the American System of Government* (Cambridge, Mass.: Harvard University Press, 1955), p. 76.

3. William O. Douglas, "An Intimate Memoir of the Brethren," *The New York Times Magazine*, Sept. 21, 1980, p. 38, at p.40.

4. K. N. Llewellyn, *The Bramble Bush* (Dobbs Ferry, N.Y.: Oceana Publications, 1969), p. 64. For a more detailed discussion of the elements of judicial reasoning see David W. Rohde and Harold J. Spaeth, *Supreme Court Decision Making* (San Francisco: W. H. Freeman, 1976), pp. 34-53. For a discussion of judicial discretion and informal norms of judicial restraint see Rohde and Spaeth, pp. 118-133; and Henry J. Abraham, *The Judicial Process*, 3rd ed. (New York: Oxford University Press, 1975), pp. 169-188. For a discussion of the impact of judicial decisions, see Stephen L. Wasby, *The Impact of the United States Supreme Court* (Homewood, Ill.: Dorsey Press, 1970).

5. Fred W. Catlett, "The Development of the Doctrine of Stare Decisis and the Extent to Which It Should be Applied," 21 *Wash.L.Rev.* 158 (1946).

6. William Zelermyer, *Legal Reasoning* (Englewood Cliffs, N.J.: Prentice-Hall, 1960), p. 29.

7. Walter F. Murphy and C. Herman Pritchett, *Courts, Judges, and Politics* (New York: Random House, 1961), pp. 367-369.

8. K. N. Llewellyn, as quoted in Carl A. Auerbach et al., eds., *The Legal Process* (San

Francisco: Chandler, 1961), p. 380.

9. Quoted in Jon D. Noland, "Stare Decisis and the Overruling of Constitutional Decisions in the Warren Years," 4 *Val.U.L.Rev.* 101, 104 (1969).

10. Robert B. McKay, "The Preference for Freedom," 34 *N.Y.U.L.Rev.* 1182, 1197 (1959).

11. Both this quote and the one in the preceding sentence are K. N. Llewellyn's (see Auerbach et al., eds., p. 380).

12. *Bradwell v. Illinois*, 16 Wall. 130 (1873).

13. *Furman v. Georgia*, 408 U.S. 238 (1972).

14. Rohde and Spaeth, pp.174-175.

15. Stuart S. Nagel, "Political Party Affiliation and Judges' Decisions," 55 *American Political Science Review* 843 (1961). See also Sheldon Goldman, "Voting Behavior on the United States Courts of Appeals, 1961–1964," 60 *American Political Science Review* 374 (1966).

16. Douglas, p. 74.

17. 367 U.S. 643 (1961).

18. Note, "Trends in Legal Commentary on the Exclusionary Rule," 65 *J. Crim. Law and Criminology* 373, 380 (1974).

19. It is unclear whether police found gambling paraphernalia or not. An early account in *The New York Times* (April 2, 1961, p. 52) reported that police did find paraphernalia. A later account (June 20, 1961, p. 1) stated that they did not.

20. Mapp testified that the materials belonged to a former boarder. However, she admitted that she saw the materials when storing the man's belongings and thereby satisfied the "knowing" provision of Ohio Revised Code § 2905.34: "No person shall knowingly . . . have in his possession or under his control an obscene, lewd, or lascivious book, magazine, pamphlet, paper, writing, advertisement, circular, print, picture . . . or drawing . . . of an indecent or immoral nature" *Mapp v. Ohio*, 367 U.S. at 668, n.3.

21. Mapp's primary claim was that Ohio's anti-obscenity law violated her First Amendment right of free speech. Although a majority of the judges on the Supreme Court of Ohio agreed, the court upheld the law because Ohio's constitution required an extraordinary majority before a court could declare a state law unconstitutional. *State v. Mapp*, 166 N.E. 2d 387 (1960).

22. Ibid.

23. *Weeks v. United States*, 232 U.S. 383 (1914).

24. *Rea v. United States*, 350 U.S. 214 (1956).

25. *Elkins v. United States*, 364 U.S. 206 (1960).

26. *Wolf v. Colorado*, 338 U.S. 25 (1949).

27. *The New York Times*, June 20, 1961, p. 1.

28. 116 U.S. 616 (1886).

29. 232 U.S. 383 (1914).

30. 338 U.S. 25 (1949).

31. 342 U.S. 165 (1952).

32. 350 U.S. 214 (1956).

33. 364 U.S. 206 (1960).

34. It is unclear whether *Weeks* made the exclusionary rule an inherent part of the Constitution or merely a supplement to it. Justice Harlan, dissenting in *Mapp v. Ohio*, assumed that *Weeks* did elevate the rule to constitutional status. 367 U.S. at 668.

35. 7 Peters 243 (1833).

36. U.S. Const., Amend. XIV, sec. 1 (emphasis added).

37. U.S. Const., Amend. V.

38. See Justice Black's lengthy dissent in *Adamson v. California*, 332 U.S. 46 (1948).

39. *Hurtado v. California*, 110 U.S. 516 (1884).

40. *Maxwell v. Dow*, 176 U.S. 581 (1900).

41. *Twining v. New Jersey*, 211 U.S. 78 (1908).

42. 268 U.S. 652 (1925).

43. Ibid., at 666.

44. The Court formally incorporated freedom of speech two years later in *Fiske v. Kansas*, 274 U.S. 380 (1927).

45. *Near v. Minnesota*, 283 U.S. 697 (1931) (press); *Hamilton v. Regents of the University of California*, 293 U.S. 245 (1934) (religion); *DeJonge v. Oregon*, 299 U.S. 353 (1937) (assembly).

46. The Court incorporated a limited Sixth Amendment right to counsel in 1932. Under special circumstances, as when a defendant is illiterate, poor, young, isolated from friends and family, and is charged with a capital offense, the state must provide free counsel. *Powell v. Alabama*, 287 U.S. 45 (1932).

47. 302 U.S. 319 (1937).

48. In *Palko*, for example, the Court held that the Fifth Amendment's guarantee against double jeopardy was not one of the "fundamental principles of liberty and justice which lie at the base of all our civil and political institutions." 302 U.S. at 328.

49. Other methods include victims of illegal searches bringing suit against offending officers, internal discipline of officers, and training police in the art of "proper" search and seizure procedures. James A. Spiotto, "Search and Seizure: An Empirical Study of the Exclusionary Rule and Its Alternatives," 2 *J. of Legal Studies* 243, 269-278 (1973).

50. 342 U.S. 165 (1952).

51. The vote was 8-0. Justice Minton did not participate.

52. The Court later reiterated that it would intervene only if the evidence had been obtained in a truly shocking manner. In *Irvine v. California*, 347 U.S. 128 (1954), the Court held that police who eavesdropped on a suspect by placing microphones in several rooms of his house, including the bedroom, engaged in "obnoxious" but not heinous actions violating due process. In *Breithaupt v. Abram*, 352 U.S. 432 (1957), the Court held that police did not violate due process by taking a blood sample from an unconscious accident victim suspected of driving while intoxicated.

53. 350 U.S. 214 (1956). The Court reasoned that the officials defied the federal rules of evidence over which it had control.

54. 364 U.S. 206 (1960). Not to do so would subvert the good faith efforts of states to abide by the Fourth Amendment.

55. K. N. Llewellyn, as quoted in Carl A. Auerbach, p. 380.

56. Here the Court elevated the exclusionary rule to constitutional status, characterizing it as "part and parcel" of the Constitution. 367 U.S. at 651. When the question was later raised as to whether *Mapp* elevated the rule, the Justices participating in *Mapp* affirmed that the Court had intentionally imputed a constitutional origin to the rule. See *Malloy v. Hogan*, 378 U.S. 1, 8 (1964); and *United States v. Calandra*, 414 U.S. 338, 360 (1974) (Brennan, J., dissenting).

57. One-half of the states that considered the rule between 1949 and 1961 wholly or partly adopted it through legislative or judicial action. Justice Clark failed to point out that twenty-four states still did not require it.

58. 367 U.S. at 657 (emphasis added).

59. "The simple truth is . . . that the Court has no easy means or objective criteria to aid it in the exercise of its judgment; indeed the judgment is largely intuition and informed guess." Leo Pfeffer, *The Liberties of an American: The Supreme Court Speaks* (Boston: Beacon Press, 1963), p. 30.

60. See note 21 above.

61. *Mapp v. Ohio*, 367 U.S. at 673, n.6 (Harlan, J., dissenting).

62. 367 U.S. at 645, n.3. Justice Douglas also addressed the question in his concurring opinion, 367 U.S. at 671.

63. Many of the Warren Court's reversals of previous decisions involved criminal procedure. Noland, at 120.

64. Today only three major provisions of the first eight amendments remain to be incorporated: the right to indictment by grand jury, the right to a jury trial in civil cases, and the right to be free from excessive bail. Henry J. Abraham, *Freedom and the Court*, 2nd ed. (New York: Oxford University Press, 1972), p. 81.

65. Robert G. McCloskey, *The Modern Supreme Court* (Cambridge, Mass.: Harvard University Press, 1972), p. 244.

66. Note, "Trends in Legal Commentary . . . ," at 380.

67. *United States v. Janis*, 428 U.S. 433, 460 (1976) (Brennan, J., dissenting).

68. For a discussion of the effects of *Mapp*, see Donald L. Horowitz, *The Courts and Social Policy* (Washington, D.C.: Brookings Institution, 1977), pp. 220-254.

69. Erwin N. Griswold, *Search and Seizure: A Dilemma of the Supreme Court* (Lincoln: University of Nebraska Press, 1975), p. 8.

70. In Minneapolis, for example, only two search warrants were issued between 1929 and 1954 and none after 1954. Ibid. See also Arlen Specter, "Mapp v. Ohio: Pandora's Problems for the Prosecutor," 111 *U.Pa.L.Rev.* 4, 5 (1962).

71. Specter, at 42.

72. Ibid., at 5.

73. Griswold, pp. 7-8.

74. Ibid.

75. See Note, "Trends in Legal Commentary. . . ."

76. For studies in which the conclusions are generally unfavorable for the rule, see Bruce A. Finzen, "The Exclusionary Rule in Search and Seizure: Examination and Prognosis," 20 *U.Kan.L.Rev.* 768 (1972); and Spiotto. A supportive study is Bradley C. Canon, "Is the Exclusionary Rule in Failing Health? Some New Data and a Plea Against a Precipitous Conclusion," 62 *Ken.L.J.* 681 (1973-74).

77. *Stone v. Powell*, 428 U.S. 465 (1976).

78. Judicial activism defies easy understanding. Noland, at 100, n.1, notes that "'[a]ctivism' is used both in the sense of a willingness to accept cases as proper for adjudication and a willingness to decide cases according to personal notions of what is desirable." It also refers to the willingness of Justices to overrule previous decisions. Using the latter definition, it is apparent that the Warren Court was an active Court. Between 1954 and 1968 it overruled thirty-six cases on constitutional grounds, an average of two reversals per term. Courts in the preceding 100 years averaged one reversal every two and one-half terms. Ibid., at 119.

79. Although "Warren Court" and "Burger Court" are only loose terms, it is true that the four Nixon appointees have tended to vote as a block. They voted together 75 percent of the time in the 1973-74 session and 69 percent in the 1974-75 term. Most of their bloc voting in the 1974-75 term occurred in criminal law cases (88 percent), the lowest in First Amendment cases (50 percent). William A. Linsley, "The Supreme Court and the First Amendment: 1974-1975," *Free Speech Yearbook 1975*, 67.

80. Wilkinson, *Serving Justice*, quoted in William B. Lockhart et al., *Constitutional Rights and Liberties*, 4th ed. (St. Paul, Minn: West, 1975), p. 169.

81. *Stone v. Powell*, 428 U.S. 465, 500 (1976) (Burger, C. J., concurring).

82. *Bivens v. Six Unknown Agents*, 403 U.S. 388, 493 (1971) (Burger, C. J., concurring in part and dissenting in part).

83. *Stone v. Powell*, 428 U.S. 465, 496 (1976). For other criticism the Chief Justice has made about the exclusionary rule, see Warren E. Burger, "Who Will Watch the Watchman?" 14 *Am.U.L.Rev.* 1 (1964).

84. For example, the Court could expand the range of situations from which police are exempt from the search warrant requirement. See Martin Shapiro and Douglas S. Hobbs, *The Politics of Constitutional Law* (Cambridge, Mass.: Winthrop, 1974), p. 497.

85. Rohde and Spaeth, pp. 35-36.

86. See David O. Foshee, "Limitation Placed on Federal Habeas Corpus Jurisdiction in Fourth Amendment Cases—A Further Erosion of the Exclusionary Rule," 4 *Loyola L.Rev.* 856, 862 (1976).

87. *United States v. Calandra*, 414 U.S. 338, 348 (1974) (emphasis added). See also *Stone v. Powell*, 428 U.S. 465 (1976).

88. 414 U.S. 338 (1974).

89. 428 U.S. 433 (1976).

90. 428 U.S. 465 (1976). State prisoners petition federal courts to review the constitutionality of their convictions in what is known as the writ of federal *habeas corpus*. Originally available only to federal prisoners (guaranteed in the Constitution), Congress in 1867 extended it to state prisoners. For a concise overview of the history of federal *habeas corpus*, see Joseph L. Shea, "The Fourth Amendment Exclusionary Rule in Federal Habeas Corpus," 37 *Louisiana L.Rev.* 289 (1976). Also, in *Harris v. New York*, 401 U.S. 222 (1971), the Court held that illegally seized evidence (that seized in violation of the rules set forth in *Miranda v. Arizona*, 384 U.S. 436 [1966]) may be used to impeach the credibility of the defendant if he or she testifies at his or her trial (see Chapter 7). The defendant who voluntarily takes the stand is under an obligation to tell the truth; the interest in justice at trial here outweighs the *speculative* value of the exclusionary rule in deterring illegal police conduct. The Court extended this line of thought in *United States v. Havens*, 446

U.S. 620 (1980) when it allowed the state to use illegally seized evidence to impeach the defendant's credibility during cross-examination when his or her testimony "reasonably suggests" such questions.

91. *Funk v. United States*, 290 U.S. 371 (1933), as quoted in William J. Cox, "The Decline of the Exclusionary Rule: An Alternative to Injustice," 4 *Sw.U.L.Rev.* 68, 77, n.47 (1972). For similar thoughts, see Benjamin N. Cardozo, *The Nature of the Judicial Process* (New Haven: Yale University Press, 1939), p. 150.

92. The last point is ironic in that *Mapp* had said the *absence* of the rule increased disrespect of criminal procedures.

93. *United States v. Calandra*, 414 U.S. at 351-352.

94. Concurring in *Gideon v. Wainwright*, 372 U.S. 335, 346 (1963).

95. Anthony G. Amsterdam, "Perspectives on the Fourth Amendment," 58 *Minn.L.Rev.* 349, 353-354 (1973-74).

96. Ibid., at 350-351.

CHAPTER TWO

Freedom of Speech

When the Allies freed the survivors of the concentration camps in 1945 they closed down stark physical reminders of a once-thriving political ideology, but they could not excise the legacy of the conflagration, which has reappeared in different forms since World War II. One recent encounter pitted two descendants of the original protagonists against each other: the National Socialist Party of America (NSPA), which believes in white supremacy but not genocide, and survivors of Nazi persecution who had settled in the heavily Jewish community of Skokie, Illinois. The dispute, which dragged out over twelve months and occupied the attention of six courts, raised a wealth of free speech issues that vividly underscore the problematic nature of First Amendment free speech.

In late 1976 the NSPA planned a series of demonstrations in Jewish communities to "expose and document" Jewish influence in American society. Party members chose Skokie as one site because they held its residents responsible for racial busing in Chicago's schools. When news of the planned demonstration slipped out, however, Skokie's residents, 40,000 of whom are Jewish and 5,000 to 7,000 of whom had lived in

32

concentration camps, reacted vocally. The controversy was fanned further by hostile phone messages made by unknown callers to villagers with Jewish-sounding names. Skokie's village president appealed to the Cook County Circuit Court to bar the demonstration from taking place. The court complied, issuing a broad injunction forbidding anyone from "marching, walking or parading in the uniform of the National Socialist Party of America; marching, walking or parading or otherwise displaying the swastika on or off their person; distributing pamphlets or displaying any materials which incite or promote hatred against persons of Jewish faith or ancestry or hatred against persons of any faith or ancestry, race or religion. . . ."[1]

NSPA leader Frank Collin filed suit with the Illinois Appellate Court to stay the injunction, but it refused. He then appealed to the Supreme Court of Illinois, which also refused to stay the injunction; finally he went to the U.S. Supreme Court.[2] Here he was successful; the High Court reversed the lower court and held that Skokie could not permanently bar the NSPA from staging its march. "If a State seeks to impose a restraint of this kind," wrote the Court, "it must provide strict procedural safeguards . . . including immediate appellate review." Because Skokie failed to provide these safeguards, its attempted injunction violated the First Amendment rights of the NSPA members. The Supreme Court sent the matter back to the lower court for its reconsideration.

Reviewing the injunction for a second time, the Illinois Appellate Court narrowed but did not scrap the injunction.[3] It deleted the part that forbade anyone from wearing Nazi uniforms, saying there was no evidence the uniforms would cause disorder. It also struck the part forbidding the distribution of materials because there was no indication the members planned to distribute inflammatory materials. It kept the injunction against the display of the swastika, however, saying the emblem amounted to what is known in legal parlance as "fighting words," that is, those inherently likely to lead to violence. On this point the court cited testimony by Jews about the effect the swastika had on them and mentioned the comment by one concentration camp survivor that "he [did] not know if he [could] control himself" if he saw the swastika in the parade. The court concluded that the swastika "as a matter of common knowledge, is inherently likely to provoke violent reaction among those of the Jewish persuasion or ancestry when intentionally brought into close proximity to their homes and places of worship. The swastika is a personal affront to every member of the Jewish faith. . . ."

NSPA leader Collin went back to court in the hopes of getting the last of the injunction reversed. This time the Illinois Supreme Court did strike down the modified injunction.[4] Citing definitive Supreme Court rulings, the judges held that the injunction violated the First Amendment rights of NSPA members. Displaying the swastika was a form of speech—symbolic rather than verbal but speech nonetheless—deserving First Amendment protection. The swastika did not amount to fighting words. The city bore a heavy burden in showing why it should enjoin the display of the swastika, a burden not met in this case.

Thus thwarted in their effort to stop the march through injunction, Skokie residents turned to another tactic. While the above litigation had been going on, the villagers passed three restrictive ordinances directly aimed at the slated march. The first set up a permit system requiring groups to post a hefty insurance bond against possible property damage before receiving permission to hold parades or assemblies. The second and third mirrored the language of the now-defunct injunction: one forbade the distribution of material inciting racial or religious hatred and the other banned demonstrations in which participants wore military-type uniforms. The controversy had now taken a different turn and NSPA strategy shifted as well. Frank Collin announced a date for the march and a new purpose: it would be held to protest the burdensome insurance-posting scheme.

In his application for a parade permit Collin described what the parade would be like. Thirty to fifty people would march in single file, he said, cooperating with police, wearing military-style uniforms, and displaying the swastika. Marchers planned to carry a party banner with a swastika on it and hold placards expressing Nazi slogans such as "White Free Speech," "Free Speech for the White Man," and "Free Speech for White America." Skokie denied Collin permission to hold the march, however, because the party could not post the $350,000 insurance bond. Collin asked the city to waive the insurance requirement but was told he could not be exempted because the proposed march violated the third ordinance by featuring people clothed in military uniforms.

Collin again went to court only this time to the federal district court and this time to grapple with legislative ordinances rather than judicial injunctions. The federal district court struck down all three ordinances as violations of the First Amendment.[5] Briefly, the insurance-posting scheme fell because most groups could not meet it so it amounted to a "drastic restriction of the right of freedom of speech and assembly." Moreover, Skokie applied it arbitrarily because the city had waived the requirement for groups such as the Northeast Skokie Property Owners Association and the American Legion. The racial slur ordinance fell because it was "subjective and impossible to clearly define" and had an excessively broad sweep. The military uniform ordinance improperly banned protected symbolic speech.

This time it was Skokie's turn to appeal and the city lost roundly. First the federal Circuit Court of Appeals upheld the lower court decision.[6] Then the U.S. Supreme Court refused to review the case, thereby by default letting the lower decision stand.[7] All avenues had been tried; with the Supreme Court's denial of certiorari the way was paved for the NSPA to hold its march. This saga of injunctions and stays, court orders and ordinances, remands, upholdings, and reversals had an ironic ending, however, when Collin moved the march to Chicago where it was held without incident.

The Skokie chronicle sandwiches a gold mine of free speech issues into a single controversy. Rarely does one find prior restraints, fighting words, symbolic speech, overbreadth, and the void-for-vagueness doctrine in such close proximity, a fact that makes this case ideal for introducing the key principles of free speech adjudication. Yet the very richness of the case is confusing. It may be helpful, therefore, to introduce a second, simpler, case to highlight the major issues of the Skokie confrontation. The case involved one Terry Dean Eaton, an Oklahoman on trial for breaking a Tulsa ordinance.[8]

It is not clear from the record exactly why Eaton was on trial but the episode at some point involved an assault on *him*. Taking the stand in his own defense, Eaton referred to "defensibility" in describing the assault and his reaction to it. The cross-examiner then asked Eaton, "What's defensibility?" and he answered, "I think that would be a place where you were able to get your feet to stand square so you would be half ready for some chicken shit that had jumped you from behind." Here the presiding judge jumped on Eaton for calling his alleged assailant "chicken shit." The judge cited Eaton for contempt of court and ordered him to pay a $50 fine plus costs. The judge was angry over Eaton's general demeanor in court but specifically mentioned only the "chicken shit" remark in his written order stating why Eaton should be held in contempt. Eaton appealed the citation on First Amendment grounds, claiming that his words were protected speech and ought not be punished. The U.S. Supreme Court wasted little time reversing the conviction. Citing an earlier ruling, the Court said that "[t]he vehemence of the language used is not alone the measure of the power to punish for contempt. The fire which it kindles must constitute an imminent, not merely a likely, threat to the administration of justice."

Several parallels exist between the Nazi case and the Eaton case. First, each is a free speech case, although Eaton's involves two simple words and the Nazi case involves an ideology having profound implications for twentieth-century politics. Second, in each case an individual or group's interest in speaking clashes head-on with a government barrier. In Eaton's case it is a contempt citation by a judge; in the Skokie case it is a judicial injunction and three ordinances. Third, the government assumes that the speech will harm society in some way. Eaton's judge feared the expletive threatened the orderly administration of justice; Skokie officials feared psychological damage to survivors of the concentration camps and upsets in public peace and order. Fourth, the government also assumes in each case that the speech itself is inherently evil—that its very nature, apart from its effect on society, makes it unworthy of First Amendment protection. Fifth, each calls upon a neutral judge to weigh the conflicting interests at stake, thereby creating an archetypal triangle in which the First Amendment stands opposite a social interest and is adjudicated by a judge who will tip the scales in one direction or the other to resolve the dispute.

Three things distinguish the cases. First, the timing of the restriction on speech differs. Eaton was punished *after* uttering the words; the NSPA was restricted *before* the march was ever held. Second, Eaton's case involved clearly articulated, verbally spoken *words*; the Nazi case involved two expressive *symbols*—military uniforms and swastikas. Third, although the speech in both cases was attacked for its nature and its effect on society, the Nazi case focused more squarely on the *inherent* worth of the expression and the Eaton case focused on the *effect* of the words.

Recall the twin themes of this volume: the Court values some liberties in the Bill of Rights more highly than others (inter-liberty gradations) and values some facets of each guarantee more highly than other facets (intra-liberty gradations). These principles help explain the backdrop against which the Supreme Court ruled on the Skokie and Eaton cases and their eventual outcomes. The protagonists in future free speech cases will differ: perhaps the state will try to restrict the Ku Klux Klan or the Communist Party or the Palestine Liberation Organization. Or, instead of courtroom expletives, a person might be penalized for wearing an offensive T-shirt in the corridors of a public courthouse or for using abusive language against a police officer. The nature of jurisprudence dictates, however, that the basic principles governing the Skokie or Eaton cases apply to analogous cases as well. By understanding the fundamentals of free speech doctrine, one is equipped to pick out common clues in the succession of speech cases coming before the Court each term no matter who the protagonists. Toward this end the remainder of the chapter examines inter- and intra-liberty gradations in free speech doctrine, using the Skokie and Eaton cases to illustrate.

FREE SPEECH AS A HIGHLY VALUED LIBERTY

The Supreme Court has elevated free speech to a "preferred" freedom within the Constitution's litany of rights and liberties. In so doing it has developed a unique battery of tests for reviewing laws that intrude on free speech. This is important because these tests favor the speech interest at stake and, when used, tip the balance in free speech disputes.

The Court first hinted that it placed the First Amendment on a high plane in *Gitlow v. New York*,[9] a 1925 incorporation case in which the Court held that First Amendment free speech bound the state as well as federal government. In a passage that seemed to indicate a "keystone" quality of the First Amendment,[10] Justice Cardozo praised free speech as "the matrix, the indispensable condition, of nearly every form of freedom."[11] The next hint came as a footnote to an opinion dealing with a subject hardly connected with civil liberties—milk controls. In an opinion reversing the Filled Milk Act, Justice Stone suggested in Footnote 4 that the Court should scrutinize laws limiting civil liberties more carefully than laws intruding on other constitutional guarantees.[12] Surely Justice Stone had little idea his footnote would become grist for as many constitutional law books as it has. The passage warrants mention, however, for its suggestive idea that civil liberties as a whole are more important than other constitutional guarantees. Later Justice Stone (by then the Chief Justice) stated it more precisely: the First Amendment was supreme among the civil freedoms. This message came in the text of an opinion, albeit a dissenting opinion:

> The First Amendment is not confined to safeguarding freedom of speech and freedom of religion against discriminatory attempts to wipe them out. On the contrary, the Constitution, by virtue of the First and Fourteenth Amendments, has put those freedoms in a *preferred position.*[13]

From footnote to dissent . . . the gradation idea had one more hill to climb to receive the due attention of a judicial principle, namely, it had to appear in the text of a majority opinion. The occasion came shortly when the Court reversed itself in the decision in which Chief Justice Stone had dissented. Justice Douglas wrote the Court opinion this time and duly incorporated Justice Stone's idea into the majority position,[14] stating forthrightly: "Freedom of press, freedom of speech, freedom of religion are in a preferred position."[15]

Once this was said and done the Justices stopped using the phrase "preferred position,"[16] but their opinions and tests still attest to the elevated regard they give to free expression. Virtually all Justices since 1919 have either written an opinion or concurred with one expressing the belief that the First Amendment is special.[17] Moreover, they have developed special "devices"[18] for examining laws that intrude on the First Amendment. Three of these are the relaxed presumption of constitutionality, the void-for-vagueness doctrine, and the overbreadth doctrine. Each stacks the odds against the government action, meaning, for example, that the village of Skokie would run into more hurdles in court by trying to prevent the Nazis from marching than it would trying to defend a prison reform measure, water purification plan, or some other policy not connected with free speech.

Relaxed Presumption of Constitutionality

A norm of judicial self-restraint is that the Court will do everything possible to preserve a statute under challenges to its constitutionality. The Court sees itself as a reviewing body—a court of last resort—not as a legislative body free to reverse congressional initiative at the slightest opportunity. Thus in reviewing a law open to several interpretations the Justices will ordinarily choose the interpretation most likely to preserve the law.[19] This principle is known as the "presumption of constitutionality." It is so well-ingrained that departures from it are worthy of special note. One departure lasted for about fifty years, from the late 1880s to 1937, when the Court struck down assorted federal controls on commerce, such as a New York law limiting the number of hours bakers could work[20] and, in doing so, seemed to presume the unconstitutionality of laws limiting private enterprise. In the late 1930s, however, a change in the Court's composition, together with the wrath of President Roosevelt, prompted the Court to revert to its normal position and again presume the constitutionality of business laws, a position it has held to this day.

A second departure began in the 1930s and involved a subject of more immediate interest to this book—civil liberties. It started with the above-mentioned Footnote 4 when Justice Stone suggested the Court should relax the presumed constitutionality of laws intruding on civil liberties,[21] continued a year later when eight members of the Court agreed that a law intruding on civil liberties should not be presumed to be constitutional,[22] and was capped nine years after that when Justice Rutledge looked back to say the Court had "declared repeatedly" that laws interfering with First Amendment rights are presumptively unconstitutional.[23] This departure lasted until the Court's composition changed in the early 1950s and the anti-Communist fervor of that decade put free speech and the Court on the defensive. At that time the Court escorted the reverse presumption doctrine "into a sort of constitutional limbo."[24]

Today the Court's position represents a compromise. For all subsequent punishments on speech (those that control speech after the fact such as Eaton's contempt citation in the "chicken shit" case), the Court *relaxes* the presumption of constitutionality; that is, it does not go so far as to reverse the presumed constitutionality but neither does it blandly presume the law is constitutional. The Court will examine the law with special care and thereby tilt the scales against it. For all prior restraints (those controlling speech in advance of its expression), however, the Court *reverses* the presumption of constitutionality.[25] As will be seen in Chapter 3, the Court is especially wary of prior restraints and their effect on a healthy system of free expression. With a prior restraint the state makes a weighty conclusion about the supposed harm of speech before the words are even emitted, thereby imagining a bundle of supposed horrors in the absence of supportive empirical information. The Nazi march case involved a classic prior restraint in which city officials tried to enjoin the march in anticipation of disorders it might cause, thereby divorcing the supposed harm from empirical evidence that disorder would result from the march. When a prior restraint is at issue the Court places a heavy burden on the state to justify the control. Hence, Clue No. 1 in the Nazi case: a prior restraint is at issue so the Court will presume the measure's unconstitutionality and place the burden on the state to prove why it should limit the speech. If history is any guide, the state will fail to meet this burden. The reverse presumption of constitutionality tilts the scales against the law in question.

Void-for-Vagueness Doctrine

The Court requires laws to be written precisely enough so as clearly to warn persons which acts are illegal. A law that is "so vague that men of common intelligence must necessarily guess at its meaning and differ as to its application"[26] may very well be struck down by the Court as void for vagueness. A vague law violates the Sixth Amendment guarantee that a criminal defendant shall be "informed of the nature and cause of the accusation" against him or her; it also violates the Fifth and Fourteenth Amendment guarantees that no one shall be deprived of liberty without "due process of law."

The vagueness doctrine applies to all laws coming before the Court, but the Justices are especially vigilant about vagueness in laws infringing on the First Amendment. "Where the First Amendment freedoms are at stake," writes the Court, "we have repeatedly emphasized that precision of drafting and clarity of purpose are essential."[27] A loosely written law leaves citizens uncertain about what is forbidden; to be safe, the theory goes, they will build a margin of error and "steer far wider of the unlawful zone" than necessary.[28] This "chills" expression and threatens the system of free speech.[29]

A not untypical law attacked on vagueness grounds was a Louisiana breach-of-the-peace statute forbidding behavior tending "to agitate, to arouse . . . to disquiet."[30] Under such a law any person who happened to arouse the emotions of others could be arrested for a breach of the peace. The statute's vague wording suggests many interpretations; the trial judge in one case gave it a highly personal construction when he concluded that it "*has* to be an inherent breach of the peace" for 1,500 black people to sing songs with lines such as "black and white together" as they waited at lunch counters to be served.[31] Three other laws challenged by litigants on vagueness grounds were the Skokie ordinances banning the dissemination of material inciting racial or religious hatred (the so-called racial slur ordinance), forbidding demonstrations in which participants wear military-style uniforms, and requiring demonstrators to post insurance bonds.

If the Court does subject a law to the vagueness test, it has two options available.[32] The less protective for free speech is for the Court to uphold the law but strike down improper applications of it. Such happened in the case of a young Seattle resident, Harold Oman Spence, who owes his clean criminal record to the "as applied" attack on vagueness.[33] Spence had fashioned a peace symbol out of removable black tape, placed it on both sides of a U.S. flag, and hung the flag upside down in his apartment window. Three police officers spotted the flag and arrested Spence for violating a state law forbidding the public display of an American flag to which had been attached any "word, figure, mark, picture, design, drawing or advertisement." Spence challenged the law on First Amendment grounds. The Justices had no objection to the content of the law, noting that it was straightforward and did not invite discriminatory enforcement,[34] but they reversed Spence's conviction on the grounds that the state improperly applied the law. Spence's flag was privately owned, displayed on private property, and did not disrupt the public order. As applied, the law violated his First Amendment rights.[35]

Another law attacked for faulty application was the insurance-posting scheme at issue in the Skokie case. In reversing the law on First Amendment grounds the U.S. District Court noted that one of its faults lay in arbitrary application. It will be remembered that the city exempted some groups such as the American Legion from having to post insurance. But on what bases were these decisions made? The court could find "no principled standards for determining which organizations are exempt" and it speculated that "[t]his device permits organizations that have the approval of the Village government to avoid the restrictions imposed on all other groups." The law's lack of precision paved the way for discriminatory enforcement.

A second option is for the Court to strike down the law on its face. The facial attack on vagueness disposes of bad laws with dispatch, unlike the as-applied approach, which may let a poor law languish indefinitely. It warns legislators that incautiously written laws will fall and is highly protective of the First Amendment.[36] In facial review the Court examines the words of the law to see if people of "common intelligence" can understand them and agree about their meaning. It recognizes that "we can never expect mathematical uncertainty from our language" so it looks at the clearness of the statute taken as a whole.[37] It struck down for facial vagueness a Cincinnati ordinance forbidding three or more persons from meeting on sidewalks and acting "in a manner annoying to persons passing by."[38] The word "annoying" is subject to many interpretations and the law invited discriminatory application by police officers.[39] The Court also struck down a New York law making it a crime to possess with the intent to sell materials "principally made up of criminal news, police reports, or accounts of criminal deeds, or pictures, or stories of deeds of bloodshed, lust, or crime."[40] The law's problem lay with the phrase "principally made up of." Newspapers spice up their copy with crime stories, and the law leaves unclear how many stories they can publish without violating the law.[41] Finally, the U.S. District Court struck down Skokie's racial slur ordinance for facial vagueness, noting that the ordinance "punishes language which intentionally incites hatred. This standard is subjective and impossible to clearly define." It went on to say that any statutes "which punish speech solely on the basis of the emotion it arouses in other persons are vulnerable to findings of vagueness."

The willingness of judges to apply the facial attack varies just as the willingness of judges to attack laws in the first place varies. Some judges assiduously avoid reviewing a law's constitutionality and, if finally persuaded that a vagueness challenge is warranted, will take the less active route and only challenge the law as applied. Other judges who are more willing to review laws are also more inclined to use the facial variant. Thus, although the facts of a case may seem to the observer to warrant a vagueness attack, he or she must consider the proclivities of the Justices in predicting whether the Court will actually use the vagueness test. The issue dividing the Court today, for example, is not the vagueness test itself but rather the appropriateness of the facial attack as opposed to the as-applied attack. The present Court seems to be less inclined to use the facial vagueness test than its predecessor.

Overbreadth Doctrine

The overbreadth doctrine is a device designed by the Court especially for First Amendment cases.[42] An overbroad law is analogous to an insect bite with the place the proboscis enters akin to the behavior the state rightfully can prevent and the swelling encircling the bite akin to protected speech that is improperly scooped up with the law's application. An overbroad law "does not aim specifically at evils within the allowable area of state control [but] sweeps within its ambit other activities that in ordinary circumstances constitute an exercise of freedom of speech or of the press."[43]

The overbreadth doctrine is closely related to the vagueness doctrine.[44] Each attacks laws that infringe on First Amendment freedoms, reduces uncertainty about what is forbidden, and prevents the chilling of expression. In addition, the Court strikes down a law either for facial or as-applied overbreadth. A law suffering from both faults was a New York statute making it a crime to "mutilate, deface, defile, or defy, trample upon or cast contempt upon, *either by words or act*" any U.S. flag.[45] The law was facially overbroad because it forbade *verbal* defilement of the flag, which is protected speech. It was overbroad as applied in the case of a man who burned a flag and at the same time said that "we don't need an American flag." It was unclear from the trial transcript whether the man had been convicted for his act or his words. The possibility that he had been punished for his words, which were protected, led the Court to reverse the conviction.[46]

The overbreadth doctrine also played a role in the Skokie case in that the U.S. District Court struck down the racial slur ordinance for facial overbreadth. The court used this test: "a law is overbroad for First Amendment purposes when, even though it is directed at unprotected speech, it can also be applied to protected speech." One of the law's problems was that it punished the "dissemination of material" and was "not aimed solely at personally abusive, insulting behavior." Even assuming that racially inflammatory speech may be controlled, the mere dissemination of racially inflammatory materials may not.

The Court struck down a number of laws for facial overbreadth in the 1960s but did not clearly say what made a law overbroad.[47] The four new Justices who joined the Court between 1969 and 1972 charged that the Court had been declaring laws unconstitutional on grounds of vagueness and overbreadth "in wholesale lots" and warned that the Court had become a "council of revision."[48] These Justices gained enough supporters by 1973 to limit facial overbreadth review somewhat. In a decision upholding a law under overbreadth challenge, the Court stated that "particularly where conduct and not merely speech is involved, the overbreadth of a statute must not only be real, but substantial as well."[49] The "substantial overbreadth" test leaves fewer laws open to facial invalidation but by no means emasculates the overbreadth doctrine.[50]

GRADATIONS WITHIN SPEECH

That free expression is important in a democratic society is incontrovertible. Freely flowing ideas promote the growth of knowledge[51] and encourage a "more capable citizenry," able to exercise its vote intelligently.[52] Free expression is also thought to be an antidote to dangerous and "noxious" doctrines because it opens their true nature to public disclosure.[53] Yet free expression can pose disservices to society. A magazine that publishes classified information on the nation's nuclear capability arguably threatens national security, a person shouting "Fire!" in a crowded theater can cause chaos and possible injuries,[54] and an arrogant journalist who recklessly maligns another person can put his or her target through unwarranted grief.[55]

Some jurists and scholars argue that speech is so important it must never be limited.[56] But these so-called absolutists have never amounted to more than a footnote in American jurisprudence; by far the more common view is that the state can limit speech and still abide by the First Amendment. An important feature of free speech law that helps one understand when the state may properly limit speech is this: courts regard some forms of speech as more useful and worthy of protection than others. To speak of "speech" as if it is a monolithic entity is to oversimplify matters because in fact there are gradations within speech.

Political speech ranks highly as a form of expression, with the Court saying that "speech concerning public affairs is more than self-expression; it is the essence of self-government"[57] and that "[w]hatever differences may exist about interpretations of the First Amendment, there is practically universal agreement that a major purpose of the Amendment was to protect the free discussion of governmental affairs."[58] Speech conveyed through conduct (symbolic speech) is less highly valued. The First and Fourteenth Amendments do not "afford the same kind of freedom to those who would communicate ideas by conduct," writes the Court, "as these amendments afford to those who communicate ideas by pure speech."[59] Commercial speech, too, falls low on the ladder of valued expression: "Even if the differences [between commercial speech and "other varieties"] do not justify the conclusion that commercial speech is valueless, . . . they nonetheless suggest that a *different degree of protection* is necessary to insure that the flow of truthful commercial speech is unimpaired."[60] Finally, at least a plurality of Justices have gone on record as saying that sexually explicit speech is an inferior form of communication. Such speech, wrote Justice Stevens in a recent opinion, "is of a wholly different, and *lesser*, magnitude than the interest in untrammeled political debate."[61]

Over the years the Court has reduced these gradations and now sees more types of speech as socially useful than ever before. It now calls entertainment "speech," saying that these words have a value, even if not part of a larger search for truth.[62] It also calls words that convey emotion "speech," saying "We cannot sanction the view that the Constitution . . . has little or no regard for that emotive function which, practically speaking, may often be the more important element of the overall message sought to be communicated."[63] Finally, reversing a tradition,[64] it now treats advertising as speech, noting that commercial messages fall within the "exposition of ideas"[65] and contain material in the "public interest."[66] Yet other gradations remain and clearly affect the way the Justices approach free speech conflicts. The following three sections describe the winnowing process by which the Justices cull protected First Amendment speech from the many utterances litigants claim are free speech. In "winnowing by fiat" the Court excludes some utterances from First Amendment protection on the grounds that they are not speech at all. In "speech–conduct distinctions" it excludes expression that is more conduct than speech. In "balancing" it takes what expression is left (that which *is* speech of the First Amendment genre) and weighs it against the danger it poses to the public. The end product is highly valued and thus "free" speech.

Winnowing by Fiat

One of the more intriguing ironies of First Amendment case law is that some speech is not speech at all. It may look like speech, being made up of words uttered or printed, and the dictionary may define it as speech, but in First Amendment parlance at least it is not speech of the sort that is given constitutional protection. The Court let it be known that some speech was not speech in the 1942 case of *Chaplinsky v. New Hampshire*:

> There are certain well-defined and narrowly limited classes of speech, the prevention and punishment of which has never been thought to raise any Constitutional problem. These include the lewd and the obscene, the profane, the libelous, and the insulting or "fighting" words — those which by their very utterance inflict injury or tend to incite an immediate breach of the peace.[67]

According to this passage four types of utterances are not First Amendment speech: obscene, profane, defamatory, and fighting. Each is ostracized because it is socially useless. Nonspeech utterances "are no essential part of any exposition of ideas"; they are "of such slight social value as a step to truth that any benefit that may be derived from them is clearly outweighed by the social interest in order and morality."[68] The significance of this winnowing by fiat is obvious: if obscenity or libel or other nonspeech is at issue, the words will receive no more protection than the act of driving down the street or painting a house inasmuch as the First Amendment has been cast out of the picture. The law will not be subject to overbreadth or especially careful vagueness review, nor will its constitutionality immediately be open to suspicion.

Winnowing by fiat gives a new meaning to the Skokie and Eaton cases because each involved allegedly "fighting words." Skokie's central argument was that swastikas, as displayed in its heavily Jewish community with its links to the Holocaust, amounted to fighting words and were not entitled to First Amendment protection. Less central to the state's argument but present nonetheless was the claim in Eaton's case that "chicken shit" also amounted to fighting words. The key in winnowing by fiat is definition: When are sexual utterances obscene? When are misstatements libelous? When are offensive or annoying words fighting? The Court has reduced *Chaplinsky*'s scope by narrowly defining each category of ostracized speech so that relatively few utterances fall within each. Moreover, while *Chaplinsky* started out ostracizing four types of speech the Court now recognizes only three: fighting words, obscenity, and defamation (see Table 2.1).

TABLE 2.1
UTTERANCES EXCLUDED AT ONE TIME OR
ANOTHER FROM FIRST AMENDMENT
PROTECTION

Form of speech	Sample case	Supporting Court passage
Epithets and personal abuse	*Cantwell v. Connecticut* (1940)	"Resort to epithets or personal abuse is not in any proper sense communication of information or opinion safeguarded by the Constitution, and its punishment as a criminal act would raise no questions under that instrument," at 309-310.
Fighting words tending to provoke an immediate breach of the peace	*Chaplinsky v. New Hampshire* (1942)	"There are certain well-defined . . . classes of speech, the prevention and punishment of which have never been thought to raise any Constitutional problem. These include . . . the insulting or 'fighting' words—those which by their very utterance inflict injury or tend to incite an immediate breach of the peace," at 572.
Obscenity	*Roth v. United States* (1957)	"We hold that obscenity is not within the area of constitutionally protected speech or press," at 485.
Slander and libel	*Beauharnais v. Illinois* (1951)	". . . libelous utterances are not within the area of constitutionally protected speech, . . ." at 250.

Fighting words   Robert Paul Cohen walked down the aisles of Los Angeles County Courthouse wearing a jacket on the back of which were written the words "Fuck the Draft."[69] One Rosenfeld addressed a public school board meeting and used the words "mother fucking" four times.[70] One Lewis, irate at the arrest of her son, intervened and called the arresting officer "g-- d--- m----- f------ police."[71] And, of course, the Nazis wanted to display the swastika and Terry Eaton said "chicken shit." The common tie of these cases is that in each the state argued that the words were fighting words and could properly be limited through breach of the peace and similar statutes. What, precisely, is a fighting utterance?

As defined by the Court, mere insults are not fighting words nor are offensive utterances nor words randomly addressed to anyone who happens to be listening. Fighting words must be specifically addressed to a target person. Moreover, they must be "inherently likely to provoke violent reaction" by the person to whom they are addressed.[72] Thus, Cohen's colorful jacket was offensive, yes, but its words were not fighting because they were not directed to a particular individual nor did they inherently provoke violence. The same can be said of the school board remarks. They were offensive and distasteful but did not meet the standard set for fighting words. Are swastikas fighting words? The Illinois Appellate Court thought so, saying the swastika "as a matter of common knowledge, is inherently likely to provoke violent reaction among those of the Jewish persuasion or ancestry when intentionally brought in close proximity to their homes and places of worship." But other courts involved in the dispute disagreed, concluding, as did the federal district court, that under standards set forth by the Supreme Court swastikas were not fighting words.

A lingering point of dissension in the fighting words doctrine concerns the so-called captive audience. The Court has said that the remedy for merely offensive words is for the viewers to "avert their eyes" rather than for the speaker to stifle the message; that is, people sitting in the courthouse corridor could look away as Robert Cohen walked by, and Skokie residents, forewarned that offensive symbols would be on display in a parade, could simply not watch the parade. But it is harder for the parents attending the school board meeting to avert their ears from offensive language. Does the presence of a captive audience alter the definition of fighting words? Justice Powell suggests that the definition be expanded to include "the willful use of scurrilous language calculated to offend the sensibilities of an unwilling audience"[73] but so far the Court has preserved its basic definition. The only change over the years has been a narrowing, not expansion, of the definition so that today fewer words fit into the fighting words category than when the Court originally conceived the concept.[74]

Obscenity   In the 1960s Massachusetts swept the 1750 book, *Memoirs of a Woman of Pleasure* ("Fanny Hill") from the bookshelves on the grounds that it was obscene.[75] Also in the 1960s Ralph Ginzburg was convicted of using the U.S. mail to send obscene material in violation of the federal code.[76] The material that he sent contained, among other things, photographs of nude interracial couples. Ginzburg went to some lengths to titillate his readers by trying to have the publication, *Eros*, mailed from the towns of Intercourse or Blue Ball, Pennsylvania, both names loaded with sexual innuendo. Finally, one Mr. Miller was convicted of sending obscene materials to a California restaurant owner who happened to open the unsolicited package with his unsuspecting mother.[77] The package contained advertisements for "adult" books that featured explicit drawings and photographs of assorted sexual activities. Fully aware that obscenity is unprotected speech, governments have passed myriad laws to control the distribution and consumption of obscene materials. But in their quest to root out obscenity, states can all too easily sweep protected sexual speech in the wake. To guard against the unwitting censure of protected expression, the Court has taken special care to develop a reasonably concise definition of obscenity.

TABLE 2.2
THE EVOLVING DEFINITION OF OBSCENITY

Total number of concurring and dissenting opinions	Decision
3	Something is obscene if, "to the average person, applying contemporary community standards, the dominant theme of the material taken as a whole appeals to prurient interests."
3	Material must be "patently offensive" as well as appealing to prurient interests to be obscene.
5	Material must be *utterly* without social importance to be obscene.
7	A book that is patently offensive and appeals to prurient interests is not obscene if it has "a modicum of literary and historical value."
4	Material may be held obscene if it is crudely and offensively marketed (i.e., if it is "pandered").
2	Obscene material appeals to prurient interests, is patently offensive, and lacks *serious* literary, artistic, political or scientific value. Obscenity may be decided through community, not national, standards.

One classic political cartoon shows the Justices happily taking front row seats, bags of popcorn in hand, before a screen in the High Court chambers, ready to preview films for obscenity. All indications are, however, that in reality the Justices approach obscenity cases with more dread than delight and more dissension than unanimity. Obscenity has turned out to be an especial quagmire in First Amendment doctrine. Called an "intractable" problem by one Justice,[78] obscenity has bred an unusual amount of confusion within the Court. Rarely do the Justices throw up their hands in despair, but they came close to doing so in 1967 when they admitted they had no agreed-upon definition of obscenity[79] and issued simple per curiam opinions on the next thirty-three obscenity cases coming before them. Justice Stewart said *he* knew obscenity when he saw it—but the Court majority did not and it was not until 1973, sixteen years after the first attempt,[80] that a Court majority finally agreed upon a definition that still is intact today (see Table 2.2). The so-called *Miller* definition of obscenity[81] is this: material is obscene if,

Case	Vote	Author of Court opinion
Roth v. United States (1957)	6–3	Brennan
Manuel Enterprises, Inc. v. Day (1962)	6–1	No agreement on an opinion for the Court
Jacobellis v. Ohio (1964)	6–3	No agreement on an opinion for the Court
"Memoirs" v. Massachusetts (1966)	6–3	No agreement on an opinion for the Court
Ginzburg v. United States (1966)	5–4	Brennan
Miller v. California (1973)	5–4	Burger

(1) taken as a whole and
(2) judged by the average person using
(3) contemporary
(4) community standards, it
(5) appeals to prurient interests in sex,
(6) is patently offensive, and
(7) lacks serious social value.

Courts consider at least loosely each part of the *Miller* definition when reviewing material for obscenity. Each element is a unique standard in itself. Consider, first, "taken as a whole": the overall theme and tone of the work must be obscene; judges will not ferret out one sexually explicit passage from a 900-page volume, for example, and dub the entire work obscene on the basis of the excerpt. Thus *Fanny Hill* may have had highly questionable isolated passages, but the Justices examined the work in its entirety, which included, among other things, a moral ("that sex with love is superior to sex in a brothel").[82] Second, "judged by the *average* person": some people are perverse, no question there, but should *their* idea of what is sexually enticing be the standard for the entire community? Suppose some people got great satisfaction from medical textbooks. It is probably safe to say most people would look at such books clinically and dispassionately. Should the books be controlled merely because they appeal to the prurient interests of one odd group of people? The "average person" standard counteracts this possibility by ensuring that material will be judged by an archetypal person in the community rather than by the most deviant group.

Third, "contemporary" standards: the public's acceptance of sexuality is subject to fairly dramatic shifts. In the early 1800s a person could be convicted of obscenity/libel for displaying a sign "showing a 'horrid and unnatural monster' which had no eyes, whose ears were misplaced and whose skin was copper-colored."[83] In the early twentieth century a censorship board found a Walt Disney film showing the birth of a buffalo obscene.[84] But by the 1970s thousands of filmgoers queued to see such uncommonly explicit films as "Deep Throat" and "The Devil in Miss Jones." The "contemporary standards" provision ensures that yesterday's ideas do not bind today's consumer of sexual expression.

Fourth, "community standards": this has posed problems for the Court. At first it indicated there was a national standard of pruriency but in *Miller* and subsequent decisions it has suggested that each community has its own notion of pruriency. Recognizing that a traveling performance of, say, "Oh! Calcutta!" would have a different reception in a sleepy North Dakota township than in New York City, the Court allows a variable standard of pruriency to flourish. This can work two ways. On the one hand it protects New Yorkers from North Dakota's idea of sexuality, but on the other hand it may cut off expression for the exceptionally curious North Dakotan. On balance this standard seems to be less protective of speech than the original national standard.

Fifth, "prurient interests": the Court dragged the word from lethargy to part of the legal lexicon in the 1957 case of *Roth v. United States*.[85] There the Court defined pruriency as "material having a tendency to excite lustful thoughts" and elaborated by referring to *Webster's New International Dictionary*: pruriency has to do with "itching, morbid, or lascivious longings; of desire, curiosity, or propensity, lewd. . . ." The material must appeal to some warped or kinky feeling—not to a mere interest or curiosity in sex. Thus, for example, enemies of Alex Comfort's *Joy of Sex* I and II would have a hard time proving that these books, supposedly written to inform and educate, satisfy *Miller's* pruriency test.

Sixth, "patently offensive": the Court assumes that some material is gross on its face.[86] By requiring material to be patently offensive as well as prurient, the Court tightens its definition of obscenity and offers greater protection to sexual speech by doing so.

Seventh, "lacks serious social value": this standard gave the Justices some trouble. At first they said material must be *utterly* without social importance.[87] Since very few works are totally devoid of redeeming value (artistic, literary, scientific), few works met this standard of obscenity. When the Court changed this to say that material must have serious value to be salvaged, it opened the way for more works to be judged obscene.

A battery of secondary tests and formulas fleshes out obscenity doctrine. For example, the Court suggests that a different definition of obscenity might apply when children make up the audience,[88] that the way a publication is advertised and sold may affect its obscenity,[89] and that indecent as well as obscene material can be controlled if it is conveyed over television or radio.[90] Each such test chips away at the method of defining obscenity by fiat by weakening the distinction between obscenity and nonobscenity. When the Court recognizes different definitions of obscenity and uses contextual as well as content clues to decide whether material is obscene, it undermines the relatively dogmatic rationale of protected versus unprotected speech without doing away with it entirely.

Defamation   Mary Alice and Russell Firestone, a young and wealthy Florida society couple, separated in 1964 amid lengthy and publicized divorce proceedings spiced with testimony about Mrs. Firestone's "extramarital escapades." The court battle gained national coverage when *Time* magazine wrote about the story in its "Milestones" section. *Time*'s account proved to be inaccurate, however; the magazine put the blame for the divorce on Mrs. Firestone, but the court had actually granted the divorce without singling out either party for fault. Mrs. Firestone sued for libel and was awarded $100,000 by a Florida Circuit Court.[91]

Another defamation case involved an advertisement a civil rights group placed in *The New York Times* in an effort to solicit funds. The advertisement contained several inaccuracies about events in Montgomery, Alabama. It said, for example, that Martin Luther King had been arrested seven times (actually it was only four); that "the entire student body" of Alabama State College protested the "truckloads" of "armed" police "ringing" the campus (actually, "most" of the student body protested the "large" numbers of police who were present but not "ringing" the campus); and that authorities padlocked the dining hall in order to "starve" the students "into submission" (authorities did not padlock the dining hall). The supervisor of Montgomery's police department claimed that the mistakes maligned the department and, by inference, him personally. He sued *The New York Times* and was awarded $500,000.[92]

A defamatory statement (an oral defamation is slander, a written defamation libel) "tends so to harm the reputation of another as to lower him in the estimation of the community or to deter third persons from associating or dealing with him."[93] Under the *Chaplinsky* rule, defamatory statements are unprotected speech, which makes guidelines spelling out what kinds of expression are defamatory very important. Common law rules about defamation at the time of *Chaplinsky* were very lax; a person making a harmful statement about someone else could be found guilty of libel.[94] But what about the innocent misstatement? Were all reporters to produce completely accurate information every time they put their pens to paper we would no longer be dealing with human beings since the human tendency to err is legion. Or what about the misstatement earnestly made by an individual who sincerely believes he or she has found the truth? Suppose a bank official called a female colleague a "g-- d--- liar" in a business meeting. Under common law the maligned individual could sue her malfactor. But suppose the woman *was* a "g-- d--- liar" and the speaker had evidence to prove she had lied in business meetings. Does the common law standard unnecessarily stifle free expression?

Perhaps because of questions like these the Court has narrowed the range of utterances that may be held defamatory and thus cast outside the reach of First Amendment protection. Its most important change since *Chaplinsky* has been that mere falsehoods are not defamatory. Instead, the plaintiff must show that the person made the false statement with "actual malice," that is, "with knowledge that it was false or with reckless disregard of whether it was false or not."[95] Thus, when the Supreme Court reviewed the police supervisor's suit against *The New York Times* it reversed the award, holding that the supervisor had not shown that the newspaper made the inaccurate statements purposely or with malice.[96] Falsehoods are inevitable in public speech, wrote the Court, and innocently made falsehoods must be protected in order for free expression to have the "breathing space" it needs to survive.

The individual's interest must not, of course, be overlooked in a defamation dispute. A person's reputation is a precious commodity that is easily lost and so must be protected. Yet some people have greater armor against defamation than others. If accusations are made against a city mayor or U.S. senator or even a police supervisor the targeted person, by virtue of his or her standing within the community, will probably be approached by members of the press and be given an opportunity publicly to rebut the charges. The banker who was called a liar in her boardroom has no immediate access to the news media, however, even if the accusation leaked out to the press. Her activities are not automatically "news" and so the banker is left without a systematic way to rebut charges that threaten her reputation. Ought the ground rules be different for the private individual against whom falsehoods or accusations have been made?

According to the Court, the doctrine does differ when private individuals are involved because, the theory goes, these people do not have easy access to the public media to rebut the charges leveled against them. They need extra protection, which comes from an addendum to the general doctrine: both the private individual and the public official must prove actual malice to collect for "presumed damages," but the private person need not prove actual malice to collect for "actual injury," whereas the public official must.[97] Thus, Montgomery's police supervisor as a public person must prove *The New York Times* printed the falsehoods about racial incidents in his city with actual malice in order to collect for damages he actually sustained as a result of the advertisement. The banker, however, need only prove her accusor made false statements in order to collect for actual damages. If the banker wants to sue for presumed injury also, she must, as with the police supervisor, prove the statements were made with actual malice.

This shows that in order to understand how the scales are tilted in a slander case it is important to know who the target of defamation is. If it is a public official (including government officials and also candidates for public office[98]), the balance favors free speech inasmuch as the words were considered to be protected. If it is a private individual, the balance shifts somewhat in that the person does not have access to the media to rebut the charges. It is easy enough to see that the police supervisor was a public official and the banker a private individual. But what about someone like Mary Alice Firestone? She is a private individual but, by virtue of her marriage to a man of high society, was in the public limelight. Florida's society-watchers were so enamoured of Mrs. Firestone's activities that she had hired a press secretary. Clearly, she had access to the media to rebut *Time*'s story that she was at fault in the divorce. Do the ground rules change in her case?

The Court has identified one other type of person who falls between the private individual and the public official but who, for defamation purposes, is treated like a public official—the "public figure."[99] Public figures have "roles of especial prominence in the affairs of society"[100] and include such people as a former athletic director[101] and a former military man active in anti-integration politics.[102] A public figure must have "thrust" himself or herself into the public view; a person who unwittingly comes into public focus through no fault of his or her own is still considered to be a private individual.[103] Consider, for example, the case of Ronald Hutchinson, a research director at Kalamazoo State Mental Hospital and adjunct professor at Western Michigan University. Part of his research, which was funded by state and federal agencies, focused on the reactions of animals to stress, as measured by jaw-clenching. Hutchinson came into the public limelight when Senator William Proxmire gave him a "Golden Fleece" award for using public money to conduct what Proxmire considered to be frivolous or inane research. Hutchinson sued for damages and the Court held that for defamation purposes Hutchinson was a private individual, not a public figure, because he was unwittingly thrust into the public limelight through no fault of his own.[104] The Senator, not the scientist, was responsible for the latter's sudden notoriety. This ruling gave Hutchinson added protection in the conflict between his reputation and the Senator's interest in free speech. The Court also held that Mary Alice Firestone was a private individual because she had not purposely thrust herself into public view,[105] a decision that gave her added protection in her suit against *Time* magazine.

In summary, winnowing by fiat excludes the "calculated falsehood"—the falsehood made with actual malice—from First Amendment speech. It no longer excludes the innocent "error and misstatement" that is "inevitable in any scheme of truly free expression and debate."[106] The line between protected and nonprotected speech has become increasingly wavy, however, in that libel requirements vary according to the target of false remarks. Now both public figures and public officials must show actual malice; with these decisions the Court decreased the amount of speech excluded by the *Chaplinsky* ruling.

Speech–Conduct Distinctions

One of the first questions the Court watcher must ask in free speech cases is whether a form of ostracized speech (fighting words, obscenity, or the calculated falsehood) is at issue because if it is the scales tilt in favor of the countervailing social interest. Another question to be asked is whether symbolic speech is at issue. If it is the ground rules again change because the conflict involves a less "pure" form of expression.

Symbolic speech is the communication of ideas through conduct. Normally the action of the message heightens its drama or impact, as illustrated by the case of the Stovers of Rye, New York, who protested high property taxes by erecting a clothesline in their front yard and stringing it with dirty clothes and rags. The next year they put up a second clothesline, equally laden with junk, and over the next four years added four more lines.[107] Conduct was central to the Stovers's protest but so was speech: the Stovers turned their home into a junkyard solely to communicate their unhappiness with high taxes. Another case involved Mary Beth Tinker, a high school student who protested the Vietnam War by wearing a black armband to school in defiance of regulations laid down by the school superintendent. Tinker engaged in conduct when she put on the armband but her purpose was to send a message.[108] Finally, NSPA members planned to engage in conduct by donning military-style uniforms and carrying a party banner with a swastika on it but the effect of the action was to convey a message. The swastika in itself speaks; it is an immediately recognizable symbol of a political ideology.

There is no simple formula for deciding when clotheslines, armbands, and swastikas are merely conduct with expressive overtones and when they become First Amendment speech, subject to the protections that status offers. Judges do seem to agree, however, that symbolic conduct will be counted as speech only if it is clearly legal conduct. An assassination, act of terrorism, or the malicious destruction of property is not excusable simply because its perpetrator attached a tangential message to it.[109] Judges also agree that conduct is protected as speech only if its sender reasonably intends to communicate an idea and the recipient interprets it as communication.[110] Thus, a person cannot act disruptively and later ascribe a communicative intent to it in the hope of reaping the privileges attached to speech. The question of intent is delicate, however,[111] as illustrated by the case of Valerie Goguen, a man arrested for "contemptuous" treatment of the U.S. flag.[112] Goguen's crime lay in walking down the street with a flag patch sewn on his trousers. Police spotted him, *assumed* he was sending a contemptuous message, and arrested him. But Goguen said nothing to the officers about a message. Without his affirmation, how is one to know whether he was in fact speaking or whether he was merely decorating his pants for a stylistic or other innocuous purpose? Conceivably he could have been sending a message of pride, as did Roy Rogers and Dale Evans when they appeared on a television special wearing flag emblems. Or, consider Alfred Tennyson Cowgill's arrest for contempt toward the flag.[113] Cowgill had fashioned a vest out of the flag but denied he wore the vest to express contempt for the flag. He had a message, he admitted, but it was to oppose "the concept that any bolt of cloth must be regarded as 'sacred'."[114] This raises the question whether one form of conduct may express different messages and, if so, whether some messages are more protected than others.

In order to separate speech from conduct the Supreme Court seems to use a continuum approach. It assumes that "the 'speech' and 'nonspeech' elements" of symbolic conduct can be distinguished.[115] Once this is done the behavior can be mentally placed on a continuum ranging from speech predominant to conduct predominant (see Figure 2.1). The more predominant the speech element the more likely is the behavior to be First Amendment speech. The more predominant the behavior element the less likely is the behavior to receive First Amendment protection. An example of a "speech predominant" behavior is a person complaining about high property taxes by talking with passersby on a street corner. The person shifts to "conduct predominant" behavior when he or she protests by refusing to pay property taxes. A person enters the middle grey area when he or she does something like erecting a junk-laden clothesline to protest taxes. Judges ruling on the Stover case disagreed about whether speech or conduct was at stake, but the final ruling classified the clothesline strategy as conduct. In separating speech from conduct judges are not so concerned with the method of communication that they overlook the importance of the ideas being communicated, however. As one observer has noted "[i]t is the *ideas* expressed, and not just a particular form of expression, that must be protected if the underlying first amendment values are to be realized."[116] Thus virtually all the people involved in the Skokie case agreed that

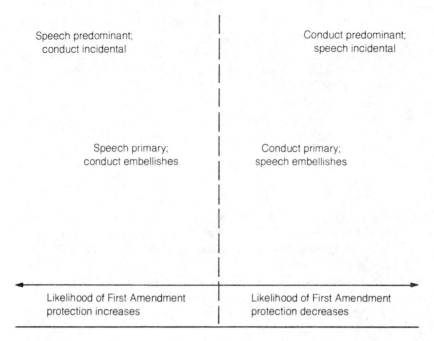

Speech predominant; conduct incidental	Conduct predominant; speech incidental
Speech primary; conduct embellishes	Conduct primary; speech embellishes
Likelihood of First Amendment protection increases	Likelihood of First Amendment protection decreases

FIGURE 2.1
PERSPECTIVE FOR VIEWING SYMBOLIC
EXPRESSION CASES

swastikas and uniforms were speech because they communicated a message.

The Court has said that "as the mode of expression moves from the printed page to the commission of public acts . . . the scope of permissible state regulations significantly increases."[117] It has also said that the First Amendment does not "afford the same kind of freedom to those who would communicate ideas by pure speech."[118] Expression becomes progressively less valued as its conduct element grows. Yet the Court tempers its continuum approach by reviewing the conduct's impact on society. As refined in the draft-card burning case of *United States v. O'Brien*,[119] the Court's test for determining when communicative conduct is excluded from First Amendment protection is this: communicative conduct is excluded if the conduct element predominates *and* burdens society by intruding on a "substantial" government interest. In *O'Brien* the Court upheld a congressional amendment to the Selective Service Act making it a crime knowingly to destroy or mutilate a draft card. At that time young men were purposely burning their draft cards to protest Vietnam policy; that is, they knowingly destroyed their cards to convey a message. The Court upheld the law under First Amendment challenge, however, saying that Congress could control the behavior element in symbolic speech if doing so furthered a "substantial government interest" which, in the law at bar, was ensuring the smooth functioning of the draft. The Justices attached two other conditions as well: the government's purpose in controlling the behavior must not be to quash speech and the limit must be "no greater than is essential."

Balancing

Intra-liberty gradations to this point have excluded obscenity, fighting words, and defamation from First Amendment protection on the grounds that they have no social utility; symbolic conduct in which harmful behavior predominates has been excluded on the grounds that it is more conduct than speech. An expression passing these two hurdles qualifies as First Amendment speech but it is not home "free" yet. Still to come is for the Court to weigh this speech against other social interests in order to see which speech the state may control. The process of balancing is potentially open-ended, but the Court has developed two variants that help restrict its arbitrary application. One type of balancing involves time, place, and manner restrictions; another is based upon the likelihood of danger. A third variant, ad hoc balancing, does little to direct balancing and may even encourage its open-endedness.

Time, place, and manner restrictions   The state may put time, place, and manner restrictions on speech. These control the trappings of speech—when, where, and how—rather than the speech itself. The First Amendment has "never been thought to give absolute protection to every individual to speak whenever or wherever he pleases, or to use any form of address in any circumstances that he chooses,"[120] writes the Court. Thus, the state may limit street parades to one at a time,[121] forbid demonstrations on a busy street during rush hour,[122] control the volume of sound trucks,[123] and forbid noisy demonstrations outside of schoolhouses.[124]

In order to qualify as a permissible time, place, and manner restriction the law must meet three conditions. First, it must be made "without reference to the content of the regulated speech";[125] that is, it must truly be a restriction *only* on the trappings of speech. A Chicago ordinance that forbade all picketing except labor picketing within 150 feet of a schoolhouse failed this test; by specifying which types of picketing could be controlled the ordinance impermissibly referred to the content of expression.[126] Second, the state must have a "significant" interest in putting on the control; it cannot make time, place, and manner restrictions for frivolous reasons. A "significant" interest might be to limit parades during rush hour in order to prevent traffic jams and the possibility of accidents. A frivolous interest might be to limit parades in order to prevent littering; the state has other ways of controlling littering that are less harmful to speech. Third, the state must "leave open ample alternative channels for communication of the information."[127] If a time, place, and manner restriction cuts off all opportunities for the individual or group to speak, it will probably not stand in court.

The question of time, place, and manner restrictions did not really arise in the Skokie case,[128] but presumably the ordinances would have failed the test. Were the ordinances content-neutral? Probably not; the uniform ordinance singled out only one type of uniform for control and the swastika provision singled out one type of emblem. The ordinances were designed to stop Nazis from marching and this bias clearly showed through. Did the state have a significant interest in restricting the parade? Protection of public peace and order usually qualifies as a significant interest, so perhaps the city could have controlled some features of the march (but not banned it altogether) had it been able to show that the restrictions would preserve public order in a volatile setting. Did the city leave other channels open to the NSPA? By banning the march the city surely foreclosed one effective channel of communication. The party could have publicized its message through letters to the editor or paid advertisements, but these avenues are not as effective nor as cheap as a well-orchestrated march, which is virtually guaranteed to bring out the press corps. The city did not leave open "ample" alternative avenues. In short, the city was not powerless to control what it perceived to be a disruptive demonstration; under certain conditions it could have imposed reasonable time, place, or manner restrictions on the march. By taking a more blunderbuss approach and imposing a prior restraint on the march, however, the city wrote off the possibility of more subtle controls.

Likelihood of danger   The judge who issued the contempt citation to Terry Eaton feared that a courtroom expletive would threaten the orderly administration of that chamber. How real must that fear be to justify penalizing speech? Could the envisioned danger be merely possible? Must it be probable? Must it be imminent? Does a judge have to wait until the courtroom is actually disrupted or until spectators actually turn cynical about courtroom decorum before he or she can control verbal outbursts? Or can a judge act under a mere suspicion that the speech will prove to be disruptive? Or, consider the Ku Klux Klan leader who staged a rally in which hooded people burned a cross and said such things as "This is what we are going to do to the niggers," "Send the Jews back to Israel" and "Freedom for the whites."[129] He was convicted of advocating "crime, sabotage, violence, or unlawful methods of terrorism," and bringing people together to advocate these things. May the state control speech that "advocates" or calls for violence even when there is no showing that anyone is actually preparing to be violent? Suppose a group of patrons is watching a Presidential news conference at a bar and one fellow in the audience says, "Someone should kill the President." May the state arrest him for advocating violence? Or must it wait for more evidence that violence is incipient? Suppose it waits too long?

One of the things the Court asks about in balancing speech with another social interest is the likelihood the speech will actually endanger the interest at stake. It has, over the course of this century, offered at least four formulas, ranging from the "bad tendency" test, which allows the state to control speech at the merest hint of danger,[130] to the presently favored "imminent and lawless action" test, which requires the state to wait until the speech is clearly an "incitement to imminent lawless action."[131] In between it tried the "gravity of the evil" test, which holds that courts must in each case "ask whether the gravity of the 'evil,' discounted by its improbability, justifies such invasion of free speech as is necessary to avoid the danger."[132] This test, like the bad tendency test, is unconcerned with the time span between the words and the danger. To "discount" the improbability of the evil is to allow free conjecture about its likelihood. Another middle-ground test is the "clear and present danger" test, which holds that the danger must be clear and present and which advises courts that it "is a question of proximity and degree."[133] By requiring the danger to be "present" the test specifies a distance in time between the words and their consequences; by requiring the danger to be "clear" the test avoids blind conjecture about the harmful tendency of the words.[134] The currently used imminent and lawless action test is the most protective of all for free speech. Closely related to the clear and present danger test, it too expresses concern over proximity and degree.

Using the imminency test, the Court struck down Eaton's contempt conviction, saying the words themselves were not enough to convict. Rather, the "fire which [the language] kindles must constitute an imminent, not merely a likely, threat to the administration of justice." In another case the Court reversed the conviction for disorderly conduct of a demonstrator who said, "We'll take the fucking street later [or again]."[135] The words were too far removed from the supposed danger to be quashed; they amounted to "nothing more than advocacy of illegal action at some indefinite future time."

Ad hoc balancing Ad hoc balancing is a sort of catch-all category referring to cases in which judges weigh the conflicting interests with no clear test to guide them.[136] It presupposes case-by-case adjudication, leaving it to the court "to strike a . . . balance in the light of its own best judgment."[137] Some observers see this as an invitation to arbitrary judicial decisions and criticize the Court for condoning and, indeed, using it.[138] One particularly controversial use of ad hoc balancing occurred in a decision the Court handed down in the wake of the anti-Communist sentiment of the 1950s and 1960s. The case involved a psychology instructor suspected of having ties with the Communist Party who was called before a subcommittee of the House Committee on Un-American Activities.[139] He refused to answer questions posed to him and was convicted of contempt of Congress. The Supreme Court upheld his conviction but did not use a clear guiding doctrine. Instead, it noted that in this case the "critical element" in weighing the individual's interest in free expression and the state's interest in controlling it is the importance of Congress's interest "in demanding disclosures from an unwilling witness." The Court examined in detail Congress's interest in anti-Communist investigation but it did not examine the instructor's interest in free association, thereby showing the malleability of ad hoc balancing. Lacking specific guidelines, it allows courts to load one side of the scale over the other.

SUMMARY

Justice Cardozo once called free speech "the matrix, the indispensable condition, of nearly every form of freedom."[140] Reflecting that sentiment, the Court has elevated the First Amendment to a high place within the Bill of Rights. Among other things, this inter-liberty gradation means the Court subjects laws intruding on the First Amendment to especially strict review. Three tests it reserves for state controls on speech are the relaxed presumption of constitutionality, the void-for-vagueness doctrine, and the overbreadth doctrine:

Relaxed presumption of constitutionality
Normally the Court presumes a law's constitutionality; however, it *relaxes* this presumption when the state imposes a subsequent

punishment on speech and *reverses* the presumption when the state imposes a prior restraint on speech.

Void-for-vagueness doctrine

The Court strikes down a law on its face or as applied if the "average person charged with its violation is necessarily left uncertain as to what conduct . . . would be enough to convict under it." All laws are open to vagueness review, but the Court pays special attention to vague laws infringing on speech because of their chilling effect on expression.

Overbreadth doctrine

The Court strikes down a law on its face or as applied if it is substantially overbroad; that is, if it "sweeps within its ambit" protected speech.

Each of these tests tips the scales so that the person's right to speak has more ballast than the state's interest in controlling speech when the two come into conflict in a court of law. Not surprisingly, therefore, people convicted of an offense will try to base their appeal on First Amendment grounds if the offense is remotely connected with expression. Yet the range of *potentially* free speech is substantially greater than the range of *actual* free speech and so the hopes of many of these people will be thwarted. This chapter reviews the assorted principles the Court uses to cull or winnow protected speech from the many utterances litigants claim are free speech. The chapter orders the guidelines into three types: winnowing by fiat, speech–conduct distinctions, and balancing (see Figure 2.2).

Winnowing by fiat is the most dogmatic of the approaches. It presupposes that some utterances so lack redeeming social value that they are not speech within the meaning of the First Amendment. It excludes fighting words, obscenity, and libelous words:

Fighting words

Fighting words are those "inherently likely to provoke violent reaction" by the person to whom they are directly addressed.

Obscenity

Obscenity is material that, taken as a whole and judged by the average person using contemporary community standards, appeals to prurient interests in sex, is patently offensive, and lacks serious social value.

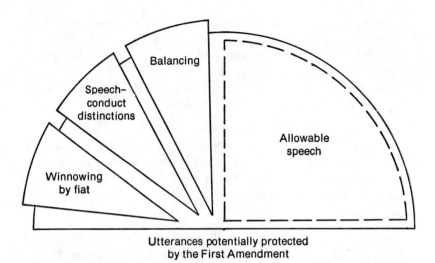

Utterances potentially protected
by the First Amendment

FIGURE 2.2
NARROWING THE SPECTRUM FROM ALL
UTTERANCES TO ALLOWABLE SPEECH

Defamation

Libelous statements are those made with knowledge of their false-hood or a reckless disregard of the truth (also known as the calcu-lated falsehood or words made with actual malice).

Speech–conduct distinctions involve expression conveyed through conduct such as the wearing of a black armband to communicate unhappiness about U.S. foreign policy. The Court has said that "as the mode of expression moves from the printed page to the commission of public acts . . . the scope of permissible state regulations significantly increases."[141] By thinking in terms of a continuum, the Court's approach here is less dogmatic than the black versus white, protected versus unprotected distinctions of winnowing by fiat. Generally speaking, the Court offers First Amendment protection to all symbolic speech except that in which conduct predominates and endangers a substantial government interest. The latter is not thought to be First Amendment speech.

Utterances not excluded in winnowing by fiat or speech–conduct distinctions join the ranks of First Amendment speech. Yet entry into the

First Amendment does not immunize speech from state control. In balancing, the Court weighs First Amendment speech against other social interests and upholds state controls on speech when the social interest outweighs the individual's interest in speaking. The Court uses three balancing mechanisms: time, place, and manner restrictions; likelihood-of-danger assessment, and ad hoc balancing:

Time, place, and manner restrictions

The state may control the "when, where, and how" of speech provided the regulation serves a significant governmental purpose, leaves open alternative channels for expression, and makes no reference to the speech's content.

Likelihood-of-danger assessment

The state may control speech that endangers society, as defined by a pre-set formula for assessing the likelihood of that danger. Currently the Court prefers a test that only lets the state control speech posing an "imminent danger of lawless action."

Ad hoc balancing

The Court decides the constitutionality of the state control on speech in a case-by-case manner in which it weighs the substantiality of the state's interest in control against the individual's interest in free speech.

Of these three, time, place, and manner restrictions intrude the least on free speech because they control the trappings rather than the content of speech. Ad hoc balancing intrudes the most because it gives broad leeway to the judge who happens to hear the appeal and opens the door for highly personal decisions. A likelihood-of-danger assessment interjects sensory observation and probability into the decision and so is an improvement over ad hoc balancing, although the protection it offers speech varies with the particular formula used. Some formulas, such as the bad tendency test, offer scant protection to speech; others, such as the clear and present danger and the imminent and lawless action tests, are more protective.

Which of these many tests will actually be used in a free speech case depends on the facts of the case, the claims raised by the parties, and the inclinations of the judges reviewing the appeal. Normally a case will focus on a single issue; for example, a person charged with flag desecration will principally argue that the act was in fact symbolic speech deserving First Amendment protection or a person charged with sending obscene material through the mails will argue that the material was not obscene under the *Miller* standard. The Skokie case that threads throughout this chapter is unusual in the large number of issues it raises and so should not be taken as typical. The many different places in which the Skokie case is used as illustration may leave the reader with the incorrect assumption that the plaintiffs used a shotgun approach, bringing up this and that claim indiscriminately. In fact, the accelerating number of issues rose only as the case went from the lowest to the highest state courts and then from the lowest to the highest federal courts and as its focus shifted from the city's effort to enjoin the march to its effort to pass laws making the march illegal. Each appeal presented a manageable conflict in which a limited number of issues came to bar. Only when the case is viewed panoramically do the issues take on a chaotic air. To clarify the relation of the case to this chapter's framework, it might be useful to list some of the things an attorney for the NSPA would include in a brief designed to persuade a court to reverse an injunction on a Nazi march.

1. Show that the march and its displays of emblems and swastikas are symbolic speech as defined by the Court and are therefore protected by the First Amendment. This will allow the attorney to overcome the barrier posed by speech–conduct distinctions.

2. Overcome the barrier posed by winnowing by fiat by demonstrating that the march, emblems, and swastikas are not excludable speech under the *Chaplinsky* ruling, that is, they are not fighting words, obscene, or defamatory. Use tests developed by the Court; for example, show that the speech is not "fighting" because it is not inherently likely to provoke violence and is not directed at a specific person.

3. Overcome the balancing barrier by showing that any danger posed by the march to public peace and order is hypothetical and speculative and does not meet the "imminent and lawless action" test.

4. Focus on the fact that the injunction is a prior restraint and is therefore presumptively unconstitutional.

5. Attack the injunction as void on its face for vagueness—that it does not give clear warning as to what is forbidden—and void as applied—that it gives indiscriminate leeway to officers in deciding whom to arrest.

6. Attack the injunction as overbroad on its face—that it punishes protected speech—and as applied—that in the present case it will be used to quash symbolic (protected) speech.

In answering these claims an attorney for the city of Skokie would present the opposite arguments: that the march is conduct and not speech; that even if it is speech it is not protected speech because it amounts to fighting words; that it poses a clear and present danger to public safety; that the danger is compelling and therefore overcomes the presumed unconstitutionality of a prior restraint; that the injunction is precise on its face and as applied; and that the injunction narrowly punishes only properly forbidden speech. The judges would then review each claim individually, reaching a decision on their interpretation of each doctrine and affected by the range of legal and extralegal influences that Chapter 1 discusses.

The tests this chapter reviews stand out for their diversity and malleability. On the one hand this opens the Court to criticism for the various and sometimes conflicting guidelines it has handed down and also for the gap that frequently looms between principle and practice. Not always acting upon its exhortations, the Court at times slips the First Amendment to a level no higher than other rights and subjects it to standards little more demanding than those governing other constitutional guarantees. Yet on the other hand the variegated array of tests is understandable and perhaps laudable. Each test was born in a unique historical period and each bequeaths to future Justices a rich assortment of precedents from which to construct principled responses to new historical eras. The Court could adopt a single standard for reviewing First Amendment cases; for example, it could follow Justice Black's suggestion and read "'no law abridging' to mean *no law abridging*"[142] and thereby give the First Amendment a spacious cast. Or, it could open all speech to ad hoc balancing and leave it to individual judges to decide each case as they see fit. This is unlikely, however, and perhaps it is testimony to the First Amendment's respected place that the Court is reluctant to impose a single standard—one possibly inflexible and nondescript after surviving the compromises necessary for final agreement—in place of the multiform yet adaptable standards it now applies.

Questions for Thought

1. How persuasive is Justice Cardozo's belief that the First Amendment is the cornerstone of all other liberties? Do you agree that any one liberty or set of related liberties is more basic than the others and acts as a foundation for them? If so, do you think the First Amendment serves that function? Why or why not? If you think another liberty is the cornerstone, which is it and why?

2. In the 1930s and 1940s the Court elevated the First Amendment to a "preferred position" among all rights and liberties. The Justices have not often

repeated the "preferred position" argument in the decades since. Is the Court letting this idea sink into oblivion? Look at recent free speech decisions to see how often and with how much intensity the Justices write about a special status for the First Amendment. Are some Justices more likely than others to make this claim in their written opinions? Do the claims "fit" the decision in the case at bar? That is, when the writer of the majority opinion talks of the special status of the First Amendment, does he then go on to rule in favor of the First Amendment interest at stake? Or are references to the First Amendment's paramountcy hollow posturing?

3. Do you agree with the Court's conclusion that some utterances are not "speech" for First Amendment purposes? The Court defines nonspeech as utterances having no social utility. This test ostracizes speech for something it does *not* possess. Might it be better to use a test that ostracizes speech only for what it *does* possess, namely content that harms society? How would this differ from the likelihood-of-danger formulation? Why use winnowing by fiat at all? Why not subject all speech, including obscenity, defamation, and fighting words, to a clear and present danger test? Would this leave more or less material open to regulation?

4. Some people suggest it is ironic Americans are so concerned about controlling obscenity but do not systematically control violent expression. Is there a persuasive reason for this difference? Does one harm society more than the other? Could violent expression meet the winnowing-by-fiat test and be excluded from the First Amendment on the grounds that it has no social utility?

5. How closely have the legislators and judges in your state heeded the winnowing-by-fiat tests suggested by the Supreme Court? Look up your state's anti-obscenity statute. How does it define obscenity? Does the definition meet the *Miller v. California* test? Look up three recent obscenity decisions handed down by the highest appellate court in your state. How have the judges construed the statutory definition? Have they made it more restrictive than *Miller*? Less restrictive? Look up several recent breach-of-the-peace or fighting words decisions handed down by your state's highest court. Have the judges used a likelihood-of-danger test? If so, which? Clear and present danger? The imminent and lawless action test? Bad tendency? Something different?

6. In *Young v. American Mini Theatres, Inc.*, 427 U.S. 50 (1976), the Court upheld a Detroit ordinance that limited the number and location of adult-only theaters. Writing for the Court, Justice Stevens treated the ordinance as a time, place, and manner restriction, but the dissenters called it a content-based regulation. Read the *Young* opinion. Do you think the ordinance was a "mere" time, place, and manner restriction? What does the decision tell us about the adequacy of the Court's method of distinguishing between time, place, and manner laws and content-based restrictions?

7. Executives in the motion picture industry have tried to preempt state controls on the content of films by setting up their own self-censorship system, first with the Code of the 1930s and then with the Motion Pictures Rating System of 1968. In doing so, however, it is possible the industry has created a worse system of censorship than one the government could constitutionally impose. Assume that the rating system, which puts the familiar "G," "PG," "R," and "X" labels on films, was set up by a city council. Would it pass constitutional review? Would it meet the substantive and procedural standards the Court has laid down for controlling First Amendment expression? See the following two sources for a description of how the industry enforces its rating system: Jane M. Friedman, "The Motion Picture Rating System of 1968: A Constitutional Analysis of Self-Regulation by the Film Industry," 73 *Colum.L.Rev.* 185, 199 (1973); Douglas Ayer et al., "Self-Censorship in the Movie Industry: An Historical Perspective on Law and Social Change," 1970 *Wisc.L.Rev.* 791 (1970).

NOTES

1. See *Village of Skokie v. National Socialist Party*, 366 N.E. 2d 347 (1977).
2. *National Socialist Party v. Skokie*, 432 U.S. 43 (1977).
3. *Village of Skokie v. National Socialist Party*, 366 N.E. 2d 347 (1977).
4. *Village of Skokie v. National Socialist Party of America*, 373 N.E. 2d 21 (1978).
5. *Collin v. Smith*, 447 F. Supp. 676 (1978).
6. *Collin v. Smith*, 578 F. 2d 1197 (1978).
7. *Smith v. Collin*, 47 U.S.L.W. 3264.
8. *Eaton v. Tulsa*, 415 U.S. 697 (1974).
9. 268 U.S. 652 (1925).
10. Justice Black extolled the First Amendment as the "keystone of our Government" in his dissent in *Dennis v. United States*, 341 U.S. 494, 580 (1951).
11. *Palko v. Connecticut*, 302 U.S. 319, 327 (1937).
12. *United States v. Carolene Products Co.*, 304 U.S. 144 (1938).
13. *Jones v. Opelika*, 316 U.S. 584, 608 (1942).
14. *Murdock v. Pennsylvania*, 319 U.S. 103 (1943).
15. Ibid., at 105.
16. See, for example, Justice Black, speaking for the Court in *Marsh v. Alabama*, 326 U.S. 501, 509 (1946), and dissenting in *Dennis v. United States*, 341 U.S. 494, 581 (1951). Justice Frankfurter vigorously attacked the preferred position idea in his concurrence in *Kovacs v. Cooper*, 336 U.S. 77 (1949) but, as C. Herman Pritchett, *The American Constitution*, 2nd ed. (New York: McGraw-Hill, 1968), p. 422, notes, Justice Frankfurter went along with *Schneider v. State*, 308 U.S. 147 (1939), which accepted a premise of the preferred position. See Robert B. McKay, "The Preference for Freedom," 34 *N.Y.U.L.Rev.* 1182, 1190-1193 (1959). This discussion owes much to McKay's thesis on the First Amendment's paramountcy.

17. McKay, at 1223-1227, lists such references made by various Justices between 1919 and 1959. For more recent statements see *Pittsburgh Press Co. v. Human Relations Commission*, 413 U.S. 376, 381 (1973) and *Southeastern Promotions, Ltd. v. Conrad*, 420 U.S. 546, 561 (1975).

18. McKay refers to them as "devices." Only three are discussed here, although others might also be covered. See, for example, William B. Lockhart et al., *Constitutional Rights and Liberties* (St. Paul, Minn.: West, 1975), p. 399, who discuss the "less drastic means" offshoot of the overbreadth doctrine.

19. *United States v. C.I.O.*, 335 U.S. 106, 121, n.20 (1948).

20. *Lochner v. New York*, 198 U.S. 45 (1904).

21. He said "There *may be* narrower scope for operation of the presumption of constitutionality" when laws touch provisions of the first ten amendments. *United States v. Carolene Products Co.*, 304 U.S. 144, 152, n.4 (1938) (emphasis added).

22. Eight Justices formed the majority in *Schneider v. State*, 308 U.S. 147 (1939), which said at 161 that "mere legislative preferences or beliefs respecting matters of public convenience may well support regulation directed at other personal activities, but be insufficient to justify such as diminishes the exercise of rights [i.e., freedom of speech and the press] so vital to the maintenance of democratic institutions."

23. Concurring in *United States v. C.I.O.*, 335 U.S. 106, 140 (1948) (footnote omitted). A similar passage is contained in the majority opinion at 121, n.20. See also *Schneider v. State*, 308 U.S. 147, 161 (1939); *Thornhill v. Alabama*, 310 U.S. 88, 95 (1940); *Thomas v. Collins*, 323 U.S. 516, 529-530 (1943). Justice Rutledge concluded that the Court's presumption is *against* the legislative intrusion into these domains when the First Amendment is at issue. *United States v. C.I.O.*, 335 U.S. at 140 (emphasis added).

24. Alpheus Thomas Mason, *The Supreme Court From Taft to Warren*, 2nd ed. (Baton Rouge: Louisiana State University Press, 1968), p. 161.

25. Chief Justice Burger said of *New York Times v. United States*, 403 U.S. 713 (1971) that "every member of the Court, tacitly or explicitly, accepted the *Near [Near v. Minnesota*, 283, U.S. 697 (1931)] and *Keefe [Organization for a Better Austin v. Keefe*, 402 U.S. 415 (1971)] condemnations of prior restraint as presumptively unconstitutional." Dissenting in *Pittsburgh Press v. Human Relations Commission*, 413 U.S. 376, 396 (1973). The reverse presumption of constitutionality also applies to racial classifications (see Chapter 5).

26. *Connally v. General Construction Co.*, 269 U.S. 385, 391 (1926).

27. *Erznoznik v. Jacksonville*, 422 U.S. 205, 217 (1975). See also *Smith v. California*, 361 U.S. 147, 151 (1959) and *N.A.A.C.P. v. Button*, 371 U.S. 415, 438 (1963). The Court first applied the vagueness doctrine to economic controls and later to laws affecting First Amendment rights. Christina M. Burkholder, "Recent Supreme Court Developments of the Vagueness Doctrine: Four Cases Involving the Vagueness Attack on Statutes During the 1972-73 Term," 7 *Conn.I..Rev.* 94, 105 (1974).

28. *Baggett v. Bullitt*, 377 U.S. 360, 372 (1964). See also Justice Black, dissenting in *Barenblatt v. United States*, 360 U.S. at 137: A vague law "leaves all persons to guess just what the law really means to cover, and fear of a wrong guess inevitably leads all persons to forego the very rights the Constitution sought to protect above all others."

29. *Dombrowski v. Pfister*, 380 U.S. 479, 487 (1965).

30. *Cox v. Louisiana*, 379 U.S. 288 (1965).

31. Emphasis added. See Burkholder, at 100.

32. This discussion is based largely on Note, "The First Amendment Overbreadth Doctrine," 83 *Harv.L.Rev.* 844, 844-845 (1970). The "as applied" and "facial" attacks apply to both the void-for-vagueness doctrine and the overbreadth doctrine discussed below. See Note, "The Void-for-Vagueness Doctrine in the Supreme Court," 109 *U.Pa.L.Rev.* 67 (1960).

33. *Spence v. Washington*, 418 U.S. 405 (1974).

34. The "statute's application is quite mechanical." Ibid., at 414, n.9.

35. The Court may narrowly construe a federal statute in order to decrease future improper applications of it, but federal courts may not narrow state statutes further than state courts have already done. Burkholder, at 110; *United States v. Thirty-Seven Photographs*, 402 U.S. 363, 369 (1971).

36. For a detailed discussion of the advantages and disadvantages of the facial attack, see Note, "Overbreadth Review and the Burger Court," 49 *N.Y.U.L.Rev.* 532 (1974).

37. *Grayned v. Rockford*, 408 U.S. 104, 110 (1972).

38. *Coates v. Cincinnati*, 402 U.S. 611 (1971).

39. Its enforcement "may depend entirely upon whether or not a policeman is annoyed." Ibid., at 614.

40. *Winters v. New York*, 333 U.S. 507 (1948).

41. On the other hand, the Court upheld under vagueness challenge a Mississippi law forbidding picketing that "obstruct[ed] or unreasonably interfere[d] with free ingress to and from" courthouses. *Cameron v. Johnson*, 390 U.S. 611 (1968). Analyzing each word, the Court concluded: "The terms 'obstruct' and 'unreasonably interfere' plainly require no 'guess[ing] at [their] meaning.' Appellants focus on the word 'unreasonably.' It is a widely used and well understood word and clearly so when juxtaposed with 'obstruct' and 'interfere.' We conclude that the statute clearly and precisely delineates its reach in words of common understanding."

    The Court also upheld a New Hampshire statute forbidding "offensive, derisive, or annoying" words. *Chaplinsky v. New Hampshire*, 315 U.S. 568 (1942). Here the Court looked approvingly on the narrow construction the state supreme court had given it. As interpreted by the court, the law forbade only words having "a direct tendency to cause acts of violence by the persons to whom, individually, the remark is addressed."

42. The Court first suggested it in *Thornhill v. Alabama*, 310 U.S. 88 (1940). For discussions of overbreadth see Note, "The First Amendment Overbreadth Doctrine."

43. *Thornhill v. Alabama*, 310 U.S. 88 (1940).

44. *Smith v. Goguen*, 415 U.S. 556, 577, n.20 (1974). See also William O. Dillingham, "Constitutional Law: Old Glory Sits Down," 26 *U.Fla.L.Rev.* 615 (1974).

45. *Street v. New York*, 394 U.S. 576 (1969) (emphasis added).

46. The Court *upheld* under overbreadth challenge an antinoise ordinance that forbade any person near an in-session school or class from "willfully mak[ing] or assist[ing] in the making of any noise or diversion which disturbs or tends to disturb the peace or good order of such school session." *Grayned v. Rockford*, 408 U.S. 104 (1972). The Court concluded that "[f]ar from having an impermissibly broad prophylactic ordinance," the city "punishes *only* conduct which disrupts or is about to disrupt normal school activities." The ordinance was "narrowly tailored" and it met the city's proper "compelling interest" of ensuring undisturbed school sessions.

47. According to the author of Note, "Overbreadth Review," at 533, the Court seemed to treat overbreadth as more of "an attitude or policy than a well-developed doctrine."

48. Justice Blackmun, dissenting in *Lewis v. New Orleans*, 415 U.S. 130, 140 (1974). "If the Court adheres to its present course," continued Justice Blackmun, "no state statute or city ordinance will be acceptable unless it parrots the wording of our opinions." For other attacks on facial overbreadth by dissenting Justices see *Coates v. Cincinnati*, 402 U.S. 611, 617-621 (1971) (White, J., dissenting); *Gooding v. Wilson*, 405 U.S. 518, 534-547 (Burger, C. J., dissenting); *Rosenfeld v. New Jersey*, 408 U.S. 901 (1972) (Powell, J., dissenting).

49. *Broadrick v. Oklahoma*, 413 U.S. 601, 615 (1973).

50. For example, the Court used the test to strike down a law forbidding drive-in theater owners from showing films containing nudity when the screen was visible from a public place, holding that this law did have a "real and substantial" deterrent effect on protected speech. *Erznoznik v. Jacksonville*, 422 U.S. 205 (1975). See also *Young v. American Mini Theatres, Inc.*, 427 U.S. 50 (1976). Because the Court has only used "substantial overbreadth" in cases involving expression other than traditional speech, it is unclear whether *Broadrick* limits the facial review of laws affecting verbal speech.

51. See John Stuart Mill, "On Liberty," in Max Lerner, ed., *Essential Works of John Stuart Mill* (New York: Bantam Books, 1961) and Thomas Jefferson, who said "[r]eason and free enquiry are the only effectual agents against error." Quoted in Walter Berns, *The First Amendment and the Future of American Democracy* (New York: Basic Books, 1976), p. 81. Justice Holmes was the first Supreme Court Justice to expand on the idea that free speech is requisite for truth. See his dissent in *Abrams v. United States*, 250 U.S. 616, 630-631 (1919). See also Justice Brandeis, concurring in *Whitney v. California*, 274 U.S. 357, 375 (1927).

52. *Cohen v. California*, 403 U.S. 15, 24 (1971).

53. "[D]iscussion affords ordinarily adequate protection against the dissemination of noxious doctrine." Justice Brandeis, concurring in *Whitney v. California*, 274 U.S. at 375. See also Chief Justice Hughes speaking for the Court in *DeJonge v. Oregon*, 229 U.S. 353, 365 (1937); Justice Black, dissenting in *Dennis v. United States*, 341 U.S. at 580; and Justice Douglas, also dissenting in *Dennis v. United States*, 341 U.S. at 588, who declared that free speech had "crippled" Communism "as a political force" in this country.

54. *Schenck v. United States*, 249 U.S. 47, 52 (1919). See also *Near v. Minnesota*, 283 U.S. 697 (1931), for a hypothetical example of the harm publication of certain information in wartime can pose to national security.

55. See, for example, Louis Nizer's account of the libel trial of Westbrook Pegler, a journalist practicing a brusque and sometimes reckless writing style. Nizer represented the man targeted by Pegler, and he convincingly recounts the personal trauma the man experienced as a result of Pegler's inaccurate reporting. Louis Nizer, *My Life in Court* (New York: Pyramid Books, 1968), chap. 1.

56. For example, Justice Douglas supported controls only on speech "so closely brigaded with illegal action as to become an inseparable part of it." *Roth v. United States*, 354 U.S. 476, 514 (1957) (Douglas, J., dissenting). Justice Black, another so-called "absolutist," read "'no law abridging' to mean *no law abridging*." *Smith v. California*, 361 U.S. 147, 157 (1959). Justice Black did, however, support controls over speech conveyed through conduct. *Tinker v. Des Moines*, 393 U.S. 503 (1969) (Black, J., dissenting).

57. *Garrison v. Louisiana*, 379 U.S. 64, 74-75 (1964).

58. *Mills v. Alabama*, 384 U.S. 214, 218 (1966).

59. *Shuttlesworth v. Birmingham*, 394 U.S. 147, 157 (1969).

60. *Virginia State Board of Pharmacy v. Virginia Citizens Consumer Council, Inc.*, 425 U.S. 748, 771-772, n.24 (1976). Reasoning that advertising is "hardier" than other speech, the Court concluded that "there is little likelihood of its being chilled by proper regulation. . . ." Ibid.

61. *Young v. American Mini Theatres, Inc.*, 427 U.S. 50 (1976). Writing only for a Court plurality, Justice Stevens went on to say there is "a less vital interest in the uninhibited exhibition of material that is on the borderline between pornography and artistic expression than in the free dissemination of ideas of social and political significance." It should be noted, however, that just the year before the Court had extended full constitutional protection to sexually explicit expression in *Erznoznik v. Jacksonville*, 422 U.S. 205 (1975).

62. *Winters v. New York*, 333 U.S. 507, 510 (1948). See Mark C. Rutzick, "Offensive Language and the Evolution of First Amendment Protection," 9 *Harv.C.R.-C.L.L.Rev.* 1, 11 (1974).

63. *Cohen v. California*, 403 U.S. 15, 26 (1971).

64. The Court had never explicitly excluded commercial speech from First Amendment protection, but observers interpreted two cases—*Breard v. City of Alexandria*, 341 U.S. 622 (1951) and *Valentine v. Chrestensen*, 316 U.S. 52 (1941)—to say the Court left commercial speech unprotected.

65. *Virginia State Board of Pharmacy v. Virginia Citizens Consumer Council, Inc.*, 425 U.S. 748 (1976). The Court reaffirmed this in cases involving advertisements by lawyers (*Bates and O'Steen v. State Bar of Arizona*, 433 U.S. 350 [1977]) and advertisement for contraceptives (*Carey v. Population Services, Int'l.*, 431 U.S. 678 [1977]). The Court leaves open the possibility the state may control advertising, particularly if it is "deceptive or misleading." *Virginia State Board of Pharmacy v. Virginia Citizens Consumer Council, Inc.*, 425 U.S. at 770-771.

66. *Bigelow v. Virginia*, 421 U.S. 809 (1975).

67. 315 U.S. 568, 572 (1942). Actually the Court first suggested this idea two years before in the case of *Cantwell v. Connecticut*, 310 U.S. 296 (1940). See Table 2.1.

68. *Chaplinsky v. New Hampshire*, 315 U.S. 568, 572 (1942).

69. *Cohen v. California*, 403 U.S. 15 (1971).

70. *Rosenfeld v. New Jersey*, 408 U.S. 901 (1972).

71. *Lewis v. New Orleans*, 415 U.S. 130 (1974).

72. *Cohen v. California*, 403 U.S. 15 (1971).

73. *Rosenfeld v. New Jersey*, 408 U.S. 901 (1972).

74. In *Chaplinsky v. New Hampshire*, 315 U.S. 568 (1942) the Court defined fighting words as those having "a *direct tendency* to cause acts of violence by the person to whom, individually, the remark is addressed" (emphasis added). In *Cohen v. California*, 403 U.S. 15 (1971), by contrast, the Court defined fighting words as those "*inherently likely* to provoke violent reaction" by the person to whom they are addressed.

75. *A Book Named "John Cleland's Memoirs of a Woman of Pleasure" v. Massachusetts*, 383 U.S. 413 (1966).

76. *Ginzburg v. United States*, 383 U.S. 463 (1966).

77. *Miller v. California*, 413 U.S. 15 (1973).

78. *Interstate Circuit, Inc. v. Dallas*, 390 U.S. 676, 704 (1968).

79. In *Redrup v. New York*, 386 U.S. 767 (1967), the Court summarized the extant definition of obscenity and then reversed the convictions of a newsstand dealer and two other persons, saying "[w]hichever of these constitutional views is brought to bear upon the cases before us, it is clear that the judgments cannot stand." Ibid., at 771. In *Redrup* and the thirty-five obscenity convictions summarily reversed on its basis in the next two years, the Justices concluded that the material in question was not obscene, but they offered no common definition of obscenity. See Herald Price Fahringer and Michael J. Brown, "The Rise and Fall of *Roth*—A Critique of the Recent Supreme Court Obscenity Decisions, " 62 *Ken.L.J.* 731, 735 (1973-74). See also Frederick F. Schauer, *The Law of Obscenity* (Washington, D.C.: Bureau of National Affairs, 1976), p. 44.

80. *Roth v. United States*, 354 U.S. 476 (1957).

81. From *Miller v. California*, 413 U.S. 15, 24-25 (1973).

82. *A Book Named "John Cleland's Memoirs of a Woman of Pleasure" v. Massachusetts*, 383 U.S. 413 (1966).

83. Beverly G. Miller, "*Miller v. California*: A Cold Shower for the First Amendment," 48 *St. John's L.Rev.* 567, 569, n.9 (1974).

84. Henry J. Abraham, *Freedom and the Court*, 2nd ed. (New York: Oxford University Press, 1972), p. 177. From Chief Justice Warren's dissent in *Times Film Corp. v. Chicago*, 365 U.S. 43 (1961).

85. 354 U.S. 476 (1957).

86. See *Manuel Enterprises, Inc. v. Day*, 370 U.S. 478 (1962).

87. *Jacobellis v. Ohio*, 378 U.S. 184 (1964).

88. *Ginsburg v. New York*. 380 U.S. 629 (1968).

89. *Ginzburg v. United States*, 383 U.S. 463 (1966). In this case the Court held that material that is "pandered"—that is, crudely and offensively marketed so as to appeal to the salacious interests of the targeted public—may be held obscene on this basis alone if it is otherwise borderline obscene.

90. *FCC v. Pacifica Foundation*, 438 U.S. 726 (1978).

91. *Time, Inc. v. Firestone*, 424 U.S. 448 (1976).

92. *New York Times v. Sullivan*, 376 U.S. 254 (1964).

93. Restatement of Torts §. 559 (1937), quoted in Joel D. Eaton, "The American Law of Defamation through *Gertz v. Robert Welch, Inc.* and Beyond: An Analytical Primer," 61 *Va.L.Rev.* 1350, 1353 (1975).

94. Ibid., at 1353. Under common law, even true statements could be proscribed if they damaged one's reputation; "truth or good motives was no defense." *Beauharnais v. Illinois*, 343 U.S. 250 (1952).

95. *New York Times v. Sullivan*, 376 U.S. 254 (1964). "Actual malice" presupposes that the defendant had "serious doubts" about the accuracy of his or her statements. *St. Amant v. Thompson*, 390 U.S. 727 (1968). It applies to criminal libel prosecutions as well as civil suits. *Garrison v. Louisiana,* 379 U.S. 64 (1964).

96. *New York Times v. Sullivan*, 376 U.S. 254 (1964).

97. *Gertz v. Robert Welch, Inc.*, 418 U.S. 323, 349-359 (1974).

98. *Monitor Patriot Co. v. Roy*, 401 U.S. 265 (1971).

99. *Curtis Publishing Co. v. Butts*, 388 U.S. 130 (1967). Although the Court offered no majority opinion, five Justices agreed that *The New York Times* rule should extend to public figures. The Court confirmed this consensus in *Gertz v. Robert Welch, Inc.*,

418 U.S. 323, 336, n.7 (1974). For a summary of the various positions taken by the Justices in *Curtis Publishing Co.*, see Gerald G. Ashdown, "*Gertz* and *Firestone*: A Study in Constitutional Policy-Making," 61 *Minn.L.Rev.* 645, 649, n.17 (1977).

100. It is possible but "exceedingly rare," for public people to become figures involuntarily. *Gertz v. Robert Welch, Inc.*, 418 U.S. 323 (1974).

101. *Curtis Publishing Co. v. Butts*, 388 U.S. 130 (1967).

102. *Associated Press v. Walker*, 388 U.S. 130 (1967).

103. *Time, Inc. v. Firestone*, 424 U.S. 448 (1976).

104. *Hutchinson v. Proxmire*, 61 L.Ed. 2d 411 (1979); *Wolston v. Reader's Digest Association*, 61 L.Ed. 2d 450 (1979).

105. *Time, Inc. v. Firestone*, 424 U.S. 448 (1976).

106. *Garrison v. Louisiana*, 379 U.S. 64 (1964).

107. *People v. Stover,* 191 N.E. 2d 272 (1963), reprinted in Haig A. Bosjamian, ed., *Dissent: Symbolic Behavior and Rhetorical Strategies* (Boston: Allyn and Bacon, 1972), p. 274-282.

108. *Tinker v. Des Moines*, 393 U.S. 503 (1969).

109. Note, "Symbolic Conduct," 68 *Colum.L.Rev.* 1091, 1111 (1968).

110. Note, "Symbolic Conduct," at 1113-1114; Louis Henkin, "Foreword: On Drawing Lines," 83 *Harv.L.Rev.* 63, 80 (1968).

111. See Note, "Symbolic Conduct," at 1109-1117; and Melville B. Nimmer, "The Meaning of Symbolic Speech Under the First Amendment," 21 *U.C.L.A.L.Rev.* 29, 35-38 (1973).

112. *Smith v. Goguen*, 415 U.S. 556 (1974).

113. *Cowgill v. United States*, 396 U.S. 371 (1970). The Court dismissed Cowgill's appeal.

114. Nimmer, at 50-51.

115. *United States v. O'Brien*, 391 U.S. 367 (1968). See also *Cohen v. California*, 403 U.S. 15 (1971), in which the Court said Cohen's behavior was "speech not based upon any separately identifiable conduct," and *Amalgamated Food Employees Union Local 590 v. Logan Valley*, 391 U.S. 308 (1968) in which the Court noted that "picketing involves elements of speech and conduct."

116. Nimmer, at 33-34.

117. *California v. LaRue*, 409 U.S. 109, 117 (1973). See also *Cox v. Louisiana*, 379 U.S. 536, 555 (1965).

118. *Shuttlesworth v. Birmingham*, 394 U.S. 147, 152 (1969).

119. 391 U.S. 367 (1968).

120. *Cohen v. California*, 403 U.S. 15, 19 (1971).

121. *Cox v. New Hampshire*, 312 U.S. 569 (1941).

122. *Cox v. Louisiana*, 379 U.S. 536 (1965).

123. *Kovacs v. Cooper*, 336 U.S. 77 (1949).

124. *Grayned v. Rockford*, 408 U.S. 104 (1972).

125. *Virginia State Board of Pharmacy v. Virginia Citizens Consumer Council, Inc.*, 425 U.S. 748, 771 (1976).

126. *Chicago v. Mosley*, 408 U.S. 92 (1972). The ordinance exempted the "picketing of any school involved in a labor dispute" but the Court noted it was "undisputed that this exemption applies only to *labor* picketing of a school involved in a labor dispute." At 94, n.2.

127. *Virginia State Board of Pharmacy v. Virginia Citizens Consumer Council, Inc.*, 425 U.S. 748, 771 (1976).

128. The dissenting judge in *Collin v. Smith*, 578 F.2d 1197, 1215 (1978) did bring the matter up, arguing that the ordinances were "facially neutral" "manner" restrictions.

129. *Brandenburg v. Ohio*, 395 U.S. 444 (1969).

130. *Gitlow v. New York*, 268 U.S. 652 (1925).

131. *Brandenburg v. Ohio*, 395 U.S. 444 (1969).

132. *Dennis v. United States*, 341 U.S. 494 (1951).

133. *Schenck v. United States*, 249 U.S. 47 (1919).

134. However, the Court hinted of the bad tendency test near the end of this opinion: "[i]f the act (speaking, or circulating a paper), *its tendency* and the intent with which it is done are the same, we perceive no ground for saying that success alone warrants making the act a crime." *Schenck v. United States*, 249 U.S. at 52 (emphasis added).

135. *Hess v. Indiana*, 414 U.S. 105 (1973). See also *Communist Party of Indiana v. Whitcomb*, 414 U.S. 441 (1974).

136. It dates from *Schneider v. State*, 308, U.S. 147 (1939).

137. Thomas I. Emerson, *Toward a General Theory of the First Amendment* (New York: Random House, 1966), p. 54.

138. See ibid., pp. 53-54. See also Justice Black, who charged that ad hoc balancing allows the Court to "'balance away' First Amendment rights whenever a majority of the Justices are impressed with a countervailing interest." Justice Black went on to say that ad hoc balancing changes the First Amendment to mean: "Congress shall pass no law abridging freedom of speech, press, assembly and petition, unless Congress and the Supreme Court reach the joint conclusion that on balance the interest of the Government in stifling these freedoms is greater than the interest of the people in having them exercised." *Barenblatt v. United States*, 360 U.S. 109, 143 (1959) (Black, J., dissenting).

139. Ibid.

140. *Palko v. Connecticut*, 302 U.S. 319, 327 (1937).

141. *California v. LaRue*, 409 U.S. 109, 117 (1973).

142. *Smith v. California*, 361 U.S. 147, 157 (1959).

CHAPTER THREE

Freedom of the Press

In the evening of October 18, 1975, Erwin Charles Simants, a handyman with borderline intelligence, killed six members of the Kellie family of North Platte, Nebraska.[1] After the shooting Simants went to his nephew's home and told him, "I've just killed the Kellies." The nephew called Simants's parents; unbelieving, Mr. Simants went to the Kellie's home and discovered the carnage for himself. He called the police and from that moment on the town of North Platte was ablaze with sirens, rumors, and fear—the last fed by a warning flashed over radio and television that a killing had taken place and "everyone should lock their doors and windows and admit no one."

A mass murder in a placid community is grist for news stories; within hours reporters from all parts of the state swept into North Platte to find out what had happened. By 1:30 A.M. police had officially released the names of the victims and identified Simants as the suspect. Even before Simants surrendered, the newspapers were filled with stories about the crime and suspect. One newspaper started off its lead story, "He was called a hothead, a loner, a drinker by those who knew him, but Erwin Charles Simants, suspected of killing six here Saturday night, remains an enigma to many." Another reported that Mr. Simants had said, "My son killed five or six people here."

If police were nervous about the amount of publicity already churning, they were even more concerned about what would happen should the details of the crime, which included rape and necrophilia, become known. By 10 the next morning Simants had come out of hiding and turned himself in. Officials scheduled a preliminary hearing, an early step in criminal procedure designed to demonstrate that a crime had been committed and that police had probable cause to believe the suspect committed it. It was likely that the details officials wanted to keep hushed up would come out in the open. By this time the judge scheduled to preside over the hearing and who would later oversee the trial itself began to worry about adverse publicity too. Not wanting to have a ruling handed down in his courtroom reversed for prejudicial publicity,[2] he decided to let reporters attend the preliminary hearing, as is customary, but to forbid them from reporting on what took place inside. To "gag" the press in this manner is not unlike giving a child a candy bar but not letting him eat it. It meant reporters sat in on a full day's hearing, heard the testimony of nine witnesses, and went home in silence.

Another slaying in another part of the country was, as far as murders go, more routine than the Simants's crime. It involved the stabbing of a solitary hotel manager by a Mr. Stevenson.[3] The prosecution of Stevenson set the case apart, however, because officials seemed to have more than the usual number of problems bringing the man to trial. Not one, but three attempts at trial ended in mistrials and as Stevenson was brought to court for the fourth time all parties hoped this would be the last. To this end Stevenson's attorney moved that the courtroom be closed to the press and public. The prosecuting attorney had no objection, so the trial judge closed the trial to everyone except those scheduled to testify. Here the "child" was forbidden from holding the candy in the first place.

The judge in each case knowingly entered a constitutional thicket. For one thing, each risked violating the Sixth Amendment's guarantee that the defendant have a public trial. For another, each severely limited the press and so risked intruding on the First Amendment. Yet the judges made their moves in the effort to promote another social interest—a fair trial for the defendant. Only the remedies differed. In Simants's case the judge imposed a classic prior restraint, which is, as discussed in Chapter 2, a control in advance of publication. The remedy in Stevenson's case was even more dramatic—cutting off information from the press in the first place.

The cases recall the principles set forth in Chapter 2, which make clear that limits on expression are subject to especially strict scrutiny. With these in mind it is perhaps not surprising that when each case reached the Supreme Court, the Justices struck down the remedy at issue. Yet these cases were introduced here to point out a dimension of First Amendment doctrine that is more specifically paired with free press than free speech law and that warrants separate treatment in this chapter. This is concern over the free flow of information. "Without the information provided by the press," writes the Court, "most of us and many of our representatives would be unable to vote intelligently or to register opinions on the administration of government generally.[4] What makes the press special is its ability to use an intermediary to disseminate ideas widely and efficiently; moreover, it is made up of reporters—"surrogates of the public"[5]—who will investigate government activities, report back to the public, and aid the public as it tries to govern the governors. When a judge gags the press or cuts it off from public courtrooms, he or she blocks the free flow of information. In a word, the judge cuts off "access" to a key source of information and so prevents the flow from beginning in the first place. But how much access is necessary for a vital First Amendment? When may the state constitutionally intrude on access? Or, on the other side of the coin, may the state take positive steps to *promote* access? The concept of access raises unique doctrinal questions and is a new dimension of First Amendment case law that this chapter will highlight.

To introduce a second dimension of press doctrine, we skip from the courtroom and criminal reporting to the automobile and dirty words. The dispute started when a New York City resident driving with his young son turned his car radio to station WBAI just as the station was airing an excerpt from a George Carlin album. The excerpt, entitled "Filthy Words," was just that—a 22-minute monologue in which Carlin repeatedly uttered some favored expletives as he mocked society's attitudes toward the words. The station played the piece as part of its discussion of contemporary language and had warned listeners that language offensive to some would be forthcoming. The listener, complaining that "[a]ny child could have been turning the dial, and tuned in to that garbage," wrote to the Federal Communications Commission (FCC) to protest.[6]

The FCC responded by issuing an order barring the broadcast of "indecent" speech from the public airwaves.[7] The U.S. Code makes it a criminal offense to broadcast "obscene, indecent, or profane language."[8] The FCC used the man's complaint as an occasion to define indecency, a task that to that point had been skirted by both the FCC and the courts. This time the FCC made it clear: indecent language is that which "describes, in terms patently offensive as measured by contemporary community standards for the broadcasting medium, sexual or excretory activities and organs, at times of the day when there is a reasonable risk that children may be in the audience."[9] The FCC did not sanction station WBAI, but it did associate the order with WBAI's license file and warn that "in the event that subsequent complaints are received, the Commission will then decide whether it should utilize any of the available sanctions it has been granted by Congress."[10]

The station appealed the order and eventually the case reached the Supreme Court in the name of *FCC v. Pacifica Foundation*, otherwise known as the "case of the seven dirty words" inasmuch as the FCC singled out seven words as indecent.[11] The Court resolved the case in favor of the FCC, upheld the indecency restriction under First Amendment challenge, and adopted the FCC's definition of indecency. This left the FCC free to penalize television and radio licensees for broadcasting "patently offensive references to excretory and sexual organs and activities."

What must come to the reader's mind is that something is amiss if the principles covered in Chapter 2 still hold true. Nowhere did that chapter mention that indecency was fair target for control. Obscenity, yes; fighting words, yes; but indecency was not singled out as unprotected speech. Why here? The case is important because it harks back to the thing that makes press different from speech, namely, that press uses an intermediary to convey ideas whereas speech is usually based on face-to-face communication. The three big intermediaries for the press are the printed word, motion pictures, and broadcasting. The *Pacifica Foundation* case introduces a key element in free press doctrine: the medium at issue affects the dispute's outcome. The Court upheld the control of indecency in *Pacifica Foundation* because broadcasting was at issue. Had the printed word or motion pictures been at issue, the Court would have reverted to the principles of obscenity control reviewed in Chapter 2 and struck down the provision as a violation of the First Amendment.[12]

The case of the seven dirty words introduces another of the intra-liberty gradations identified in this book, namely, that free press doctrine varies with the medium at issue. Generally speaking, the press is "freest" when the print medium is involved, somewhat less free when motion pictures are at issue, and the least free when broadcasting is at stake. But a caveat comes to mind. In the two criminal reporting cases reviewed at the beginning of this chapter, the judges made no distinction between reporters working for newspapers or for broadcasting stations. All reporters, regardless of medium, fell under sweeping restraints at the hands of trial court judges and all were "liberated" from the controls by the Supreme Court. Could it be that the type of speech (such as criminal reporting as opposed to dirty words) had some bearing on the intensity of inter-media gradations?

This chapter reviews inter-media gradations in free press doctrine by developing a four-pronged definition of "free" press and noting how each part differs for the print and broadcast media.[13] In doing so, however, it is careful to point out how these differences are modified by the nature of the speech at issue. The law on free press is complex and defies easy generalizations, but the Court watcher who knows two things about a case—the medium and type of speech at issue—has two important clues in understanding how the Justices will approach the dispute.

FOUR INDICATORS OF A FREE PRESS

Virtual Absence of Prior Restraints

One indicator of a free press must be the virtual absence of prior restraints. Sir William Blackstone leveled an early indictment of prior restraints when he wrote that the "liberty of the press consists in laying *no* previous restraints upon publications."[14] American jurists have not been quite so vehement about prior controls, but they have inherited the English distaste for such restraints. The Supreme Court calls vigilance against them the "chief"[15] and "leading"[16] purpose of the First Amendment. It also writes that prior restraints are the "most serious and least tolerable infringement on First Amendment rights."[17]

A prior restraint forbids expression before it is communicated, in contrast to a subsequent punishment, which sanctions it after. A prior restraint "prevent[s] communication from occurring at all," whereas a subsequent punishment "allows the communication but imposes a penalty after the event."[18] Cases involving prior restraints are always newsmakers; when the Supreme Court agrees to review this kind of control the decision invariably promises to be "landmark" or "major" or "definitive." The Skokie case would not have received nearly as much attention had it not centered around a prior restraint, and neither would the gag order at issue in the preliminary hearing of Erwin Simants. What is it about a prior restraint that so arouses jurists?

One "evil" of a prior restraint is that it undercuts the basic principle in American jurisprudence that the accused is entitled to a trial before being deprived of his or her liberty.[19] When the state imposes a prior control, it *presumes* that the material (the "accused") is guilty and prevents it from having its day in court. No one knows whether the expression actually will harm society because it has not had a chance to be received by the public. Thus the trial judge in Simants's preliminary hearing presumed that reporters were going to publish every lurid detail of the crime and that whatever publicity came out of the hearing would hurt Simants's right to a fair trial. He could just as easily have warned reporters not to publish certain details and advised them of the dangers leaks would cause. If the feared consequences did, indeed, happen, then the judge could take steps to remedy them, such as moving the trial to another jurisdiction. At least the reporters and information would have had their day in court. A prior restraint is not unlike the system of preventive detention the British tried out on suspected IRA terrorists. Detaining suspects on the grounds that they *may* commit crimes is anathema to American criminal procedure; likewise, gagging speech on the grounds that it *may* endanger society is anathema to the First Amendment.

A prior restraint also undercuts the principle that the accused is entitled to a trial by an impartial judge. Criminal procedure separates the roles of prosecutor and judge. The prosecutor builds the case against the defendant and has a vested interest in winning a conviction; the judge is supposedly neutral and acts as the impartial arbiter in the trial itself. In a prior restraint, however, the state acts both as a prosecutor and judge. First it builds the case against the expression and then it declares the speech guilty. Combining these roles violates an established principle of Fifth and Fourteenth Amendment due processes.

A third problem with a prior restraint is that it chills speech and press. "The special vice of a prior restraint," writes the Court, "is that communication will be suppressed, either directly or by inducing excessive caution in the speaker, before an adequate determination that it is unprotected by the First Amendment."[20] A prior control causes people to "steer far clear of the unlawful zone" and in so doing restricts protected as well as unprotected speech.

Written word   Were we to limit this discussion to the written word we would undoubtedly conclude that the press is "free" because the Court allows virtually no prior controls on print material. "According to our accepted jurisprudence," writes the Court, "the First Amendment erects a virtually insurmountable barrier between government and *the print media* so far as government tampering, in advance of publication, with news and editorial content is concerned."[21]

To illustrate how closely the Court follows its own counsel one only need look at cases in which the government tried to enjoin newspapers (that is, get a court order preventing publication or distribution). The

Court struck down the attempted injunctions in all major cases. For example, it struck down a statute empowering the state to file suit to enjoin print publishers from distributing "malicious, scandalous and defamatory" material in the 1931 case of *Near v. Minnesota*.[22] In the twin 1971 cases of *New York Times v. United States* and *Saxbe v. Washington Post, Inc.*, it prevented the government from enjoining the newspapers from publishing Vietnam policy papers leaked to the press by Daniel Ellsberg.[23] The Carter administration's attempt to enjoin a magazine from publishing details of the making of a hydrogen bomb likewise ended unsuccessfully.[24] The Court has also struck down injunctions preventing groups from distributing leaflets and in one such case reiterated that "[a]ny prior restraint on expression comes to this Court with a 'heavy presumption' against its constitutional validity."[25]

We have also seen how the Court struck down the gag order at issue in Simants's preliminary hearing. The judge who imposed the order in that case was well aware of the risk he was taking, and another judge advised him that he would be "opening a can of worms" by restraining the press in advance of publication. The judge went ahead with the order because in his mind when the First and Sixth Amendments clash "the right of the free press must be subservient to the right of the accused to have due process." The Court cast its weight on the side of free press, however, and, noting the distaste for prior restraints filtering through American history, struck the gag order down on First Amendment grounds.

None of this is to say that prior restraints on written material are always unconstitutional. In *Near v. Minnesota* the Court said it would allow restraints on material directly threatening national security, such as releases revealing the "number and location of troops."[26] Concurring in the Pentagon Papers cases Justice Brennan said the state could restrain material "inevitably, directly, and immediately" causing "the occurrence of an event kindred to imperiling the safety of a transport already at sea"[27] and Justices Stewart and White indicated they would prevent disclosure of material "surely" resulting in "direct, immediate, and irreparable damage to our Nation or its people."[28] Moreover, it denied review, and therefore let stand, a Fourth Circuit Court decision upholding censorship of Victor Marchetti's book *The CIA and the Cult of Intelligence*.[29] The CIA contended that Marchetti had signed away his right to write about top secret CIA activities when he contracted to join the agency in the first place. The Fourth Circuit decision meant Marchetti's book went to print with 168 blank spaces tantalizingly interspersed throughout. But the sweep of decisions and dicta alike suggest on the whole a nearly universal antagonism of the Court to prior controls on the print medium, particularly when newsworthy information is at stake.

Broadcasting   Over 97 percent of American households own at least one television set and presumably that many own radios as well.[30] The average child watches almost seven hours of television daily and the average adult falls not far behind. It is no exaggeration to say that broadcasting transmits more information, imparts more entertainment, elicits more trust,[31] and captures more time of Americans than any other single medium. It is therefore ironic that so many commentaries on First Amendment doctrine are based almost solely on decisions handed down in the context of the print word while broadcasting decisions are either excluded or footnoted as a curious aberration. The author of one otherwise comprehensive book on obscenity, for example, noted only of broadcasting that "the analysis of what can or cannot be permitted on the airwaves is wholly unlike that for determining obscenity in other contexts."[32]

An accurate analysis of the status of free press requires that broadcasting be brought into the fold. Under the assumption that broadcasting is "different," judges have developed a separate body of law for speech transmitted over the public airwaves. The task here is not to say whether or not this assumption is correct but, rather, to incorporate these principles into the larger body of free press law in order to see how it affects the vitality of the First Amendment. As it turns out, one finds a less vigorous system of free press after bringing broadcasting into the mainstream commentary than when only the print media are discussed. The Court has repeated that it is "idle to posit an unabridgeable First Amendment right to broadcast comparable to the right of every individual to speak, write, or publish."[33] The lesser status accorded the broadcast word clearly appears in the doctrine of prior restraint.

Consider, first, policy relating to advertising. Cigarettes have been attacked from all quarters in the past twenty years and the government has taken a number of measures to warn the public about the dangers of smoking, including the requirement that cigarette manufacturers print a warning label on cigarette packages. One of its more dramatic and controversial moves was to ban cigarette advertising altogether from the air. The Court approved this prior restraint,[34] which led to a dual system that permitted cigarette advertising in the print media but not in broadcasting. The First Amendment implications of the decision were unclear, however, because at that time the Court did not treat commercial speech as First Amendment speech. Shortly after the cigarette decision the Court extended First Amendment status to commercial speech in a case involving newspapers.[35] Would this change the apparent ease with which the government struck one form of advertising from the air?

The Court has made clear that commercial speech on television and radio is not entitled to the same added protection given commercial speech in the print media and has, therefore, indirectly approved the dual system now at work. In dicta in one case the Court cautioned that it need not "comment here on the First Amendment ratifications of legislative prohibitions of certain kinds of advertising in the electronic media, where the 'unique characteristics' of this form of communication 'make it especially subject to regulation in the public interest'."[36] In a second advertising case it again distinguished broadcasting from the print media by stating that "the special problems of the electronic broadcast media are likewise not in this case."[37]

Broadcasting's lesser status in prior restraint doctrine is more dramatically shown in the web of affirmative prior controls placed on broadcast licensees (see the final section of this chapter, on public access). An affirmative prior restraint differs from a classic prior restraint, which tells producers what they may *not* show, by telling producers what they *must* show. Consider, for example, the absence of televised movies featuring Ronald Reagan during the 1980 Presidential campaign. A target for jokes in the popular press, the lack of Reagan movies reflects a serious issue for it is the result of the equal time rule set down by Congress in the Communications Act of 1934.[38] The rule requires a licensee who lets one candidate for public office use the airwaves to give an equal opportunity to other candidates for the same office to use the airwaves also. It is hardly surprising that licensees opted to expunge Reagan movies from their programming; at two hours a movie the licensees would be hard pressed to find equal time for the other candidates.

Or, consider the affirmative restraint at issue in *Red Lion Broadcasting Corp. v. FCC*.[39] The dispute started when Fred Cook, an investigative reporter, called the Reverend Billy James Hargis a bigot in a magazine article on the political right. Hargis, who broadcast a regular 15-minute radio show from 200 stations, used his time on the air one day to retaliate with accusations of his own against Cook. Wanting to rebut the charges, Cook wrote letters to the 200 stations claiming he had a right to respond over the air. He did, too, under the FCC's personal attack rules, which require a broadcast licensee to give a person singled out for attack over the air free time to respond. These rules are a subset of the broader fairness doctrine, which holds that when a "controversial issue" of "public importance" is aired, the broadcaster must ensure that each side of the issue is given fair coverage. Yet 150 of the stations either did not respond to Cook's letters or turned down his request. He then went to court in a dispute that eventually reached the Supreme Court and that featured one rebellious radio station claiming the personal attack rules violated the First Amendment and the FCC claiming the rules were within their constitutional scope of power. The Court sided with the FCC, holding that some measure of control of the airwaves is necessary to "preserve an uninhibited marketplace of ideas in which truth will ultimately prevail."

All these rules—the equal time rule, fairness doctrine, and personal attack rules—tell producers what they must show and so amount to prior restraints, albeit of a different kind from the negative restraints at issue in the gag order or Nazi march cases. To tell a radio licensee it must give Cook rebuttal time is to "tamper with editorial content in advance of publication"; the Court has made clear that advance tampering is unconstitutional for the print medium.[40] Moreover, in a sense the affirmative prior control is not so different from the classic prior restraint after all; by forcing the licensee to air a 15-minute rebuttal, for example, the personal attack rules prevent the station from airing whatever program would have been scheduled in those minutes had the rules not been laid down.

What is it about broadcasting that justifies this system of prior controls? Why did the Court uphold the personal attack rules in *Red Lion* when it struck down an analogous rule for newspapers? Clearly, the nature of the medium is critical here. But, what exactly is broadcasting's distinguishing feature? Of all the so-called "unique" features of broadcasting,[41] the scarcity theory reappears the most often to justify prior affirmative restraints. If licensees want something to blame for the elaborate system of controls under which they labor, they may well blame an iceberg for it was the ramming of a block of ice by the British steamship *Titanic* that triggered controls over the airwaves. It seems that after the fatal collision, the steamship's crew members tried to radio land for help and found their distress calls blocked by radio signals on the mainland. They eventually got through, of course, but the muddled radio spectrum clearly hindered rescue efforts and gave rise to the Radio Act of 1912. This law, the first to regulate the airwaves, set up a system of emergency signals based on the Morse Code and also set up a licensing system in which radio operators had to obtain licenses from the Secretary of Commerce and Labor before being allowed to operate.[42]

The *Titanic* incident presaged the confusion yet to come because it showed what happens when too many stations vie for too few airwave frequencies. In 1920 only three radio stations operated in the country but only five years later 578 were broadcasting, having "sprung up like mushrooms across the land."[43] Ironically, the more stations there were the less the listeners could enjoy; more often than not they heard jumbled programs and screeching static because two or more stations competed for each of the ninety available channels. Residents of one community, for example, turned on their radios three Sundays running only to find two churches broadcasting services at the same time and frequency.[44]

Broadcasting relies on an electromagnetic spectrum. The spectrum has only a limited number of frequencies so when too many people try to use the spectrum the frequencies are overloaded. As happened in the early days of radio, "[w]ith everybody on the air, nobody could be heard."[45] In short, broadcasting relies on a scarce resource. Moreover, the electromagnetic spectrum is a public resource on the order of a national park that belongs to the public generally rather than to any private business or businesses. Under the assumption that a public resource must be regulated in the public interest, Congress passed the Radio Act of 1927, which superseded the Radio Act of 1912. It set up the Federal Radio Commission to allocate licenses to broadcasters so that only one station would broadcast at the same time and on the same frequency. It also gave the FRC power to allocate and control on the basis of "public convenience, interest, or necessity."

Seven years later Congress passed the Communications Act, which superseded the Radio Act, and set up the present Federal Communications Commission as the watchdog of the public airwaves. The Act gave the FCC power to allocate licenses, again in the "public convenience, interest, or necessity,"[46] reiterated the equal time rule for candidates that had originally been set up in the 1927 Act, and added the kernel of the fairness doctrine. Later Congress modified the fairness doctrine so that today it is two-pronged: first, it bids the licensee to seek out public issues to discuss ("the broadcaster must devote a reasonable percentage of . . . broadcast time to the coverage of public issues") and, second, it must give equal opportunity for both sides of the controversial issue to be presented (the broadcaster's "coverage of these issues must be fair in the sense that it provides an opportunity for the presentation of contrasting points of view").[47]

In short, regulation got a foothold in broadcasting because this form of press uses an intermediary in short supply, unlike the print medium, which relies on freely available resources—paper, printing presses, ink—and motion pictures, which also use plentiful resources—cameras, film, projectors. But the scarcity rationale is persuasive only as a justification for time, place, and manner restrictions over who uses the airwaves and when. Is there another rationale for the content restrictions of the fairness doctrine and equal time rule?

Another of broadcasting's "unique" features mentioned by jurists is its reliance on a public forum. As mentioned above, the electromagnetic spectrum is thought to be akin to a public street or park owned by everyone. Just as public streets are open to all who want to use them, the theory goes, so should the electromagnetic spectrum be open to all who want to use it. But the spectrum's scarce nature makes this impossible. The second best solution, then, is to ensure openness among those who do use the spectrum through such content regulations as the fairness doctrine. It was for this reason that the Court ruled in favor of the FCC in *Red Lion*. "It is the right of the viewers and listeners, not the right of the broadcasters, which is paramount," wrote the Court.[48] The broadcaster's right to air what he or she wants is tempered by the fact that the broadcaster is using a public resource and must take into account the public's need to have a wide variety of ideas aired. Were Reverend Hargis to go unrebutted, the public would have received only a one-sided presentation of an issue of political importance.

Recall the Court's warning that the First Amendment "erects a virtually insurmountable barrier between government and the print media so far as government tampering, in advance of publication, *with news and editorial content* is concerned."[49] For the print medium, the fact that newsworthy information is at issue vividly signals that the government must keep its hands off. Yet, ironically, for broadcasting the presence of newsworthy information signals the propriety of government controls. Newsworthy information is public interest material and is open to controls designed to ensure the spectrum be used in the public interest. The same information that triggers hands-off treatment for the print medium is the very information that triggers a network of affirmative prior controls in broadcasting. Thus, it is a great overgeneralization to conclude that prior restraints are virtually absent in free press doctrine. In the history of the print medium, yes, but in the history of broadcasting, no. Since the bulk of information transmitted through the press today goes through the public airwaves, one must conclude that the press is not as free as first appears, at least for this particular indicator of a "free" press—the virtual absence of prior restraints.

Strict Tests for Reviewing Subsequent Punishments

Most controls on press and speech are subsequent rather than prior; that is, they punish expression after it has been uttered. Though not shunned as heartily by jurists, subsequent punishments still can dampen free press and, if not watched carefully, threaten the system of free expression. Moreover, sometimes it is hard to tell the difference between a subsequent and a prior control, which means the former can pose the same evils as the latter.[50] Z. Chafee once noted that "a death penalty for writing about socialism would be as effective as a censorship."[51] He meant that some subsequent controls are so severe as to amount to a prior restraint. An example might be the FCC's licensing power over broadcast licensees. The FCC's weapon in making sure that the airwaves are used in the public interest is its power to withdraw, withhold, or issue only a short-term license to broadcasters. Every three years broadcasters apply for renewal of their license; the FCC can issue one of its sanctions if it feels the station has failed to live up to its responsibilities as a licensee. The FCC calls license revocation a subsequent punishment; but one can make a strong case that the FCC's ability to deny a license is the ultimate prior restraint, for when the Commission does revoke a license, it cuts off the station's ability to speak again. In short, subsequent punishments are important in a system of free expression and the strictness of the tests used to review these punishments must stand as one of the indicators of a "free" press.

To define "strict" tests, we draw on the battery of tests covered in Chapter 2 and come up with a mix that is highly protective of free expression. Some tests are based on the strength of the state's interest in controlling speech and range from the protective (the state's interest must be "substantial," "important," or "compelling") to the less protective (the state need only show a "reasonable" interest in control). Other tests focus on the expression itself, asking how likely it is that the words will endanger someone or something. These also range from the protective (the "imminent and lawless action" test) to the less protective (the "bad tendency" test). A third group of tests asks whether the state has other methods for meeting the given interest. This, the "least drastic means" test, requires the state to show it has chosen the method posing the least hardship for the First Amendment.

The Court uses one or the other of these tests depending on the issue at bar, the claims raised by litigants, and its own composition. The most protective formula is this: the state may control the press only if the expression poses a "clear and imminent danger" to a "substantial" state interest and the control chosen is the "least drastic" measure available. If the Court deletes or dilutes one or more of these components, it leaves the press that much less "free" as a result.

Written word   In most cases the Court's treatment of the written word meets the standard presented here. To illustrate, consider a typical subsequent punishment on the press set in the state of Virginia. The state had set up a judicial inquiry and review commission to investigate reports of wrongdoing in the judicial system. By law and the state constitution, the proceedings were to be kept secret; a state law provided for the punishment of anyone who published information about the commission's investigations while underway. During the course of an investigation of a judge, a newspaper in Virginia published the name of the man under review and was fined $500 for doing so. Newspaper publishers challenged the law on the grounds that it violated the First Amendment. What standard of review should be used to examine the law?

The Supreme Court took a highly protective stance in this case, holding that "the substantive evil must be extremely serious and the degree of imminence extremely high before utterances can be punished."[52] This test, a variant of the clear and present danger test, paid special attention to the proximity of the danger (the "danger must not be remote or even probable: it must immediately imperil") and the degree of danger ("extremely serious"). The Court also used the least-alternative-means test and concluded that Virginia could have taken less drastic measures to meet its interest in a fair and secret hearing. Although the Court did not examine the strength of the state's interest in this case, in other cases involving newspapers it has required the interest to be "substantial."[53] It is especially wary of laws proscribing newspapers from publishing information on the public record.

Broadcasting The First and Fourteenth Amendments "command *nothing less* than that the States may not impose sanctions for the publication of truthful information contained in official court records open to public inspection."[54] The Court handed down this forceful statement in a case involving television. At issue was a state statute making it a misdemeanor for the media to identify a rape victim. After a news reporter on a local television station broadcast the name of one young rape (and murder) victim, the girl's father brought suit for privacy invasion and the law came under attack. The Court wasted little time striking down the statute. It seems the law intruded on a highly valued type of speech — factual material on the public record — and there was no question in the case at hand that the material was published accurately. Any citizen could go to the public courthouse and find out the name of the rape victim; the press then could not be forbidden from reporting on information to which the public is entitled.

Both this case and the case involving the Virginia judicial review commission involved information on the public record, that is, information recorded in log books in government offices and available to any enterprising citizen. It is information in the public domain and must be freely available for the governed to oversee their governors. It is, in short, high order speech and when it is at issue the unique nature of broadcasting has no bearing. Thus, for this particular type of speech the Court uses the same protective tests regardless of the medium through which it is conveyed.

Once we move from the sanctuary of factual information on the public record, however, we return to a dual set of standards, with the Court using less protective tests for broadcasting than for the print medium. Away go the imminent and lawless action and substantial state interest tests and in comes the FCC with its relatively free arm of control. Through its licensing power and its ability to sanction stations in other ways, the FCC directs the content of television and radio programs in subtle and not-so-subtle ways. The Communications Act defines the ground rules for this regulation in two places. In one it forbids the FCC from "censoring" material[55] and in another it advises the commissioners to regulate only if "public interest, convenience, and necessity" require it.[56] The "public interest" standard is oblique, however, and the Supreme Court gives the FCC broad scope in using it. Unlike the print medium, in which the Court has said the state must act only if it has a "substantial" interest in doing so, the Court has said only that the FCC cannot deny or revoke a license "capriciously."[57] This relaxed standard for reviewing subsequent punishments in broadcasting sets that medium apart from the print medium.[58]

An even clearer example of inter-media differences in press doctrine comes in the area of sexual speech. Here we return to the "case of the seven dirty words" described in the introduction to this chapter.[59] In that case the Court upheld the provision in the U.S. Code that sanctions indecency in broadcasting: "Whoever utters any obscene, indecent, or profane language by means of radio communication shall be fined not more than $10,000 or imprisoned not more than two years, or both."[60] The Court has struck down similar laws involving the print and film media,[61] so this leaves broadcasting as the only medium through which the state may penalize merely indecent speech. Moreover, the FCC and lower courts define obscenity more broadly in the context of television and radio than in the print and film media, meaning that stations can lose their licenses or be fined for airing material that would not be found obscene in other media.[62]

What is it about broadcasting that justifies this different standard for subsequent punishments? Joining the scarcity and public forum rationales is a third supposed "unique" feature of broadcasting—its intrusive nature. Courts point to this characteristic in explaining why they are justified in using singular standards for controlling offensive speech over the air. Broadcast material is received in the most private of contexts, the theory goes—the home. It is a "guest in the American home" and must obey the etiquette expected of a visitor. One of its gaffes is unexpectedly to expose its owner to offensive material as he or she switches channels in search of an acceptable program; another is its accessibility to children The dial switcher is a sort of captive audience who deserves added protection so as not to be offended unwillingly; the child must be protected because he or she, too, may unwittingly be exposed to questionable material. According to the FCC, broadcasting is "uniquely accessible" to children. Unlike offensive magazines, which parents can hide, the television sits in the center of the living room and is freely available to the child when the parent is not watching.

This discussion of broadcasting's intrusive character shows how the nature of the speech at issue affects how clearcut the inter-media differences in free press doctrine will be. Information on the public record is highly valued and so the Court uses virtually identical standards to govern its control in the broadcast and print media. Sexual speech is less highly regarded, however, and here the inter-media differences are abundantly clear. In a sense the Court is saying that for highly regarded speech (public record information) the nature of that speech supersedes differences in the nature of the media but for less valued speech (sexual speech) the nature of the medium is centrally important for deciding which standards of review should be used. Differential treatment is permissible in the latter case but not in the former.

Access of Press to Information

The press is a watchdog. It helps "expose deception in government" and "bare the secrets of government and inform the public."[63] The First Amendment's free press clause helps protect the press's responsibility and, as the Court has written, that amendment serves "the governed, not the governors;"[64] it is an arm of the public, not the state. This model recalls the trustee legislator whose constituents trust him or her to examine documents and hear testimony in Congress and then vote as he or she sees fit. The trustee legislator frees the people from having to do the work themselves; they can rely on someone else to vote in the public interest. Similarly, the press is like the trustee legislator; reporters listen, investigate, and examine in order to free the people from having to "bare the secrets of government" themselves.

The press also plays a vital role in informing the public about issues not directly related to government. Newspapers and broadcasters explore more than political issues; they also let the public know about social changes, they feature stories on families and individuals who are unusual in some way, and they generally inform the public about what life is like for other people. Because daily activities ultimately relate in some way or another to how the country is governed and the demands the public places on the government, gathering of social news is as much a function of the press as is the gathering of political news. Reporters investigate and examine in order to free the people from having to "bare" the way of life of Americans themselves.

For this model to work the press must be able to enter the world of the governors and have some freedom to gather social-interest news. Reporters must be free to interview people, examine documents, and sit in on meetings. In a word, they must have "access" to the news. The greater the access, the healthier and more robust the press; thus, a third indicator of a free press relates to the free access of reporters to information. The question then centers around how much access is "enough" to warrant saying the press is free. It is clear that access cannot be absolute, no more than can any other right or liberty. The Supreme Court fiercely guards the privacy of its own sessions, foreignn policy counsels sit in secrecy, sensitive congressional committee hearings take place without outsiders, grand juries are off-limits to reporters, and the government has an elaborate classification system by which it tries to keep many documents from the press and public. Whether one thinks these constraints are justified or not, they show that access is limited by national security and other interests.

Access is a fairly new concept in free press case law and its place in First Amendment theory is open to speculation. The least aggressive view is that access is a social interest only loosely connected with the First Amendment. This puts access on a par with other social interests and, doctrinally, merely tells the government not to interfere with it arbitrarily. One case, for example, arose when the White House denied a press pass to a reporter. The man went to court, claiming that his First Amendment rights had been violated. The court presumed the man's need to have access to the White House was a social interest, not a constitutional right, and said the government could deny the pass so long as it did not act arbitrarily.[65] Such a position does not offer much protection to access.

A more aggressive position is that access to information is a constitutional right lodging in the First Amendment.[66] This elevates the stature of access considerably. If access is a constitutional right, it receives added protection; for example, if a law intrudes on access courts will call out a forceful battery of tests (substantial state interest, clear and present danger, and so on) to review the law and in so doing tilt the scales to the side of the reporter. If, in the White House press pass case, the court had treated access as a constitutional right, it would have demanded more than that the government not deny the pass arbitrarily. For example, it might have requested the White House to show it had a substantial reason for not giving the man the pass he wanted.

The most aggressive view is that access is a constitutional right *and* that it entitles the press, as watchdog, to privileges over and above those available to the public generally. Consider, for example, the case of Paul M. Branzburg, a reporter for a Louisville daily newspaper.[67] Branzburg's assignment was to explore the drug culture and to do so he established contacts with various users and sellers of drugs. In 1969 the paper printed one of his stories about two people who brought in about $5000 a week from marijuana sales. The story featured a picture of hands working with marijuana on a table. Two years later the paper printed Branzburg's account of the two weeks he spent among drug users in Frankfort, Kentucky. One must presume that the drug users would not have let Branzburg observe their illegal goings-on had they suspected he would turn them in. Yet Branzburg was put to the test twice. Following each story he received a subpoena to appear before a grand jury "to testify in the matter of violation of statutes concerning use and sale of drugs." Among other things he refused to give the names of people he saw working with the illegal drug.

Grand juries are bodies of laymen who assemble to decide if enough evidence exists to indict a person for a crime. They investigate, study incriminating evidence, and interview persons who might have knowledge of a crime and who committed it. A citizen called upon to testify before a grand jury either goes or risks being cited for contempt of court. Branzburg refused to answer questions on the grounds that, as a news reporter, he had a special First Amendment privilege not to divulge certain information. He claimed that if he were to testify he would "destroy the relationship of trust which he [enjoyed] with those in the drug culture." The drug users would no longer talk with Branzburg—in effect, cutting off access to him—and this would hamper the ability of reporters "to cover the views and activities of those involved in the drug culture." Thus, Branzburg tried to make a link between grand jury testimony and the free flow of information that is essential to a free press. If he were forced to testify he would lose his sources; this in turn would "suppress vital First Amendment freedoms." If he were given special consideration and excused from testifying, he would preserve his sources and be free to gather news for public consumption. Branzburg asked for a privilege not granted to the public generally in order to further his newsgathering and, by inference, the free press.

For the purposes of this chapter the most aggressive view is taken as evidence of a "free" press. The press is freest when the Court treats the public's access to information (and the press as part of that public) as a constitutional right, not merely a social interest. Such a view requires the government to limit access only if it can show a compelling or substantial reason for doing so. Moreover, the right of access sometimes grants reporters privileges beyond those accorded to the general public, as in the case of Branzburg. It is presumed that realistically the public cannot gather information on some subjects itself; it is forced to rely on reporters. If, to promote the press's role as watchdog, concessions must occasionally be made to reporters to promote a freely flowing information, then these extra privileges should, in accordance with First Amendment free press, be granted.

Written word   To find out how free the written press is as defined above, we need to know what happened to Paul Branzburg. In that case as in others before it,[68] the Court refused to grant privileges of access to reporters beyond those available to the public generally. The Court discussed the importance of grand jury investigations in the control of crime, thereby alluding to the harm that would result if people were exempt from grand jury testimony. The harm to the free press of grand jury testimony by Branzburg and others is less clear, however. The Court was not persuaded by Branzburg's claim that his newsgathering abilities would be hampered by his grand jury appearance. Thus, weighing these two things—the public interest in law enforcement versus the "consequential, *but uncertain*, burden on news gathering"—the Court ruled on the side of law enforcement. This, of course, left open the possibility that reporters could secure added privileges if they were able clearly to show that free press would be hurt without these privileges. Branzburg's problem was that he failed to convince the Justices that grand jury subpoenas intruded on the free flow of information. Rather, concluded the Court, the "sole issue before us is the obligation of reporters to respond to grand jury subpoenas as other citizens do and to answer questions relevant to an investigation into the commission of a crime."

In other cases, too, the Court has declined to give the press, as the public's surrogate, extra privileges beyond some minimal concessions such as giving reporters "special seating and priority of entry (in public trials) so that they may report what people in attendance have seen and heard."[69] Thus, the public does not have the right to interview prisoners and neither does the press.[70] The public cannot withhold information from grand juries and neither can the press. Also, the press is bound by the law of privacy just as are other citizens; for example, a lower federal court upheld a state law barring press and public from executions, saying that the privacy of the condemned person (in the case at bar of Gary Gilmore) predominated over other social interests.[71]

Although the press has not succeeded in securing privileges, it has benefitted from a 1980 decision according constitutional status to access to information.[72] The occasion for this decision was the closure case used in the introduction to this chapter in which a judge closed off a trial to the public and press completely. It is clear that courtroom closing runs head-on into the Sixth Amendment guarantee that the defendant have a public trial. It is less clear, however, whether that same closing also conflicts with the First Amendment guarantee of free press. In 1979 the Court had said the defendant had a constitutional *right* to a public trial, but the public had only a social *interest* in access to a preliminary hearing.[73] This left open the possibility that a trial judge could close not only a preliminary hearing but also the trial itself to the press and public if some countervailing interest demanded it. The decision left the First Amendment—with its battery of protective tests—out of the picture. In the 1980 case, the Court soothed the fears of reporters by making clear that the public and press also had a constitutional right, based on the First Amendment, to open trials. It reached this decision by recounting the deeply ingrained history and tradition of open trials in this country and by pointing to the public's right to information generally that inheres in the First Amendment.

This ruling added another hue to the meaning of First Amendment free expression. Free speech does not simply give the freedom to speak; it also "carries with it some freedom to listen." The First Amendment contains a right to "receive information and ideas" and this extends to the courtroom: "The explicit, guaranteed rights to speak and to publish concerning what takes place at a trial would lose much meaning if access to observe the trial could . . . be foreclosed arbitrarily." It should be pointed out that the Court made clear this right of access is confined to public places only. Thus, the press and public are entitled to listen in on proceedings in the courtroom because it is a public place; they are not entitled to access to a prison or other institution not "shar[ing] the long tradition of openness."[74]

Broadcasting The Court heard Paul Branzburg's appeal at the same time it listened to the claims of Paul Pappas, a television reporter-photographer who watched what was going on at Black Panther head-quarters at a time of racial unrest in New Bedford, Rhode Island. Pappas did not write a story about his observations, but he was called upon by a grand jury two months later to testify about what he saw. The outcome of his appeal was the same as that of Paul Branzburg: the Court decided the two together and held that neither Pappas nor Branzburg could refuse to testify on First Amendment grounds. The point is that the Court lumped a newspaper and television reporter together in framing doctrine relating to the access of the press to information. For once the doctrine for both major media is the same. Here it denied something to both types of reporters; in the closure case it granted something—access to trials—to both types of reporters. Generally, when newsgathering is at stake the Court does not distinguish between the media. Why not?

Inter-media differences level off in newsgathering because the activity has nothing to do with the reporter's medium. Newsgathering revolves around the reporter's activities in the street, courtroom, government offices, libraries. It precedes activities in the editorial room and for that reason is unaffected by the nature of the medium, which arises only when the information is conveyed to the public. The arguments of broadcasting's uniqueness—its scarcity, reliance on a public resource, or intrusive nature—are irrelevant at the point of newsgathering and thus cannot be used to justify differential treatment of reporters. Thus the same conclusion on access to information extends to broadcasting as to the written word: access is an interest and a constitutional right but it does not give extra concessions to reporters as surrogates for the public's right to access to trials and other public sources of information.

The one area in which differences do arise is when the television reporter's camera equipment makes this reporter more troublesome than the print reporter with his or her pad and pencil. Thus, trial judges, with the American Bar Association's consent, have limited broadcast reporters by barring their paraphernalia from trials.[75] Such is a time, place, and manner restriction, however, and does not prevent broadcasting reporters from giving their employers the same substantive information as print reporters.

Access of the Public to the Press

"Open debate and discussion of public issues are vital to our national health," writes the Court. "On public questions there should be 'uninhibited, robust, and wide-open' debate."[76] One ingredient for open debate is, as described in the preceding section, access of reporters to information so the press can transmit information to the public. But debate is a two-way process. A second ingredient must relate to the public's ability to talk back. If the press speeds the dissemination of information about the government so, it stands to reason, can it facilitate transmission of the public's voice. A fourth indicator of a free press—"access of the public to the press"—refers to the public's ability to use the press to send ideas. Its relation to the other kind of access is shown in Figure 3.1.

Let us use an economic analogy to point out problems raised by access of the public to the press. One can liken the First Amendment system of free expression to the economic marketplace, with a couple of substitutions. The economic marketplace traffics commodities; the marketplace of expression barters ideas. The economic marketplace features buyers and sellers of goods; the marketplace of ideas involves the buyers (public) and sellers (press) of information. Classical capitalist

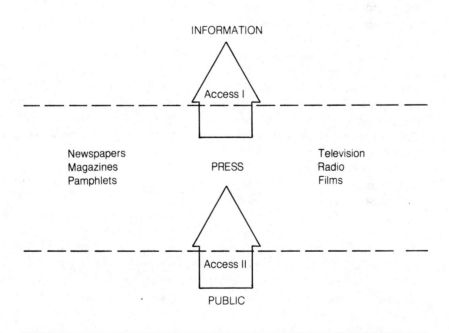

FIGURE 3.1
TWO FORMS OF ACCESS PROMOTING THE
FREE FLOW OF INFORMATION

theory suggests that the economic marketplace will thrive if left to itself and that imbalances will correct themselves. Likewise, traditional free press theories hold that diversity of ideas can only come from a press unencumbered by state controls. But, anyone familiar with twentieth-century economics will recognize that economists have turned to government controls to promote competition and no longer believe a free reigning market serves the buyer's interests. Analogously, might government controls over the press be necessary to protect the public in the marketplace of ideas?[77]

For the purposes of this chapter, the press is deemed free to the extent that classical capitalism reigns, that is, to the extent that access is achieved without state controls over the content of the press. This position is compatible with the earlier criticism of prior restraints because most laws designed to guarantee public access to the media are affirmative prior controls and bring on the same evils as negative restraints. If the state were to mandate access through, for example, right-to-reply statutes for newspapers, it would tell the press what it must publish and thereby prevent press executives from publishing material of their own choice in the same space or time slot. This position still holds that access of the public to the press is necessary for press vitality; it simply suggests that this access must be achieved voluntarily or through indirect controls such as strict enforcement of antitrust statutes.

Written word   Pat L. Tornillo was running for the Florida House of Representatives in 1972 and, we may presume, was incensed when he read two attacks on him in the editorial pages of the *Miami Herald*.[78] Both zeroed in on Tornillo's activities as leader of the Classroom Teachers Association, in particular his role in a 1968 teachers' strike. A passage in the first editorial said, for example, "Call it whatever you will, it was an illegal act against the public interest and clearly prohibited by the statutes. . . . We cannot say it would be illegal but certainly it would be inexcusable of the voters if they sent Pat Tornillo to Tallahassee to occupy the seat for District 103 in the House of Representatives." Wanting to defend his record and that of the CTA, Tornillo asked the *Miami Herald* to print a reply. The newspaper declined and Tornillo went to court, pressing charges against the newspaper for failing to abide by Florida's right-to-reply statute, which said in part that if a newspaper "assails the personal character of any candidate" it shall, if asked by the candidate, publish a free reply "in as conspicuous a place and in the same kind of type" as the original attack. Failure to print a reply was a misdemeanor.

The Florida right-to-reply statute is a classic example of enforced access of the public to the press. Florida's legislators had viewed with misapprehension changes in the newspaper business over the years that turned a "true marketplace of ideas . . . in which there was relatively easy access to the channels of communication" to a monopolistic juggernaut closing off access to most people wanting to convey their views. The legislators joined a growing body of observers who also worried about the effect mergers and other signs of big business in newspapers would have on the average person's chances of penetrating the media. To them the threat to freely flowing information was so great as to warrant dramatic remedies. If the capitalist moguls of publishing would not voluntarily open up their newspapers, then the government would have to find ways to do it for them. An enforced right-to-reply to a personal attack was one such way.

The Supreme Court's reaction to enforced access to the print medium is straightforward. The state may, through antitrust statutes, control the growth of monopolies in the publishing business and so indirectly promote access,[79] but it may not promote access through interference with the content of publishing. Antitrust enforcement is a time, place, and manner restriction that controls the conditions under which newspapers operate. Right-to-reply statutes are content-based restrictions, however, that amount to prior controls over the content of published material. As such they cannot stand under the First Amendment. Moreover, concluded the Court, far from promoting the free flow of information, enforced access "dampens the vigor and limits the variety of public debate." The Justices wasted little time in striking down Florida's law as a violation of First Amendment free speech. At least for the written word, classical capitalism holds sway and, in light of the fourth indicator of a "free" press, one must conclude that the written word passes the test.

Broadcasting Take the Florida right-to-reply statute, change a few minor details, move the controversy from newspapers to broadcasting—and the outcome reverses itself. The equivalent of the Tornillo case in broadcasting is *Red Lion Broadcasting Corp. v. FCC*, a decision reviewed earlier in this chapter in which Fred Cook demanded that a radio station grant him equal time to rebut the charges Billy James Hargis had leveled against him over the air. Cook, as Tornillo, was attacked in the press; Cook, as Tornillo, requested response time; and Cook, as Tornillo, made this response under the authority of government policy. The differences lay in the medium in question (Cook was attacked over the air, Tornillo in a newspaper) and in the governing agency (Cook relied on the FCC's personal attack rules, Tornillo on Florida's right-to-reply statute). The even larger difference lay in the outcome. Whereas the Court struck down Florida's right-to-reply law, it specifically upheld the right-to-reply rules that had been set forth for broadcasting.

The FCC's personal attack rules are another classic example of enforced access. If a television or radio licensee airs "an attack . . . upon the honesty, character, integrity or like personal qualities of an identified person or group" during the discussion of a controversial issue, the broadcaster must notify the attacked individual within a week and give him or her a reasonable opportunity to respond.[80] These rules are only a small part of a much larger set of FCC-enforced rules designed to promote public access to broadcasting. As discussed earlier, these rules center around the fairness doctrine, which requires broadcasters to seek out controversial issues for exploration on the air and to give reasonable coverage to the different sides of the controversy. Under the auspices of these rules, people bring all kinds of complaints to the FCC, which then reviews the facts, interprets the rules, and hands down its decision. Plaintiffs unhappy with the decision may then appeal to the federal courts.

Another example of an access case involved Walter Baring, a politician running in the Nevada Democratic primary for a position in the U.S. Congress.[81] Baring wanted to buy some 5-minute advertising slots from a Las Vegas television station but was told the station sold only 60-second slots except in the middle of the night, from 1:30 A.M. to 6:00 A.M., when it would sell longer periods of time. He complained to the FCC on the basis of what is known as the reasonable access rule for candidates for federal office. Congress launched the rule as part of the 1972 Federal Election Campaign Act in order to make sure these candidates had "adequate opportunity to present and discuss their candidacies and hence provide the voters with information necessary for the responsible exercise of their franchise."[82] Under it broadcasters must make a reasonable effort to give free time to candidates or give them reasonable opportunities to buy their own time. Hearing Baring's complaint, the FCC held that the Las Vegas station failed to live up to the law. By letting candidates elaborate on their views only "during the hours when the vast majority of the potential voting audience is asleep," the station failed to live up to its obligation to ensure access for the politicians.

Another example of the variety of claims tossed about by the FCC involved a two-part showing of the CBS comedy "Maude," in which the leading character discovered she was pregnant. In one scene Maude, her husband, and her daughter discussed the possibility of an abortion in a dialogue the Long Island Coalition for Life saw as "pro-death." The Coalition complained to the FCC on the grounds that the program amounted to a personal attack on "all present and future unborn children" and called for rebuttal time. The FCC rejected the claim,[83] but the fact that existing rules led the group to believe it could respond to entertainment shows how extensive the web of access rules is.

The elaborate system of enforced access in broadcasting clearly differs from the "classical capitalism" that reigns over the newsprint industry and, as defined by the fourth indicator of free press, points to a less vigorous First Amendment when broadcasting is brought into the scene. Yet the irony of enforced access in broadcasting is that the government has done it in order to promote the free flow of information. Listen to the Court in *Tornillo*: "Government enforced right of access inescapably 'dampens the vigor and limits the variety of public debate'." But the same Court in *Red Lion* argues that government-enforced access in broadcasting is essential for vigorous public debate. Here the scarcity theory again comes into play. Whereas anyone can set up a printing press, gain access to the world of publishing, and rebut whatever charges have been filed, not just anyone can make use of the airwaves. Were the government not to intervene, the theory goes, public discussion would be limited to whatever the station licensees wanted it to include. Thus, vigor comes from regulation.

Although the system of enforced access distinguishes broadcasting from the printed word, in two other doctrinal areas the print and broadcast media are the same. First, the Court allows indirect controls akin to antitrust regulation for broadcasting as well as for newspapers. In the 1940s the FCC limited the number of television or radio stations one owner could have in the same community; then it limited the total number of stations one owner could have regardless of location; and in 1970 it began limiting cross-media ownership, first with radio and television and then with broadcasting-newspaper combinations.[84] Second, for neither print nor broadcasting has the Court gone so far as to say the public has a constitutional *right* of access to the media.[85] Thus, at the most basic level broadcasting doctrine is not really so much different from print doctrine. The web of policy designed to promote access both directly and indirectly in broadcasting is, at root, based on the supposition that the public has an *interest* in penetrating that medium. The unique features of broadcasting are not enough, however, to change the meaning of the First Amendment for that medium only. The public has an interest in access to the press that is strong enough to warrant special policy for broadcasting, but this interest is not sufficiently strong nor the features of broadcasting so different as to grant the public a constitutional right of access to the press for any medium.

SUMMARY

Press differs from other First Amendment expression by its reliance on an intermediary to communicate ideas. Unlike speech, religion, and assembly, which involve face-to-face expression, press puts a medium between the sender and recipient of a message. Today three major media make up press—the printed word, motion pictures, and broadcasting.[86] The medium can keenly affect the impact of an idea. Sometimes nothing can surpass the well-honed written word as a medium for creating moods; other times a surreptitious photograph keeps alive the adage that a picture is worth a thousand words. Motion pictures and broadcasting add the auditory impact to a message; for example, when ordering the Nixon tapes to be made publicly available a federal court judge noted that "one who listens to the tapes—the inflections, pauses, emphasis and the like—will be better able to understand the conversations than one who only reads the written transcripts that have been published."[87]

The person trying to decide which medium to use to convey an idea would do well not only to consider which medium most enhances the punch of that idea but also to ask whether the message can legally be sent through the chosen medium. Doctrinally the press is multidimensional and variegated, with the Court using differing standards depending on the medium at issue, with the result that sometimes free press doctrine is monolithic, other times dichotomous, and still other times tripartite.[88] In order to chart the intra-liberty gradations within First Amendment free press, this chapter identifies four indicators of a "free" press and uses them as a standard to compare and contrast doctrine for the print and broadcasting media. It suggests that the press is "freest" when the following conditions obtain:

(1) Prior restraints are virtually absent;
(2) subsequent controls are imposed only for a compelling state interest clearly endangered by the press;
(3) reporters have a constitutional right of access to information and may exercise that right even if it means they are granted privileges not available to the public generally; and
(4) public access to the press is achieved without state laws directly mandating it.

These indicators encompass not only prior and subsequent controls as discussed in Chapter 2 but also access, a concept intimately associated with free press. Access helps promote a freely flowing body of information unencumbered by barriers between reporters and information and between the public and press (see Figure 3.1). It should be noted that putting values on these indicators is inescapably an individual decision, so readers may disagree that one or another condition is important for a "free" press. The purpose of the exercise, however, is to create a standard from which intra-liberty gradations can be assessed. Therefore, the nuances of each indicator are less important than creating a single definition of free press from which one can chart differences and similarities for the printed word and broadcasting.

The cases reviewed in this chapter show that, generally speaking, the press is freer for the print medium than for broadcasting. Yet exceptions arise that more often than not are a function of the type of speech at issue. This means that the observer should be aware of the speech involved in a case—is it truthful speech on the public record? controversial political speech? sexual speech?—in order to understand the way in which courts will approach the conflict.

The chapter shows that press doctrine *is the same* (and the press equally free) for the print and broadcasting media in the following conditions:

Newsgathering, or access of reporters to information

Newsgathering takes place before the medium is used to convey the story; hence the medium has little bearing on the reporter's activities. Reporters for both newspapers and television have a constitutional right of access to information (for example, judges cannot close off a judicial proceeding without a compelling reason for doing so) but neither is granted privileges beyond those available to the public generally (compare the outcome of Paul Branzburg's case and Paul Pappas's appeal). The doctrine for each medium almost but not quite meets the standard for a free press suggested in this chapter.

Subsequent controls over truthful information contained in the public record

No press, regardless of medium, can be penalized for conveying information available on the public record such as the name of a crime victim. This type of expression is highly valued and transcends any differences in the media as a reason for control.

Access of the public to the press

The state may indirectly promote access to both media through enforcement of antitrust statutes.

Press doctrine *differs* for each medium in the following conditions:

Prior restraints—negative

The state cannot "execute" a newspaper by enjoining its publication without the most compelling of reasons. The FCC can "execute" a broadcast licensee, however, by denying it a license renewal merely by showing that the licensee did not broadcast in the public interest.

Prior restraints — affirmative

The state may not tell a print publisher what he or she *must* publish any more than it can tell the publisher what *not* to publish (recall *Miami Herald v. Tornillo*). However, the state has set up an elaborate set of rules telling broadcasters what they *must* publish (recall *Red Lion v. FCC*).

Prior restraints — political speech

Prior controls on political speech are the *least* excusable for the printed word. However, controversial speech in the public interest is the *most* likely to prompt affirmative prior controls in broadcasting under such rules as the fairness doctrine.

Prior restraints and subsequent controls — sexual speech

The state may censor or penalize only obscenity in the print medium (*Miller v. California*), but the state may censor or penalize obscenity *and* indecency in broadcasting (*FCC v. Pacifica Foundation*).

Access of public to press

The state may not directly enforce access to the print medium (*Miami Herald v. Tornillo*), but it may do so in broadcasting (*Red Lion Broadcasting Corp. v. FCC*).

In summary, accurate information on the public record is valued and protected speech for both the printed word and broadcasting. Public interest material is also highly valued but the *way* it is protected differs for each medium. The Court has held that to protect public interest speech in printed publications, the state must keep its hand off; to protect public interest speech in broadcasting, however, the state may have to intervene in a positive sense to encourage diversity in programming. Sexual speech, on the other hand, is not highly valued; here the state may intervene in a negative sense to forbid merely offensive (indecent) material from being aired.

Inter-liberty gradations in free press doctrine have been building since Congress passed the Communications Act of 1934 and empowered the Federal Communications Commission to regulate broadcasting in the public interest. It is likely, however, that the era of inter-media differences in press law has peaked and that we will now see a convergence in the law. This is due to an interesting trend of the 1970s in which the media themselves have become more alike. In contrast to earlier decades in which new technology created *different* conduits for sending information (motion pictures, then radio, then television), the technology of the 1970s and 1980s has helped reporters and entertainers use *common* conduits. The centerpiece of this media convergence is the coaxial cable, which captures broadcast signals and sends them to individual homes. The cable, which can bring up to fifty channels to each subscriber, can do the work that was once done by motion picture theaters (all-movie channels such as Home Box Office and Showtime bring advertisement-free films to the home viewer soon after their release to the general public and videodisk and videotape attachments let consumers buy films for repeated playing) and by printed publications (teletext systems show pages of printed information on the television screen and bring closer the day that viewers can "read" the daily newspaper through their television sets). As the media become more alike, it is reasonable to expect the law to become simpler.

If a convergence toward a single constitutional standard is likely, one may well ask what the nature of that standard will be. Will the Court free broadcasting from some of its controls and move it closer to the standard now governing the print medium? Or will the Court add controls to the nonscarce print and cable industries and move the law closer to the regulated world of broadcasting? The Court has only just begun to hand down pertinent decisions, so it is too early to predict with any certainty the direction media law will go. But it does appear that so far the cards are weighted in favor of a convergence toward broadcasting. In two decisions the Court approved new controls on the cable[89] and in another it approved new controls on newspapers,[90] thereby bringing two nonscarce media closer to the broadcasting standard. On the other hand, in the 1981 case of *Chandler v. Florida*,[91] in which the Court held that television in the courtroom is not inherently unconstitutional, the Justices lifted some *time, place, and manner* controls on broadcasting and brought the medium more in line with the print medium. Also, in *FCC v. WNCN Listeners Guild*[92] the Court upheld an FCC ruling that lifted restrictions on radio licensees. Nowhere to be found, however, is a solid convergence case that lifts controls on the *content* of television. The fairness doctrine, equal time rules, and other affirmative controls still stand untouched.

In short, free press is a continually changing guarantee if for no other reason than that the intermediaries for transmitting information also change steadily. Each improvement in or addition to extant media bids the Court to consider its effect upon the system of free expression. The first time the Court faced a new medium—films—it reacted by ostracizing it from the First Amendment for fifty years.[93] The second time—with broadcasting—the Court accepted the medium as First Amendment material but gave it fewer protections than it accorded the more traditional media. If history is any guide the Court will continue to incorporate broadcasting into the fold and do the same, albeit gradually, for new media forms. Thus, when we conclude that press is freer for the print than the broadcast medium, we must recognize that these gradations may very well level in the future, at least insofar as they relate to differences in the nature of the media. Gradations based upon the nature of the speech at issue may still continue, however, recalling similar gradations in free speech doctrine reviewed in Chapter 2.

Questions for Thought

1. Jurists and legislators put extra controls on telecommunications because the "scarcity theory" says the medium depends upon a scarce natural resource and must be regulated in the public interest. See, for example, *FCC v. Pacifica Foundation*, 438 U.S. 726 (1978). Cable television shakes up this theory, however, by freeing telecommunications from the electromagnetic spectrum and opening up the field to forty or more channels (with transmissions flowing through a coaxial cable) where only one could operate before. Should the scarcity theory still apply? How should scarcity be defined? Jurists traditionally look at the nature of the resource upon which the medium depends to define scarcity. But what about practical things such as the cost of abundant resources? The newspaper industry, for example, is based upon paper and other easily available resources but very few people can afford to compete with newspaper conglomerates. Does this make the printed word a scarce medium? How, in short, should scarcity be defined? Which media are scarce? Is scarcity a valid rationale for controlling the press?

2. Jurists and legislators also limit telecommunications because they say television has an intrusive character that allows it to invade the privacy of the citizen's home more readily than other media. See *FCC v. Pacifica Foundation*, 438 U.S. 726 (1978). All-movie channels such as Home Box Office and Showtime come to the homes of subscribers who deliberately decide to pay an extra monthly fee for the service, however. These consumers are more like the deliberate consumers of printed publications and are thus less likely to have their living room unexpectedly invaded by offensive programming. Today there are virtually no controls over pay-TV. Should the presently minimal controls over these special channels be strengthened to bring them into line with the detailed controls over broadcasting? Or should the FCC loosen its controls over broadcasting in order to bring that medium closer to the relatively free standard for cable TV? Would Congress violate the First Amendment if it forbade indecency in all-movie channels? (The Court upheld indecency control in broadcasting in *FCC v. Pacifica Foundation*.)

3. A California judge in *Fording v. Landau*, 54 Cal. Rptr. 177, 181, affirmed per curiam, 388 U.S. 456 (1967), said that the same message has a greater impact and can be controlled earlier when transmitted by motion pictures than by the printed word (see note 88 to this chapter). Do you agree that violence, grief, sex, and other emotions and messages can be explored more persuasively and with greater impact through certain media? If yes, does this justify more stringent controls on that medium?

4. Some states have started to allow televised trials. This raises constitutional problems because it puts several constitutional rights against one another, including these: the defendant's Sixth Amendment right to a public trial, the public's Sixth Amendment right to a public trial, the defendent's Sixth Amendment right to a fair trial, the public's First Amendment right to know, and the press's First Amendment right to gather information. In which way does television in the courtroom affect each? Do you favor televised trials? What does your answer tell about the relative value you place on each of these rights?

NOTES

1. The facts are from *Nebraska Press Association v. Stuart*, 427 U.S. 539 (1976) and the report of this case in Fred W. Friendly, "A Crime and Its Aftershock," *The New York Times Magazine*, March 21, 1976, p. 17.
2. See Friendly, p. 87. The judge had said, "I kept thinking of *Sheppard v. Maxwell*. . . . I didn't care what was in the paper; I just didn't want to be reversed." In the *Sheppard* case (384 U.S. 333 [1966]) the Court reversed a murder conviction because the trial judge had failed to restrain garrulous reporters.
3. *Richmond Newspapers, Inc. v. Virginia*, 65 L.Ed. 2d 973 (1980).
4. *Cox Broadcasting Corp. v. Cohn*, 420 U.S. 469 (1975). See also L. A. Powe, Jr., "Or of the [Broadcast] Press," 55 *Texas L.Rev.* 39, 40 (1976).
5. *Richmond Newspapers, Inc. v. Virginia*, 65 L.Ed. 2d at 987.
6. The facts are from *FCC v. Pacifica Foundation*, 438 U.S. 726 (1978.)
7. *Pacifica Foundation*, 56 F.C.C. 2d 94 (1975).
8. 18 U.S.C. §1464 (1976).
9. *Pacifica Foundation*, 56 F.C.C. 2d 94, 98 (1975).
10. Ibid., at 99.
11. 438 U.S. 726 (1978).
12. In interpreting other laws that forbid both indecency and obscenity, the Court has held that only obscene matter may be controlled. See, for example, *Hamling v. United States*, 418 U.S. 87 (1974), in which the Court reached this conclusion as it interpreted a federal statute barring the mailing of any "obscene, lascivious, indecent, filthy or vile" item. See also *United States v. Orito*, 413 U.S. 139 (1973), reaching the same conclusion for a federal statute barring the use of a common carrier for the interstate and foreign transport of any "obscene, lewd, lascivious, or filthy" item. Each of these cases involved media other than broadcasting.

13. Films are left out of the analysis in order to simplify the thesis. For the most part doctrine relating to films and the print medium is the same. For exceptions, see note 88 below.

14. Quoted in *Near v. Minnesota*, 283 U.S. 697, 713 (1931).

15. Ibid.

16. *Lovell v. Griffin*, 303 U.S. 444 (1938).

17. *Nebraska Press Ass'n v. Stuart*, 427 U.S. 539 (1976).

18. Thomas I. Emerson, "The Doctrine of Prior Restraint," 20 *Law and Contemp. Problems* 648, 651 (1955).

19. For a thorough discussion of the evils of prior restraints, see ibid.

20. *Pittsburgh Press Co. v. Pittsburgh Comm'n on Human Rights*, 413 U.S. 376, 390 (1973).

21. *Miami Herald Publishing Co. v. Tornillo*, 418 U.S. 241, 259 (1974) (White, J., concurring).

22. *Near v. Minnesota*, 283 U.S. 697 (1931).

23. 403 U.S. 713 (1971).

24. *United States v. Progressive*, 467 F. Supp. 990 (1979); *Morland v. Sprecher*, certiorari filed June 2, 1980, 47 U.S.L.W. 3838.

25. *Organization for a Better Austin v. Keefe*, 384 U.S. 333 (1966).

26. 283 U.S. 697 (1931).

27. *New York Times v. United States*, 403 U.S. 713, 726-727 (1971).

28. Ibid., at 730 (Stewart and White, JJ., concurring).

29. *Alfred A. Knopf, Inc. v. Colby*, 509 F. 2d 1362 (4th Cir. 1975), certiorari denied, 421 U.S. 992.

30. Note, "The Limits of Broadcast Self-Regulation Under the First Amendment," 27 *Stan.L.Rev.* 1527, 1548 n.91 (1975).

31. "[N]early one-half of all adults consider television the most believable news medium among newspapers, magazines, radio and television." Ibid.

32. Frederick F. Schauer, *The Law of Obscenity* (Washington, D.C.: Bureau of National Affairs, 1976).

33. *FCC v. Pacifica Foundation*, 438 U.S. 726, 748 (1978).

34. It summarily affirmed a lower court decision to this effect. *Capital Broadcasting Co. v. Acting Attorney General*, 405 U.S. 1000 (1972).

35. *Bigelow v. Virginia*, 421 U.S. 809 (1975).

36. Ibid., at 825, n.10.

37. *Virginia State Board of Pharmacy v. Virginia Citizens Consumer Council, Inc.*, 425 U.S. 748, 773 (1976).

38. 47 U.S.C. § 319 (a) (1976).

39. 395 U.S. 367 (1969).

40. *Miami Herald Publishing Co. v. Tornillo*, 418 U.S. 241, 259 (1974) (White, J., concurring).

41. For a description of broadcasting's supposed "uniqueness," see *FCC v. Pacifica Foundation*, 438 U.S. 726, 749 (1978). See also Henry Goldberg and Michael Couzens, "'Peculiar Characteristics': An Analysis of the First Amendment Implications of Broadcast Regulation," 31 *Fed. Communications L.J.* 1, 26-33 (1978).

42. Steven J. Simmons, "Fairness Doctrine: The Early History," 29 *Fed. Communications L.J.* 207, 219 (1976).

43. Quoted in ibid., at 214.

44. Ibid., at 217.

45. *Nat'l Broadcasting Corp. v. United States*, 319 U.S. 190, 212 (1943).

46. 47 U.S.C. §307 (a) (1976) and 47 U.S.C. § 307 (d) (1976).

47. See Simmons, at 208, quoting from the FCC.

48. 395 U.S. 367, at 390.

49. *Miami Herald Publishing Co. v. Tornillo*, 418 U.S. 241, 259 (1974) (White, J., concurring) (emphasis added).

50. Because publication is a "multistage process" involving writing, printing, publishing, distributing, and selling, a subsequent control for one stage is a prior control for the next. M. Glenn Abernathy, *Civil Liberties Under the Constitution* (New York: Dodd, Mead, 1974), p. 344.

51. Quoted in ibid., at 335.

52. *Landmark Communications, Inc. v. Virginia*, 435 U.S. 829 (1978).

53. See, for example, *Mills v. Alabama*, 384 U.S. 214 (1966).

54. *Cox Broadcasting Corp. v. Cohn*, 420 U.S. 469, 495 (1975) (emphasis added).

55. 47 U.S.C. § 326 (1976): "Nothing in this chapter shall be understood or construed to give the Commission the power of censorship over the radio communications or signals transmitted by any radio station, and no regulation or condition shall be promulgated or fixed by the Commission which shall interfere with the right of free speech by means of radio communications."

56. The FCC, "if public convenience, interest, or necessity will be served thereby, . . . shall grant to any applicant therefore a station license . . . from time to time for a term of not to exceed three years . . . if the Commission finds that public interest, convenience, or necessity would be served thereby" 47 U.S.C. § 307 (d) (1976).

57. *Nat'l Broadcasting Corp. v. United States*, 319 U.S. 190, 226-227 (1943).

58. For example, the Court's standard in *Nat'l Broadcasting Corp. v. United States* contrasted with other decisions of the 1940s in which the Court suggested that statutory limitations on speech were presumptively unconstitutional. See, for example, *United States v. Congress of Indus. Organizations*, 335 U.S. 106, 121 n.20 (1948); *Thomas v. Collins*, 323 U.S. 516, 529-530 (1943); and *Schneider v. New Jersey*, 309 U.S. 147, 161 (1939).

59. *FCC v. Pacifica Foundation*, 438 U.S. 726 (1978).

60. 18 U.S.C. § 1464 (1976).

61. See note 12 above.

62. See, for example, *In re Sonderling Broadcasting Corp.*, 27 RR 2d 285, affirmed sub. nom. *Illinois Citizens Comm. for Broadcasting v. FCC*, 515 F. 2d 397 (D.C. Cir. 1975).

63. *New York Times v. United States*, 403 U.S. 713, 717 (Black, J., concurring). The press also gives the citizen "the information needed for the intelligent discharge of his political responsibilities." *Gannette Co., Inc. v. DePasquale*, 61 L.Ed. 2d 608, 632 (1979) (Powell, J., concurring).

64. *New York Times v. United States*, 403 U.S. at 717 (Black, J., concurring).

65. *Sherrill v. Knight*, 569 F. 2d 124 (D.C. Cir. 1978).

66. This question was at issue in *Gannette Co., Inc. v. DePasquale*, 61 L.Ed. 2d 608 (1979), and *Richmond Newspapers, Inc. v. Virginia*, 65 L.Ed. 2d 973 (1980).

67. *Branzburg v. Hayes*, 408 U.S. 665 (1972).

68. See, for example, *Pell v. Procunier*, 417 U.S. 817 (1974): "The Constitution does not . . . require government to accord the press specific access to information not shared by members of the public generally."

69. *Richmond Newspapers, Inc. v. Virginia*, 65 L.Ed. 2d 973 (1980).

70. *Pell v. Procunier*, 417 U.S. 817 (1974).

71. *Garrett v. Estelle*, 556 F.2d 1274 (5th Cir. 1977). See also *Galella v. Onassis*, 353 F. Supp. 196 (S.D.N.Y. 1972), in which the court upheld a lower court order forbidding news photographer Galella from coming within a specified number of feet of Jacqueline Kennedy Onassis. Onassis's interest in privacy outweighed Galella's interests in taking pictures of her.

72. *Richmond Newspapers, Inc. v. Virginia*, 65 L.Ed. 2d 973 (1980).

73. *Gannette Co., Inc. v. DePasquale*, 61 L.E. 2d 608 (1979).

74. *Richmond Newspapers, Inc. v. Virginia*, 65 L.Ed. 2d 973 (1980).

75. The American Bar Association adopted Canon 35 of its Judicial Ethics barring photographs in courtrooms after the Bruno Hauptmann trial in the 1930s and later expanded the ban to include television cameras. Donald Gillmor and Jerome Barron, *Mass Communications Law: Cases and Comment*, 3rd ed. (St. Paul, Minn.: West, 1979), p. 534. Today, one-half the states and all the federal courts bar cameras from courtrooms. ibid., pp. 536-540. The Judicial Conference of the United States reaffirmed its ban on television coverage of federal courtroom proceedings in 1980. See *The New York Times*, September 28, 1980, p. 61.

76. *New York Times v. United States*, 403 U.S. 713, 724 (1971).

77. Scholars are divided on the wisdom of using the government to promote access of the public to the press. Some opine that the press has become monopolistic, is big business that closes off access to people having unusual views, and censors speech in its own preference for stability. To them, dramatic ills in the free marketplace of ideas call for remedies involving government controls. See, for example, Jerome Barron, "Access to the Press—A New First Amendment Right," 80 *Harv.L.Rev.* 1641 (1967). Other scholars see problems of access too but do not see government controls as the answer. To them, free press must protect the publisher; other constitutional guarantees such as free speech and free assembly protect the public's right to speak. See, for example, John C. Merrill, *The Imperative of Freedom: A Philosophy of Journalistic Autonomy* (New York: Hastings House, 1974). They also doubt that controls actually will promote press diversity. They favor voluntary methods of promoting public access, such as encouraging newspapers to use an op-ed page (Hillier Krieghbaum, "The 'Op-Ed Page' Revisited," 54 *Saturday Review* 91, Nov. 13, 1971), and appointing an internal ombudsman to ensure a fair coverage of issues in the newspaper or television station (Samuel L. Becker, "Mass Communications and the First Amendment: An American Dilemma," 1 *Freedom of Speech Newsletter* 16 [1975]).

78. *Miami Herald Publishing Co. v. Tornillo*, 418 U.S. 241 (1974).

79. *Associated Press v. United States*, 326 U.S. 1 (1945).

80. For a thorough discussion of the FCC's personal attack rules, see Andrew O. Shapiro, *Media Access* (Boston: Little Brown, 1976), pp. 192-222.

81. *Summa Corp.*, 43 F.C.C. 2d 602 (1973). See Shapiro, p. 41.

82. *Licensee Responsibility Under Amendments to the Communications Act Made by the Federal Election Campaign Act of 1971*, 47 F.C.C. 2d 516, 517 (1974). See Shapiro, p. 40.

83. *Diocesan Union of Holy Name Societies*, 41 F.C.C. 2d 297 (1973). See Shapiro, p. 205.

84. For a history of these policies, see *FCC v. Nat'l Citizens Comm. for Broadcasting*, 431 U.S. 775 (1978).

85. *Columbia Broadcasting System, Inc. v. Democratic Nat'l Committee*, 412 U.S. 94 (1973).

86. Generally speaking, the print medium includes typescript, drawings, pictures contained in newspapers and magazines, leaflets and pamphlets, and books. Motion pictures include films shown in theaters. Broadcasting covers television and radio programs transmitted over the public airwaves. This typology overlooks the leveling of distinctions being brought about by such technological innovations as cable television.

87. *United States v. Mitchell*, 551 F. 2d 1252 (D.C. Cir. 1976).

88. The one area in which the print medium and films diverge is in the control of obscenity. Under the assumption that each method of expression presents its own problems (*Times Film Corp. v. Chicago*, 365 U.S. 43 [1961]), the Court allows licensing for films that it would probably not allow for books and print materials. First, it allows censors to screen films for obscenity *before* their first public showing. Such a scheme would probably not stand for the print medium. See Lee J. Bollinger, Jr., "Freedom of the Press and Public Access: Toward a Theory of Partial Regulation of the Mass Media," 75 *Mich.L.Rev.* 1, 23-24 (1976). See also Schauer, p. 232; *Freedman v. Maryland*, 380 U.S. 51, 60-61 (1965); and *Bantam Books, Inc. v. Sullivan*, 372 U.S. 58, 70 n.10 (1963). The Court justifies this difference by pointing to the different nature of films. It reasons that books go directly to book sellers from the press so any screening will delay their public distribution. Films, on the other hand, are scheduled before they are shown, thereby giving courts time to decide whether the films are obscene and making it less likely that screening will actually delay the film's public showing. *Freedman v. Maryland*, 380 U.S. at 60-61.

   Second, the Court uses a slightly different substantive standard of obscenity for films than for print materials. The Court uses the *Miller v. California* definition for both media (413 U.S. 15 [1973]), but it indicates that filmed material may reach the *Miller* threshold before comparable printed material. For example, it said that "motion pictures possess a greater capacity for evil, particularly among the youth of a community, than other modes of expression" (*Interstate Circuit, Inc. v. Dallas*, 390 U.S. 676, 690 [1975]), and it affirmed without comment a lower court decision in which the judge said in part that "[b]ecause of the nature of the medium, we think a motion picture of sexual scenes may transcend the bounds of the constitutional guarantee long before a frank description of the same scenes in the written word" (*Fording v. Landau*, 54 Cal. Rptr. 177, 181, affirmed per curiam, 388 U.S. 456 [1967]). See L. A. Powe, Jr., "Cable and Obscenity," 24 *Cath.U.L.Rev.* 719, 723-724 (1975).

89. *United States v. Southwestern Cable Co.*, 392 U.S. 157 (1968) and *United States v. Midwest Video Corp.*, 406 U.S. 649 (1972). But see *FCC v. Midwest Video Corp.*, 440 U.S. 689 (1979), in which the Court drew the line on FCC controls over cable.

90. *FCC v. Nat'l Citizens Comm. for Broadcasting*, 436 U.S. 775 (1978).

91. *Chandler v. Florida*, 49 U.S.L.W. 4141 (January 27, 1981).

92. *FCC v. WNCN Listeners Guild*, No. 79-824 (decided by the Supreme Court March 25, 1981).

93. In *Mutual Film Corp. v. Industrial Commission of Ohio*, 236 U.S. 230, 244 (1915) the Court held that motion pictures were not part of First Amendment press: "the exhibition of moving pictures is a business, pure and simple, originated and conducted for profit, like other spectacles, not to be regarded, . . . as part of the press of the country or as organs of public opinion." It was not until 1952, in the case of *Joseph Burstyn, Inc. v. Wilson*, 343 U.S. 495, 501 (1952), that the Court recognized films as a "significant medium for the communication of ideas" and hence part of the First Amendment.

CHAPTER FOUR

Freedom of Religion ‖

Freedom of religion stands out as one of the more predominant concerns to the framers of the Bill of Rights. In its early draft form the First Amendment guaranteed a "freedom of conscience," which debates and correspondence show to have meant freedom of religious thought. The early Americans acted to protect their religious conscience because they feared, for one thing, the state might impose an official religion on them and, for another, the state would restrict religions through taxation schemes, religious oaths, and other intrusive policies. And rightly did these people fear the state—the government is only a reflection of its people and the very groups so concerned about tolerance to their own creeds were less than angelic when it came to tolerating other religions.

The range of religious persecution, both outright and unwitting, in U.S. history is broad and fascinating, in part because the range of religions practiced is so varied. Mormons, Shakers, Quakers, the "I Am" movement of Guy Ballard, Christian Scientists, Catholics, Baptists, Zen Buddhists—believers in these creeds and hundreds more have practiced their beliefs in the 200 years of this country's independence. It is not surprising that religions have directly conflicted with one another or that   113

elected officials, beholden to their own religions and those of their constituents, have acted less than hospitably to the practices of others.

Religious history in this country is dotted with outright prejudice—Illinoisans driving Mormons to the wild and locust-infested
plains of Utah, the Know-Nothings with their blatant hostility toward
Catholics, anti-Moonie parents forcibly kidnapping their children from
what they perceive to be the brainwashed grip of religious dictators, and
rules preventing atheists from holding public office—which vouch for the
easy ability of Americans, even those professing to be deeply religious, to
intrude on the freedoms of others in the name of their own evangelizing.
More often, however, religious persecution and intolerance comes from
ignorance. Thus, it is more from lack of awareness than evil intrigue that
Muslim prisoners suffer when faced with meals laced with pork and pork
fat, that atheist residents of Moscow, Idaho, must pass a stone engraving
of the Ten Commandments on their main thoroughfare, and that minor
religions find they are denied tax-exempt status because their faith fails
to meet some of the earmarks of a "religion" as defined by the majority.
Surely not all injustices will be erased in the name of religion, yet a series
of small injustices add up to an ambience of intolerance that bodes ill for
a system of free religion. It is to maintain a healthy religious milieu that
two separate but interrelated religion clauses appear in the First
Amendment.[1]

The free exercise clause of the First Amendment warns Congress not
to "prohibit the free exercise" of religion. It is consanguineous with the
free speech and press clauses in that all three guarantee a freedom to
think, speak, and act without arbitrary government restraint. Their
common tie leads the Court to use similar tests to review laws intruding
on religious speech as it does to review laws interfering with free speech
in general. For example, it allows the state to restrict the free exercise of
religion only if it has a "compelling," "paramount,"[2] or "highest order"[3]
interest in doing so; the expression poses a clear and present danger to
that interest;[4] and the state has no less intrusive way of meeting the
interest.[5] It upholds time, place, and manner restrictions provided they
meet the three criteria described in Chapter 2; and it presumes the
unconstitutionality of prior restraints on religion.

The establishment clause, which warns Congress to "make no law
respecting an establishment of religion," is an oddity within the First
Amendment. Unlike the speech, press, and free exercise clauses, which
ward off repressive laws, the establishment clause wards off promotional
laws that aid one religion over another or religion in general over
nonreligion. It guards against subtle promotion such as financial aid to
religious schools as well as more blatant promotion such as enforced

school prayers. Because the establishment clause is different in nature from free exercise, the Court has developed tests solely for it. But this does not divorce establishment entirely from free exercise, however. Although conceptually distinct, the two clauses eventually interlock. Their relationship is contradictory rather than complementary, and their Janus-like character poses one of the more sensitive constitutional dilemmas for the state. If the government passes policy designed to protect free exercise, it risks establishing religion and thereby violates the Constitution. If it makes no move when it sees free exercise rights abridged, however, it risks violating the free exercise rights of religious groups and here also violates the Constitution. The two clauses give conflicting directions to the state and place upon it the delicate task of framing policy that straddles the two guarantees but intrudes on neither.

To illustrate, consider a lower court case involving a brother and sister attending a junior high school in New Hampshire.[6] Along with 20 percent of the other students, they were Apostolic Lutherans. As part of their creed, they eschewed television, radio, motion pictures, acting, and singing and dancing to "worldly" music as well as certain subjects, such as the public discussion of sexual and family relations. These tenets unavoidably brought the students into conflict with the school for it used audiovisual materials in class and taught a health course covering sexual topics and mandated by the state for all students. At first, in order to protect the free exercise rights of the Lutheran students, school administrators excused them from the room whenever audiovisual materials were used. However, these departures disrupted the classroom and upset the remaining students who the Lutherans taunted as "sinners" as they left the room. Administrators then changed policy and made the Lutherans stay in the room with a choice of "placing their heads on the desk, turning their chairs away, or standing in the back of the classroom" when teachers used audiovisual aids. As before, they refused to excuse the students from the health course. Unsatisfied with this policy, the siblings' parents filed suit against the superintendent of schools, alleging violations of their free exercise of religion. Specifically, they claimed the practices undercut family and church efforts to teach religious values and threatened them as parents with "eternal damnation" for exposing their children to forbidden activities.

From the parents' point of view this picture is bleak, for it shows them fearing the worst possible afterlife and their children stoically standing at the back of classrooms while their schoolmates watch films and televised broadcasts. But consider the choices from the school's point of view. First, it could *do nothing* and let school practices go on as scheduled without thinking of the Lutherans. This would leave it to the

Lutherans to accommodate themselves to school practices by setting up their own school system, staying away from classes when audiovisual materials were used, and shunning the health course. This option puts other interests before those of the minority religion but in doing so it threatens the religion's free exercise rights. It is rarely practicable for a religion to set up its own school system, so this leaves staying away from certain classes as the only real choice for the Lutherans. But this penalizes the students for freely exercising their religion. Students not taking the health course may have trouble graduating and those boycotting classes may do poorly on exams. When the state does nothing, the free exercise of a minority religion suffers (and incidentally, the state risks establishing the majority religion over the minority religion). Given this possibility, the state may elect to *do something* to protect the free exercise of the minority religion. It may, in the example at hand, do something minor such as allowing students to leave the room, or something greater such as offering separate courses without audiovisual aids or setting up a separate health course. This would enhance the free exercise rights of the Lutherans, but it would interfere with other social interests by forcing taxpayers to underwrite the costs of separate courses, teachers to develop two sets of assignments and exams, and some students to be responsible for more material than others. By using state facilities to protect free exercise, the school board risks advancing and impermissibly establishing a religion (and incidentally threatening the free exercise rights of the nonpreferred religions). Herein lies the contradictory messages of the two clauses. If the government ignores religions, it may interfere with their free exercise by default and thereby violate the free exercise clause. If it takes steps to protect free exercise, it risks aiding that religion and thereby violating the establishment clause. The two clauses spar rather than complement and one gains at the expense of the other.[7]

The meaning of free religion depends upon the Court's interpretation of the establishment clause taken alone, the free exercise clause taken alone, and the two clauses taken together. Establishment cases involve laws promoting religion; Court decisions tell when the state may aid religion in its effort to satisfy one or another social interest. Free exercise cases involve laws restricting religious practices; Court decisions tell when the state may control religion in its effort to satisfy another social interest. The clauses come together when the state does something to protect free exercise and in the process aids that religion. Court decisions here tell how much intrusion the state may make on one of the clauses in order to ensure the vitality of the other. This balances two facets of religion against each other, in contrast to the clauses taken alone, which balance religion against another social interest. As such it recalls the balancing of two press interests in access cases. Intra-right balancing is especially sensitive because it leaves one facet of a constitutional right the loser. Court decisions telling which face of a right should predominate reveal much about the character of that right.

ESTABLISHMENT

The establishment clause warns Congress to pass "no law respecting an establishment of religion." Despite its absolute language it, as are other First Amendment guarantees, is relative rather than absolute. In the words of the Court, "the Nation's history has not been one of entirely sanitized separation between Church and State. It has never been thought either possible or desirable to enforce a regime of total separation."[8] Nor has a clean separation been achieved. Some governmental aid to religion is innocuous, unquestioned, and not even realized. For example, fire fighters respond to fire alarms on tax-exempt church property without thought of its establishment overtones,[9] church officials use civil rights to resolve internal disputes,[10] and recipients of GI Bill payments, welfare, or other government grants may spend part of their money to support their religion.[11] Other benefits are more obvious and also more controversial. They include giving tax-exempt status to places of worship and monetary grants to sectarian schools. There are, in short, different degrees of establishment with some more dangerous (and more likely to be unconstitutional) than others. Figure 4.1 shows two ways in which establishment varies: by subtlety and by specificity.

In regard to subtlety, establishment ranges from "actual" to "incipient." Actual establishment occurs when the state inaugurates an official religion as did Emperor Constantine when he established Christianity as the official religion of Rome, England when she created the Church of England as the official state church, and the American colonies when Massachusetts, Connecticut, and New Hampshire established the Congregational Church and Virginia, North Carolina, and South Carolina established the Church of England.[12] Incipient establishment is the more common today; it occurs when the government encourages or advances a religion short of creating a state church. It occurred when the government gave block sums of money to religious schools and tax credits to parents of parochial school children.[13] The First Amendment's wording that Congress "shall make no law *respecting* an establishment of religion" shows it forbids more than actual establishment.

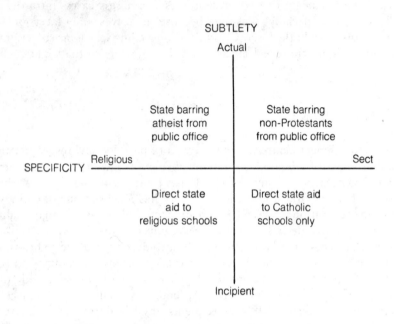

FIGURE 4.1
DIMENSIONS OF ESTABLISHMENT

Establishment also ranges on a specificity dimension from "religious" to "sect." Religious establishment promotes religion over nonreligion and is the more general form. It occurred when school officials required students to recite an "interdenominational" prayer[14] and when another school district released students from class to study religion elsewhere in the building.[15] Sect establishment promotes one particular creed over another and occurred when school authorities required students to recite the Lord's Prayer[16] and when city officials applied an ordinance in such a way as to allow Catholics and Protestants but not Jehovah's Witnesses to use city parks for church services.[17] Some Justices argue that Sunday closing laws promote Christianity, with its Sunday sabbath, over Judaism and other creeds celebrating a Saturday sabbath.[28]

Chief Justice Warren once observed that law "floats on a sea of religious ethics."[29] One can continue this metaphor by saying that law in the United States floats on a sea of religious ethics and possibly even on a sea of Protestant ethics. Part of the runoff from this spiritual sea is largely symbolic, such as the call for the "Protection of Divine Providence" in the

Declaration of Independence and references to God on money and in Congressional ceremonies. However, the runoff also surfaces in the perspective or weighted starting point from which legislators make laws and the Court interprets them. "We are a religious people whose institutions presuppose a Supreme Being," writes the Court.[20] These deeply rooted values boldly appear in policy-making, with legislators passing varied and inventive laws promoting religion over nonreligion and Protestantism over non-Protestantism. One of the more protracted and visible examples is the dogged effort of state and federal lawmakers to allow prayers inside schoolhouses. Another is the effort of officials to forbid the teaching of evolution in public schools because of its challenge to the biblical account of creation.[21] For the most part the Court strikes down these efforts and therefore moderates the religious bias of legislators. It does not level the bias, however, in that the Justices too are products of the country's religious heritage. Religious values, no matter how subtle, underlie the Court's definition of religion and the tests it uses to interpret the First Amendment's religion clauses. These values weigh the scales so that the Court starts from a skewed point in deciding establishment cases and subtly prefers religion over nonreligion and at times Christianity and even Protestantism over other creeds. The inclination toward judicial establishment is tentative, to some degree unavoidable, is punctuated with exceptions, and reveals an often overlooked feature of the meaning of free religion today.

Religious Establishment

In its first modern interpretation of the establishment clause, the Court adopted Jefferson's call for the state to maintain a "wall of separation" between itself and the church:

> Neither a state nor the Federal Government can set up a church. Neither can pass laws which aid one religion, aid all religions, or prefer one religion over another. Neither can force nor influence a person to go to or to remain away from church against his will or force him to profess a belief or disbelief in any religion. No person can be punished for entertaining or professing religious beliefs or disbeliefs, for church attendance or non-attendance. No tax in any amount, large or small, can be levied to support any religious activities or institutions, whatever they may be called or whatever form they may adopt to teach or practice religion. . . . In the words of Jefferson, the clause against establishment of religion by law was intended to erect "a wall of separation between Church and State."[22]

This instruction bids the government to do nothing either to advance or inhibit religion. It relegates the government to a nonentity or neutral agency making no acts affecting religion in a repressive or promotional sense. But complete neutrality is a celestial idea rather than pragmatic guide. The government cannot stand in total isolation from religion.[23] Its mere presence affects religion and even state inaction touches upon a church's fortunes, as illustrated by the case of the Apostolic Lutherans. As such, the wall theory's impracticability surfaced early — in the very case in which the Court expressed it in fact. Alongside the stringent "wall of separation" passage, the Court upheld a state plan to pay bus fares for parochial school students, reasoning that the plan benefitted the children, not the schools and religion. The plan undeniably aided religion by making it easier for children to attend sectarian schools and therefore ran abreast of the Court's warning that "no tax in any amount, large or small, can be levied to support any religious activities or institutions." The discrepancy between dicta and holding made the case everyman's decision. In the words of one commentator, the decision "may hold the record for being cited most often as a precedent on opposite sides of the same question."[24]

Since the state cannot stay completely aloof from religion, most state policy will incidentally affect religion, either to aid or inhibit it. The question then becomes whether one effect is more acceptable than the other; that is, whether the state should err on the side of beneficence or on the side of hostility as it strives for neutrality. The Supreme Court calls the former "benevolent neutrality";[25] we call the latter "malevolent neutrality."[26] The first promotes religion over nonreligion, the second favors nonreligion over religion. In a sign that it operates on a sea of religious ethics, the Court prefers to err in favor of religion. On the one hand it has specifically rejected malevolent neutrality by denouncing policy that shows a "callous indifference to religious groups" if doing so prefers "those who believe in no religion over those who do believe."[27] Stating that the First Amendment does not make it "necessary for government to be hostile to religion and to throw its weight against efforts to widen the effect scope of religious influence,"[28] the Court advises the government to stop striving for neutrality when that quest harms religion. After specifically rejecting malevolent neutrality, the Court implicitly accepted benevolent neutrality. It "follows the best of our traditions," writes the Court, when the government "respects the religious nature of our people and accommodates the public service to their spiritual needs."[29] State neutrality need not stem from "a callous indifference" to religion, but may at times be benevolent.[30] Such weighted neutrality is part of the historical flavor of American life.[31]

> We are a religious people whose institutions presuppose a
> Supreme Being. We guarantee the freedom to worship as one
> chooses. We make room for as wide a variety of beliefs and
> creeds as the spiritual needs of man deem necessary. We sponsor
> an attitude on the part of government that shows no partiality to
> any one group and that lets each flourish according to the zeal of
> its adherents and the appeal of its dogma. When the state
> encourages religious instruction or cooperates with religious
> authorities by adjusting the schedule of public events to sectarian
> needs, it follows the best of our traditions.[32]

The Court puts the benevolent neutrality principle to work in taxation cases. The federal government and almost every state exempt places of worship from taxation. These exemptions follow a Western tradition dating from the Emperor Constantine's exemption of Christian churches after he converted to Christianity in the Fourth century.[33] Their purpose was originally sectarian, but legislators now defend them for secular reasons, equating them with exemptions granted to other nonprofit organizations.[34] Inescapably, however, they benefit religion and, in upholding tax exemptions in 1970, the Court opined that the accommodation they make to religion is essential for the free exercise of religion. The Court wrote that "there is room for play in the joints productive of a benevolent neutrality which will permit religious exercise to exist without sponsorship and without interference."[35]

After it made clear its preference for benevolent over malevolent neutrality, the Court went on to specify the limits it would place on incidental benefits to religion. Benevolent neutrality does not give the state *permission* to err on the side of beneficence; it merely says that if the government must err as it strives for neutrality, it should err on the side of religion rather than nonreligion. Benevolent neutrality "gives room for play in the joints" only and past a certain point incidental aids turn from benevolent neutrality to outright establishment. The Court uses a three-pronged test to decide when the state has passed that point.

First, the law's primary *intent* must be secular with any religious benefits following incidentally, not purposefully. For example, the Court approved New Jersey's plan to reimburse parents of children attending private schools for bus fares.[36] It noted that the state passed the statute with a secular purpose in mind—to protect the children by giving them safe transportation—and the resulting aid to sectarian schools was only incidental to the policy. Second, the law's primary *effect* must be neither to advance nor inhibit religion.[37] Failing this test was a New York law giving money ($30 to $40 per pupil) to sectarian schools for "maintenance and repair" of the building designed to ensure the "health, welfare and safety" of students.[38] Although the law's intent was secular, its primary effect was to benefit religion. Among other things, the state gave the money to the schools in block sums without legislative oversight, raising the possibility the schools could use the money for religious activities rather than snow removal, heating, and other tasks for which it was intended. Another law failing this test reimbursed parochial schools for books and instructional materials.[39] Here again the effect was to aid the school and hence advance religion. A law passing the test loaned textbooks to sectarian schools, and thereby aided the child rather than the school.[40] Third, the law must not excessively entangle the government with religion.[41] Under this test the Court struck down a Rhode Island program supplementing the salaries of private school teachers.[42] The legislators stipulated that the money only supplement salaries for secular instruction and, to ensure this set up an elaborate scheme of legislative oversight that amounted to excessive governmental entanglement. The Court also struck down a New York plan to reimburse private schools for administering state-required tests[43] and a law giving tax credits to parents of parochial school children[44] for excessive church–state interaction. However, it upheld under this test a congressional plan to grant, on a one-time basis, federal money to religious colleges for buildings used for secular instruction[45] and a South Carolina scheme to use state bonds to back construction at colleges, including a Baptist college.[46] It is no accident that the laws passing the excessive entanglement test involved colleges and the laws failing it involved secondary schools. The Court feels religion is less pervasive in religious-based colleges, making it easier for the state to make sure the money will not be used for sectarian purposes.[47]

Another sign of the Court's basic sympathy with religion is its interpretation of Title VII of the Civil Rights Act of 1964, which forbids job discrimination on the basis of religion. The Equal Employment Opportunity Commission (EEOC) enforces Title VII and deals with some obvious cases of religious discrimination, such as the case of a young man who was offered a job but then lost it to a less educated Gentile applicant after the man revealed he was Jewish.[48] More sensitive questions arise when an employer's practices are neutral on their face but discriminatory in effect as, for example, job schedules forcing employees to work on Saturdays. Posing no problem for Protestants or Catholics, Saturday work inconveniences Orthodox Jews, Seventh Day Adventists, members of the World Wide Church of God, and others who observe Saturday sabbaths. At first the EEOC did nothing to combat policies neutral on their face but discriminatory in effect, and the Supreme Court tied on a vote on the question and thereby let stand the EEOC position.[49]

Then in the late 1960s the EEOC changed positions and bade employers to make "reasonable accommodations" to the religious interests of employees and applicants in order to prevent discriminatory effects. In 1972 the Court addressed the intent–effect question in the area of racial discrimination and concluded that discriminatory policies violated Title VII even if the employer did not intend to discriminate.[50] Thereafter Congress made formal the EEOC's lead, requiring employers to make reasonable accommodations to a worker's religious beliefs.[51] To illustrate, the EEOC concluded that a hospital failed reasonably to accommodate a nurse who resigned rather than trade her scarf (worn for religious reasons) for the nurse's cap personnel said she had to wear,[52] and that a bank violated Title VII by dismissing a teller who refused to attend morning business meetings that started off with a prayer.[53] Reasonable accommodation tends more to establish religion over non-religion than vice versa, but it is limited by the Court's holding that employers need not accommodate to the point of imposing "undue hardship" on their business.[54] Thus, the Court ruled in favor of TWA for firing a worker who refused on religious grounds to work Saturdays. [55] TWA contended that the man's refusal to substitute for a vacationing co-worker on Saturdays interfered with tasks "critical to airline operations" and burdened the other workers. The Court agreed, holding that reasonable accommodation did not force an employer to "carve out a special exception" to its practices or "discriminate" against other workers in order to accommodate to the religious needs of its workers.

Sect Establishment

Definition of religion The word "religion" has a secular origin, deriving from a Latin word meaning "to bind, to bind back," which involved a secular call for self-restraint.[56] Throughout America's history, however, religion has taken a distinctly theological meaning, with lexicographers and judges pairing it with a deity.[57] The self-restraint of the Latin *religare* now revolves around dedication to theistic principles in particular rather than moral principles in general. An Oklahoma court, for example, defined religion as the belief in a supreme being with the belief itself "exercising power over human beings by volition, imposing rules of conduct with future rewards and punishments."[58] A New York court defined it as a bond between man and God with the purpose of giving to "God the worship due to Him as the Source of all being and the principle of all government of things."[59]

For many decades the Supreme Court equated religion with a belief in a supreme being. In 1890 it opined that religion referred "to one's views of his relations to his Creator, and to the obligations they impose of reverence for his being and character, and of obedience to his will."[60] This definition treaded on sect establishment; by limiting religion to a tie between a supreme being and an individual, the Court excluded great Eastern nontheistic creeds such as Buddhism, Taoism, and Confucianism[61] and lesser-known Western religions such as Unitarian Humanism.[62] The definition had little practical import in 1890, however, because at that time most American religions embraced a God. But by mid-twentieth century, fissures appeared in the hegemony of God-centered religions as Americans began experimenting with a rich variety of Eastern religions such as the International Society for Krishna Consciousness and the Divine Light Mission of Guru Maharaj Ji, and ethical creeds such as Zen Buddhism and Transcendental Meditation.[63] Due to exposure to other religions from travel and mass communications and the search for new answers in the aftermath of two world wars, Americans increasingly turned to hitherto little-known and exotic creeds. When the state resisted in one way or another, the new believers went to court, joining the ubiquitous appeals on court dockets filed by Jehovah's Witnesses, Christian Scientists, and other minority believers whose creeds had long conflicted with state policies.

The Supreme Court revised its definition of religion in 1965 by holding that belief in a God need not be a condition of a religion.[64] Its opinion arose in a case during the Vietnam War involving conscientious objection. In setting forth the requirements for attaining conscientious objector status, Congress had stated that religion involved an "individual's belief in relation to a Supreme Being." The Court broadened that definition by saying that a person could receive conscientious objector status on religious grounds by showing he held a sincere belief that "occupies a place in [his] life parallel to that filled by the Orthodox belief in God." Although an improvement over its 1890 definition in that it removed belief in a Supreme Being as a necessary precondition of religion and thereby moved away from sect establishment, the Court's conception still had establishment overtones because it involved a young man who declined to say whether he believed in a God. The Court allowed that a person ambiguous about his belief in God could still receive religious-based C.O. status, but it cautioned that it was not deciding an appeal by an avowed atheist. This left open the possibility that the Court could deny C.O. status to an atheist, and as long as this possibility exists the Court embraces a definition of religion that favors theistic over nontheistic creeds.

Definitional matters are important because courts face assorted cases requiring them to weed out bona fide from frivolous religious claims. Just as persons act in a variety of ways and later try to claim their behavior was speech warranting special protection, so do persons act without thought to religion and later try to draw a religious connection in order to reap additional protection.[65] For example, one lower court held that Stanley Oscar Brown made such a spurious claim when he argued that he had been fired because of his "personal religious creed" that Kozy Kitten People Cat Food increased his energy.[66] To identify a religion for First Amendment purposes courts have suggested several guidelines. First, following the above Supreme Court holding, the creed must include a belief in a God or a life force that occupies a parallel place in the believer's life.[67] Second, it must embrace more than a "merely personal moral code,"[68] a criterion that sounded the deathknell for Oscar Stanley Brown because the district court judge said Brown's penchant for cat food was no more than a set of "personal moral preferences." Third, a religion must have associational ties,[69] or what one court called a "gregarious association openly expressing the belief,"[70] together with some unifying tenets or rituals.[71] This criterion excluded from religious tax exemption a minister who spread his gospel through radio broadcasts and pamphlets and who had no congregation.[72] The congregation need not be formal or large, however. One court agreed that a "self-styled 'peyote preacher'" whose retinue numbered only six persons[73] had formed a religious society. Fourth, the person filing the claim on religious grounds must demonstrate he or she is a sincere believer. Sincerity is a particularly knotty question for judges, and it is fraught with subjective potential. Judges look to such things as the length of time a person has held the beliefs. One judge invalidated a mother's religious claim in a child custody suit because her religion apparently only arose during the course of the custody proceedings.[74] The mother argued that she was unconstitutionally denied custody because she refused to seek psychiatric testing for religious reasons. In rejecting the sincerity of this claim, the judge pointed out that the mother had seen psychiatrists earlier with no apparent religious conflict and that her refusal could properly be admitted as evidence. Judges also look to the historical pattern of the person's behavior. For example, in upholding the right of an Orthodox Jewish prisoner to keep his beard in defiance of prison rules, a district court noted that he scrupulously followed Jewish law regarding facial hair in the past and thereby raised a serious claim.[75] Another judge inferred a woman's sincerity by her willingness to go to jail rather than serve as a juror in violation of her religion.[76] Courts also look to the principles of the church with which a person is affiliated to determine if his or her claim is sincere.[77] Men affiliated with the Society of Friends (Quakers), for example, easily gain C.O. status because the Quakers are known for their position on the immorality of war.[78] And, in the case of the bearded prisoner, the court verified that Jewish law does indeed proscribe beard cutting.[79] Overseeing all these criteria is the judiciary's care not to question the truth or falsity of the religious belief itself.[80] "Religious experiences which are as real as life to some may be incomprehensible to others," wrote the Court, "yet the fact that they may be beyond the ken of mortals does not mean that they can be made suspect before the law."[81] When faced with what they consider to be a fantastic creed, judges may not conclude that the beliefs themselves are incomprehensible. Thus, the judge ruling on Oscar Stanley Brown's appeal avoided commenting on the belief itself, as did the Supreme Court when confronted with the curious "I Am" movement of Guy W. Ballard.[82] Because this guideline removes attention from the belief's content, it reduces the chances that sect establishment will bias judges as they distinguish between religious and nonreligious creeds for First Amendment purposes.

Court tests The American heritage is Protestant. The men who put their names on the Declaration of Independence were, save one, Protestant; the framers of the First Amendment were Protestant; and the philosophers from whom early political figures derived their ideas were Protestant.[83] Protestantism and its correspondent values permeated early U.S. history even though the proportion of devout practitioners was small. To the extent that a "Protestant world view" underlies contemporary law, sect establishment occurs. An analysis of Court decisions shows a Protestant world view predominating over Catholicism and to a lesser extent a Christian over a Judaical world view. The trend, however, is away from rather than toward sect establishment.

Protestantism over Catholicism emerges in the Court's wall of separation theory, even with its benevolent neutrality modifications.[84] The "wall" theory mirrors a predominantly Protestant world view that the family is the nurturing seat of religion. The Protestant believes religion is a private experience whose perpetuation is sealed through family instruction and church worship. The Catholic, on the other hand, looks beyond the family and place of worship to perpetuate his or her creed. Catholicism relies on a host of institutions—family, church, parochial school, papacy—for nurturance. To the Catholic "the total separation of faith from the experience of everyday life is impossible,"[85] and religion weaves throughout his or her daily life and institutions. Thus, Court decisions warning Congress not to aid religious institutions fall more heavily on Catholicism than Protestantism inasmuch as the former embraces a larger number of institutions. For example, the Court upholds tax exemptions for church buildings but strikes down tax credits to parents who send their children to private schools. By allowing benefits to formal places of worship, which happen to be the Protestant's center of religious activity, but denying benefits to church schools, which happen to be essential appendages of religion for Catholics, the Court totters on sect establishment.[86]

This greater burden on Catholics is magnified by the twentieth century trend toward the active state,[87] in which the government gives increasing amounts of aid to hospitals, schools, orphanages, and other social institutions. At the same time that secular institutions depend more and more upon state grants for their fortunes, courts strictly limit aid to sectarian institutions. The denial of aid to religious institutions in the twentieth century has a sharper impact than in the nineteenth century because it drives a larger wedge between secular and sectarian fortunes than when neither received aid in the nineteenth century. Two Court doctrines modify this disproportionate impact on Catholicism, however. The benevolent neutrality principle condones incidental benefits to religion, and the Court has used it to approve policies aiding church schools. The principle is more congenial to Catholicism's expanded world view than the "wall" theory, and the Court's endorsement of it reflects a movement away from sect establishment (even though it also moves the Court closer to religious establishment). The "child benefit" principle, enunciated in decisions approving textbook loans[88] and reimbursements for parochial students' bus fares,[89] has the same effect. It focuses on the individual receiving the aid and disregards that person's religious connections.[90]

A lesser form of sect establishment prefers Christianity over Judaism and surfaces in the Court's decisions on Sunday closing laws. Most states restrict, in some way or another, the work and commerce that may take place on Sundays. The laws date from thirteenth-century England where they were imposed by the Crown in deference to the Eighth Commandment: "Remember the sabbath day, to keep it holy. Six days you shall labor, and do all your work; but the seventh day is a Sabbath to the LORD your God; in it you shall not do any work."[91] Their presence today raises questions of sect establishment, inasmuch as Judaism and some Christian creeds celebrate Saturday sabbaths. The Court reviewed these laws in four cases in 1966, two of which involved Jewish store owners who argued that state laws requiring them to close their stores on Sunday imposed a double hardship on them because they closed their store both on Sunday (by law) and Saturday (by the dictates of their faith) and therefore lost two business days per week.[92] The Court upheld each law under challenge that it violated equal protection and the First Amendment's religion guarantees. The Court conceded the religious origin of the statutes but concluded that the laws had long since become secular in purpose. They allowed for a day of rest for employees and were an integral part of our secular culture: "People of all religions and people with no religion regard Sunday as a time for family activity, for visiting friends and relatives, for late sleeping, for passive and active entertainments, for dining out, and the like."[93] In dissent, Justice Douglas argued that the laws intruded on the free exercise rights of believers celebrating a Saturday sabbath and also established Christianity over other religions:[94] when "the State uses its coercive powers . . . to compel minorities to observe a second Sabbath, not their own, the State undertakes to aid and 'prefer one religion over another'—contrary to the command of the Constitution."[95] In a later decision, however, the Court ruled in favor of a Seventh Day Adventist fired for refusing to work on Saturdays on religious grounds and then denied unemployment benefits.[96] Basing its decision on free exercise grounds, the Court said the law forced the woman to choose between free exercise and employment, and therefore burdened her freedom to practice religion. The decision's recognition of the interests of people celebrating a Saturday sabbath modified the sect establishment threatened in the Sunday closing laws cases.

FREE EXERCISE OF RELIGION

Hundreds of religious creeds coexist in the United States today; each sets forth a singular set of prescriptions by which its followers model their daily lives. Some religions instruct their believers to spread the word of God through face-to-face proselytizing, others forego systematic proselytizing. Some religions use drugs as part of their religious services, others use wine, still others foresake rituals. Some religions forbid worship of graven images such as the U.S. flag, others tightly pair their creed with patriotic displays. Some religions counsel their followers to shun medicine, others sanction the power of medicine along with the power of prayer. The amalgam of religious practices inevitably brings religions into conflict with equally diverse secular laws. Free exercise of religion is a relative rather than an absolute right,[97] so the question is not whether religious practices can be controlled; instead, it concerns when the state can limit the free exercise of religion.

The Court uses the same tests for free exercise as it uses for free speech: the state may only restrict religious practices that clearly and imminently endanger an important social interest. For example, it reversed breach-of-the-peace convictions of Jehovah's Witnesses who had played religious records to passersby on public sidewalks, concluding that the proselytizers may have irritated passersby but did not clearly endanger public peace and order.[98] It also affirmed a lower court decision excusing a woman from jury duty, noting that her refusal to serve posed no demonstrable danger to the smooth operation of the jury system.[99] The Court used the compelling-state-interest test in a case involving a school requirement that children salute the flag in school despite their religious scruples not to worship a false god. The Court held that the state had not met its burden of showing the need for the compulsory exercise. In general, the more tangible the social interest at stake, the more likely the Court is to uphold the state law or practice designed to protect it. On the one hand it has upheld very few practices designed to protect such abstract things as patriotism.[100] On the other hand, it has upheld state practices protecting tangible goals such as the health and safety of its citizens. Consider sample cases dealing with manifestations of religious beliefs, behaviors central to the religion's perpetuation, and rituals of the church service itself.

Many religions manifest their creeds with ideas about the inviolability of the body, thus giving courts ample opportunity to rule on cases involving public health and safety. In the area of autopsies, for example, many cities use their police power to require autopsies on persons who died of unknown causes or under suspicious circumstances. However, some religions object to tampering with the body after death; Orthodox Jews, for example, believe the soul is concentrated in the blood, that the body in death is as holy as the body in life, and that autopsies intrude on a still inviolable soul.[101] In one recent case an Orthodox Jew objected to the scheduled autopsy on his son, an outwardly healthy young man who suddenly collapsed and died in his home.[102] The city empowered the medical examiner to perform an autopsy inasmuch as the cause of death was not explained beyond a reasonable doubt. An appellate court ordered the autopsy to proceed, holding that the state has a "compelling" interest in determining whether unexplained deaths have a criminal connection that "outweighed the interests of the father in his religious tenets." The state's interest lay in its police power to "safeguard the peace, health and good order of the community."

Cases involving blood transfusions position another religion, the Jehovah's Witnesses, against the state. Jehovah's Witnesses read the Bible literally and interpret passages such as Leviticus 17:13,14 ("You must not eat the blood of any sort of flesh, because the soul of every sort of flesh is its blood") to forbid the "ingestion" of blood through transfusions.[103] A believer who does not do everything in his or her power, short of violence, to avoid ingesting blood faces excommunication by the congregation.[104] Exercising its power to protect the life and safety of its citizens, the state occasionally seeks court-ordered blood transfusions on people likely to die without transfusions. Courts usually rule in favor of the state if it can show transfusions are clearly necessary for the health and welfare. For example, one court approved involuntary transfusions for a seven and one-half month pregnant woman after doctors testified that the treatment was necessary to save the lives of both mother and fetus;[105] another court ordered a transfusion for a young accident victim with a potential for a long and healthy life who needed a transfusion to survive.[106] On the other hand, courts will defer to the religion if the state cannot demonstrate a clear danger to public interests. Such occurred in the case of a middle-aged woman with no children who made clear her religious objections to blood transfusions.[107] The fact that she had no children mitigated the danger her death would pose to the public welfare. The Court has also upheld enforced vaccinations in the interest of public health,[108] and it refused to hear, and thereby let stand, two lower court decisions upholding fluoridation of local water supplies over religious objections.[109]

The Court applies similar tests to practices central to the religion's perpetuation. Again, the Jehovah's Witnesses have clashed with the state. Public evangelism is critical to the perpetuation of their religion (they follow Mark 16:15: "Go ye into all the world, and preach the gospel to every creature" and Acts 20:20, which tells how Paul went "publickly and from house to house").[110] Occasionally their proselytizing intrudes on other social interests, such as public quiet and personal privacy. The Court has struck down ordinances that limited the public speaking of Jehovah's Witnesses,[111] their ability to distribute leaflets door to door,[112] and their freedom to solicit contributions without first paying a license tax.[113] In a celebrated case involving the Amish, the Court allowed Amish parents to withdraw their children from public schools after the eighth grade to continue their education within the religious community.[114] Normally very protective of society's interest in universal education, the Court allowed this exception, noting that lengthy public school instruction would harm the perpetuation of the Amish society and that education in the Amish community successfully produced hard-working and "very law-abiding members of society." On the other hand the Court upheld as a proper police power a statute forbidding children from selling newspapers and periodicals in public places as applied in the case of a Jehovah's Witness who accompanied a young girl selling biblical tracts.[115]

Finally, courts use similar tests for rituals used in church services themselves. On the one hand, courts uphold restrictions on practices dangerous to the believers. For example, southern courts have upheld laws forbidding the use of poisonous snakes in religious services.[116] Snake-handling is central to a Tennessee-based religious sect known as The Holiness Church of God in Jesus Name[117] and the sect itself originated when George Went Hensley gathered a following on the basis of his interpretation of Mark 16:18: "They shall take up serpents; and if they drink any deadly thing, it shall not hurt them; they shall lay hands on the sick, and they shall recover."[118] If denied the right to hold the snakes, believers would also be denied the opportunity to "confirm the Word of God."[119] A circuit court enjoined the practice in 1973 on the basis of an old statute forbidding snake-handling after two people in the sect died of strychnine poisoning (drinking any "deadly thing" is also part of the service). The Tennessee Supreme Court upheld the injunction on the basis of common law nuisance, reasoning that the state "has the right to guard against the unnecessary creation of widows and orphans" (twenty-nine people had died from snake-handling since 1910).[120] On the other hand, courts strike down controls on practices not intruding on an independent social interest, even if the practices are illegal. Such occurred during Prohibition when courts looked the other way at wine used during religious services, and more recently when a California court affirmed the right of a church to use an illegal drug (peyote) after satisfying itself that the drug was central to the church creed.[121]

Although the Court uses the same tests for free religion as for free speech, the tests have a greater effect on the system of free expression when applied in the religious context. The reason is that free exercise clearly embraces behavior but free speech does not. Free speech embraces the freedom to think and speak, but it only includes action so tied with expression that it amounts to communicative conduct. By contrast, free "exercise" by its very nature subsumes conduct. People arrested for talking with passersby about religion may base their appeal on speech *or* free exercise grounds, but parents who withdraw their children from public schools in order to educate them within the religious community will, if challenged, justify their acts on free exercise grounds only. "The freedom to believe is absolute," writes the Court, "but in the nature of things," the freedom to act "cannot be."[122] Thoughts, words, and actions lie on a continuum. The Court treats words as the behavioral manifestations of one's freedom to think in free speech cases but treats acts as manifestations of that freedom in free exercise cases. Thus, when the Court rules in favor of the First Amendment in free exercise cases it embraces behavior as well as speech and accords it all the attention befitting a right falling within a "paramount" amendment. Free exercise's multiplier effect on free expression is illustrated by the law on conscientious objection. A conscientious objector is exempt from military duty because he has voiced abhorrence to war on religious grounds. The University Military Training and Service Act of 1948 exempts from service those people opposed to war because of their "religious training and belief" and specifically excludes people opposing the war for "essentially political, sociological, or philosophical views or a merely personal moral code." This means political pacifists must participate in war but religious pacifists need not. The law grants more protection to those acting on their religious beliefs than to those acting on political beliefs.

THE TWO CLAUSES TOGETHER

The two clauses together raise a number of dilemmas. The one highlighted here occurs when the state fears inaction will hurt free exercise so it designs policy to protect these rights but in the process it establishes or aids that religion. Quixotically, it ensures the vitality of one religion clause but only at the expense of the other. This dilemma is common; it arose in the case of the Apostolic Lutherans and underlies most aid-to-education policies. For example, fearing that parents will be financially unable to send their children to church schools under the burden of dual payments (paying taxes to support public schools and paying tuition to church schools), New York legislators set up a plan to grant tax credits to low-income parents who sent their children to sectarian schools.[123] If the state did nothing, it risked burdening free exercise; if it did something, it risked promoting religion over nonreligion and, more particularly, Catholicism over non-Catholicism inasmuch as Catholic schools benefitted disproportionately from the plan. Establishment in turn intrudes on the free exercise rights of nonestablished religions and the litany of rights and injuries travels full circle.

Preferably, the government should pursue policy designed to leave an insulating channel between the two clauses in order to prevent their intersection.[124] However, as the Court notes, "it may often not be possible" to promote one right without intruding on the other.[125] Therefore, more often than not, one facet of free religion must bow to the other. The question is whether the state should aim to protect free exercise even if doing so amounts to a "callous indifference to religious groups." The Court leans toward the former with its benevolent neutrality approach. Given the choice between doing nothing (and thereby hurting free exercise) or doing something (and thereby risking establishment), the Court elects to protect free exercise provided three tests are met: the primary intent is not to promote religion, the primary effect does not aid religion, and the state does not become excessively entangled in the religion in the process. The approach conforms with the Court's preference for religion over nonreligion and is a manifestation of religious establishment. It also gives a new dimension to free exercise by broadening it to mean more than the absence of restrictive laws. Because the state may promote free exercise, the First Amendment guarantee gains a positive cast and stands apart from the "purer liberty" cast of free speech and press.

SUMMARY

Freedom of religion is a two-pronged liberty with the free exercise clause protecting worshippers from state interference and the establishment clause ensuring that the government not prefer religion over nonreligion or one creed over another. Free exercise is akin to free speech, press, and assembly; the establishment guarantee recalls Fourteenth Amendment equal protection in its role as a grand equalizer that makes sure the state treats people equally, regardless of their religious belief. Of the two clauses, establishment is the more problematic and has occupied the brunt of the Court's attention. Establishment has at least four variants—religious, sect, actual, and incipient—each of which poses different threats in the contemporary United States. At the time the First Amendment was framed, actual establishment (both religious and sect) was a robust possibility because established churches were common in Europe in general and England in particular.[126] On the other hand, in 1791 Americans feared incipient establishment less because this variant is a corollary of the active state and the government at that time did not pour aid into social sectors. Today, however, as the state distributes goods and services and aids myriad secular and sectarian institutions, it risks benefitting religion in a more subtle fashion, thereby making incipient establishment the more likely possibility. This shift has led some commentators to suggest that the Court reviews twentieth-century legislation, which threatens incipient establishment, under inappropriate eighteenth- and nineteenth-century standards designed with actual establishment in mind.[127] They argue this hurts religious freedom in two ways. First, by taking excessive care to avoid aiding religion, courts insert a growing wedge between the fortunes of secular and sectarian institutions and thereby hurt free exercise more than necessary. Second, in order to ensure some groups not be preferred over others, legislators take religion into account, and thereby distinguish between groups on the basis of a fundamental right (religion) and violate equal protection in the process.[128] By using religion to ensure that all are treated equally, in other words, legislators unconstitutionally discriminate against people on the basis of religion. The child-benefit theory, expressed in school aid cases only, partially circumvents this problem by focusing on the recipient of the aid and not his or her religion.

It is hard to say whether religious or sect establishment is a more immediate threat in the contemporary United States, partly because of weaknesses in the distinction itself. Religious and sect establishment inextricably overlap, with sect establishment by nature encompassing religious establishment as well. It appears, however, that religious establishment is the more immediate threat; the Court's recent observation that religion does not require a belief in God[129] moves it farther from sect establishment, but its benevolent neutrality and accommodation doctrines suggest religious establishment.

Although each religion clause has a separate structure that is fairly straightforward when studied independently, at some point the two clauses must be studied together for a full understanding of freedom of religion. It is here that one becomes aware of a tension within freedom of religion that results from the inverse relation between the two clauses. Rather than existing independently (see Figure 4.2A), if unregulated, the two clauses eventually intersect (see Figure 4.2B). Both of the clauses "are cast in absolute terms," writes the Court, and "either of which, if expanded to a logical extreme, would tend to clash with the other."[130] The Court's policy is to try to keep an insulating channel between the two clauses in order to prevent their intersection (see Figure 4.2C). It does not always succeed, however, and the tension between the two clauses is responsible for inconsistencies in the Court's interpretation of freedom of religion.[131] The tension should not be taken as purely troublesome, however, for it bequeaths a test for judicial interpretation. Whereas the balancing of each right separately places religion against another social interest, the balancing of the two rights together places religion against religion. The contradiction between the clauses advises judges that the logical limit of the free play of one occurs when it encroaches on the free play of the other.

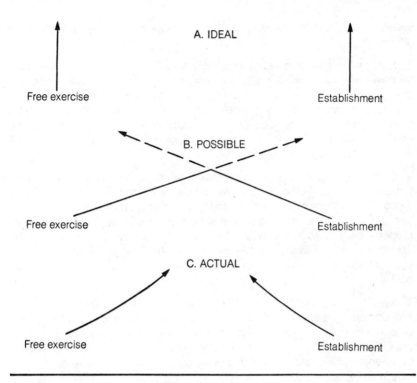

FIGURE 4.2
THREE KINDS OF RELATIONSHIPS BETWEEN
THE FREE EXERCISE AND ESTABLISHMENT
CLAUSES: IDEAL, POSSIBLE, ACTUAL

Questions for Thought

1. Court dicta would have us believe that the free exercise of religion, as a First Amendment right, is a preferred freedom which the state may control only for compelling reasons. But states sometimes limit religion for arguably less than compelling reasons. Consider, for example, a contempt-of-court ruling against a Moslem who refused for religious reasons to testify against another Moslem. A lower court upheld the ruling, saying that the state had a compelling interest in maintaining the "effective operation of a court of justice." *State v. Bing*, 253 S.E. 2d 101 (S.C. 1979). Is the orderly administration of justice a compelling state interest? Think of other situations in which religion interferes with state interests. Suggest a test for determining when the state's interest is so important as to justify limiting one's free exercise of religion. Does this test differ from the one you would use for limiting free

speech in general? In what ways are free exercise of religion and free speech different?

2. How persuasive is this chapter's argument that the Court prefers Protestantism over Catholicism? Do any of the Court's decisions suggest a preference for Catholicism over Protestantism? See Henry J. Abraham, *Freedom and the Court*, 3rd ed. (New York: Oxford University Press, 1977) for tabular summaries of the Court's religion decisions to 1977. Could we add a section to this chapter on sect establishment of Christianity over Judaism? Sect establishment of Christianity over Islam?

3. Some formerly neutral policies may amount to religious establishment today. Consider, for example, tax exemptions for church properties. Originally thought to signal governmental neutrality, the policies today may amount to a decided preference for religion because they put extra burdens on other property owners who do pay taxes. What is the policy toward religious tax exemptions in your state? Has this policy changed in the last decade or so? Do you think your state's policy establishes religion over nonreligion? Why or why not?

4. Ever since the Supreme Court held that school prayers violated the First Amendment, proponents of prayers have tried to add a constitutional amendment guaranteeing the right of voluntary prayers in schools. If added to the Constitution, this amendment would confuse the already existing conflict between the establishment and free exercise clauses by adding a third religion clause. Look up proposed wordings of the school prayer amendment. Suppose it is added to the Constitution. Suppose a parent claims school prayers violate his or her rights under the establishment clause and the school board claims the prayers are permissible under the new amendment. Which guarantee—the establishment clause or the prayer clause—should come out stronger in the balance? Is the prayer clause any different from the free exercise clause?

5. The New York Board of Regents composed a supposedly nondenominational prayer to be recited by children every morning in school. The prayer read "Almighty God, we acknowledge our dependence upon Thee, and we beg Thy blessings upon us, our parents, our teachers, and our country." The Court struck it down as a violation of the First Amendment in *Engel v. Vitale*, 370 U.S. 421 (1962). Is there such a thing as a nondenominational prayer? Try writing a prayer that does not prefer Christianity over non-Christianity. Is it possible to write one that does not prefer religion over nonreligion? Would this "prayer" still be by definition a prayer? A professor of psychology at a Christian college in Winona Lake, Indiana, begins his classes with prayer. One day he gave a passage from Scripture: "Be transformed by the renewal of your minds." See Kenneth Briggs, "Evangelical Colleges Reborn," *The New York Times Magazine*, December 14, 1980, p. 140, at p. 154. Assume that he taught at a public school. Is the passage religious? How important is the fact that the passage came from the Bible? Would it help to call such sessions periods of

"reflections" instead of prayer? What if the obvious intent is prayer, even if it is called something else?

6. What makes a creed a religion? Is Zen Buddhism a religion? Identify the common links of Zen with a God-oriented religion. What are the fundamental elements of a religion? Look up unusual religions in a book such as the *Dictionary of American Religion*. Find one that most typifies a religion. What do your choices say about your values of what makes a creed a religion?

7. One way of visualizing the Court's religion decisions is to use the dialectical model developed in Chapter 5, with point A (thesis) being the free exercise clause, point B (antithesis) being the establishment clause, and point C (synthesis) representing the Court's attempt to resolve the contradictory tug between the two amendments. Using the skewed triangles such as those in Figures 5.2 and 5.5 as a guide, take the Court's decisions on aid to public schools and impressionistically place point C to the right of center if the decision preferred establishment and to the left of center if the decision preferred free exercise. Line up the triangles to see the position of the point C syntheses in relation to one another. Is there a trend over time to veer to the right or left? Use Henry Abraham's tables of religion decisions as a guide to school aid decisions up to 1977 (cited in question 2 above).

NOTES

1. The Court incorporated the free exercise clause in *Hamilton v. Regents of the University of California*, 293 U.S. 245 (1934) and the establishment clause in *Everson v. Board of Education*, 330 U.S. 1 (1947).

2. *Sherbert v. Verner*, 374 U.S. 398, 403, 406 (1963).

3. *Wisconsin v. Yoder*, 406 U.S. 205, 215 (1972).

4. *W. Virginia State Board of Education v. Barnette*, 319 U.S. 624, 639 (1943).

5. *Sherbert v. Verner*, 374 U.S. at 407.

6. *Davis v. Page*, 385 F.Supp. 395 (1974).

7. The Court recognizes that it "may often not be possible to promote free exercise without intruding on establishment. *Committee for Public Education v. Nyquist*, 413 U.S. 756, 788 (1973).

8. Ibid., at 760.

9. See *Zorach v. Clauson*, 343 U.S. 309, 312-313 (1952).

10. Donald T. Kramer, "Annotation—Supreme Court Cases Involving Establishment and Freedom of Religion Clauses of Federal Constitution," 37 L.Ed. 2d 1147, 1169-1170 (1973).

11. *Committee for Public Education v. Nyquist*, 413 U.S. at 804 (Burger, C. J., concurring in part and dissenting in part).

12. Sanford H. Cobb, *The Rise of Religious Liberty in America* (New York: Burt Franklin, 1902), pp. 70-72.

13. *Committee for Public Education v. Nyquist*, 413 U.S. 756 (1973).

14. *Engel v. Vitale*, 370 U.S. 421 (1962). The prayer was: "Almighty God, we acknowledge our dependence upon Thee, and we beg Thy blessings upon us, our parents, our teachers, and our country."

15. *Illinois ex rel. McCollum v. Board of Education*, 333 U.S. 203 (1948).

16. *School District of Abington Township v. Schempp*, 374 U.S. 203 (1963).

17. *Fowler v. Rhode Island*, 345 U.S. 67 (1953).

18. *McGowan v. Maryland*, 366 U.S. 420, 577 (1966) (Douglas, J., dissenting).

19. Quoted in Walter G. Muelder, "Protestants, Catholics and 'Free Exercise'," 8 *Cumberland L.Rev.* 77, 80 (1977).

20. *Zorach v.Clauson*, 343 U.S. 309, 313 (1952).

21. See *Epperson v. Arkansas*, 393 U.S. 97 (1968), and *Scopes v. State*, 289 S.W. 363 (1927). Consider also a recent reappearance of the creationist–evolution controversy in the Sacramento case of *Creation-Science Research Center v. Board of Education.*

22. *Everson v. Board of Education*, 330 U.S. 1, 15-16 (1947).

23. *Walz v. Tax Commission*, 397 U.S. 664, 669 (1970).

24. James C. Kirby, Jr., "Everson to Meek and Roemer: From Separation to Detente in Church–State Relations," 55 *N.Caro.L.Rev.* 563, 564 (1977).

25. See, for example, *Walz v. Tax Commission*, 397 U.S. at 676-677.

26. See, for example, *Zorach v. Clauson*, 343 U.S. at 314.

27. Ibid.

28. Ibid.

29. Ibid.

30. Ibid.

31. Kramer, at 1165.

32. *Zorach v. Clauson*, 343 U.S. at 313-314.

33. John D. Brancato, "Characterization in Religious Property Tax Exemption: What Is Religion? — A Survey and a Proposed Definition and Approach," 44 *Notre Dame Lawyer* 60, 62 (1968).

34. See ibid., at 63.

35. *Walz v. Tax Commission*, 397 U.S. at 669.

36. *Everson v. Board of Education*, 330 U.S. 1 (1947).

37. *McGowan v. Maryland*, 366 U.S. 420 (1966).

38. *Committee for Public Education v. Nyquist*, 413 U.S. 756 (1973).

39. *Lemon v. Kurtzman*, 403 U.S. 602 (1971).

40. *Meek v. Pittenger*, 421 U.S. 349 (1975).

41. *Walz v. Tax Commission*, 397 U.S. 664 (1970). Jurists feel the entanglement guideline will prevent strife between churches as well as between church and state. See Kirby, at 569.

42. *Lemon v. Kurtzman*, 403 U.S. 602 (1971).

43. *Levitt v. Committee for Public Education and Religious Activity*, 413 U.S. 472 (1973). The Court feared the state would intervene to make sure testing was not intermingled with instruction.

44. *Committee for Public Education v. Nyquist*, 413 U.S. 756 (1973). It also struck down, on excessive entanglement grounds, Ohio's law giving a $90 tuition

reimbursement to each child attending a private (including sectarian) school. *Essex v. Wolman*, 409 U.S. 808 (1972).

45. *Tilton v. Richardson*, 403 U.S. 672 (1971). The Court did, however, strike down a provision that the government's interest in the use of the buildings would cease at twenty years.

46. *Hunt v. McNair*, 413 U.S. 734 (1973).

47. See Kirby, at 572. See also *Roemer v. Maryland Public Works Board*, 426 U.S. 736 (1976), in which the Court upheld a Maryland law granting noncategorical grants to private colleges, including sectarian schools.

48. Example from Casenote, "Title VII—Religious Discrimination—Employer's Duty to 'Reasonably Accommodate' Employee's Religious Practices—*Hardison v. Trans World Airlines, Inc.*, 527 F. 2d 33 (8th Cir. 1975)." 9 *Creighton L.Rev.* 795, 801 n.36 (1976).

49. *Dewey v. Reynolds Metal Co.*, 429 F. 2d 324 (6th Cir. 1970), affirmed by an equally divided Court, 402 U.S. 689 (1971).

50. *Griggs v. Duke Power Co.*, 401 U.S. 424 (1971).

51. Casenote, "Title VII . . . ," at 802.

52. Example from Casenote, "Title VII . . . ," at 811-812.

53. *Young v. Southwestern Savings and Loan Association*, 509 F. 2d 140 (5th Cir. 1975).

54. 42 U.S.C.A. § 2000e (j) (1974). See Casenote, "Title VII . . . ," at 799 n.23.

55. *Trans World Airlines, Inc. v. Hardison*, 432 U.S. 63 (1977).

56. John D. Brancato, "Characterization in Religious Property Tax Exemption: What Is Religion?—A Survey and a Proposed Definition and Approach," 44 *Notre Dame Lawyer*, 60, 68 (1968), quoting from *Estate of Hinckley*, 58 Cal. 457, 512 (1881).

57. *Fellowship of Humanity v. County of Alameda*, 315 P. 2d 395, 399 (1957).

58. *McMasters v. State*, 207 P. 566, 568 (1922). See Brancato, at 67.

59. *Nikulnikoff v. Archbishop of the Russian Orthodox Greek Catholic Church*, 255 N.Y.S. 653, 663 (Sup.Ct. 1932). See Brancato, at 68.

60. *Davis v. Beason*, 133 U.S. 333, 342 (1890).

61. See, for example, *Fellowship of Humanity v. County of Alameda*, 315 P. 2d 395, 404 (1957); and Brancato, at 68-69.

62. The Unitarian Humanist holds that the idea of God hinders religion with unnecessarily burdensome questions. *Fellowship of Humanity v. County of Alameda*, 315 P. 2d at 404.

63. John E. LeMoult, "Deprogramming Members of Religious Sects," 46 *Fordham L.Rev.*, 599, 600 (1978).

64. *United States v. Seeger*, 380 U.S. 163 (1965).

65. For example, some groups falsely call themselves religious in order to claim tax-exempt status. See Brancato, at 60. See also Charles M. Whelan, "Church in the Internal Revenue Code: The Definitional Problems," 45 *Fordham L.Rev.*, 885, 927-928 (1977), which tells of the leader of the Universal Life Church of Modesto, California, who, in a television interview, admitted doing this.

66. *Brown v. Pena*, 441 F.Supp. 1382, 1384 (S.D.Fla. 1977). Brown contended that his employer violated Title VII of the Civil Rights Act of 1964, which forbids discrimination on the basis of religion.

67. *United States v. Seeger*, 380 U.S. 163 (1965).

68. Ibid., at 186.

69. 66 Am.Jur. 2d 653, 758 (1964).

70. *Fellowship of Humanity v. County of Alameda*, 315 P. 2d at 406, quoted in Donald A. Giannella, "Religious Liberty, Nonestablishment, and Doctrinal Development. Part I. The Religious Liberty Guarantee," 80 *Harv.L.Rev.* 1381, 1430 (1967).

71. Brancato, at 74. For example, Peace Haven, an allegedly religious community in New York, did not qualify for tax-exempt status because it had "no tenets, ritual, dogma or other characteristics of a religious organization except, possibly, the solicitation of funds." *In re Peace Haven*, 25 N.Y.S. 2d 974 (Sup.Ct. 1941), quoted in Brancato, at 76.

72. *Mordecai F. Ham Evangelistic Association v. Matthews*, 189 S.W. 2d 524 (1945), as cited in Brancato at 74.

73. *In re Grady*, 394 P. 2d 728 (1964).

74. *In re marriage of Gove*, 572 P. 2d 458 (1977).

75. The prisoner had, with one exception, not cut his beard in the past. He allowed the one trimming for medical reasons and followed strict procedures for the cutting.

76. *In re Jenison*, 125 N.W. 2d 588 (1963), vacated and remanded in light of *Sherbert v. Verner*, 374 U.S. 14 (1963).

77. Anita Bowser, "Delimiting Religion in the Constitution: A Classification Problem," 11 *Valparaiso U.L.Rev.* 163, 182 (1977).

78. See, for example, Henry J. Abraham, *Freedom and the Court*, 3rd ed. (New York: Oxford University Press, 1977), p. 253, who notes that the federal draft act passed during World War I "exempted from combat only members affiliated with some 'well-recognized religious sect or organizations,' such as 'peace churches' or a 'pacifist religious sect' like the Quakers."

79. *Moskowitz v. Wilson*, 432 F.Supp. 947 (1977).

80. Bowser, at 182; John E. LeMoult, "Deprogramming Members of Religious Sects," 46 *Fordham L.Rev.* 599, 611 (1978).

81. *United States v. Ballard*, 322 U.S. 78, 86-87 (1944).

82. Ibid.

83. Walter G. Muelder, "Protestants, Catholics and 'Free Exercise'," 8 *Cumberland L.Rev.* 77, 90 (1977).

84. This is the argument of Nancy H. Fink, "The Establishment Clause According to the Supreme Court: The Mysterious Eclipse of Free Exercise Values," 27 *Cath.U.L.Rev.* 207 (1978).

85. Ibid., at 252-253.

86. Ibid.

87. See ibid., at 218.

88. *Board of Education v. Allen*, 392 U.S. 236 (1968).

89. *Everson v. Board of Education*, 330 U.S. 1 (1947).

90. See *Committee for Public Education v. Nyquist*, 413 U.S. at 802 (Burger, C. J., dissenting in part).

91. Found in Exodus 20:8-11. See *McGowan v. Maryland*, 366 U.S. at 566-567 (Douglas, J., dissenting).

92. *McGowan v. Maryland*, 366 U.S. 420 (1966); *Gallagher v. Crown Kosher Super Market*, 366 U.S. 517 (1966); *Two Guys from Harrison–Allentown v. McGinley*, 366 U.S. 582 (1966); *Braunfeld v. Brown*, 366 U.S. 599 (1966).

93. 366 U.S. at 451-452.

94. 366 U.S. at 572 (Douglas, J., dissenting).

95. Ibid., at 577 (Douglas, J., dissenting).

96. *Sherbert v. Verner*, 374 U.S. 398 (1963).

97. *Cantwell v. Connecticut*, 310 U.S. 296, 303-304 (1940).

98. *Cantwell v. Connecticut*, 310 U.S. 296 (1940).

99. *In re Jenison*, 125 N.W. 2d 588 (1963). Vacated and remanded in light of *Sherbert v. Verner*, 374 U.S. 14 (1963). See also 2 A.L.R. 3d 1392, 1394.

100. For example, in *Torasco v. Watkins*, 367 U.S. 488 (1961), the Court struck down a state requirement that candidates for public office declare a belief in God.

101. "The soul touches all parts of the living body, but its greatest concentration is in the blood. A post-mortem tampers with the body and the blood and therefore contravenes religion." *Snyder v. Holy Cross Hospital*, 352 A. 2d 334, 337 n.4 (1976).

102. Ibid.

103. "Constitutional Law — Freedom of Religion — Blood Transfusions May Be Administered to Expectant Mother Despite Her Religious Objections if Necessary to Save Her Life or That of Her Child," 10 *Villanova L.Rev.* 140, 140 n.1 (1965).

104. Ibid., at 140-141 n.3.

105. *Raleigh Fitkin–Paul Morgan Memorial Hospital v. Anderson*, 201 A. 2d 537 (1964).

106. *John F. Kennedy Memorial Hospital v. Heston*, 279 A. 2d 670 (1971).

107. *In re Estate of Brooks*, 205 N.E. 2d 435 (1965).

108. *Jacobsen v. Massachusetts*, 197 U.S. 11 (1905). The case did not involve religion, but later courts have interpreted it as applying to religion. See *Sadlock v. Board of Education*, 58 A. 2d 218 (1948).

109. The Court denied certiorari to appeals arising from *De Aryan v. Butler*, 260 P. 2d 98 (1953); and *Dowell v. Tulsa*, 273 P. 2d 859 (1954).

110. See *Murdock v. Pennsylvania*, 319 U.S. 105, 108 (1943).

111. *Douglas v. Jeanette*, 319 U.S. 157 (1943).

112. *Marsh v. Alabama*, 326 U.S. 501 (1946); *Martin v. Struthers*, 319 U.S. 141 (1943).

113. *Murdock v. Pennsylvania*, 319 U.S. 105 (1943).

114. *Wisconsin v. Yoder*, 406 U.S. 205, 214 (1972).

115. *Prince v. Massachusetts*, 321 U.S. 158 (1944).

116. See, for example, *State ex rel Swann v. Pack*, 527 S.W. 2d 99 (Tenn. 1975). The Supreme Court declined to review the case and therefore let stand the court's decision upholding an anti-snake-handling statute. *Pack v. Tennessee*, 424 U.S. 954 (1976). See also *State v. Bunn*, 336 U.S. 942 (1949), in which the Supreme Court denied certiorari and thus left standing another anti-snake-handling law.

117. See *State ex rel Swann v. Pack*, 527 S.W. 2d 99, 104 (Tenn. 1975), certiorari denied, *Pack v. Tennessee*, 424 U.S. 954 (1976). See also Comment, "*State ex rel Swann v. Pack*: Self-Endangerment and the First Amendment," 65 *Ky.L.J.* 195, 218 (1976-77).

118. Comment, "Snakehandling and Freedom of Religion, *State v. ex rel Swann v. Pack*, 527 S.W. 2d 99 (Tenn. 1975)," 1976 *Wash.U.L.Q.* 353, 353 n.1 (1976); Comment, "*State ex rel Swann . . . ,*" at 214 n.97.

119. Comment, "*State ex rel Swann . . . ,*" at 212.

120. Lisa Alther, "'They shall take up serpents'," *New York Times Magazine*, June 6, 1976, p. 18.

121. *People v. Woody*, 394 P. 2d 813 (1964).

122. *Cantwell v. Connecticut*, 310 U.S. 296, 303-304 (1940).

123. *Committee for Public Education v. Nyquist*, 413 U.S. 756 (1973).

124. *Walz v. Tax Commission*, 397 U.S. 664, 668-669 (1970).

125. *Committee for Public Education v. Nyquist*, 413 U.S. at 788.

126. Fink, at 218, 261.

127. Ibid., at 218.

128. Ibid., at 220. See also Giannella, at 1381, 1383-1384; and *Committee for Public Education v. Nyquist*, 413 U.S. at 799, 802 (Burger, C. J., dissenting in part).

129. *United States v. Seeger*, 380 U.S. 163 (1965).

130. *Walz v. Tax Commission*, 397 U.S. at 668-669.

131. The Court realizes the inconsistencies of some of its decisions. See *Walz v. Tax Commission*, 343 U.S. at 669.

CHAPTER FIVE

Equal Protection
of the Law

The laws in this country affect everybody and everything; are churned out in an endless procession of legislative, executive, and bureaucratic edicts; and threaten the devoted anarchist with suffocation. For all their variety, however, a common dimension emerges in the laws when one stops to think about them: virtually all divide people and/or objects into groups.[1] Sift through a random sampling of laws and one will find a recurring system of classification, division, categorization. A New York law forbade aliens from holding civil service jobs, thereby creating two classes of people—aliens and citizens—and treating each differently.[2] A Minnesota statute put partisan candidates ahead of nonpartisan candidates on the electoral ballot and thereby gave the edge to party affilates;[3] an Oklahoma law let business persons but not opticians sell eyeglasses without prescriptions;[4] and a Massachusetts law on the hiring and firing of police officers created ten age-based classes in one section alone.[5]

Many laws divide people on the basis of age, setting up different retirement, driver's license, liquor sales, and voting schemes for people above and below a certain age. Still others distinguish between men and women, residents and nonresidents, low-income and high-income   143 groups, and legitimate and illegitimate offspring. Classification is the basis for our legal codes and, in the normal course of events, is presumed to be valid. Laws need not "operate with rigid sameness upon all persons";[6] so long as the state has a rational reason for discriminating between groups of people it may do so. Among other things, classifications help make government efficient. By presuming that all people under the age of sixteen are too young to drive, for example, a state saves itself from time-consuming, individualized decisions that would arise if each person were allowed to petition for a driver's permit whenever he or she felt competent to drive.[7]

This is not to say that all classifications are laudable. Some have a tawdry or offensive side and are based on emotions, misconceptions, or simple prejudice. Detailed southern laws in the late nineteenth and twentieth century set up separate hospitals, drinking fountains, telephone booths and even courtroom Bibles[8] for the white and black races. One wonders what possible administrative expediency these laws were designed to promote. More likely, lawmakers set them up out of primitive racism, hardly a rational state purpose. A more recent example of an arbitrary classification comes from a provision Congress inserted in the Food Stamp Act that denied stamps to people who lived together but were unrelated by blood or marriage. An examination of congressional debates showed that the provision bespoke the lawmakers' contempt for "hippies."[9] Such classifications discriminate in the prejudicial rather than neutral sense of the term[10] and have no place in a system of enlightened and reasonable law-making. Judicial deference to classifications stops when they are arbitrary, invidious, or offensive.[11]

The Fourteenth Amendment's equal protection clause is the Constitution's chief overseer of classifications; litigants use it to challenge widely assorted laws.[12] The clause, which warns states not to "make or enforce any law" that denies "to any person within its jurisdiction the equal protection of the law,"[13] ensures that legislators will discriminate between people only if the classification is rational and is fairly related to the reason for passing the law in the first place. The clause does not forbid discrimination per se. Instead, it searches for fairness and legitimacy, weeding out only those capricious laws failing to serve a proper state purpose.

The equal protection clause is no more monolithic than First Amendment free speech or press, however. Just as the Court uses different free speech tests depending on the type of expression at issue and different free press tests depending on the medium in question, so does it use different equal protection formulas depending on key issues in the case at bar. To understand the bases for intra-liberty gradations in equal protection doctrine, consider the grievances of Louise Levy, Veragene Hardy, and K. Leroy Irvis.

Louise Levy was a Louisiana woman who went to the Charity Hospital in New Orleans complaining of chest pains, fatigue, and dizziness. The doctor looked at her briefly and sent her home with tranquilizers. A week later she returned with worsened symptoms and this time the doctor recommended that Miss Levy see a psychiatrist. Her problem quite definitely was not psychosomatic, however; unbeknownst to either patient or doctor the woman was suffering from hypertensive uremia. Untreated, she was dead within ten days. Miss Levy's sister filed suit under the state's wrongful death statute on behalf of Levy's five children. Before the plaintiffs even got a chance to argue the hospital's culpability, however, a district court dismissed the suit on the grounds that the children did not have the right to recover damages. It turns out that Levy's children were all illegitimate and Louisiana's wrongful death statute allowed only legitimate children to collect for the death of their mother. The plaintiffs went to court again, this time contending that Louisiana's law violated their right to equal protection of the laws.

Veragene Hardy was a twenty-seven-year-old California woman who wanted to be a police officer. She applied for a position with the Oakland Police Department, passed the written test, but failed to pass the physical ability test. The test required applicants to "run 300 feet . . . , scale a 6-foot wall . . . , walk across a balance beam, run another 300 feet, register 75 pounds on a grip dynamometer device, and drag a 140-pound dummy for 50 feet, raising it to a 2-foot platform, all within 2½ minutes." Hardy could do everything but scale the wall and she failed in the two attempts given her. She was not the only female applicant in this position; it seems that 85 percent of the male applicants passed the test but only 15 percent of the females did. Under department rules Hardy could retake the test after four months but she chose instead to bring suit, claiming among other things that the test discriminated against her on the basis of sex and violated her right to equal protection of the laws.

K. Leroy Irvis was a black man who went to the Harrisburg, Pennsylvania, chapter of the Moose Lodge with a friend who was a member of the Lodge. Once inside, Irvis was refused service because he was a black man in a white man's fraternal club; Lodge membership was restricted to "male persons of the Caucasian or White race above the age of twenty-one years, and not married to someone of other than the Caucasian or White race, who are of good moral character, physically and mentally normal, who shall profess a belief in a Supreme Being. . . ." Irvis went to court, claiming violation of his Fourteenth Amendment rights.

One thing that distinguishes these equal protection cases is the type of classification at issue. *Levy v. Louisiana*[14] involved a classification deliberately written into the law and known as a *de jure* or "by law" discrimination. *Hardy v. Stumpf*,[15] on the other hand, involved a secondary, unstated discrimination resulting from a deliberate classification. When a discrimination is the unwitting result of a classification, it is known as a *de facto* or "in fact" discrimination. In Hardy's case the deliberate classification was between those who could and those who could not scale a six-foot wall, but the unwitting discrimination was between men and women inasmuch as women failed the test in disproportionate numbers. *Irvis v. Moose Lodge #107*[16] involved a deliberate discrimination, to be sure, but one imposed by a private fraternal club, not by the state. The Fourteenth Amendment warns no "state" to deny to its citizens the equal protection of the laws and would seem not to apply here, but then again, one may ask if Pennsylvania really were totally divorced from the Moose Lodge. It did, after all, issue a liquor license to the club, Moose members pay land tax, and the Lodge benefits from city fire and police services. Perhaps what appears to be a private discrimination is not so private after all.

Of these three types of classifications — de jure, de facto, and private — the first is most clearly attached to the Fourteenth Amendment and, appropriately, is the basis for most equal protection appeals. The other two are more problematic, however, and their relation to equal protection review is less clear. Should the state be held responsible under the Fourteenth Amendment for discriminations it unintentionally fosters? Should it be held responsible for discriminations its liquor licenses or utilities clients enforce? Just how far does the authority of the Fourteenth Amendment reach? Might it be less forceful for de facto and private discriminations than for relatively clear-cut de jure classifications?

Another thing distinguishing the *Levy, Hardy,* and *Irvis* cases is the identity of the group targeted by the classification. *Levy* attacked a law discriminating against illegitimate children, *Hardy* challenged a practice falling heavily on women, and *Irvis* involved a rule burdening racial minorities. Other laws and practices single out homosexuals, students, fat people, motorcycle drivers, single people, and linguistic minorities for differential treatment. Inasmuch as our legal structure is based on classification, *someone* will always be hurt by laws and practices. If everyone targeted by a law were successfully to challenge it in court, the system would collapse. Yet if no one contested unfair classifications, the tentacles of prejudice would have a stranglehold over the country, leaving us with racially segregated schools, male-only law schools, and businesses devoid of handicapped workers. Might it be that some classifications are inherently less acceptable than others, simply because of the type of group burdened? Might racially based classifications, for example, be automatically suspect because of the odious history of racism in this country, but age-based classifications, which have not been used so prejudicially, be more acceptable?

What we are leading up to with these three cases is a set of gradations within equal protection doctrine that give clues about how judges will approach Fourteenth Amendment appeals. As it turns out, a litigant's chances of winning an equal protection suit depend, among other things, on the type of classification at issue (is it de jure, de facto, or private?) and on the group targeted by the classification (racial minorities? women? illegitimates? motorcycle drivers?). Generally speaking, the chances of victory are greatest with de jure racial classifications and poorest with de facto or private discrimination, with assorted chances in between. Figure 5.1 presents a schematic overview of equal protection's

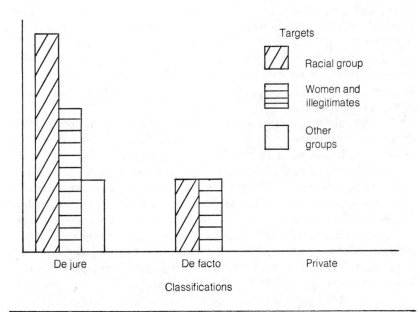

FIGURE 5.1
GRADATIONS IN EQUAL PROTECTION'S
STRENGTH ACCORDING TO TARGET AND
TYPE OF CLASSIFICATION

gradations. Roughly equating height of the bar with clout, it shows the classifications most and least likely to fall under equal protection challenge. Figure 5.1 also depicts the organization of the chapter, which will first review principles attending de jure classifications and then the law on de facto and private discrimination.

Figure 5.1 is tidy, but where would the mystery and intrigue of constitutional law be if equal protection doctrine were as pat as the figure makes it out to be? Thus, one must expect caveats. Equal protection is one of the more steadily changing areas of civil liberties, led in its long march by racial minorities as pioneers. Racial prejudice has clung to U.S. history like a magnetic albatross and has stubbornly cropped up in new forms. For decades racial minorities have raised assorted issues under equal protection's banner as they assaulted one, then another, vestige of racism, each time bidding the Court to modify and revamp equal protection's application. For the most part the Court has responded by moving forward with equal protection, applying it in new and original ways. Using a dialectical analogy, one may say that a particular form of racism is the status quo or "thesis" and the lawsuit filed by racial minorities the suggestion for change or "antithesis." The thesis and antithesis then enter a state of conflict and the Court's response under the Fourteenth Amendment can either be a return to the status quo, in which case no progress is made, or it can be a new use of the equal protection clause, in which case a "synthesis" has been achieved. Racial minorities have attacked de jure, de facto, and private discrimination, thereby giving the Court an opportunity to shape a new synthesis for each area.

Racial minorities still raise questions in court, but it appears that their role as pioneers has been at least momentarily surpassed by other groups which also want to benefit from the protection offered by the Fourteenth Amendment. Watching racial successes with the Fourteenth Amendment in the 1950s and 1960s, these groups—most notably women—began to march their grievances before the courts in the late 1960s, again with equal protection in the lead. The interesting thing now is to see to what extent the Court is willing to extend to the new groups the same advances it granted to racial minorities. Assume, with reference to Figure 5.2, that A is the thesis for de jure racial discrimination (a network of laws burdening blacks), B is the antithesis (litigation), and C is the synthesis (an equal protection test for reviewing discriminatory laws). Assume that A' is the thesis for de jure sexual discrimination (a network of laws burdening women) and B' the antithesis (litigation). The next question is whether the Court will reach a synthesis (C') that is the same as the earlier C; in other words, will the Court afford the same equal

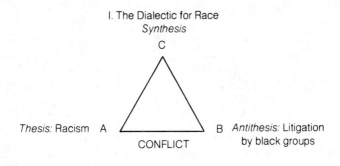

I. The Dialectic for Race
Synthesis
C

Thesis: Racism   A

CONFLICT

B   *Antithesis:* Litigation
by black groups

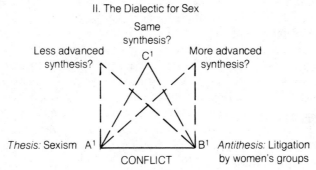

II. The Dialectic for Sex

Same
synthesis?

Less advanced
synthesis?

C^1

More advanced
synthesis?

Thesis: Sexism A^1

CONFLICT

B^1 *Antithesis:* Litigation
by women's groups

FIGURE 5.2
QUESTIONS POSED BY THE EVOLUTION OF
EQUAL PROTECTION DOCTRINE

protection remedy for sexual discrimination as for racial discrimination? Its options are several. It could decline to use equal protection at all, thereby leaving the status quo intact; it could reach a less aggressive synthesis, thereby introducing another gradation in equal protection doctrine; it could reach the same synthesis, thereby leveling out equal protection doctrine; or it could make a more aggressive synthesis. We can ask the same question for de facto and private discrimination and the answer is the same for each: more often than not the Court extends a slightly less aggressive test for discrimination other than race. Like an inchworm, equal protection doctrine takes a dramatic step when new racial issues are raised but then backs off, creating a new middle position when other groups try to benefit from the racial synthesis. It appears that not only is equal protection litigation becoming more diverse in the 1970s and 1980s but so also is equal protection doctrine taking on more complex tones and hues. Thus, to appreciate the exact claims raised by the Levy children, Veragene Hardy, and Leroy Irvis, we must first understand the gradations of equal protection doctrine and the logic upon which they are based.

DE JURE CLASSIFICATIONS

As a result of the dialectic, the Court has three tests for reviewing de jure classifications. They are known in judicial parlance as minimum scrutiny, moderate scrutiny, and strict scrutiny. Under minimum scrutiny most laws will stand, under strict scrutiny most will fall. The record is mixed for moderate scrutiny, but more laws fall than stand under it. The Court, for example, examined Louisiana's wrongful death statute under moderate scrutiny and the law fell. Obviously, by knowing which test the Court will use, the observer is armed with a good clue as to the outcome of the test. The tricky part lies in trying to figure out what test it will select. In essence equal protection review is a two-step process in which the Court first screens the law to decide which test to use and then applies the test. Since screening stacks the odds, it turns out to be the more important step. The following sections review the substance of each test and tell what the Court looks for in screening laws brought to it on equal protection grounds.

Strict Scrutiny

The strict scrutiny test assumes the law's unconstitutionality. In contrast to the usual procedure in which the plaintiff carries the burden of showing why the law should be struck down, under strict scrutiny the state carries the burden of showing why the law should stand. It is up to the state to show that the classification furthers a "compelling," "paramount," or "cogent" state interest.[17] The state must also show the classification is the "least burdensome" way of meeting the interest. To show the difficult task this poses to the government, consider that the Court has only upheld classifications under strict scrutiny twice.[18]

The discriminating reader will realize that strict scrutiny is remarkably similar to the tests used to review prior restraints on speech. As discussed in Chapter 2, the Court presumed the unconstitutionality of prior restraints, bade the state to show a "compelling" interest for the act, and asked that the prior restraint be the least burdensome way of meeting the interest. Thus, we see here another intra-liberty gradation in our litany of rights guaranteed in the amendments to the Constitution.

When the state intrudes on the First Amendment or passes certain types of classificatory laws, it infringes on something so fundamental as to prompt extraordinary standards of review.[19] What kinds of classifications are so odious as to prompt strict scrutiny when challenged on equal protection grounds?

To answer this, consider a Virginia law the Court reviewed under strict scrutiny in 1967.[20] The law, an antimiscegenation statute, made it a crime for black and white people to intermarry. It stated, in part, that if "any white person and colored person shall go out of this State, for the purpose of being married, and with the intention of returning, and be married out of it, and afterwards return to and reside in it, cohabiting as man and wife, they shall be punished. . . ." In June of 1958 Mildred Jeter, a black woman, and Richard Loving, a white man, left Virginia for Washington, D.C., to marry. When they returned to their home state they were arrested and convicted for violating the code. The judge sentenced them to one year in prison but suspended the sentence for twenty-five years on the condition that the Lovings leave the state for twenty-five years.

This law shows racism at its ugliest. If the law on its face left any doubt about the prejudice that underlay it, consider the words of the trial judge in sentencing the Lovings ("Almighty God created the races white, black, yellow, malay and red, and he placed them on separate continents. . . . The fact that he separated the races shows that he did not intend for the races to mix") and of the state court in describing the legislative intent of the law (it was designed "'to preserve the racial integrity of its citizens,' and to prevent 'the corruption of blood,' 'a mongrel breed of citizens,' and 'the obliteration of racial pride'.").

Virginia's law was only one of many that distinguished between people on the basis of race. These other laws, too, seemed to be based on prejudice rather than any dispassionate, rational purpose; one wonders, in fact, whether any racially based law that treats blacks as a separate class is completely separate from racism. Given the entrenched history of racism in this country, one may logically assume that racial classifications are prejudicial clssifications. This leaves them immediately open to suspicion; they are, in legal parlance, "suspect." In the 1940s the Court reviewed a racial classification under strict scrutiny for the first time, noting that classifications restricting a single racial group are "immediately suspect" and must be subjected to the "most rigid scrutiny."[21] Herein the Court begat a new tenet of equal protection review: when a law classifies on the basis of a "suspect criterion," it will be subject to strict scrutiny. How, though, does one know a "suspect criterion" when one sees it?

Inasmuch as the first suspect criterion identified by the Court was race, it is not surprising that the earmarks of such a criterion are tailored to fit racial classifications. One indicator of a suspect criterion is that it is based on a trait over which the individual has no control, that is, on an "accident of birth."[22] Second, a suspect criterion burdens a group easily singled out by physical or other attributes for unfair treatment, that is, a "discrete and insular minority."[23] Third, it burdens a politically powerless group.[24] Fourth, legislators have used the criterion out of prejudice rather than to satisfy a rational state interest and, fifth, have used the criterion to subject the targeted group to a "long and unfortunate history" of "purposeful unequal treatment."[25]

Racial classifications fit all these indicators and amount to the classic "suspect criterion." Racial traits are beyond the individual's control; one is born with skin tones of white, black, yellow, or brown and can do nothing to change that. Moreover, the mere color of one's skin has been used to create a discrete minority in this country and has led to worse, not better, treatment for that group. This group is politically less powerful than majority groups, and legislators have, because of blunt prejudice, used race to subject that minority to a lengthy history of discrimination. The Court has also called national origin[26] and alienage[27] suspect criteria, bringing to three the number of criteria that automatically bring on strict scrutiny.

It is clear that strict scrutiny is reserved for odious classifications. Some classifications, as we have just seen, are suspect because of the criterion on which they are based. But others are suspect because they intrude on something precious in our lives. Suppose a state's criminal code required the forced sterilization of all habitual criminals.[28] The law distinguishes between habitual and nonhabitual criminals and does not bring on strict scrutiny because it is not based on a suspect criterion. Its effect, however—to sterilize a person—is dramatic. Or, consider the effect of Virginia's antimiscegenation law. It, too, is dramatic for it tells citizens whom they may and may not marry. Marriage brings with it a twenty-four-a-day spouse; it is one of the more private decisions filled with more implications than perhaps any other in life. A classification that intrudes on the marital decision represents a grave intrusion of the state into our daily lives.

In recognition of this other odious side of classifications, the Court treats some classifications as suspicious because they intrude on something basic. In particular, the Court will subject laws intruding on a "fundamental" right to strict scrutiny. Childbearing is a fundamental right, so is marriage. But how do we know that? How does one know a fundamental right when one sees it? The Court defines a fundamental right as one rooted in the Constitution. Some fundamental rights are explicitly stated in the Constitution, such as the First Amendment right of free speech or the Sixth Amendment right to a speedy trial. Others are only inferentially a part of the Constitution. Though not specifically stated in the document, implicit rights are part of its spirit and give "life and substance" to stated rights.[29] For example, as discussed in Chapter 3, the Court stated that the public has a constitutional right of access to information. Access is nowhere mentioned in the document, but it nurtures and sustains the stated First Amendment right of free press. The Court has also held that we have a constitutional right to privacy (see Chapter 6). But privacy, like access, is not mentioned in the document. It is a constitutional right because it logically flows from a stated right (the "mother" rights for privacy are in the First, Third, Fourth, Fifth, and Ninth Amendments[30]). So too does the right to interstate travel flow from a stated right—the Fourteenth Amendment right to liberty.[31]

We see that Virginia's antimiscegenation law hit a double-header when it came to the Court for screening. Not only was it based on a suspect criterion—race—but it intruded on a fundamental right—marriage. Either is enough to prompt strict scrutiny.[32]

Minimum Scrutiny

Minimum scrutiny is the patriarch of equal protection's three tests. Until the Court surprised observers by using an unusually strict test in the 1940s on a racial classification, minimum scrutiny was the only test used. As a traditional, typical test it defers to the legislature and is not particularly rigorous. Under this test courts presume the law's constitutionality; few laws fail to withstand it. It has five main parts, as depicted in Figure 5.3. Its multifaceted nature should not be taken to mean it is more complex or problematic than the relatively straightforward strict scrutiny test; instead, it has simply been around longer and so the Court has had ample opportunity to make its constituent parts clear.

The first requirement of minimum scrutiny is that the classification itself be reasonable. Judges presume reasonableness unless the group challenging the law takes it upon itself to show that the classification is instead "patently arbitrary" or capricious.[33] Second, the classification on its face must treat all people within each class equally. An Oklahoma law providing for the sterilization of all habitual criminals except those convicted of white-collar crimes failed this subtest because it did not treat all members of a class (habitual criminals) alike.[34] Third,

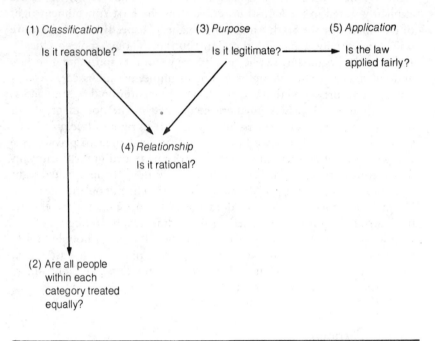

FIGURE 5.3
FIVE COMPONENTS OF THE MINIMUM
SCRUTINY TEST

the law's purpose must be proper. The Court struck down a provision of the Food Stamp Act denying food stamps to unmarried or unrelated co-habitants for failing this subtest.[35] Legislative debates showed that Congress passed the bill to discourage communal living by "hippies," and this moralizing reflected "invidious discrimination" rather than a proper state purpose. Fourth, the relationship between the classification and its purpose must be rational. The Court struck down a law forbidding the sale of birth control devices to single people on the grounds that the law had no rational relationship between the classification and its purpose (to discourage premarital sex).[36] Assuming that the law's purpose is proper, the Court could see no logical way that withholding birth control devices from single persons could discourage them from having sexual relations. Similarly, a southern court struck down a school superintendent's order that no parent of an illegitimate child could be hired because the order bore no rational relation to the school's intention of only hiring people with good moral characters;[37] among other things, giving birth to an illegitimate child several years past had no direct bearing on the parent's moral behavior at the present time. Fifth, the law as applied must treat all persons within a class equally. The Court struck down a San Francisco ordinance for failing this subtest. The policy required all owners of laundries housed in wooden buildings to secure operating licenses (supposedly a safety measure), but the record showed the city used the rule routinely to deny licenses to Chinese laundrymen only.[38]

If this is the substance of minimum scrutiny, how does the Court decide when to use it? Actually, there is no deliberate decision to use minimum scrutiny because the Court applies it as a matter of course *unless* shown that the conditions warranting stricter review are present. The Court is predisposed to use minimum scrutiny; the burden is put on plaintiffs to show the presence of extraordinary conditions that call for the lifting of that predisposition. Consider, for example, the case of the aging police officer, one Murgia. Under Massachusetts law Murgia had to retire from the force at age fifty but, feeling that he was fit enough to continue working past that age, Murgia filed suit, claiming that the mandatory retirement law violated his right to equal protection. It was in Murgia's best interest for the Court to review the law under strict scrutiny, so in part of his appeal he tried to lift the Court's normal proclivity to use minimum scrutiny. He argued, first, that the criterion upon which the law was based—age—was a "suspect criterion" and, second, that the law intruded on a fundamental right—his right to work. He failed to persuade the Court on either count, however, so the Justices used minimum scrutiny. Under this lax test the Court upheld the mandatory retirement provision as a reasonable way of meeting the rational state interest in protecting the public welfare.[39]

Moderate Scrutiny

Moderate scrutiny is a middle-range test that is more rigid than minimum scrutiny but not as rigid as strict scrutiny. It requires the law to further an "important" state purpose (stronger than minimum scrutiny's "legitimate" state purpose but weaker than strict scrutiny's "compelling" state purpose) and asks whether there is a "substantial" relation between the classification and the purpose (stronger than minimum scrutiny's "reasonable" relation).[40] Under it laws are more than likely to fail. We mentioned earlier in the chapter that the Court struck down Louisiana's wrongful death statute (the one discriminating against illegitimate children) under moderate scrutiny.[41] How did it decide to use a middle level of review?

If the reader has taken the discussion thus far at its face value he or she may now be wondering why the Court did not subject the wrongful death statute to strict scrutiny. The stated legislative purpose was to "discourage bringing children into the world out of wedlock." Supposedly, the theory goes, this and other laws that treat illegitimates less well than legitimates will cause a man and woman to think twice before creating an illegitimate child. If the law affects extramarital liaisons, it intrudes on a highly personal kind of familial and sexual decision that bears all the earmarks of a "fundamental" right and, in fact, the Court in *Levy* did note that the law affected a fundamental right of familial privacy.

Moreover, legitimacy of birth seems to meet at least some of the indicators of a suspect criterion. A child's illegitimacy is an accident of birth over which he or she has no control. There is evidence that legislators have passed laws burdening the bastard for prejudicial reasons. Not only has the bastard long been the target of scorn and bias but, in the southern states at least, illegitimacy has been greater among blacks than whites. Perhaps it is not surprising that laws discriminating among illegitimates tend to lump together in the South; more than one observer has suggested that anti-illegitimacy statutes are in reality anti-black statutes.

In other respects, though, illegitimacy may not meet the indicators of a suspect criterion. Illegitimates can be identified through court records, but they wear no badge — such as skin color — that makes them a "discrete and insular minority." Nor do they stand out as a politically powerless group, largely because they have not tried to unite as an interest group in the first place. They have long been discriminated against, with a tradition dating to the English common law that made a bastard a *filius nullius*, or "child of nobody,"[42] but one wonders just how "unfortunate" and disastrous such discrimination has been.

Thus it appears that legitimacy of birth is an "almost suspect" criterion that could, with a gentle prod, be subject to strict review and not complicate equal protection doctrine in any way. In fact, such might make the doctrine more consistent. Recall that the Court has called alienage and national origin suspect criteria. These two bases of classification are arguably no less suspect than legitimacy of birth.

To explain why the Court did not subject Louisiana's wrongful death statute to strict scrutiny, one must venture away from a literal reading of equal protection doctrine and consider extralegal factors impinging on the Court. In a way illegitimates just picked the wrong time to challenge classifications. Had they been recognized as a group with legitimate civil rights grievances a decade or so earlier, they too might have enjoyed the added equal protection the Court gave blacks with its strict standard of review. As it turns out, much of the decision to use strict review hinges not on "accidents of birth" and "long and unfortunate" histories of discrimination but rather on the predilections of the Justices.

By the mid-1960s the Court had established a two-pronged, strict–minimum scrutiny model of equal protection. Referring to the dialectical process depicted in Figure 5.2, one can see that the Court used minimum scrutiny until litigants challenged racial classifications on equal protection grounds and thereby introduced an antithesis (B) to the thesis of racism (A). The Court resolved the conflict by developing a new test—strict scrutiny—and thereby creating a new synthesis (C). The modus vivendi lasted only a short time, however, because the number of groups raising equal protection claims surged dramatically in the 1960s and 1970s. Encouraged by the successful efforts of blacks to use the Fourteenth Amendment as a weapon for attacking egregious laws, other social groups began filing suit under the same amendment. The most visible of these were women, who began to question the many laws using gender as a basis of classification. They were followed by prisoners, the handicapped, homosexuals, linguistic minorities, and others targeted by burdensome laws but who previously had little hope of using the equal protection clause as a weapon. Up to that point the Court had subjected all classifications other than those based on race, national origin, and ancestry to minimum scrutiny, thereby giving little incentive to other groups to use the Fourteenth Amendment.

Many of the new litigants tried to show that the laws discriminating against them were based on suspect criteria. Among these were illegitimates, as illustrated in the *Levy* case, and women. As we have seen, illegitimacy of birth meets at least some of the indicators of a suspect criterion; a strong case can also be made that gender is suspect. Gender is as much an accident of birth as race—a person has no control over his or her sex—and it is, except for an infinitesimal number of people who have undergone the scalpel, immutable. Moreover, sex-based classifications create discrete and easily identifiable groups, one of which—women—is politically under-represented. And, perhaps most importantly, male-dominated legislatures have passed these laws with stereotypical or prejudicial motives and have created a sorry history of discrimination in doing so. Underlying many sex-based laws has been a paternalistic theory that women have limited capabilities and must be protected by society. Paternalism was at the root of a Michigan law, for example, forbidding women to tend bar unless their fathers or husbands were also bartenders.[43] The rationale was that the male figures could protect the women from what could turn out to be a dangerous job. It was also the basis for a Florida law exempting women from jury duty because they would be taken away from their rightful place in the home if called to serve as jurors.[44] The law made a presumption—that women should stay in the home while men worked and served outside of the home—that amounts to stereotypical thinking. Stereotypes are in turn the basis for prejudice, or conclusions about a group based upon gross generalizations rather than reasoned inquiry. It makes little difference that women themselves pushed for some of these protective laws early in the century. Once the arbitrary basis upon which they are formed is recognized, paternalistic laws become prejudicial laws and meet one of the indicators of a suspect criterion.

The "sorry history of discrimination" resulting from paternalistic laws has been well-documented by the raft of books on women's status in U.S. society published in the last two decades. Despite a battery of laws designed to undo the injuries of past discrimination, women today still earn 60 percent of what men do, are shunted into low-paying jobs with little chance of advancement, and struggle to upend deep-seated notions of their physical and mental inferiority. Just as the Court uses strict scrutiny as a weapon for compensating for past wrongs to racial minorities (the rationale is that as a discrete and politically powerless group blacks need extra judicial help in catching up with white society), so does it make sense that the Court use strict scrutiny to compensate women for the lingering effects of sexism. Blacks point to the *Dred Scott* decision, a decision in which the Court declared blacks not to be citizens in the meaning of the Constitution, as a symbol of their sorry history of discrimination.[45] An analogous nineteenth-century decision for women was *Bradwell v. Illinois*,[46] in which the Court upheld a law denying women the right to practice law in the state of Illinois. In pulling the career of Myra Bradwell out from under her, the Court pointed out women's God-given duty to be the nurturer in the home rather than a provider in the workplace.

Other things being equal, it is possible the Court would have recognized gender and legitimacy of birth as suspect criteria in the late 1960s or early 1970s. But other things were not equal in that nearly half of the Justices who had shaped and polished the two-pronged model died or retired in a short period of time. In a position to replace them was a President who made no secret of the fact that he disdained Justices who scrutinized legislation too closely. President Nixon set out to replace the departing Justices with strict constructionist counterparts, that is, Justices who would interpret the Constitution narrowly and forsake the willingness of the Warren Court to review laws and practices for their constitutionality. Deprived of some of its creators and joined by some of its detractors, the two-pronged model faced an uncertain future.

Impinging on this reluctant Court were not only new claims of suspect criteria but also claims that one or another right was "fundamental." Again the Burger Court found itself in a web not of its own making, this time the web of dicta handed down by Warren Court Justices that left a "legacy of anticipations" about possibly fundamental rights.[47] Although the Warren Court did not go so far as to say the right to work or the right to education was fundamental, it broadly hinted that such rights were constitutionally based and ought to be protected by close Fourteenth Amendment scrutiny.[48]

The new Justices were not eager to expand the list of suspect criteria or of fundamental rights because doing so would expand the number of laws subject to strict scrutiny. Since strict scrutiny virtually guarantees the law will fail, it is hardly surprising that the Justices hesitated to add to the opportunities to use the test. Perhaps had the civil rights movement not spread so quickly the Justices would have extended strict scrutiny here and there, but the spiraling of demands created a domino atmosphere with no clear end once the expansion of fundamental rights and suspect criteria began.

Although philosophically disinclined to create the same synthesis for sexism as for racism (point C′ on Figure 5.2), the Court was not blind to discrimination against women and other groups. Thus, it did shun one option—maintain the status quo—in favor of another—create a synthesis but one less active than C′. Herein was born moderate scrutiny. The Court first suggested it in a 1971 case involving a typical sex-based classi- fication—one quietly hidden in the statute books that alone had little significance but that, when taken together with a legion of other discriminatory laws, created a paternalistic and prejudicial milieu that left women as second-class citizens in their own land. At issue was an Idaho law giving automatic preference to the father in the administration of estates.[49] The law provided that when "several persons" claimed to administer an estate and each was "equally entitled to administer" it, "males must be preferred to females." The reason for this preference was similar to the reason for most classifications, namely, administrative expediency. By creating classes of people, the state is freed from the need to make individual case-by-case decisions and this speeds bureaucratic processing. The litigants in the Idaho case, for example, were Sally and Cecil Reed, parents of a young son who died. As mother and father, each had equal claim to administer their son's estate. Who shall be granted that right in case of a dispute? If the law did not say, it is possible the Reeds would go to court and in so doing slow down the administrative process. Thus the law went one step further and said that in case of disputes the male shall be given the right. Normally this would prevent the need for a lawsuit. With the Reeds, however, it caused a lawsuit because Sally Reed filed suit under the equal protection clause, claiming the law arbitrarily discriminated against women.

The Supreme Court struck the law down in an historical decision that marked the first time it overturned a sex-based classification on equal protection grounds. Using the new moderate scrutiny test, the Court struck the law down for failing to serve an "important" state interest. One commentator has called moderate scrutiny "minimum scrutiny with bite."[50] The description is apropos because the test borrows from both low-level and high-level review. In screening, the test is close to minimum scrutiny in that the Court uses it for classifications it normally would subject to low-level review. In application, however, the test approximates strict scrutiny because under it laws do fail. One such example is the law in *Reed v. Reed*; another is Louisiana's wrongful death statute. In that decision too the Court took an almost suspect criterion—legitimacy of birth—and subjected it to a test heftier than minimum scrutiny but not as strong as strict scrutiny.[51]

We can see now the pioneering role race has played in the doctrine for de jure classifications. Faced with litigants who claimed that de jure racial discrimination deprived them of their Fourteenth Amendment rights, the Court created a new test (point C on Figure 5.2) for reviewing racially based classifications. Later, the Court faced litigants who claimed that other classifications deprived them of their right to equal protection of the laws. The Court decided to move beyond the status quo for two of these groups—women and illegitimates—and it created a synthesis for them, albeit one that did not go so far as that for blacks. The Court has largely maintained the status quo for other groups such as homosexuals or the aged, using the traditional minimum scrutiny test, which rarely succeeds in striking down a law.

Table 5.1 summarizes the screening and application of the three scrutiny tests. The precise elements of each test are less important than the principle they illustrate, namely, that equal protection is a graduated right with differing levels of clout depending on the type of classification at issue. The observer who knows the criterion on which a law is based and the right on which it infringes is armed with two bits of information that go a long way in predicting the outcome of the equal protection claim.

Affirmative Classifications

The doctrine reviewed to this point has involved laws that burden a targeted group, such as a law foreclosing wrongful death compensation to illegitimates or cutting off women from the administration of estates. The 1960s and 1970s were decades of education for our society in that the massive growth of equal protection cases revealed the extent and variety of negative classifications in the statute books. Under court directives and voluntary actions, state and federal legislatures excised many of the discriminatory laws from the books or modified them so they would no longer burden one group. State legislators deleted lingering Jim Crow laws, which set up different swimming pools, parks, and other facilities for members of the black race, and changed the wording of sexually discriminatory estate, trust, and other laws. This is not to say that all discriminatory laws have been deleted but rather that legislators, whether happily or not, took steps to make legal codes more equitable and the society less discriminatory.

Once this is done one wonders just how much it has actually helped to eradicate discrimination. True, from this point on the government may no longer discriminate, but what about the decades of discrimination that have left blacks, other minorities, and women as marginal members of society who do not share equally in the economic wealth, political bases of power, and general upward mobility that mainstream citizens enjoy? Ending school segregation is laudable, but does it help the black child whose parents and grandparents attended inferior schools, had fewer skills to show for it, and passed on the culture of poverty to him or her? It is commendable that law schools are no longer closed to women, but how quickly can one undo the damage caused by generations of male-only law schools that kept the number of female lawyers extremely low? The litigation that has infused a new neutral cast to the legal codes is, argues some observers, little more than window-dressing that spruces up the exterior but fails to dig out the rotten foundation caused by decades of neglect. With this presumption in mind some judges, legislators, and civil rights groups have called for the state to do more than passively end discrimination: they want the state to take positive steps to remedy past discrimination—that is, to go to work on the ailing foundation.

The Supreme Court itself gave the impetus to the idea that the state had a duty affirmatively to undo the past effects of discrimination. It looked to the area where the civil rights movement originally came together—school segregation—and saw that despite the ringing words of

TABLE 5.1
THREE TESTS FOR REVIEWING DE JURE
CLASSIFICATIONS: STRICT, MODERATE, AND
MINIMUM SCRUTINY

	I. Screening laws to decide which equal protection test to use		
	Strict scrutiny	Moderate scrutiny	Minimum scrutiny
Conditions of use	(1) The law is based on a "suspect" criterion (an accident of birth connected with a long and unfortunate history of discrimination) or (2) the law affects an explicit or implicit fundamental right.	The law is based on an "almost suspect" criterion (one meeting only one or two indicators of a suspect criterion).	The law classifies on the basis of a "nonsuspect" criterion.
Frequency of use	Used rarely (only race, national origin, and alienage are suspect criteria)	Used rarely (only gender and illegitimacy are "almost suspect" criteria)	Used frequently
Sample Case	*Loving v. Virginia* (1967) The Court struck down Virginia's law forbidding miscegenation. The law was based on a suspect criterion (race) and intruded on an implicit fundamental right to choose one's marriage partner.	*Craig v. Boren* (1976) The Court struck down Oklahoma's law allowing women to buy beer at an earlier age than men. The law was based on an almost suspect criterion (gender).	*Massachusetts v. Murgia* (1976) The Court upheld Massachusetts's mandatory retirement plan for police officers. Age is not a suspect or almost suspect criterion and work is not a constitutional right.

Brown v. Board of Education in 1954[52] declaring de jure school segregation unconstitutional, southern schools remained segregated.[53] The law books had changed and now took on an aura of racial equality but tampering with words had little effect on the realities of southern education. Thus the Court turned *Brown* from the entrée to the apértif and took further steps to end segregation. In 1968 it held that the Fourteenth Amendment authorized the state not merely to end segregation but to encourage integration and gave school boards the "affirmative

TABLE 5.1 continued

	II. Applying the appropriate equal protection test		
	Strict scrutiny	Moderate scrutiny	Minimum scrutiny
Test itself	——	——	Is the classification reasonable?
	Does the law further a *compelling* state purpose?	Does the law further an *important* state purpose?	Does the law further a *legitimate* state purpose?
	——	Is there a *substantial* relation between classification and purpose?	Is there a *rational* relation between the classification and its purpose?
	——	——	Are all people within each category treated equally?
	——	——	Is the law applied fairly?
	Can other less burdensome alternatives meet the compelling state purpose?	——	——

duty to take whatever steps might be necessary" to end segregation "root and branch."[54] The decision bade school boards to use busing and other methods to integrate schools. But in order to set out busing plans, the school boards had to talk about black school districts and white school districts and where the bus routes should go and who should be bused. In short, the Court's "root and branch" directive meant that the state had to use race as a criterion to develop integration policy. This was another racial classification but with a difference: it bade the state to use race for altruistic rather than prejudicial purposes in order to undo discrimination, not further it.

The notion of affirmative classifications soon gained a foothold in American policy, especially with the birth of Executive Order 11246, which forbids federal contractors and subcontractors from discriminating on the basis of race, color, religion, sex or national origin *and* requires these employers to take "affirmative" steps to ensure that all applicants and employees have equal opportunities for work and promotion. The order affects many businesses, including those selling goods to the government or accepting federal funds and companies that in turn contract with the original contractors; it sent these businesses scurrying about appointing affirmative action officers and setting up affirmative action plans showing that they were making a good-faith effort to recruit and appoint minorities and women. A later order put the same task on the federal government itself as an employer, and various states have set up their own policies to remedy past discrimination.[55] To administer affirmative action plans businesses and governments find themselves amassing numbers and figures showing how many skilled minorities and women are in the immediate area, how many have been hired, fired, and promoted, and how many are expected to be hired in the future. The policy is complex and detailed, but the point is that it uses criteria normally subject to strict or moderate scrutiny. The difference, as with school busing plans, is that the classifications are affirmative rather than negative. The constitutional question this raises is whether the same principles covered above and summarized in Table 5.1 still apply when an affirmative classification is at stake. If so, we need offer no addendums to Table 5.1. But if not, we have uncovered a visible offshoot of equal protection doctrine that warns of postscripts to the three-test framework.

Since affirmative classifications have only recently come before the Court, it is still too early to say just what the developing doctrine will look like. The Court has reviewed enough classifications to show, however, that it views affirmative racial classifications as different animals for equal protection purposes than negative classifications (it has not yet reviewed affirmative sexual classifications). In *University of California Board of Regents v. Bakke*,[56] a case involving a racial quota system the UC-Davis Medical School had set up to promote the admission of racial minorities, the Court declined to address the question of which level of scrutiny it should apply, but four of the Justices went on record as saying they would subject affirmative classifications to a less stringent test than negative racial classifications.[57] The decision itself gave some clue: it upheld the use of race as a factor in admissions, although it struck down the rigid quota imposed by admissions officials. Then, in 1980, the Court upheld a congressional law requiring state and city governments receiving federal funds for public works projects to contract 10 percent of those funds with businesses owned and operated by racial minorities.[58] Here the Court said in effect that the Constitution was color blind for prejudicial classifications (that is, that they must be subject to the most rigid of scrutiny) but not for classifications designed to remedy past effects of racial discrimination. Citing its school busing decisions, the Court noted that "[j]ust as the race of students must be considered in determining whether a constitutional violation has occurred, so also must race be considered in formulating a remedy." The Court documented the existence of racial discrimination in contracting and business opportunities, thereby establishing that Congress had a proper motive in trying to remedy the problem, and then held that Congress's method (using race as a factor in the allocation of contracts) was permissible. However unclear is the exact test the Court used to review the law, it is clear that the three-test framework does not survive intact when affirmative classifications are at issue.

It is interesting to note that once again racial issues are serving as pioneers in equal protection doctrine. In de jure negative classifications the special odiousness of racial laws led the Court to develop a new position of strict scrutiny. Later, when other groups tried also to benefit from the distant new position the Court backed away and created a middle-level moderate scrutiny test. Now again racial litigation (this time by whites) has led the Court to put a new quirk in the three-test framework by using a less strict standard of review for affirmative racial classifications. One would expect other groups (notably men contesting affirmative action for women) to bring grievances to court. It remains to be seen whether the Court will reply with the same synthesis (which is still unclear) for sex-based affirmative classifications as for racially based affirmative action.

DE FACTO CLASSIFICATIONS

A classic example of a de facto classification is the one used to introduce this chapter involving the aspiring police officer, Veragene Hardy. The reader will recall that Hardy was thwarted in her effort to get on the Oakland police force because she failed in her two attempts to scale a six-foot wall. She brought suit under the equal protection clause not because it was unconstitutional to distinguish between scalers and nonscalers but because, she argued, the classification fell more heavily on women than men and so amounted to a gender-based discrimination. Here one must look not to the wording of the law or regulation but to its *effect*, in contrast to de jure classifications, for which the content "on its face" is important.

It is possible that a large number of classifications have piggyback or de facto classifications attached to them. As with any constitutional question the doctrinal issue involves drawing a line between all-out warfare on a problem and doing nothing about it. The Court is neither absolutist nor escapist; generally it will meet a problem with a midway solution of one form or another. Thus, it recognizes the existence of de facto discrimination, but its approach has been more diluted than with de jure classifications. One can conclude this is one area in which Fourteenth Amendment equal protection is not forcefully applied.

The Court first considered the constitutional implications of de facto discrimination in the context of school segregation. *Brown v. Board of Education* had struck down de jure segregation as practiced in the southern states, but then an ironic thing happened. The country started seeing bastions of racially segregated schools not in the deep South but in the northern cities where de jure segregation had never been practiced. The phenomenon was a typical example of de facto discrimination in that it was directly the result of racially imbalanced housing, which had occurred by law.[59] Schools in this country are neighborhood schools and neighborhoods in the northern cities were black or white in part because city codes had forbidden whites from selling to blacks. Small wonder, then, that black neighborhoods begat black schools and white areas created predominantly white schools. Litigants went to court with the equal protection clause in tow, claiming that the Fourteenth Amendment forbade de facto discrimination. The Court's response to civil rights groups was not reassuring in that it said the Fourteenth Amendment forbids only *intentional* de facto segregation, not school segregation that is the unintentional result of imbalanced housing.[60]

It is very hard for litigants to prove a malevolent intent on the part of legislators. Thus it was a relief to civil rights activists that in two subsequent decisions the Court made it easier for them to show intentional segregation. First, if a school district at one time segregated by law, stopped doing so, but still remained segregated, the Court would *presume* the district intended to discriminate.[61] By presuming a discriminatory intent the Court shifts the burden to the state to prove it is not intentionally discriminating. Whoever bears the burden of proof in a dispute is at a disadvantage. Second, the Court will make this presumption for an entire school district even if only a "significant proportion" of it was once segregated by law.[62]

Here again racial activists were pioneers in equal protection doctrine. The Court's response to their claims was not forceful, but it did amount to a new position because for the first time the Court said the Fourteenth Amendment attacked at least one type of de facto discrimination—intentional discrimination. Would it take the same position for sex-based de facto discrimination? It did in a decision that brought racial and sexual classifications to the same point in equal protection doctrine,[63] but the Court has not gone further and made it easier for women's groups by shifting the burden to the state. Thus, once again the Court has taken a new position (point C synthesis) for race but a less forceful position for gender-based discrimination. Like an inchworm, equal protection doctrine moves forward and back, all the while showing a basic gradation: it exudes more clout for racial than other classifications.

How does all of this affect Veragene Hardy? Her appeal got no further than the California Supreme Court; that body held there was no de facto discrimination in the case.[64] At issue was not a gender-based classification, held the court, but rather a classification "between those persons—male and female—who can climb the wall and those—again of both sexes—who cannot." Thus, only minimum scrutiny need be applied and the state had a rational reason for requiring its officers to be able to climb fences the height of others in the city of Oakland. "The job analysis survey, upon which the physical performance test is based, indicated Oakland police officers in routine performance of their duties must occasionally scale walls or fences. With a city fence limit of six feet, it is reasonable to require police officer applicants to scale a six-foot wall as a prerequisite to becoming an Oakland police officer."

To be sure, the Court has left equal protection dulled as a weapon for attacking de facto racial and sexual discrimination, but this does not mean de facto classifications enjoy free reign. When the Constitution does not give the remedy for which interest groups hope, they still have ample opportunities through the legislative arena. One of the statutory giants in civil rights is the Civil Rights Act of 1964. One of its chapters, Title VII, made de jure discrimination in employment on the basis of race, religion, sex, and national origin illegal. Title VII has proved to be powerful indeed in promoting equality in the work force. Is it possible that Title VII can be read to forbid de facto discrimination as well? Could Veragene Hardy claim the Oakland police department violated a federal law by requiring a test that discriminated against women in effect if not in so many words?

Such a question was put to the Court in a case involving an intelligence test the Duke Power Company gave to its workers in deciding who should be hired and promoted.[65] Neutral on its face, the test in effect discriminated against blacks because a disproportionate number of them failed the test, probably because it was culturally biased. One worker challenged the test, claiming the company violated Title VII and that the law forbade de facto as well as de jure discrimination. In an important decision, given the significance of Title VII, the Court agreed. Sometime later, in a case involving height and weight requirements for prison guards that had the effect of weeding out all female applicants, the Court held that Title VII outlawed unintentional de facto discrimination against women too.[66] In this area, then, doctrine affecting race and women is the same and the point C′ synthesis for women mirrors the point C synthesis for race: to raise a claim under Title VII, the plaintiff need only prove that a de facto discrimination exists. He or she need not prove the employer intended to discriminate. Thus, Veragene Hardy challenged the fence scaling requirement on Title VII as well as equal protection grounds. Although it would be easier for the flow of this narrative to say that Hardy won her case, as it turns out the California high court ruled in favor of the police department, saying that no matter how one cut it fence-scaling is a skill the Oakland police department can require of its officers.

PRIVATE CLASSIFICATIONS

The last of the three cases used to introduce this chapter has yet to be discussed—that of Leroy Irvis, the black man refused service at the Harrisburg chapter of the Moose Lodge. The form of prejudice that causes groups to refuse to consort with members of other races is deep seated and is perhaps the hardest to root out of a society. It is also the type of discrimination the equal protection clause is least able to handle.

The discrimination foisted upon Leroy Irvis is "private," as opposed to the "public" classifications that have been the topic of the chapter to this point. It also occurs in the area of sex, when restaurants and clubs deny admission or entrance to women. The barrier placed before Debra Millenson, for example, is not unlike that felt by Irvis.[67] In 1972 Millenson went to a hotel restaurant known as the Men's Grill with some male and female companions and was refused service because of the Grill's policy of serving only men. The Grill proudly displayed its reasoning in the hotel advertisement inviting "Lunch for the liberated male." The advertisement went on to say, "Women, Bless them. They're the most delightful creatures on earth. But there are many times when a man prefers the company of other men. To discuss business, for instance, politics, sports, or, of course . . . women." Perhaps men do like to dine in the company of their own sex; perhaps whites do find it important to bar racial minorities from the doors of their clubs. But such closed clubs and establishments pose enough of a danger to the groups excluded to send them to court, basing their claims, among other things, on equal protection.

A century ago the Court examined the words of the Fourteenth Amendment, which say "no State" shall deny to its citizens the equal protection of the laws, and concluded that the amendment limits only public discrimination of the sort at issue in *Loving v. Virginia* and *Levy v. Louisiana.*[68] Private discrimination practiced by individual citizens, businesses, and social groups fell outside of the Fourteenth Amendment's oversight. This left the private school free to deny admission to blacks and women, the social club free to set its own rules about who to admit, and the shopowner able to refuse to hire racial minorities. The Court handed down this ruling in a case involving a comprehensive congressional law that outlawed racial discrimination in hotels, restaurants, and other places of public accommodation. Congress had based its authority to outlaw private discrimination on the Fourteenth Amendment, but the Court cut this authority out from under Congress by saying that the Fourteenth Amendment could only be used to attack discrimination enforced by the state. Freed from the oversight of the Fourteenth Amendment, white citizens went about excluding blacks from hotels, cafes, amusement parks, and swimming pools and so solidified a dual, black–white society in the South.

The Court's decision in 1883 enervated the Fourteenth Amendment, insofar as private discrimination was concerned, for the next sixty-one years. Then in 1944 the Court opened up an intriguing possibility. The case involved a classic example of discrimination: Texas refused to let blacks participate in Democratic party primaries, saying that the party was a private organization untouched by the Fourteenth Amendment.[69] Black plaintiffs claimed that the policy denied them a number of rights, including their Fourteenth Amendment right to equal protection. The Court agreed that the party itself was private, but it noted that the party's functions were so closely imbedded with Texas's election activities—which are public—as to make "party action . . . the action of the state." It then struck down the discrimination on the basis of the Fifteenth Amendment. Despite the fact that the decision ultimately rested on the Fifteenth and not the Fourteenth Amendment, it was suggestive of other things, namely this question: might discrimination that appears to be private be so tightly interwoven with state policy as to be public discrimination and therefore forbidden by the Fourteenth Amendment?

Four years later the Court affirmed this possibility by holding that private discrimination becomes public when the discriminators use the courts to enforce their prejudice.[70] The two decisions framed the concept of state action. It occurs when the state is so involved with a private discrimination as to be responsible for it. If the state is responsible for the discriminatory practice, then the practice is open to Fourteenth Amendment review. Here was a way for litigants to get around the Court's 1883 ruling: if they could prove state action, they stood a chance of getting the practice reversed on constitutional grounds. Thus, Leroy Irvis claimed, in ways to be discussed below, that the state was ultimately responsible for the Moose Lodge's refusal to admit and serve blacks, and Debra Millenson claimed the state was responsible for her inability to be served in the Men's Grill.

The problem facing judges in state action cases is to decide at which point an activity shifts from the private to the public sphere. Some activities are clearly private, such as a homeowner's decision not to invite people of other races to his or her house for dinner. Others are clearly public, such as a city's refusal to hire racial minorities for government jobs. But what about the Moose Lodge, that private fraternal organization with a constitution limiting membership to morally righteous white males? The club may be private on its face, but it does interact with the state in some capacity; for example, its meeting place is subject to state fire code inspection, is taxed by the state, and serves liquor after applying for and receiving a liquor license from the state. This activity falls into the fuzzy grey area between clearly private and clearly public practices. But then again even the racist homeowner pays taxes. One can make the case that some degree of government involvement underlies all of our activities.[71] At what point does mere state involvement turn to state responsibility? As Figure 5.4 shows, a threshold point must be made in order to tell when Fourteenth Amendment protection comes into play. This is the doctrinal question in cases of private discrimination.

The Court has offered a three-part test for deciding when state action has occurred:[72]

(1) the state involvement must be "significant";[73]

(2) the involvement must be explicit, as when the state "put its weight on the side of the [activity] by ordering it";[74] and

(3) the state must have intended to discriminate.[75]

The test is fairly rigid and under it very few acts amount to state action. What, though, does the test mean for Debra Millenson and Leroy Irvis? Irvis based his state action claim on the liquor license held by the

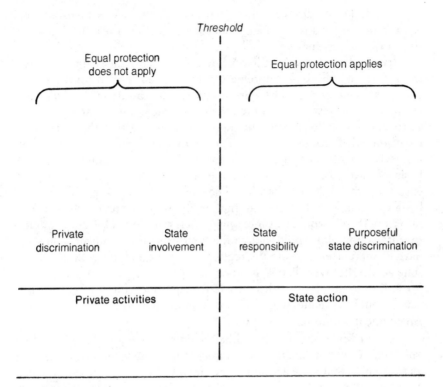

Threshold

Equal protection
does not apply

Equal protection applies

Private
discrimination

State
involvement

State
responsibility

Purposeful
state discrimination

Private activities

State action

FIGURE 5.4
CONTINUUM OF DISCRIMINATION FROM
PRIVATE TO PUBLIC

Harrisburg chapter of the Moose Lodge. In Pennsylvania, as in most states, the government regulates the sale of liquor. A business must obtain a license before being allowed to sell liquor and getting a license involves some deference to state regulations. In Pennsylvania, for example, a liquor licensee must follow building code rules, give the names of its employees to the state, and forbid "lewd, immoral or improper entertainment" in order to keep the license. Moreover, and this was the crowning point for the lower court's decision that Irvis did have a state action claim, the liquor licensee of a social club may keep the license only if he or she will "adhere to all the provisions of [the club's] constitution and by-laws." This means the Moose Lodge *had* to discriminate to keep its license. In the eyes of the U.S. District Court, this rule and the other regulations showed that Pennsylvania had "insinuated itself into a position of interdependence" with the Moose Lodge and was responsible for its discrimination. Since state action was involved, the equal protection clause applied. Under strict scrutiny, the refusal to serve Irvis was unconstitutional.

Irvis's victory was short-lived, however, because the Lodge appealed the ruling and the U.S. Supreme Court reversed.[76] Here one sees the continued reluctance of the Court to venture into the arena of private discrimination. Its test says that the state involvement must be so significant as to be akin to "ordering" the discrimination and that the state must have "intended" to discriminate. The Court could find no evidence that Pennsylvania used its liquor code intentionally to discriminate on the basis of race; moreover, its activities did not "in any way foster or encourage racial discrimination." The Court did look skeptically on the by-laws argument and agreed that if the state were to enforce the provision then it would be sanctioning discrimination. This does amount to state action and would violate the Fourteenth Amendment. Thus we have it: mere licensing and the regulations that go along with it are not state action, but were Pennsylvania to deny a license to the Moose Lodge for failing to go along with its by-laws requiring whites-only, then the state would be endorsing racial discrimination and the Fourteenth Amendment would come into play.

Debra Millenson also based her claim on the liquor license held by the Men's Grill but she, too, was unsuccessful. The federal court hearing her case held that state action was not involved because Millenson failed to show that the "state licensing system encourages, mandates, or affirmatively authorizes the admission policies of the grill." It is interesting to compare her case with one brought by Nely Johnson against another Men's Grill, this one in Milwaukee.[77] Johnson and her friends periodically tried to be seated and served in the Grill but were always refused. The owner decided to take legal action in order to stop the disruption so he got in touch with the Assistant City Attorney and police. Together they worked up a plan for the owner to call the police if the women refused to leave his restaurant; then the officers would get the women's names and give the list to the owner, who in turn would take legal action against the women. When Johnson went to the restaurant in the summer of 1972 the owner put the plan into action, calling the police and getting the names of the women from the officer. Johnson went to court to enjoin the male-only policy; the court said that in this case state action was involved, the equal protection clause was binding, and that the exclusion of women failed to stand under the moderate scrutiny test. The key here is the procedure, which put the Assistant City Attorney and the police in a position of *enforcing* a discrimination.

If the equal protection clause is not a good bet for the Irvises and Millensons of the country, they might try the legislative arena instead. For private discrimination, as for de facto discrimination, laws provide relief when the Constitution does not. It will be recalled that Congress's first attempt to outlaw private dicrimination ended when the Court said the Fourteenth Amendment did not give Congress authority to pass such a law.[78] A century later Congress passed a similar law, only this time it grounded its authority in the Constitution's commerce clause, reasoning that proprietors of hotels, restaurants, and transportation facilities interfered with the flow of human commerce from state to state when they prevented blacks from sleeping, eating, and traveling with whites. The Court upheld the law as a legitimate exercise of congressional power.[79] The same law, the Civil Rights Act of 1964, forbids job discrimination on the basis of race, color, religion, sex, or national origin. It reaches all businesses employing more than fifteen persons and is an effective way of attacking private discrimination in the work place.

Congress outlawed another form of private discrimination—white homeowners refusing to sell homes to black buyers—under the authority of the Thirteenth Amendment;[80] the Court upheld portions of it in a case alleging discrimination against white employees[81] and in the case of a private school that refused to admit black students.[82] Congress has also hit at various types of private discrimination against women. Title IX of the Educational Amendments Act is the most encompassing. It denies federal funds to schools—including private schools—practicing sexual discrimination in hiring of workers, counseling of students, sports programs, and other activities. The law does not affect private schools that do not receive federal funds, however, nor does it have much weight for private schools that receive only a small amount of federal funding and would rather do without the money than cope with the rules of Title IX. Moreover, as things now stand, the law does not forbid boys-only and girls-only schools below the college level.[83]

In short, in the area of private discrimination racial litigants once again acted as the pioneers by setting legal grievances in action. The Court responded with its state action doctrine—not a forceful position but at least a move away from the status quo—and created a point C synthesis. Later, when women attacked private discrimination too, the Court responded with the same synthesis. Thus, doctrine for racial and sexual classifications seems to be the same, and equal protection emerges as a somewhat dulled instrument for reaching private discrimination. For private discrimination as for de facto discrimination, legislative remedies seem to be preferable.

SUMMARY

The Fourteenth Amendment was framed and ratified shortly after the Civil War with the newly emancipated American black in mind.[84] It, together with the Thirteenth Amendment, which forbade slavery, and the Fifteenth Amendment, which guaranteed voting rights to black citizens, was deliberately brought into the Constitution to secure equal rights for a class of people who had been treated as second- and third-class citizens. It therefore makes sense that blacks have long turned to the Fourteenth Amendment in their quest to make their theoretical equality a reality in a society plagued by stubborn pockets of racism. This has made blacks the pioneering force in equal protection doctrine; they, more than other litigants, have posed problematic questions to the courts and have motivated judges actively to frame and shape a body of law that gives substance to the equal protection guarantee. Less expected, however, has been the basic gradation in equal protection doctrine that judges have created between racial minorities and other groups claiming discrimination. Looking over the doctrine as a whole, one can see this basic gradation for de jure, de facto, and private discrimination, although it is clearest for de jure classifications. Its effect is to make the Fourteenth Amendment an instrument of greater weight for racial discrimination than for other types of discrimination.

The intra-liberty differences in equal protection can be illustrated and summarized by way of the dialectic triangle introduced in Figure 5.2. The core model for race has three points: A is the status quo (racial discrimination), B is the litigation by blacks asking the Court to use equal protection to attack the particular form of discrimination at issue (de jure, de facto, or private), and C is the Court's response if it chooses to make one. In dialectical terms, A is the thesis, B the antithesis, and C the synthesis. Once a synthesis has been reached for blacks, we assume that other groups will want to share the reward and will, if they suffer from the same type of discrimination, go to court citing point C as precedent for attacking discrimination against them. Since the most active litigants of late have been women, let us create a second triangle based on sexual classifications. Here A' is the status quo (sexual discrimination), B' the antithesis (litigation by people hurt from sex-based classifications who cite C as precedent), and C' the synthesis. If equal protection doctrine is to be the same for women as for blacks, C' will be the same as C. If equal protection doctrine is to be graduated, however, C' will be either more or less forceful than C. Table 5.2 summarizes gradations in equal protection doctrine for de jure, de facto, and private discrimination.

TABLE 5.2
GRADATIONS IN APPLICATION OF
FOURTEENTH AMENDMENT EQUAL
PROTECTION ACCORDING TO TARGET

Target	Synthesis	Sample case
DE JURE DISCRIMINATION		
Racial	Classifications are reviewed under *strict* scrutiny.	*Hirabayashi v. United States* (1943)
Sexual	Classifications are reviewed under *moderate* scrutiny.	*Reed v. Reed* (1971)
DE FACTO DISCRIMINATION		
Racial	The Fourteenth Amendment applies only if the discrimination is intentional.	*Arlington Heights v. Metropolitan Housing Development Corp.* (1977)
	The Court will presume intentional discrimination in any school system once segregated by law.	*Swann v. Charlotte-Mecklenburg Board of Education* (1972)
Sexual	The Fourteenth Amendment applies only if the discrimination is intentional.	*General Electric Co. v. Gilbert* (1976)
	The Court has not yet held it will presume intentional discrimination in situations involving previous gender discrimination.	
PRIVATE DISCRIMINATION		
Racial	The Fourteenth Amendment applies only if what appears to be private discrimination is in fact state action (the state is significantly and intentionally involved in the discrimination).	*Smith v. Allright* (1944); *Shelley v. Kraemer* (1948)
Sexual	The Court has not directly ruled on this, but lower courts have ruled the same as for private racial discrimination.	E.g., *Stearns v. Veterans of Foreign Wars,* 395 F.Supp. 138 (1975).

What Table 5.2 does not discuss is litigation by groups other than racial minorities and women. For the most part these groups, such as prisoners, homosexuals and the aged, have not persuaded the Court to develop a new synthesis for them, although they have enjoyed occasional victories. For example, aliens may count on strict scrutiny of laws discriminating against them and illegitimates may count on moderate scrutiny of discriminatory laws. On the other hand, groups such as homosexuals have received very little protection under the Fourteenth Amendment. Courts subject laws discriminating against homosexuals to minimum scrutiny and are unconcerned with de facto discrimination (for example, do antisodomy statutes in effect fall more heavily on

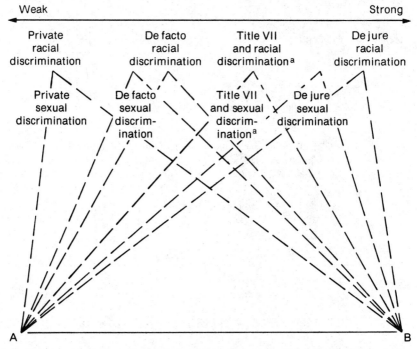

^aThe Court's position on Title VII is included to illustrate another of its positions when confronted with racial and sexual discrimination. The Court treats racial and sexual discrimination under Title VII the same: the statute forbids even unintentional discrimination against racial minorities (Griggs v. Duke Power Co. [1971]) and women (Dothard v Rawlinson [1977]).

FIGURE 5.5
GRADATION IN EQUAL PROTECTION'S
STRENGTH ACCORDING TO TYPE OF
CLASSIFICATION

homosexuals and therefore amount to a de facto discrimination?) or with private discrimination. If these groups are taken into account, one sees even more gradations in equal protection doctrine, with an advanced synthesis for blacks, a less advanced synthesis for women, and no new synthesis for other groups. This does not necessarily mean the Court has specifically rejected a new synthesis; it may only mean the Court has not yet had the occasion to rule on that point of law.

Table 5.2 also fails to discuss the gradations by type of classification. As noted at the beginning of this chapter, equal protection's strength varies by the group targeted, by the classification under review, *and* by the nature of the classification itself. Taking part II of Figure 5.2 as a model, we can impressionistically move point C to the right or left to reflect the relative clout of equal protection for de jure, de facto, and private classifications (see Figure 5.5). Figure 5.5 is another way of summarizing the theme used to introduce the chapter (Figure 5.1).

Questions for Thought

1. The Court strictly scrutinizes classifications based on race, religion, alienage, and national origin. The Justices say they will subject a criterion to strict scrutiny if it is an accident of birth, creates a discrete and insular minority, and has been purposely used by legislators to further a long and unfortunate history of discrimination. Read the original strict scrutiny cases—*Korematsu v. United States*, 293 U.S. 214 (1944) for race and *Graham v. Richardson*, 403 U.S. 365 (1971) for alienage. See also Justice Powell's opinion concurring in part and dissenting in part in *Keyes v. School District No. 1*, 413 U.S. 189, 220 (1973). What kind of evidence does the Court use to decide if the criterion meets the test stated above? Is the evidence as persuasive for alienage as for race? Read *Frontiero v. Richardson*, 411 U.S. 677 (1973), in which a Court majority failed to subject sex-based classifications to strict scrutiny. What kind of evidence did it look for there? What does *Frontiero* tell us about the values of the Justices? Is the Court's refusal to put sex-based classifications to strict scrutiny partly a "political" rather than a doctrinal decision?

2. The Court struck down a sex-based classification in *Reed v. Reed*, 404 U.S. 71 (1971). In *Reed* and in *Craig v. Boren*, 429 U.S. 190 (1975), the Court developed the "moderate scrutiny" test for reviewing burdensome sex-based laws. At the date of this writing, however, the Court has not decided under which standard to review *affirmative* sex-based policies designed to redress past discrimination against a sex by aiding members of that sex. See *Kahn v. Shevin*, 416 U.S. 351 (1974). Should the Court review affirmative sex-based

policies under the same standard—moderate scrutiny—as burdensome laws? Under strict scrutiny? Minimum scrutiny? Another standard altogether?

3. The Court says that criteria beyond an individual's control ("accidents of birth") should be strictly scrutinized. But most human traits are accidents of birth and it is unclear at what point they become off-limits for policy-makers. Consider the policy of Oral Roberts University that denies admission to fat people. The University's academic dean denies that the policy is discriminatory and says it affects only the "individual who is voluntarily overweight simply from eating too much too often." See *The New York Times*, October 9, 1977. But the director of the local chapter of the American Civil Liberties Union says the policy discriminates against "individuals with minor health problems, disabilities and imperfections." Some studies show that a person's diet in the first few months of life does much to determine that person's weight later in life. Inasmuch as a baby has no control over what it is fed, does this make obesity an accident of birth? If Oral Roberts University were a public institution, would its policy stand under the Fourteenth Amendment?

4. Most judges read marriage laws to say they only legalize contracts between men and women, not between men and men or women and women. This conforms with traditional definitions of marriage such as the English common-law view that marriage is a "voluntary union for life of one man to one woman to the exclusion of all others." See *The New York Times*, April 27, 1975, p. 49. How is marriage defined by statute in your state? Assume your state defines marriage as a bond between a man and a woman. Is this a sex-based law? Under what standard of review should it be scrutinized? Would it withstand Fourteenth Amendment review? Suppose the Equal Rights Amendment were added to the Constitution (the ERA reads in part that "Equality of rights under the law shall not be denied or abridged by the United States or by any State on account of sex"). Would laws limiting marriage to heterosexual unions stand under the ERA? Why or why not?

5. A male tennis player who used surgery and hormones to become Renee Richards, a *female* tennis player, tried to enter the U.S. Open Tennis Championships as a woman. The U.S. Tennis Association asked Ms. Richards to submit to the Barr body-sex determination test, which tells whether a person has two 'X" chromosomes, a mark of the female sex. The Tennis Association did not ask other players to submit to the test, however, and Ms. Richards claimed that the Association violated her rights under the state human rights law. *Richards v. U.S. Tennis Association*, 400 N.Y.S. 2d 267 (1977). Assume that Richards claimed the Tennis Association also violated her Fourteenth Amendment right to equal protection. Is a sex-based classification at issue? Under what standard should the policy be reviewed? Does it violate the Fourteenth Amendment?

NOTES

1. "[A]ll legislation involves classification." 16 Am.Jur. 2d, Constitutional Law, § 494 (1964).

2. *Sugarman v. Dowell,* 413 U.S. 634 (1973).

3. *Ulland v. Growe,* 262 N.W. 2d 412 (Minn. 1978).

4. *Williamson v. Lee Optical Co.,* 348 U.S. 483 (1955).

5. See *Massachusetts Board of Retirement v. Murgia,* 427 U.S. 307, 380 n.1 (1976).

6. 16 Am.Jur. 2d, Constitutional Law, § 489 (1964).

7. For example, in order to prevent "fraudulent" marriages in which a man and woman aware of the man's impending death marry solely so the wife will receive survivor's benefits when the husband dies, Congress inserted a section into the Social Security Act giving survivor's benefits only to a widow married more than nine months before her husband's death. *Weinberger v. Salfi,* 422 U.S. 749 (1975). The provision created a class by presuming that all short-term marriages were collusive. Congress meant the classification to simplify social security administration by freeing administrators from probing each suspicious marriage. After a short-term widow challenged the law on equal protection grounds, the Court upheld it, saying it furthered administrative efficiency. Ibid. (The Court noted that by creating a class Congress prevented "large numbers of individualized determinations.") The Justices admitted the law hurt some legitimate widows but said this cost was offset by the fact that the law helped others by preventing delays in social security benefits caused by investigation of possibly fraudulent marriages.

8. Paul Oberst, "The Strange Career of *Plessy v. Ferguson,*" 15 Ariz.L.Rev. 389, 413 (1973).

9. The Court struck down the provision in *United States Dept. of Agriculture v. Moreno,* 413 U.S. 528 (1973).

10. Discrimination in the neutral sense means to "distinguish accurately." *The Random House Dictionary of English Language* (New York: Random House, 1967). Discrimination in the prejudicial sense refers to a "prejudiced or prejudicial outlook, action, or treatment" when prejudice is "an opinion or leaning adverse to anything without just grounds or before sufficient knowledge" or "an irrational attitude of hostility directd against an individual, a group, a race, or their supposed characteristics." *Webster's New Collegiate Dictionary* (Springfield, Mass.: G. and C. Merriam, 1977).

11. The "prohibition of the Equal Protection Clause goes no further than the invidious discrimination." *Williamson v. Lee Optical,* 348 U.S. 483 (1953).

12. The due process clause of the Fourteenth and Fifth Amendments also guards against unfair laws; but litigants more often than not challenge classifications on equal protection grounds because this guarantee offers a "more explicit safeguard of prohibited unfairness" than due process. *Bolling v. Sharpe,* 347 U.S. 497, 499 (1954).

13. As interpreted by the Court, the Fifth Amendment due process clause, which limits the federal government, subsumes the notion of equal protection so litigants can challenge federal laws on equal protection grounds under the Fifth Amendment's auspices.

14. *Levy v. Louisiana,* 391 U.S. 68 (1968).

15. *Hardy v. Stumpf,* 576 P. 2d 1342 (1978).

16. *Irvis v. Moose Lodge #107*, 407 U.S. 163 (1972).

17. See *United States v. O'Brien*, 391 U.S. 367, 376-377 (1968).

18. *Hirabayashi v. United States*, 320 U.S. 81 (1943); *Korematsu v. United States*, 323 U.S. 214 (1944). *Hirabayashi* upheld a curfew imposed upon persons of Japanese ancestry; *Korematsu* upheld an executive order excluding all such people from military areas in California. The author of Note, "Of Interests, Fundamental and Compelling: The Emerging Constitutional Balance, 57 *Boston U.L.Rev.* 462 (1977) suggests that "only the interest of self-preservation" meets the compelling state interest test.

19. The extraordinary standard for free speech and some classifications both date to the same Footnote 4 in the case involving adulterated milk (see Chapter 2). In that note Justice Stone suggested that laws intruding on civil liberties ought to be examined more carefully than other laws; he mentioned laws affecting "discrete and insular minorities" in particular. *United States v. Carolene Products Co.*, 304 U.S. 144, 152 n.4 (1938). Six years later the Court graduated this parenthetical reference to majority doctrine by strictly scrutinizing a classification—one based on race—for the first time. *Korematsu v. United States*, 323 U.S. 214 (1944). The Court upheld the law but in passing noted that classifications that restrict a single racial group are "immediately suspect" and must be subjected to "the most rigid scrutiny."

20. *Loving v. Virginia*, 388 U.S. 1 (1967).

21. *Korematsu v. United States*, 323 U.S. 214 (1944).

22. *Weber v. Aetna Casualty and Surety*, 406 U.S. 164, 175 (1972).

23. *United States v. Carolene Products Co.*, 304 U.S. 144, 152-153 n.4 (1938).

24. Are the group's members "relatively powerless to protect their interests in the political process"? *San Antonio School District v. Rodriquez*, 411 U.S. at 105 (Marshall, J., dissenting).

25. Ibid.

26. *Oyama v. California*, 332 U.S. 633, 644-646 (1948).

27. *Graham v Richardson*, 403 U.S. 365 (1971). The Court reached this conclusion primarily because aliens are a "discrete and insular minority."

28. See, for example, *Skinner v. Oklahoma*, 316 U.S. 535 (1942).

29. *Griswold v. Connecticut*, 381 U.S. 479 (1965).

30. *Griswold v. Connecticut*, 381 U.S. 479 (1965). The First Amendment contributes the right of association (itself an unstated right), the Third the freedom from soldiers quartered in one's home, the Fourth the freedom from unreasonable searches and seizures, and the Fifth the freedom from forced self-incrimination. These freedoms form penumbras that create a right to privacy when combined with the Ninth Amendment's guarantee that rights exist other than those enumerated in the Constitution. See chapter 6 for a fuller discussion of the constitutional bases for the right to privacy.

31. *Shapiro v. Thompson*, 394 U.S. 618 (1969). Similarly, the right to vote is a "fundamental right because preservative of all rights." *Harper v. Virginia Board of Elections*, 383 U.S. 663 (1966).

32. If litigants are fighting to protect a fundamental right, they can also challenge the law's constitutionality under the particular guarantee designed to protect that right. Equal protection is not the only grounds for contesting an arbitrary classification; the wise litigant will challenge the law on other constitutional grounds too. For example, litigants who challenged a Chicago ordinance that forbade all picketers except labor

picketers from marching near a classroom raised both First and Fourteenth Amendment claims—the First Amendment because free expression was at stake and the Fourteenth Amendment because a classification between labor and nonlabor picketers was involved. As it turned out, the Court used a rigid standard of review based on First Amendment doctrine. *Police Department of Chicago v. Mosley*, 408 U.S. 922 (1972). Some commentators suggest that equal protection is superfluous when an explicit constitutional right is at stake. See Gerald Gunther, *Cases and Materials on Constitutional Law*, 9th ed. (Mineola, N.Y.: The Foundation Press, 1975), p. 789; and Laurence M. Tribe, *American Constitutional Law* (Mineola, N.Y.: The Foundation Press, 1978), p. 1006.

33. *Flemming v. Nestor*, 363 U.S. 603, 611 (1960).

34. *Skinner v. Oklahoma*, 316 U.S. 535 (1942).

35. *United States Department of Agriculture v. Moreno*, 413 U.S. 528 (1973).

36. *Eisenstadt v. Baird*, 405 U.S. 438 (1972).

37. *Andrews v. Drew Municipal Separate School District*, 507 F. 2d 611 (5th Cir. 1975).

38. *Yick Wo v. Hopkins*, 118 U.S. 356 (1886).

39. *Massachusetts Board of Retirement v. Murgia*, 427 U.S. 307 (1976).

40. See, for example, *Reed v. Reed*, 404, U.S. 71 (1971).

41. Actually the Court was unclear about the standard of review it used in *Levy* and its companion case, *Glona v. American Guarantee and Liability Insurance Co.*, 391 U.S. 73 (1968). For a clearer use of moderate scrutiny of classifications based on legitimacy of birth, see *Trimble v. Gordon*, 430 U.S. 762 (1977).

42. See 10 *Am.Jur. 2d*, Bastards, § 8 (1963).

43. *Goesaert v. Cleary*, 355 U.S. 464 (1948).

44. *Hoyt v. Florida*, 368 U.S. 57 (1961).

45. *Dred Scott v. Sandford*, 19 How. 303 (1857).

46. *Bradwell v. Illinois*, 16 Wall. 130 (1873). Wrote Justice Bradley in concurrence, the "paramount destiny and mission of woman are to fulfill the noble and benign offices of wife and mother. This is the law of the Creator."

47. Gunther, pp. 657-665.

48. See, for example, *Massachusetts Board of Retirement v. Murgia*, 427 U.S. 307 (1976). In dissent, Justice Marshall cites several Court passages lauding the right to work: "[The right to work] is of the very essence of the personal freedom and opportunity that it was the purpose of the [Fourteenth Amendment] to secure." *Truax v. Raich*, 239 U.S. 33 (1915). "[The right to work is] an inalienable right; it was formulated as such under the phrase 'pursuit of happiness' in the Declaration of Independence. . . . This right is a large ingredient in the civil liberties of the citizen." *Butchers' Union Co. v. Crescent City Co.*, 111 U.S. 746 (1884). "Liberty means more than freedom from servitude, and the constitutional guarantee is an assurance that the citizen shall be protected in the right to use his powers of mind and body in any lawful calling." *Smith v. Texas*, 233 U.S. 630 (1914). See also *Wisconsin v. Yoder*, 406 U.S. 205, 213 (1972), in which the Court noted that "[p]roviding public schools ranks at the very apex of the function of a state." The Court declined to call the right to education fundamental in *Brown v. Board of Education*, 347 U.S. 483, 493 (1954). In *Weinberger v. Salfi*, 422 U.S. 749, 772 (1970), it declined to call the right to welfare fundamental ("a noncontractual claim to receive funds from the public treasury enjoys no constitutionally protected status"). See also *Dandridge v. Williams*, 397 U.S. 471 (1970).

49. *Reed v. Reed,* 404 U.S. 71 (1971).

50. Gunther, p. 661.

51. See note 41 above.

52. 347 U.S. 483 (1954).

53. *Brown* only required "state neutrality allowing 'freedom of choice' as to schools to be attended so long as the State itself assured that the choice was genuinely free of official restraint." *Keyes v. School District No. 1,* 413 U.S. 189, 220 (1973) (Powell, J., concurring in part and dissenting in part).

54. *Green v. New Kent County School Board,* 391 U.S. 430 (1968). See also *Keyes v. School District,* 413 U.S. at 220-221 (Powell, J., concurring in part and dissenting in part).

55. Executive Order 11357.

56. 438 U.S. 265 (1978).

57. Justices Stevens, Stewart, Rehnquist, and Chief Justice Burger based their decisions on statutory rather than constitutional grounds and did not address the constitutional question. Justices Brennan, White, Marshall, and Blackmun looked for and found an "important and articulated" purpose and suggested a standard of review " 'not strict in theory and fatal in fact,' . . . but strict and searching nonetheless." Justice Powell argued for strict scrutiny.

58. *Fullilove v. Klutznik,* 65 L.Ed. 2d 902 (1980). See also *United Jewish Organizations of Williamsburgh, Inc. v. Carey,* 430 U.S. 144 (1977), in which the Court used less than strict scrutiny to uphold New York's reapportionment plan that used race to enhance black voting representation. Like affirmative action, the plan benefitted a racial group at the same time it burdened another group, in this case New York's Hasidic Jewish community (the plan divided the Hasidic community into two districts and split its voting strength).

59. De facto school segregation is "racially identifiable schools whose imbalance is the product of external factors other than the force of law or the action of school authorities." Note, "De Facto School Segregation and the 'State Action' Requirement: A Suggested New Approach," 48 *Ind.L.J.* 304, 312 (1973).

60. *Village of Arlington Heights v. Metropolitan Housing Development Corp.,* 429 U.S. 262 (1977).

61. *Swann v. Charlotte-Mecklenburg Board of Education,* 402 U.S. 1 (1972). See also *Columbus Board of Education v. Penick,* 61 L.Ed. 2d 666 (1979), in which the Court held that Columbus, Ohio, was still under the obligation to disestablish school segregation that was purposely imposed before the 1954 decision of *Brown v. Board of Education.*

62. *Keys v. School District No. 1,* 413 U.S. 189 (1973). The Court limited this line of law in *Milliken v. Bradley,* 418 U.S. 717 (1974), however, by holding that the city's obligation stopped at interdistrict busing when the record gave no evidence of the city's intent to segregate across district lines. The Court did suggest interdistrict remedies might be in order "where the racially discriminatory acts of one or more school districts *caused* racial segregation in an adjacent district, or where district lines have been deliberately drawn on the basis of race" (emphasis added).

63. *Califano v. Goldfarb,* 430 U.S. 199 (1977).

64. *Hardy v. Stumpf,* 576 P. 2d 1342 (1978).

65. *Griggs v. Duke Power Co.*, 401 U.S. 424 (1971).

66. *Dothard v. Rawlinson*, 433 U.S. 321 (1977).

67. *Millenson v. New Motel Monteleone, Inc.*, 475 F. 2d 736 (1973).

68. *Civil Rights Cases*, 109 U.S. 3 (1883). The Court struck down a sweeping congressional statute forbidding theaters, parks, public transportation, hotels, and other businesses from denying access to blacks, saying that the Fourteenth Amendment authorized Congress only to redress "the operation of state laws, [and] the action of state offices."

69. *Smith v. Allright*, 321 U.S. 649 (1944).

70. *Shelley v. Kraemer*, 334 U.S. 1 (1948).

71. The Court recognizes that some state interaction with private activities is inevitable and must be tolerated: "The Court has never held . . . that discrimination by an otherwise private entity would be violative of the Equal Protection Clause if the private entity receives any sort of benefit or service at all from the State, or if it is subject to state regulation in any degree whatever. Since state-furnished services include such necessities of life as electricity, water, and police and fire protection, such a holding would utterly emasculate the distinction between private as distinguished from state conduct. . . ." *Moose Lodge #107 v. Irvis*, 407 U.S. 163, 173 (1972).

72. The Court makes clear, however, that it "cannot apply a precise formula" to decide when the state is responsible for discrimination and says this would be an "impossible task" which it has "never attempted." *Burton v. Wilmington Parking Authority*, 365 U.S. 715, 722 (1961). See Note, "State Action and the Burger Court," 60 *Virginia L.Rev.* 840, 841 (1974), and Justice Douglas in *Keyes v. School District No. 1*, 413 U.S. 189, 215 (1973) (dissenting), quoting *United States v. Texas Education Agency*, 467 F. 2d 848: "We need not define the quantity of state participation which is a prerequisite to a finding of constitutional violation. Like the legal concepts of 'the reasonable man,' 'due care,' . . . and 'beyond a reasonable doubt,' the necessary degree of state involvement is incapable of precise definition and must be defined on a case-by-case basis."

73. *Burton v. Wilmington Parking Authority*, 365 U.S. 715, 722 (1961).

74. *Jackson v. Metropolitan Edison Co.*, 419 U.S. 345 (1974). See David Z. Nevin, "State Action: The Significant State Involvement Doctrine After *Moose Lodge* and *Jackson*," 14 *Idaho L.Rev.* 647, 649 (1978).

75. See Note, "De Facto School Segregation . . . ," at 311.

76. *Moose Lodge #107 v. Irvis*, 407 U.S. 163 (1972).

77. *Johnson v. Heinemann Candy Co., Inc.*, 402 F.Supp. 714 (1975).

78. *Civil Rights Cases*, 109 U.S. 3 (1883), striking down the Civil Rights Act of 1875.

79. *Heart of Atlanta Motel, Inc. v. United States*, 379 U.S. 241 (1964), decided along with *Katzenbach v. McClung*, 379 U.S. 294 (1964).

80. *Jones v. Alfred H. Mayer Co.*, 392 U.S. 409 (1968). At issue were restrictive covenants that prevented blacks from buying property from whites.

81. *McDonald v. Santa Fe Trail Transportation Co.*, 427 U.S. 273 (1976).

82. *Runyon v. McCrary*, 427 U.S. 160 (1976).

83. The Court divided equally on the issue and therefore let stand a lower court decision holding that sex-segregated schools below the college level are permissible. *Vorchheimer v. Philadelphia*, 430 U.S. 703 (1977).

84. In the *Slaughter-House Cases,* 16 Wall. 36 (1873), the Court noted that "the one pervading purpose" of the Thirteenth, Fourteenth, and Fifteenth Amendments was to secure "the freedom of the slave race, the security and firm establishment of that freedom, and the protection of the newly made freeman and citizen from the oppression of those who had formerly exercised unlimited dominion over them." In *Strauder v. West Virginia,* 100 U.S. 303 (1880), the Court noted that Congress "primarily designed" the Fourteenth Amendment to protect the "colored race." It reiterated its earlier words from the *Slaughter-House Cases:* "we doubt very much whether any action of a State, not directed by way of discrimination against the negroes, as a class, will ever be held to come within the purview of [the Equal Protection Clause]."

CHAPTER SIX

The Evolution of Constitutional Rights |

Rights

People speak casually about rights, claiming they have the "right" to receive welfare, discipline a child, use contraceptives, ride a motorcycle without a helmet, or do any number of other everyday activities. Technically, however, an interest is only a right if it is legally enforceable. In legal parlance a right is "that which one has a legal claim to do,"[1] it is "firmly established" in the law, and it is "undisputed or undisputable."[2] Thus, to speak precisely about rights one must keep in mind the difference between claimed and actual rights.[3] One must also be aware that each broadly claimed right may in fact have several subunits, some of which are recognized legally and others not. Consider, for example, the broadly claimed right to treatment. This generic right has many subcomponents. Is one referring to a right to medical treatment? psychiatric care? preventive medicine? Does one have in mind the right to treatment for all citizens? or only institutionalized people? only poor people? Also, it is often the case that the subunits of a broadly claimed right have differing legal statuses. The Supreme Court has held that institutionalized mental patients have a limited *constitutional* right to psychiatric treatment,[4] for example, and some states have laws giving mental patients a *statutory* entitlement to psychiatric care.[5]

185

The pool of claimed or prospective rights changes with the flow of political issues. One rarely heard of a "right" to die, for example, before medical advances made it possible for a person to linger indefinitely in a life–death hiatus and before court action focused national attention on Karen Ann Quinlan, a comatose woman suffering brain death but kept alive by an artificial respirator.[6] The denouement of claimed rights differs; some fade as political interest in them dies, others languish under repeated litigation, and only some actually receive legal recognition. Of the forms of recognition accorded a right — generally constitutional, statutory, or common law — constitutional recognition is the most prized. A right grounded in the Constitution evokes special authority and respect. When balanced against other social interests, the scales automatically tilt in its favor with courts requiring the state to show a "compelling" interest before limiting it. Moreover, a constitutional right applies nationally by virtue of its association with the "Supreme Law of the Land."

The constitutional path is elusive. Few claimed rights actually graduate to that status, yet the Court does occasionally "add" new rights to the Constitution through its interpretation of the individual guarantees in that document. After the Supreme Court broadly defines an unstated constitutional right, it, along with the lower courts, then entertains questions, rules on points of law, and adds meaning and substance to the roughly hewn generic right. The present chapter reviews the methods by which the Court recognizes unstated constitutional rights; the chapter then reviews the contribution of lower courts to the development of new constitutional rights. The chapter uses one important unstated right — the right to privacy — as a case study to illustrate the making of a constitutional right; it then focuses on the right of the individual to resist medical care to illustrate how lower courts have shaped and enriched the meaning of one subunit of the right to privacy.

CONSTITUTIONAL RIGHTS AND THE SUPREME COURT

Many claim the Constitution's skeletal nature is its strength. "For the Constitution to go beyond elementary provisions," said Woodrow Wilson, "would be to lose elasticity and adaptability. . . . If it could not stretch itself to the measure of the times, it must be thrown off and left behind, as a by-gone device; and there can, therefore, be no question that our Constitution has proved lasting because of its simplicity."[7] Similarly, Justice Jackson wrote, "the great expounders of the Constitution have always insisted that the strength and vitality of the Constitution stem from the fact that its principles are adaptable to changing events,"[8] and another jurist opined that the Constitution "does little more than lay a foundation of principles. . . . It is a corner-stone, not a complete building; or, rather, to return to the old figure, it is a root, not a perfect vine."[9]

The belief that the Constitution ought to bend with the times else it become brittle and fractured gives a mandate to the Court as the Constitution's overseer to keep it vital through interpretation. "We are under a Constitution," said Charles Evans Hughes, "but the Constitution is what the judges say it is."[10] Tempering the Court's directive to infuse contemporary values into the document are judicial norms of self-restraint that, among other things, warn courts not to rule on a constitutional question if it can be avoided, not to entertain constitutional questions in a friendly lawsuit, not to rule on a moot dispute, nor to rule on a political question more appropriately falling within Congress's jurisdiction.[11] The Justices caution that they must not "hastily import" their own views into the Constitution[12] or interfere with its basic continuity.[13]

Individual Justices and Courts respond differently to the mixed permissiveness and restraint under which they operate. The Vinson Court stepped boldly when it reversed the presumption of constitutionality for laws intruding on First Amendment rights and so did the Warren Court when it strictly scrutinized racial classifications. The Burger Court has read the Fourteenth Amendment broadly in its busing decisions but has declined to expand several avenues of doctrine handed down by its predecessor, such as its use of moderate rather than strict scrutiny on gender-based classifications. Of the many approaches to constitutional expansion jurists have taken at one time or another, seven stand out (see Table 6.1). The literal approach is the narrowest and jurists who use it confine their reasoning to a literal reading of the constitutional guarantee at issue, asking what meaning the words themselves suggest.[14] Although the approach may have dramatic results,[15] as when Justice Black literally read the First Amendment to mean Congress shall pass "no" law intruding on free speech, the approach admits few unstated rights into the Constitution. Under the historical approach jurists will broaden the meaning of individual guarantees if they are persuaded the framers intended such growth to take place;[16] for example, the Court examined the framers' intentions in a case asking whether a twelve-person jury was essential to the Sixth Amendment's guarantee of a fair trial. Concluding that the twelve-person jury was an "historical accident" only, the Court held that the defendant could have a fair trial with fewer than twelve members on his jury.[17]

TABLE 6.1
APPROACHES TO AN EXPANDED
INTERPRETATION OF STATED
CONSTITUTIONAL RIGHTS

Approach	Essence	Sample use
Literal	Is this right inherent in the words of the Constitution themselves?	The right to free speech is absolute in light of the First Amendment's warning that Congress shall pass "no law" abridging the freedom of speech. *Smith v. California* (Black, J., dissenting)
Historical	Do debates and other documents show the framers intended this interpretation?	A trial can be fair with fewer than twelve jurors; records show the tradition of twelve jurors originated by historical accident, not by a rational calculation by the Constitution's framers. *Williams v. Florida* (1970)
Zone	Does this right inhere in a zone surrounding a stated constitutional right?	The right to receive information inheres in the right to free speech. *West Virginia Board of Pharmacy v. Virginia Citizens Consumer Council, Inc.* (1976)

The zone approach ventures farther from the Constitution's text than the previous approaches. Jurists who use it see unstated, subsidiary rights radiating from a stated constitutional right in a penumbra or zone. The Court holds that freedom of association radiates from the First Amendment freedom of assembly, and the right to receive information is a logical extension of the right to free speech. With the "overlapping zone" approach, Justices combine individual zones to create new unstated rights. For example, Justice Douglas grounded a right to marital privacy in the combined privacy zones emanating from the First, Third, Fourth, Fifth, and Ninth Amendments.[18] A fifth approach uses the Ninth Amendment as an enabling clause to admit unstated rights into the Con-

TABLE 6.1 continued

Approach	Essence	Sample use
Overlapping zones	Do two or more zones together create an unstated constitutional right?	The right to marital privacy inheres in the combined zones of privacy emanating from the First, Third, Fourth, Fifth, and Ninth Amendments. *Griswold v. Connecticut* (1965)
Ninth Amendment as enabling clause	Is the right held in reserve by the Ninth Amendment's guarantee that "[t]he enumeration in the Constitution, of certain rights, shall not be construed to deny or disparage others retained by the people"?	The right to marital privacy lodges in the Ninth Amendment. *Griswold v. Connecticut* (1965) (Goldberg, J., concurring)
Due process as enabling clause	Is the right a part of Fifth or Fourteenth Amendment "life, liberty or property"?	The woman's right to decide whether to bear a child inheres in Fourteenth Amendment liberty. *Roe v. Wade* (1973)
Natural law	Is the right a timeless feature of "our modern conception of human being"?	Fourteenth Amendment liberty includes rights "so rooted in the traditions and conscience of our people as to be ranked as fundamental." *Palko v. Connecticut* (1937)

stitution.[19] Justice Goldberg grounded the right to marital privacy in it,[20] and litigants have unsuccessfully claimed that the Ninth Amendment allows a constitutional right to a clean environment.[21] A sixth, and most common, approach uses Fifth and Fourteenth Amendment due processes as an enabling clause for admitting new rights into the Constitution. Due process warns the government not to deprive a person of life, liberty, or property without due process of law. As the Court decides whether a litigant's interest is part of this trilogy of rights, it opens up the Constitution to a broader meaning; for example, it grounded a woman's right to an abortion in Fourteenth Amendment liberty.[22] The natural law approach ventures the farthest from the Constitution's text; under it

Liberty

jurists will admit as part of the Constitution rights arising from the "philosophy, history and traditions of Western democracy"[23] that are "essential to our modern conception of human being."[24]

Of these avenues for broadening the Constitution's meaning, due process stands out as the most heavily traveled and might even be called the keystone of the expanding Constitution. Due process is an "elusive concept"[25] that is "less rigid and more fluid" than other guarantees in the Bill of Rights.[26] In spirit it is thought to be a "natural" or "fundamental" right that exists in the state of nature and need not be written to be owed to all people.[27] In fact it dates from twelfth-century English common law and more precisely the Magna Carta of 1215, which states in part that the rights of no "free man" will be deprived "except by the lawful judgment of his peers and by the law of the land." "Due process of law" means today what the "law of the land" meant in King John's time:[28] it forbids the state from acting arbitrarily, capriciously, or unreasonably and it embraces timeless notions of justice, fairness, and decency.[29] The Court has used it both to identify substantive new rights and to widen the jurisdiction of stated constitutional rights.

Recognizing New Rights

A litigant claiming due process protection must first persuade the Court that the state has intruded on his or her life, liberty, or property.[30] If the Court agrees that the particular interest is part of this trilogy, it essentially brings that interest into the Constitution's ambit and gives it constitutional status. As interpreted, "life" means more than physical existence; it also means "the right to enjoy life."[31] "Property" means more than mere ownership; it also includes the "right to acquire, use, and dispose" of one's possessions.[32] "Liberty" is a "broad and majestic" right to which the Court gives a "spacious" case.[33] Fourteenth Amendment liberty includes freedom of contract[34] as well as personal freedoms such as the parent's liberty to educate his or her child as the parent sees fit,[35] freedom of speech,[36] and the right to bodily integrity,[37] travel,[38] live and work where one wishes,[39] and to "acquire useful knowledge, to marry, establish a home, and bring up children."[40] It even includes the right of a woman to end her pregnancy.[41]

Litigants base due process claims either on the procedures by which the state deprived them of their life, liberty, or property or on the content of the authoritative law itself. The first is called procedural due process; it "refers to the manner in which a law, an ordinance, an administrative practice, or a judicial task is carried out."[42] Discussed in Chapter 7, procedural due process warns the government to follow fair, reasonable, and noncapricious steps before depriving a person of life, liberty, or property.[43] For example, California police failed to meet even minimum due process standards when they forcibly pumped a suspect's stomach in their search for morphine capsules;[44] Illinois did the same when it refused to allow a suspect to talk with his lawyer despite his repeated requests to do so.[45]

The second grounds on which litigants bring claims is called substantive due process; it refers to the substance of a law or practice that deprives a person of life, liberty, or property. In substantive review, the Court examines the law to ensure that it is not "unreasonable, arbitrary or capricious."[47] If a fundamental right is at stake, the Court requires the state's interest in passing the law to be compelling, the law to have a real and substantial relation to the legislative purpose, and the means chosen by the legislature to impinge upon the right the least of all means available to the state for meeting its goal.[48] If a nonfundamental right is at stake, the Court requires only that the state's interest be "permissible," the law to have a "rational" relationship to the legislature's purpose,[49] and the law to be one over which the legislature has jurisdiction.[50] In short, the Court uses the due process clause to open up the Constitution when it decides a litigant's claimed right is (1) fundamental and (2) is part of life, liberty, or property (see Figure 6.1).

Widening the Jurisdiction of Stated Rights

The First Amendment states that "Congress" shall not infringe on speech, press, assembly, or religion; it is the only provision in the Bill of Rights explicitly to say which government it limits. The other amendments more obliquely state that "excessive bail shall not be imposed" or "the right of the people to be secure in their persons . . . shall not be violated."[51] Whatever uncertainty the lack of nouns raised the Court clarified in the 1833 case of *Barron v. Baltimore*, in which it held that the Bill of Rights limited only the federal government.[52] The holding may have indeed comported with the framers' intent, but it meant that citizens enjoyed their supposedly inalienable rights only vis-á-vis the federal government and not at the hands of state governments.

When Congress framed the Thirteenth, Fourteenth, and Fifteenth Amendments after the Civil War, it made clear that the new restrictions applied to the states. The Fourteenth Amendment states that no "state" shall deprive a person of life, liberty, or property without due process of law and, when paired with the Fifth Amendment's holding that the federal government shall not deprive a person of life, liberty, or property without due process of law, gives the due process guarantee universal

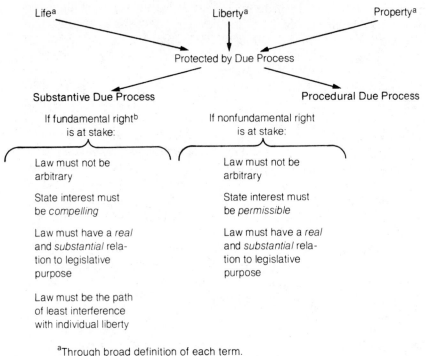

^aThrough broad definition of each term.

^bThrough recognition of fundamental right for strict due process review.

FIGURE 6.1
PLACES IN DUE PROCESS REVIEW WHERE THE
COURT CAN BROADEN CONSTITUTIONAL RIGHTS

application in this country. Less clear, however, is whether the meaning of life, liberty, and property is the same for the federal and state governments. Shortly after the Fourteenth Amendment's ratification, litigants went to court claiming that Fourteenth Amendment life, liberty, and property subsumed all the provisions in the Bill of Rights.[53] If the Court were to accept the argument, the decision would effectively undo *Barron v. Baltimore* and bring the state governments under the same restrictions as the federal government. The Court initially resisted the suggestion that the Fourteenth Amendment changed the reach of the Bill of Rights, although it did hold that due process extended to all rights necessary for "fundamental fairness," some of which might coincidentally be in the Bill of Rights.[54] Then, in the early twentieth century the

Court held that three provisions in the Bill of Rights—free speech, press, and religion—were part of Fourteenth Amendment liberty and must be respected by state governments.[55] Several years later it held that in special circumstances Fourteenth Amendment liberty also included the Sixth Amendment's right to counsel.[56] Each of these decisions "incorporated" (absorbed, nationalized) parts of the Bill of Rights into Fourteenth Amendment liberty; in 1937 the Court held that it would incorporate any guarantees that were "of the very essence of a scheme of ordered liberty."[57] With each incorporation decision the Court absorbs a guarantee in the Bill of Rights into Fourteenth Amendment liberty and thereby requires the states to follow due process standards before intruding on it. In this way incorporation expands the Constitution not by creating new rights but by extending existing rights to the people in a greater number and variety of instances. As of today the Court has incorporated virtually all of the provisions in the first eight amendments. As summarized by Laurence Tribe, the Court has used due process to protect:

> The right to just compensation (*Chicago, B. & Q. R. Co. v. Chicago*, 166 U.S. 226 (1897); the first amendment freedoms of speech (*Fiske v. Kansas*, 274 U.S. 380 (1927), press (*Near v. Minnesota*, 283 U.S. 697(1931), assembly (*DeJonge v. Oregon*, 299 U.S. 353 (1937), petition (*Hague v. CIO*, 307 U.S. 496 (1939); free exercise of religion (*Cantwell v. Connecticut*, 310 U.S. 296 (1940); and non-establishment of religion (*Everson v. Board of Education*, 330 U.S. 1 (1947); the fourth amendment rights to be free of unreasonable search and seizure (*Wolf v. Colorado*, 338 U.S. 25 (1949); and to exclude from criminal trials evidence illegally seized (*Mapp v. Ohio*, 367 U.S. 643 (1961); the fifth amendment rights to be free of compelled self-incrimination (*Malloy v. Hogan*, 378 U.S. 1 (1964) and double jeopardy (*Benton v. Maryland*, 395 U.S. 784 (1969); the sixth amendment rights to counsel (*Gideon v. Wainwright*, 374 U.S. 335 (1963); to a speedy (*Klopfer v. North Carolina*, 386 U.S. 213 (1967) and public (*In re Oliver*, 333 U.S. 257 (1948) trial before a jury (*Duncan v. Louisiana*, 391 U.S. 145 (1968); to an opportunity to confront opposing witnesses (*Pointer v. Texas*, 380 U.S. 400 (1965); and to compulsory process for the purpose of obtaining favorable witnesses (*Washington v. Texas*, 388 U.S. 14 (1967); and the eighth amendment right to be free of cruel and unusual punishments (*Robinson v. California*, 370 U.S. 600 (1972).[58]

The Court has not incorporated the right to indictment by grand jury,[59] the right to jury trial in civil suits involving over $20, nor has it clearly said that the Eighth Amendment's ban against excessive bail applies to the states.[60] It has not decided one way or the other on the Second Amendment's right to bear arms or the Third Amendment's ban on quartering soldiers in private homes.[61]

By incorporating only some of the Bill of Rights, the Court takes what is called a "selective incorporation" position. This contrasts with the "no incorporation" position it took in the years immediately following the Fourteenth Amendment's ratification[62] and the "total incorporation" position urged by some Justices.[63] In what is known as "ultra-incorporation"[64] the Court also absorbs implicit as well as stated constitutional rights; for example, in the decision in which it created the right to marital privacy, the Court also applied that right to the states.[65] Finally, the Court incorporates not only the right itself but also its essential baggage. In *Mapp v. Ohio* the Court incorporated the exclusionary rule as part of the Fourth Amendment. In another case the Court incorporated a defendant's legal right to be found guilty "beyond a reasonable doubt" as part of his or her right to a fair trial: "we explicitly hold," wrote the Court, "that the Due Process Clause of the Fourteenth Amendment protects the accused against conviction except upon proof beyond a reasonable doubt."[66] Table 6.2 places the Court's actual position on incorporation among several theoretical positions to show its relatively liberal stance on the matter. By strategically using the due process clause the Court has added considerable breadth to the Constitution.

THE RIGHT TO PRIVACY: A CASE STUDY

Over a century ago John Stuart Mill wrote that there is a "circle around every individual human being, which no government . . . ought to be permitted to overstep." He went on to say that "no one who professes the smallest regard to human dignity will call into question" the need for "some space in human existence" that is "sacred from authoritarian intrusion."[67] Such respect for the individual's autonomy is a recurring motif in the American heritage. One need not reach far into U.S. jurisprudence before coming across Justice Brandeis's oft-repeated declaration that "the right to be let alone is the most comprehensive of rights and the right most valued by civilized men."[68] Although in the early years of the republic the "right to privacy" had no clear apologist, with neither the Constitution, statutory law nor common law mentioning it, today the right to privacy is a prominent constitutional right.

The making of the constitutional right to privacy spans more than eighty years; it began with privacy's establishment in the common law following an 1881 case in which a woman in the throes of labor was visited by her doctor and a man she thought was also a physician.[69] Later finding out the stranger was not a physician, she brought suit. The Court held that the man had "entered under fraudulent pretenses" and ruled in favor of the woman; although the Court did not specify the grounds for recovery, it noted that the woman had a "legal right to the privacy of her apartment at such a time."[70] Then in 1890 Samuel Warren and Louis Brandeis published an article on the "Right to Privacy" in the *Harvard Law Review* in which they argued that the right to privacy lay in the spirit if not the words of the common law.[71] Claiming that early torts of trespass and battery built a zone of physical privacy around the individual[72] and later torts of slander and libel added a zone of spiritual privacy,[73] Warren and Brandeis "pieced together"[74] these pillars of tort law to identify an independent legal right to privacy. The article was well-received in the legal community and a court first recognized an independent legal right to privacy in 1904.[75]

The right to privacy next unfolded in the statutory law starting with New York, which acted after a state court refused to entertain the privacy claim of a woman whose likeness was used without her consent to advertise flour.[76] The court's refusal to grant relief to the woman, whose picture appeared on thousands of flyers over the caption "Flour of the Family," aroused public ire and prompted the New York legislature to pass a law forbidding the "unauthorized use of a person's name or picture for advertising or trade purposes. . . ."[77] Within twenty years most states passed similar laws in a development that helped turn an inchoate respect for autonomy into a tangible legal right.

In the meantime, the Supreme Court began laying the framework for privacy's constitutional basis. Using the zone approach, at one time or another it tied privacy to the First, Third, Fourth, and Fifth Amendments. The First Amendment, which ensures one's freedom to believe, speak, worship, and associate, protects the privacy of the individual's personality.[78] The Third Amendment, which prohibits the peacetime quartering of soldiers in homes without the owner's consent, protects the privacy of a person's home.[79] The Fourth Amendment, which gives people the right to be "secure in their persons, houses, papers, and effects, against unreasonable searches and seizures," protects a person's living space.[80] The Fifth Amendment, which protects a person from forced self-incrimination, gives one control over the amount of private information he or she will make public. Next, using the overlapping zone approach the Court combined the Fourth and Fifth Amendments to conclude that together they produced a right of "personal security, personal liberty, and private property" and protected the sanctity of one's

TABLE 6.2
RANGE OF JUDICIAL POSITIONS ON
INCORPORATION[a]

◄————————————   More restraintist   ——————————►

No incorporation of explicit rights: no incorporation of implicit rights.	*No* incorporation of explicit rights: will incorporate implicit rights.	*Selective* incorporation of explicit rights: no incorporation of implicit rights.
See, e.g., *Twining v. New Jersey* (1908).	See, e.g., Harlan, J., concurring in *Griswold v. Connecticut* (1965).	

[a]Table prepared with the aid of Leonard G. Ratner, ''The Function of the Due Process Clause,'' 116 *University of Pennsylvania Law Review*, 1056 (1968).

home and life privacies.[81] Finally, the Court used the due process clause to hold that private parental decisions about educating children were part of the Fourteenth Amendment liberty and thereby part of the Constitution.[82]

In 1965 the Court tapped these strains of precedent to recognize an independent constitutional right to privacy in a pivotal case involving a state law forbidding the sale or use of birth control devices.[83] An earlier challenge to the law had wended its way to the Supreme Court, but the Justices refused to rule on its merits because the law was not being enforced.[84] Protagonists thus opened up a public center for planned parenthood, arranged for the center's director and one of its physicians to be fined for selling birth control devices to married couples, and worked the grievance back up to the Supreme Court. This time in the

TABLE 6.2 continued

──────────────── More activist ─────────────▶		
Selective incorporation of explicit rights; will incorporate implicit rights.	*Total* incorporation of explicit rights; no incorporation of implicit rights.	*Total* incorporation of explicit rights; will incorporate implicit rights.
Current Court Position		
See, e.g., Goldberg, J., concurring in *Griswold v. Connecticut* (joined by Warren, C.J., and Brennan, J.): "Although I have not accepted the view that 'due process' as used in the Fourteenth Amendment incorporates all of the first eight Amendments, . . . I do agree that the concept of liberty protects those personal rights that are fundamental, and it is not confined to the specific terms of the Bill of Rights."	See, e.g., Black and Douglas, JJ., dissenting in *Cohen v. Hurley* (1961); *Irving v. California* (1954); and concurring in *Rochin v. California* (1952).	See, e.g., Murphy and Rutledge, JJ., dissenting in *Wolf v. Colorado* (1949), and *Adamson v. California* (1948).

case of *Griswold v. Connecticut* the Court struck the law down, saying it interfered with a fundamental constitutional right to marital privacy. The law's special flaw was its control over the *use* of birth control devices because the state would have to intrude into the bedroom and strike at the heart of the marriage relationship in order to enforce it. Justice Douglas wrote the lead opinion and used the overlapping zone approach to ground marital privacy in the Constitution. He said that privacy was inherent in the First, Third, Fourth, Fifth, and Ninth Amendments and, when combined, they created a new product larger than the sum of their parts. Douglas's approach was analogous to that of Warren and Brandeis in their seminal law review article. Whereas Warren and Brandeis created a legal right to privacy from overlapping torts, Douglas created a constitutional right to privacy from overlapping constitutional amendments (see Tables 6.3 and 6.4).

TABLE 6.3
PRIVACY AS AN INDEPENDENT LEGAL RIGHT

I	II
Tort law ————gave rise to ————▶	legal right to privacy
Privacy as part of torts, such as	*Privacy as independent legal right via*
—assault —battery —libel —trespass	—Warren and Brandeis's *Harvard Law Review* article of 1890 —*Pavesich v. New England Life Insurance Company* (1904) First court to recognize privacy as an independent legal right. Courts in most jurisdictions followed suit.

TABLE 6.4
PRIVACY AS AN INDEPENDENT
CONSTITUTIONAL RIGHT

I	II
Constitutional law ——gave rise to ——▶	constitutional right to privacy
Privacy as part of individual constitutional guarantees	
—First Amendment protects one's right to associate freely with others. See, e.g., *NAACP v. Alabama* (1958).	*via*
—Third Amendment guards against quartering of soldiers in peacetime without owner's permission. See *Katz v. United States* (1967).	—*Griswold v. Connecticut. Griswold* gave independent constitutional status only to the right to marital privacy. *Roe v. Wade* (1973) and other cases expanded the right. See Table 6.5.
—Fourth Amendment forbids unreasonable searches and seizures and protects the sanctity of one's home. See, e.g., *Warden v. Hayden* (1967).	
—Fifth Amendment forbids forced self-incrimination and gives the individual a "private enclave where he may lead a private life." *Murphy v. Waterfront Commission of New York Harbor* (1964).	

Other Justices in *Griswold* agreed with the result but used different methods for grounding marital privacy in the Constitution. Three used the Ninth Amendment as an enabling clause and two used Fourteenth Amendment due process as an enabling clause.[85] Two Justices dissented, with Justice Black writing that he could not "rely on the Due Process Clause or the Ninth Amendment or any mysterious and uncertain natural law concept as reason for striking down this state law."

Although as the first decision recognizing privacy as an independent constitutional right, *Griswold* was the north star in privacy law, it was an inelegant decision with a panoply of opinions and no single rationale for its landmark ruling. As often happens with pioneering decisions, *Griswold* suggested a direction but did not lay down the roadwork and so the Court set about clarifying it soon after. First, the Court clarified the content of the right to privacy in a task that was important because *Griswold* left unclear whether the new right focused on sex, marital sex, sex for procreation, or marital relations in general. In several post-*Griswold* decisions the Court held the heart of the constitutional right to privacy lay in a "cluster" of personal choices relating to procreation[86] that gives to the individual the right to decide "whether or not to bear or beget a child."[87] After *Griswold* gave married couples the right to decide whether to conceive a child, a second decision gave unmarried couples[88] and a third decision gave minors[89] the same right. A fourth decision gave women the right to decide whether to bear a child (the right-to-abortion decision)[90] and a fifth granted this right to underage unmarried women.[91] Radiating from this privacy core are offshoots of the right to privacy relating to personal decisions about "marriage, family relationships, and child rearing and education."[92]

Second, the Court clarified privacy's constitutional basis. In three significant decisions the Court abandoned *Griswold*'s overlapping zones approach and turned instead to due process as an enabling clause, stating simply that decisions relating to procreation were part of Fourteenth Amendment liberty (see Table 6.5). When all procreation cases are taken together, *Griswold* turns out to be a footnote in a series of due-process-based decisions. "After *Griswold* it was easy," one commentator noted. "As often happens, the Court largely forgot the difficulties of justification in *Griswold* and assumed and built on the result."[93]

The making of the constitutional right to privacy took eighty-four years, if one starts with the first mention of privacy in a judicial opinion and ends with *Griswold*. Yet these dates are only rough markers. One could move the beginning date back to the first libel and slander laws, as did Warren and Brandeis, and do away with the ending point inasmuch as the right to privacy is still evolving. Privacy is a complex right,

TABLE 6.5
CASES OUTLINING THE BORDERS AND BASES
FOR THE CONSTITUTIONAL RIGHT TO
PRIVACY

Case	Decision	Constitutional basis
Meyer v. Nebraska (1923)	Citizens have the right to study German in a private school. Decision struck down a state statute barring teaching of foreign languages to children.	Due process
Pierce v. Society of Sisters (1925)	Parents have the right to educate their children in private schools. Decision struck down an Oregon statute requiring parents to send children to public schools.	Due process
Skinner v. Oklahoma (1942)	The right to procreation is fundamental. Decision struck down state statute providing for sterilization of habitual criminals.	Equal protection
Loving v. Virginia (1967)	Citizens have the right to marry the person of their choice. Decision struck down Virginia law forbidding the intermarriage of any "white person" with any "colored person."	Due process and equal protection
Griswold v. Connecticut (1965)	A married couple has the right to decide whether it wants to beget a child. Decision struck down a state statute forbidding the sale and use of birth control devices.	Overlapping zones

generally defined as the "right to be let alone,"[94] or "the exclusive access of a person . . . to a realm of his own,"[95] but it is more manageable as a concept if subdivided into some of its main variants. One useful typology divides the right to privacy into three kinds.[96] Privacy of *intimate decisions* is the kind protected by *Griswold* and it grants the individual the freedom to make personal decisions without restrictions by the state.

TABLE 6.5 continued

Case	Decision	Constitutional basis
Eisenstadt v. Baird (1972)	An unmarried person has the right to decide whether he or she wants to beget a child. Decision struck down a state law allowing sale of birth control devices only to married persons.	Equal protection
Carey v. Population Services Int'l. (1977)	Minors have the right to decide whether to beget a child. Decision struck down a New York law forbidding the sale or distribution of contraceptives to persons under sixteen.	Due process
Roe v. Wade (1973)	A woman has the right to decide whether to abort her pregnancy (the right is unqualified in the first three months but qualified in the last six months). Decision struck down a state abortion law that forbade abortions except when the mother's life was at stake.	Due process
Planned Parenthood v. Danforth (1976)	A married woman has the right to decide without the knowledge or consent of her husband whether to abort her pregnancy. An underage unmarried woman has the right to decide without the consent of her parents whether to abort her pregnancy. Decision struck down a state statute requiring a woman to obtain her husband's or parent's consent before aborting her pregnancy.	Due process

Privacy of *repose* grants the individual "freedom from anything that disturbs or excites" and gives him or her a zone of "calm, peace, and tranquility."[97] It is violated by noisy loudspeakers, unsolicited erotic mail or, to give a specific example, by the seventeen-day "occupation" by landlords of a tenant's apartment after the tenant refused to leave the building.[98] Privacy of *sanctuary* protects the individual from "other persons . . . seeing, hearing, and knowing," and allows him or her to decide how much of his personal sphere is laid open to public inspection.[99] Sanctuary is violated when someone publishes embarrassing facts about a person, puts a person in a false public light, or uses another person's name or likeness without his consent.[100] A national magazine intruded on one Dorothy Barber's sanctuary when it published a story of Ms. Barber's trip to a hospital for an ailment that left her eating voraciously at the same time she was losing weight.[101] The article, entitled "Starving Glutton," was capped by a picture of Ms. Barber in her hospital bed with the caption "Insatiable-Eater Barber." Each type of privacy may be further subdivided into intrusions by private and public agencies, resulting in a six-part typology of privacy violations (see Table 6.6).

By pointing out some of privacy's hues, we see that *Griswold* and its progeny elevated to constitutional status only one facet of privacy—that of decisions relating to marriage, child-rearing, and procreation. Yet the right to privacy has endless variants that may warrant statutory or common law, if not constitutional, status. To a large degree the whittling of these facets of privacy occurs in the lower courts, where judges hear many claims that never reach the high bench. One commonly litigated question involves the individual's right to resist compulsory medical care, which is also part of the privacy of intimate decisions. Several Court decisions suggest that this right exists on the constitutional level, but the Court's rulings in the area are only suggestive and abstract. In the lower court arena, however, judges have fielded enough varied appeals to define the nature and extent of this right. The remainder of this chapter reviews the ways lower courts refine Supreme Court decisions and then uses the right to resist medical treatment to illustrate how lower courts have refined one facet of a constitutional right recognized by the Court.

TABLE 6.6
EXAMPLES OF TYPES OF PRIVACY VIOLATIONS

	Private intrusions (by fellow citizens)	State intrusions (by government)
Repose	Company advertising by noisy loudspeaker	Advertisements in a city's bus fleet
Sanctuary	Magazine publishing a lurid story about a person	Police distributing list of known shoplifters to businesses
Intimate decisions	Private hospital refusing to perform abortions	State law forbidding the use of birth control devices

CONSTITUTIONAL RIGHTS AND THE LOWER COURTS

The Supreme Court sits at the apex of an extensive network of federal and state courts. Ninety-four district courts, eleven courts of appeal, the United States Supreme Court, and assorted specialty courts make up the federal judicial system. A typical state system contains justices of the peace, municipal courts, county courts, one or two intermediary appellate courts, a final appellate court, and an array of specialty courts. State and federal courts intersect at the Supreme Court, where the Justices review appeals arising from both court systems. Lower court law is known variously as common, case, decisional, and judge-made law. It is not "written" in the same sense as statutory law, but the opinions of presiding judges do give it a written dimension. Judge-made law is the synthesis of judicial decisions[102] and is built as judges interpret statutes, constitutions, and suggest answers to questions not addressed by statutes or constitutions.[103] It is a cumulative body of law that grows as judges modify and build on its precedent in response to social changes.[104] Technically it binds only the courts in the jurisdiction in which it is framed. Although this works against a national "common law," it still allows a national flavor to form around the bodies of common law as judges influence one another and bequeath jointly tapped principles and interpretations.

Although the Supreme Court is the chief developer and interpreter of constitutional rights, it acts in concert with lower courts, whose role in the making of civil rights also deserves attention. In sheer numbers of cases entertained, the lower courts outdo the Supreme Court many times over; in 1972, for example, only 3,654 cases were filed in the Supreme Court, as opposed to 143,216 in the U.S. district courts and 14,535 in the appellate courts.[105] Moreover, lower court rulings often stand as the final say on a matter because the Court declines to review most appeals reaching it and grants full hearings for very few of those it does review. Typically it disposes of a case through a summary affirmance or reversal or by remanding the case for further lower court review; for example, in its 1973–74 term the Court disposed of almost 4,000 cases but decided only one-tenth of these on their merits and wrote full opinions in only 147.[106]

In addition to relieving the Supreme Court's workload, lower courts also supplement the Supreme Court's doctrine. Supreme and lower court interaction takes place in several ways. First, lower courts help ferret out coherent questions of law from the array of seemingly discrete questions posed by litigants. They help extract the common denominators of cases and consolidate issues for possible Supreme Court review. When Warren and Brandeis identified a right to privacy in their law review article, for example, they took on a task normally assumed by lower courts: they extracted a common dimension from a mass of cases, put a label on it, gave it a peculiar identity, and thus helped focus legal inquiry.[107] In the 1960s, lower courts helped shape a body of environmental law from principles of administrative, constitutional, public health, tort, and property law and looked for the environmental implications of property, trespass, and nuisance law.[108]

Second, lower courts help develop answers to these new legal questions; although the Court is technically bound only to follow its own precedent, it does draw from lower court precedent. For example, in deciding whether the Fourth Amendment allows police to use trickery to gain entry to a home, the Court approvingly cited a lower court formula which said that "entrance gained by fraud or other use of deception for the purpose of effecting an arrest is constitutionally permissible so long as force is not employed."[109] Similarly, obscenity questions gestated for decades in the lower courts; when the Court handed down its first obscenity case on its merits, it referred to principles developed in lower courts.[110] Also, in one decision the Court struck down a state scheme in which a commission intimidated book distributors into withholding questionable books from the public.[111] In concluding that such schemes look informal but are blatant censorship in fact, the Court cited lower court decisions reaching the same conclusion.

Third, lower courts supplement and build upon Supreme Court rulings after they have been handed down. After the Supreme Court rules on a particular appeal, litigants pose related legal questions in cases involving different facts. As the case with a new twist works its way up the appellate ladder, presiding judges distinguish its facts from the past case and apply the same or modified rules of law. For example, in *Miranda v. Arizona* the Court held that police must warn a suspect in a criminal investigation of his or her right to silence and to the assistance of counsel and that police must give this warning the moment the suspect is no longer free to leave.[112] It may not always be clear to police when this point begins, however, so in reviewing different appeals lower courts have helped identify this point. Among other things, judges have held that it almost always occurs when questioning takes place in a police car but does not automatically occur when the suspect initiates the conversation or when it takes place in the suspect's car.[113] Lower courts have also fleshed out Supreme Court rulings in the matter of who may consent to a police search. The Court held that a motel clerk could not consent to the search of a tenant's room,[114] but it left open whether parents, friends, and business partners could give consent on behalf of the suspect. Fielding these questions, lower courts held in three cases that parents could validly give consent on behalf of their child (the Court denied certiorari and thereby let stand each ruling)[115] and that a person could consent to a search of a jointly owned business when the partner was absent (the Court denied certiorari and thereby let stand two of these decisions).[116]

Lower courts do not always supplement in the positive sense and, through innocent misinterpretation or deliberate intransigence, may improperly or incompletely enforce Supreme Court rulings. For example, during one ten-year period the Court remanded 175 cases to lower courts for "further action 'not inconsistent with' the decision of the Court" and of the 46 cases litigated further, "the party successful in the Supreme Court was unsuccessful in the state court following the remand" less than half of the time.[117] A classic example of deliberate lower court evasion occurred after the Court's racial integration decision of *Brown v. Board of Education*[118] when, among other things, southern courts upheld state tactics defying *Brown*.[119] In recent years lower courts have forged ahead of the Burger Court in framing new protections in civil liberties, especially in the area of the defendant's rights. For example, one lower court made *Miranda v. Arizona* retroactive whereas the Supreme Court did not,[120] and another rejected the Court's holding that the state may introduce in court evidence seized in violation of *Miranda* in order to impeach a defendant's testimony.[121]

THE RIGHT TO RESIST MEDICAL CARE: A CASE STUDY

The issue of compulsory medical care is primarily of twentieth-century vintage. This century has seen the growth of the active state, in which the government legislates on a scale unheard of 100 years ago. Among other things, the state now uses its police powers to require vaccinations, blood tests, and water fluoridation in the name of the public welfare. This century also has witnessed impressive advances in medical technology. Whereas hospitals once were places to ease patient discomfort, they now are places where physicians save or prolong life through new surgical techniques, potent medicine, and extraordinary medical equipment. Confrontations between state and individual arise in various settings. Some arise when a child needs medical care and the parents refuse to allow it for religious or other reasons. The state then assumes its role as parens patraiae[122] and seeks custody of the child in order to treat him or her. Others arise when the state brings child neglect charges against parents who refuse to treat a child and still others involve adults who refuse to allow treatment on themselves, usually for religious reasons. A typical confrontation occurs when a Jehovah's Witness refuses a life-saving blood transfusion because his or her religion forbids the ingestion of blood or when an individual kept alive through artificial means wishes to die naturally.

The Court has ruled on few cases involving compulsory medical care, but it has handed down decisions on related matters that give clues about the dimensions of the individual's right to resist treatment. First, its freedom-of-religion decisions, some of which involve believers refusing medical treatment on religious grounds, make clear that the right to free exercise ends when it endangers the public health and welfare. Second, its privacy-of-procreation decisions point to the sanctity of the patient–physician relationship.[123] "The right of privacy has no more conspicuous place than in the physician–patient relationship," wrote Justice Douglas. "The right to seek advice on one's health and the right to place reliance on the physician of one's choice are basic."[124] In its abortion decisions the Court held that a woman's decision to have an abortion in the first trimester of pregnancy was one between her and her physician and no one, not even spouse or parent, had the power to intrude on that choice. Third, the privacy of procreation decisions grant the individual freedom of choice over a particular form of medical treatment—that involving procreation—and imply that one may have freedom of choice over other kinds of treatment as well. Fourth, the Court's search and seizure decisions show it reads the Fourth Amendment's prohibition of unreasonable searches and seizures of "*persons*, houses, papers, and effects" to protect the sanctity and integrity of the human body.[125] *Schmerber v. California*,[126] *Breithaupt v. Abrams*,[127] and *Rochin v. California*[128] each allows the state to intrude on a suspect's body only if the effort will yield evidence, the procedure is routine and not shocking, and the procedure is done in a sanitary manner by professionals. The suspect's right to bodily integrity is fundamental and the Court incorporated it in *Rochin v. California*.[129]

Each of these lines of law can be tapped to support the position that a right to resist medical treatment inheres in the constitutional right to privacy. The Court also suggests limits on the right, however, stating as early as 1905 that "one does not have an unlimited right to do with one's body as one pleases."[130] In the balance, the individual's right to bodily privacy ends when enjoyment of that right endangers the public health and welfare. Thus, the Court has upheld mandatory smallpox vaccinations,[131] the compulsory sterilization of mentally defective people,[132] and controls on abortion during the last two trimesters of pregnancy.[133]

In reviewing the many appeals involving compulsory medical care that arise, lower court judges have held to the general thesis that the individual's interest in protecting the privacy of his or her own body is strong but may nevertheless be limited when public health and welfare demand it. Because an unwanted intrusion on one's body is an assault under common law,[134] it is an established point of law that an adult of sound mind has the right to refuse medical treatment.[135] This right ends, however, when the individual's refusal to be treated endangers the public, so courts have upheld compulsory vaccinations in a community ravaged by an epidemic disease,[136] vaccination in a community without an epidemic disease (in order to prevent such a disease from burgeoning),[137] a state requirement that men be free from venereal diseases before being issued a marriage license,[138] a requirement that a prospective university student have chest X-rays to show he or she does not have tuberculosis,[139] and the hospitalization of a tubercular patient who resisted treatment on religious grounds.[140]

The right to resist treatment is shortened when life-saving care is at stake but does not disappear altogether. Although judges disagree on the matter, they tend to see some deaths as less harmful to society than others and will respect the individual's wish to die if his or her death will pose little burden to society. Judges look to such things as the patient's age, family position, and prognosis for a healthy productive life to decide how much the death would burden society. On the one hand courts have upheld the right of a seventy-two-year-old recluse with only one distant living relative to refuse a life-saving amputation of his gangrenous legs[141] and the granting of guardianship to the father of a comatose woman having no chance of recovery so that he might order the disconnection of her life-supporting equipment.[142] On the other hand courts have not respected the individual's wish to refuse life-saving treatment in the following cases: a mother with a seven-month-old child who refused a blood transfusion on religious grounds,[143] a father of four children who also refused treatment for religious reasons,[144] and a twenty-two-year-old accident victim with a potential for a full and healthy life whose mother resisted treatment on her behalf on religious grounds.[145] Courts also consider the nature of the treatment itself and are more likely to respect the patient's wishes if the treatment intrudes greatly on his or her body. Whereas courts regularly order simple life-saving procedures such as blood transfusions, they are less likely to order such practices as amputations[146] or overbearing life-support systems.[147] Another thing judges consider is the soundness of the patient's mind. In upholding a patient's right to refuse a life-saving gangrene operation, one court emphasized that it found the patient mentally competent to make that momentous decision.[148] Another court upheld a patient's refusal to have a blood transfusion during surgery, noting that the patient was fully competent to make this decision, which dramatically increased the surgical risks.[149] When faced with the case of a disoriented woman brought to a hospital who had earlier objected to blood transfusions on religious grounds, a third court granted her wish to refuse life-saving transfusions, noting that she had earlier informed her physician repeatedly of her wish while mentally lucid.[150] As these cases make clear, religious freedom is of relatively low importance when a patient's life is at stake and generally loses in the balance.

The right to resist treatment is also weakened when the case involves a parent or guardian acting on behalf of a child. Because it is an established point of law that a parent may not knowingly expose his or her child to ill health or death,[151] courts in virtually all cases rule in favor of the state when a parent resists medical treatment for a child suffering from serious illness or injury.[152] Judges have upheld a finding of neglect of a mother who refused to treat her child suffering from either arthritis or rheumatic fever and whose condition was worsening.[153] Courts have ordered tonsillectomies or adenoidectomies for three children suffering from chronic infections and facing hearing losses whose father refused to treat them for religious reasons;[154] involuntary plastic surgery for a grossly disfigured child whose parents kept him at home because of his condition and whose educational development suffered as a result;[155] and a court-ordered blood transfusion for a pregnant woman whose refusal to submit to the transfusion endangered the life of the fetus.[156] Generally, the religious basis of the parents' claim does not strengthen their case, so courts have upheld the compulsory vaccination[157] and blood transfusions of children against the religious objections of their parents.[158] The parents' claim *is* strengthened in two circumstances: when the treatment is risky or its effectiveness doubtful,[159] and when the child's ailment is not serious. For example, in a turn-of-the-century case a court did not find parents in neglect for refusing to treat their child for rickets in view of the fact that treatment sometimes adversely affected the patient and that the parents' nervousness was understandable in that they had already lost seven children.[160] In another case a court declined to deprive a father of custody of his child after he failed to seek medical care for the child's speech impediment.[161] On the other hand courts have upheld compulsory cancer surgery for a child even though the chance for a cure was only 50/50 because the likelihood of a cure without the operation was virtually zero.[162] Similarly a court upheld compulsory treatment for a polio-stricken child, noting that the operation was certain to be successful and that the child would just as certainly deteriorate without it.[163]

Taken together the outcomes of these cases define the boundaries of the individual's right to resist medical treatment. The individual's claim is strongest when he or she is a mentally competent adult whose refusal to be treated poses no harm to society. The individual's claim weakens when life-saving treatment is at stake but even here extenuating conditions affect his or her claim. The patient's claim to resist is strongest when he or she is a mentally competent adult with no dependent relatives and the life-saving treatment intrudes greatly on his or her body. The patient's claim weakens when his or her mental competency is in doubt, there are dependents, the patient is capable of being a productive member of society if cured, the treatment is relatively unobtrusive, the chances of recovery are great, and when the refusal is made on behalf of a child.

SUMMARY

The "provisions of the Constitution are not mathematical formulas having their essence in their form," wrote Oliver Wendell Holmes, "they are organic living institutions."[164] It is a norm of American jurisprudence that the Court breathes life into an essentially stationary Constitution and in so doing from time to time recognizes rights that are implicitly rather than explicitly a part of the Constitution. Of the approaches for reading new rights into the Constitution, the Court most often uses Fifth and Fourteenth Amendment due process as an enabling clause. Justice Frankfurter has called due process "perhaps the most majestic concept in our whole constitutional system." Through it the Court has indeed kept the Constitution flexible. First, it uses the life, liberty, and property trilogy of the due process clause to expand the number of rights falling within the Constitution's ambit. The right to marital privacy, the right to interstate travel, and the right to abort a pregnancy all joined the Constitution through the Court's interpretation of Fourteenth Amendment liberty. Second, it uses Fourteenth Amendment liberty to expand the jurisdiction of rights explicitly stated in the Constitution. Through incorporation the Court broadens the Constitution's meaning not necessarily by creating new rights but by enlarging the reach of existing rights. The Court has incorporated most of the guarantees in the first eight amendments, including some implicit rights, and it brings along in incorporation essential features of the rights, not just the core of the right itself.

The making of a constitutional right is generally a long evolutionary process, as illustrated by the right to privacy. Typically a right is first taken seriously as a contender right, sits through a period of precedent-building, is recognized as a constitutional right, and then matures as its facets receive constitutional, statutory, and/or common law recognition. Warren and Brandeis elevated the right to privacy to a serious legal concept in their *Harvard Law Review* article; then the Court built lines of precedent in the first half of the twentieth century tying privacy in one form or another to the Constitution. Finally, privacy received specific constitutional recognition in the 1965 case of *Griswold v. Connecticut*; the right matured in several post-*Griswold* cases in which the Court gave it a more even character, stating that it embraces the right to make intimate decisions relating to contraception, procreation, marriage, family relationships, and child rearing—and grounding it squarely in Fourteenth Amendment liberty.

Privacy's maturation does not end at this point, however, because litigation produces a steady stream of appeals alleging that one or another interest is part of the constitutional right to privacy. Lower courts field many of these appeals and it is here that judges refine the right only roughly carved out by the Supreme Court. The right to resist medical care is an example of a right that appears to be part of the constitutional right to privacy but one that the Court has not directly addressed. The Court has bequeathed suggestive principles, such as its holding that "one does not have an unlimited right to do with one's body as one pleases" and its abortion decision grounding a woman's control over her body in Fourteenth Amendment liberty. But it has been in the lower court arena that judges have entertained legal questions relating to compulsory medical care. Only by looking at these decisions can one say that the individual has a "right" to refuse medical treatment. As defined by the lower courts, the right is not absolute nor even particularly far-reaching but, were it not for these decisions, the right, truncated as it may be, would not be defined at all. In the absence of Supreme Court rulings on the matter, lower court judgments stand as the final authority in the making of one facet of a generic right recognized by the Supreme Court.

Questions for Thought

1. Technology brings a steady stream of new issues to the study of civil rights. Of the technological changes affecting privacy, those dealing with the beginning and ending of life are particularly interesting. Consider fetal experimentation, in which researchers use voluntarily or involuntarily expelled human fetuses to study the causes and prevention of premature deaths, birth defects, and other maladies. Fetal experimentation is not new but is now getting more attention because liberalized abortion laws have made more fetuses available for research. Three legal problems stand out. First, when does life begin? Read the Supreme Court's opinion in its abortion decision, *Roe v. Wade,* 410 U.S. 113 (1973). What does the Court say about the beginning of life? Some people define the beginning of life as the point of "brain life" when the fetus has the "capacity for human intelligence, including consciousness, self-awareness and other generally recognized cerebral functions." See Maggie Scarf, "The Fetus as Guinea Pig," *The New York Times Magazine,* October 19, 1975, p. 13, at 89. Do you agree with this definition? Or have you come across a definition you prefer instead? Second, when, if ever, must the bodily privacy of the fetus be recognized as a constitutional right that cannot be denied without due process of law? Does the beginning of life correspond with the beginning of the constitutional right to privacy? Or are two different points of time at issue? Third, the Court has said that viability begins around the third trimester of pregnancy and at this point the state may forbid abortions. See *Roe v. Wade,* 410 U.S. 113 (1973). Should this same time be used to restrict fetal experimentation? Or should the state be able to control experimentation on nonviable fetuses too? What is the social interest in fetal experimentation? How would you respond to arguments that experimentation will ultimately save lives? (Scarf, p. 90, for example, notes that fetal experimentation in the 1940s helped researchers develop the polio vaccine.)

2. Black's Law Dictionary contains a traditional, so-called "circulatory death" definition of death: "The cessation of life; the ceasing to exist; defined by physicians as a total stoppage of circulation of the blood, and a cessation of the animal and vital functions consequent thereon, such as respiration, pulsation, etc. . . ." Note, "Legislation: The Need for a Current and Effective Statutory Definition of Death," 27 *Okla. L. Rev.* 729 (1974). Artificial life-support systems now can keep a patient "alive" beyond this point, however, and some policy-makers use the "brain death" definition of death instead: "A person will be considered medically and legally dead if, . . . there is the absence of spontaneous brain function. . . ." Note, "Legislation . . . ," at 733, n.26. What is the statutory definition of death in your state? Has it changed in the last decade or so? Might there be stages of death for use in different conditions; namely, a circulatory definition for the disconnection of artificial life-support systems but a brain death definition for removal of organs for transplants? Or should a single definition of death be used?

3. California recently passed a living will statute that allows a spouse or parent to order extraordinary life-support measures to be stopped in the event the person is injured, incapacitated, and has no hope of recovery. The statute contains an important exemption: it forbids termination of extraordinary life-support systems for pregnant women. Assume you are a judge asked to interpret this exemption in a case involving a comatose pregnant woman with no hope of recovery who is kept alive on an artificial respirator. Should the exemption apply to women in all stages of pregnancy or only those with viable fetuses? Does the right to privacy of the mother come into play? How about the family's right to make intimate decisions? (After all, these members are the ones who would have raised the child.) If it appears the child will be born with brain damage, does the situation differ from one in which parents decide to abort a defective fetus in a healthy, conscious mother? Does the statute discriminate invidiously between pregnant and nonpregnant women in violation of the Fourteenth Amendment equal protection clause?

4. Susan Ruby, Valerie Diamond, and Lynn Pearl are the fictitious names of three severely retarded teenage girls whose families tried to have them sterilized. Frightened by recent controversies over involuntary sterilizations of hospitalized mental patients, doctors at the University of Connecticut Hospital refused to perform the operations. See *The New York Times*, October 2, 1977, p. 1. The girls' families charged that hospital authorities violated their familial right to make "intimate and personal" decisions by refusing to perform the operations. Whose rights are the stronger—the parents' right to make decisions relating to their retarded daughters or the daughters' right to inviolable bodies? In this particular case the parents sought major surgery involving the removal of the uterus, not a simple tubal ligation, because they wanted to stop the girls from menstruating. They claimed that menstruation was "extremely traumatic" for the girls and brought on tantrums so severe in one of them that she had to be restrained. Should the type of operation affect the balancing of privacy interests? Why or why not?

5. *Beckwith v. Beckwith*, 355 A. 2d 537 (D.C. App. 1976) involved a divorce proceeding in which the husband claimed his wife committed adultery; he said he could support this claim by having a blood test taken of his son to establish paternity. The judge in the case did order the blood test of the son. He denied that the test violated the child's privacy and noted that the test was done in a reasonable manner and was likely to establish paternity. In this case the privacy of the child's body was intruded upon not for his own health but for another social interest. Whose rights are strongest in this case? Does it make a difference that the three people are members of the same family? Does the nature of the intrusion (a simple blood test) make a difference? What if the "child" were of age and resisted having the blood test?

6. Several commentators have suggested that we have a constitutional right to a quality environment, based on the liberty clause of the Fifth and Fourteenth Amendments and the enumeration-of-rights clause of the Ninth Amend-

ment. Read Justice Douglas's opinion in *Griswold v. Connecticut*, 381 U.S. 479 (1965), in which he used the overlapping zones approach to recognize a new constitutional right, and Justice Goldberg's concurrence, in which he based the right to privacy on the Ninth Amendment. Develop a position paper outlining the constitutional bases for a right to environmental quality. Use the two models suggested by *Griswold v. Connecticut,* along with any others you choose. How persuasive do you think a constitutional basis for environmental quality is?

NOTES

1. *Words and Phrases,* "Right," 357.

2. *Words and Phrases,* "Legal Right," 475.

3. Rights are most commonly based on constitutions, statutes, and the common law. Each source creates a positive, or man-made right, in contrast to timeless and ageless natural rights, which need not be stated in law to be binding. For example, a person's "right" to due process is thought to be a natural, eternal right that antedated the Constitution.

4. *O'Connor v. Donaldson,* 422 U.S. 563 (1975). The Court did not create an affirmative right to treatment but instead bade the state either to treat or release a patient not dangerous to himself or herself or to others.

5. See, for example, Congress's efforts to give this right to involuntarily confined mental patients in Washington, D.C. D.C. Code § 21-562 (Supp.V.1966). See *Rouse v. Cameron,* 373 F. 2d 451 (D.C.Cir. 1966).

6. *In re Quinlan,* 355 A. 2d 647 (1976), certiorari denied *sub. nom. Garger v. New Jersey,* 429 U.S. 922 (1976). The respirator was detached with judicial permission, but Miss Quinlan continued to live.

7. Quoted by Saul K. Padover, *The Living U.S. Constitution* (New York: Praeger, 1953), p. 57.

8. Quoted in Percival E. Jackson, ed., *The Wisdom of the Supreme Court* (Norman: University of Oklahoma Press, 1962), p. 52.

9. Quoted in Padover, p. 57.

10. Quoted in ibid., p. 58.

11. *Ashwander v. Tennessee Valley Authority,* 297 U.S. 288, 345-348 (1936).

12. "Our peculiar security is in the possession of a written Constitution. Let us not make it a blank paper by construction." T. Jefferson, quoted in M. Frances McNamara, ed., *2000 Famous Legal Quotations* (Rochester, N.Y.: The Lawyers Co-operative Publishing Co., 1967).

13. "A Provision of the Constitution . . . does not mean one thing at one time and an entirely different thing at another time." *Home Building and Loan Association v. Blaisdell,* 290 U.S. 398, 448 (1934) (Sutherland, J., dissenting).

14. See Tom Gerety, "Redefining Privacy," 12 *Harv.C.R.-C.L.L.Rev. 233 (1977).*

15. See David W. Rohde and Harold J. Spaeth, *Supreme Court Decision Making* (San Francisco: W. H. Freeman, 1976), pp. 41-42.

16. This approach adds to the Constitution "rather specific values that text or history show the framers actually to have intended and which are capable of being translated into principled rules." Robert H. Bork, "Neutral Principles and Some First Amendment Problems," 47 Ind.L.J. 1, 17 (1971).

17. *Williams v. Florida*, 399 U.S. 78 (1970).

18. *Griswold v. Connecticut*, 381 U.S. 479 (1965).

19. "The enumeration in the Constitution of certain rights, shall not be construed to deny or disparage others retained by the people." U.S. Const., Amend. IX.

20. *Griswold v. Connecticut*, 381 U.S. 479 (1965) (Goldberg, J., concurring).

21. See, for example, *Tanner v. Armco Steel Corporation*, 340 F.Supp. 532 (S.D.Tex. 1972).

22. *Roe v. Wade*, 410 U.S. 113 (1973).

23. Note, "Of Interests, Fundamental and Compelling: The Emerging Constitutional Balance," 57 *Boston U.L.Rev.* 462, 470 (1977).

24. Henry David Aiken, "Life and the Right to Life," in James M. Humber and Robert F. Almeder, eds., *Biomedical Ethics and the Law* (New York: Plenum Press, 1976), p. 470.

25. *Hannah v. Larche*, 363 U.S. 420 (1960).

26. *Crocker v. California*, 357 U.S. 433 (1958).

27. 16 Am.Jur. 2d § 330 n.19. "Another natural right is the natural affection between the parents and offspring" 16 Am.Jur. 2d § 330. A man-made right, by contrast, is established in an organized society and includes such things as the right to education or medical care.

28. The Supreme Court treats the two terms interchangeably. *Davidson v. New Orleans*, 96 U.S. 97 (1878). See also Leonard G. Ratner, "The Function of the Due Process Clause," 116 *U.Pa.L.Rev.* 1048, 1049 (1968): "It has long since been demonstrated that the phrase 'due process of law' is a variation of Magna Carta's 'according to the law of the land'."

29. 16 Am.Jur. 2d § 546, at 939: "Due process has to do with the denial of fundamental fairness, shocking to the universal sense of justice."

30. See, for example, *Morrissey v. Brewer*, 408 U.S. 471 (1972) and *Ingraham v. Wright*, 430 U.S. 651 (1977). Because due process guards only against state and not private acts, the Court must also assure itself that state action is involved. *District of Columbia v. Carter*, 409 U.S. 418 (1973).

31. Samuel D. Warren and Louis D. Brandeis, "The Right to Privacy," 4 *Harv.L.Rev.* 193 (1890). As Warren and Brandeis said at 195, the coming of civilization "made it clear to men that only a part of the pain, pleasure, and profit of life lay in physical things."

32. *Buchanan v. Warley*, 345 U.S. 60 (1917).

33. Charles L. Black, Jr., *Perspectives in Constitutional Law* (Englewood Cliffs, N.J.: Prentice-Hall, 1970), p. 77. It has done this at least since *Allgeyer v. Louisiana*, 165 U.S. 578 (1897). Liberty gives one the right "to enjoy those privileges long recognized at common law as being essential to the orderly pursuit of happiness by free men" (*Meyer v. Nebraska*, 262 U.S. 390 [1923]) and "to [enjoy] life while existing." 16 Am.Jur. 2d § 359 (1964).

34. The Court struck down a series of laws between 1897 and 1937 on the ground that they interfered with the contractual freedom of employers and employees. For a review of the major cases of the so-called "Lochner era" and excerpts from them, see Gerald Gunther, *Cases and Materials on Constitutional Law*, 9th ed. (Mineola, N.Y.: The Foundation Press, 1975), pp. 571-576. Among the laws that fell during this era was a law setting up minimum wages for women (*Atkins v. Children's Hospital*, 261 U.S. 525 [1923]) and a law limiting the number of hours bakers could work (*Lochner v. New York*, 198 U.S. 45 [1905]).

35. *Meyer v. Nebraska*, 262 U.S. 390 (1923).

36. *Gitlow v. New York*, 268 U.S. 652 (1925).

37. *Rochin v. California*, 342 U.S. 165 (1952).

38. *Aptheker v. Secretary of State*, 378 U.S. 500 (1964).

39. *Allgeyer v. Louisiana*, 165 U.S. 578 (1897).

40. *Meyer v. Nebraska*, 262 U.S. 390 (1923).

41. *Roe v. Wade*, 410 U.S. 113 (1973).

42. Henry J. Abraham, *Freedom and the Court*, 2nd ed. (New York: Oxford University Press, 1977), p. 111.

43. Procedural due process does not dictate the exact method the government must follow but rather requires the government to carry out its selected method fairly. See, for example, *Babineaux v. Judiciary Commission*, 341 So. 2d 396 (1977).

44. *Rochin v. California*, 342 U.S. 165 (1952).

45. *Escebedo v. Illinois*, 378 U.S. 478 (1964).

46. Abraham, p. 110.

47. *Nebbia v. New York*, 291 U.S. 502 (1934).

48. The Court has said that "even though a governmental purpose is legitimate and substantial, that purpose cannot be pursued by means that broadly stifle fundamental personal liberties when the end can be more narrowly achieved." *Aptheker v. Secretary of State*, 378 U.S. 500 (1964).

49. See Note, "*Roe* and *Paris*: Does Privacy Have a Principle?" 26 *Stan.L.Rev.* 1161, 1166-1167 (1974).

50. The Court strikes down laws exceeding Congress's constitutionally mandated powers. For example in 1905 it struck down on due process grounds a law limiting the number of hours bakers could work, saying the law exceeded the state's Tenth Amendment police powers. *Lochner v. New York*, 198 U.S. 45 (1905).

51. See, for example, David Fellman, *The Defendant's Rights Today* (Madison: The University of Wisconsin Press, 1976), pp. 16-17; and Black, p. 75.

52. *Barron v. Baltimore*, 32 U.S. (7 Peters) 243 (1833).

53. At least the provisions of the first eight amendments.

54. *Twining v. New Jersey*, 211 U.S. 78 (1908). See Bernard F. Cataldo, et al., *Introduction to Law and the Legal Process*, 2nd ed. (New York: John Wiley & Sons, 1973), p. 117.

55. See the discussion in Chapter 1 of the gradual expansion of the Fourth Amendment, culminating in *Mapp v. Ohio*, 367 U.S. 643 (1961).

56. *Powell v. Alabama*, 287 U.S. 45 (1932).

57. *Palko v. Connecticut,* 302 U.S. 319, 325 (1937). It also incorporates "fundamental principles of liberty and justice which lie at the base of all our civic and political institutions" (*Herbert v. Louisiana,* 272 U.S. 312,316 [1926]) and rights "so rooted in the traditions and conscience of our people as to be ranked as fundamental" (*Snyder v. Massachusetts,* 291 U.S. 97, 105 [1934]). See Paul G. Kauper, "Penumbras, Peripheries, Emanations, Things Fundamental and Things Forgotten: The Griswold Case," 64 *Mich.L.Rev.* 235, 236 (1965). In practice, other factors, such as the nature of individual Justices and the political climate of the time, determine which rights will be incorporated.

58. Laurence H. Tribe, *American Constitutional Law* (Mineola, N.Y.: The Foundation Press, 1978), pp. 567-568.

59. *Hurtado v. California,* 110 U.S. 615 (1884).

60. Lower courts assume that it does. See Fellman, p. 19.

61. See ibid., pp. 18-19.

62. See, for example, *Twining v. New Jersey,* 211 U.S. 78 (1908); *Maxwell v. Dow,* 176 U.S. 581 (1900); and *Hurtado v. California,* 110 U.S. 516 (1884).

63. See Justice Black dissenting in *Adamson v. California,* 332 U.S. 46 (1948).

64. Peter W. Lewis and Kenneth D. Peoples, *The Supreme Court and The Criminal Process* (Philadelphia: W. B. Saunders, 1978), p. 67.

65. *Griswold v. Connecticut,* 381 U.S. 479 (1965).

66. *In re Winship,* 397 U.S. 358 (1970).

67. Quoted in Chester J. Antieau, *Modern Constitutional Law,* Vol. I (Rochester, N.Y: The Lawyers Co-operative Publishing Co., 1969), p. 146.

68. *Olmstead v. United States,* 277 U.S. 438 (1928) (Brandeis, J., dissenting).

69. *De May v. Roberts,* 9 N.W. 146 (1881). See Gerety, p. 264.

70. William J. Prosser, "Privacy," 48 *Cal.L.Rev.* 383, 389 (1960).

71. Samuel D. Warren and Louis D. Brandeis, "The Right to Privacy," 4 *Harv.L.Rev.* 193 (1890).

72. Ibid., at 193. The woman in labor could have rested her case on trespass or even battery inasmuch as the stranger had touched her. See Gerety, at 263-264; Prosser, at 389.

73. The awareness of the "intense intellectual and emotional life, and the heightening of sensations which came with the advance of civilization, made it clear to men that only a part of the pain, pleasure, and profit of life lay in physical things." Warren and Brandeis, at 195.

74. Prosser, at 384.

75. *Pavesich v. New England Life Ins. Co.,* 50 S.E. 68 (1904).

76. *Roberson v. Rochester Folding Box Co.,* 64 N.E. 442 (1902).

77. See *Cason v. Baskin,* 20 S. 2d 243, 249 (1944). The court in *Roberson v. Rochester Folding Box Co.,* 64 N.E. 442 (1902) had suggested that the legislature would be a more appropriate place than the judiciary for protecting privacy. See M. C. Slough, *Privacy, Freedom and Responsibility* (Springfield, Ill.: Charles C. Thomas, 1969), pp. 34-35.

78. See, for example, *Gitlow v. New York,* 268 U.S. 652 (1925).

79. See *Poe v. Ullman,* 367 U.S. 497, 549 (1961) (Harlan, J., dissenting).

80. The Court interpreted the Fourth Amendment narrowly until it held in *Katz v. United States*, 389 U.S. 347 (1967) that the Fourth Amendment protected people, not places.

81. *Boyd v. United States*, 116 U.S. 616 (1886).

82. *Meyer v. Nebraska*, 262 U.S. 390 (1923); *Pierce v. Society of Sisters*, 268 U.S. 510 (1925).

83. *Griswold v. Connecticut*, 381 U.S. 479 (1965).

84. *Poe v. Ullman*, 367 U.S. 497 (1961).

85. Justice Douglas had deliberately avoided using the due process clause lest it provoke cries that the Court was returning to substantive due process reminiscent of the Lochner era.

86. This cluster does not create a right to sexual privacy. The state may still regulate sexual activities such as sodomy that are unrelated to procreation. The Court has not ruled on the merits of antisodomy statutes, although it did deny certiorari and therefore let stand a lower court reversal on privacy grounds of a married couple's sodomy conviction. *Cotner v. Henry*, 394 F. 2d 873, certiorari denied 393 U.S. 847 (1968). However, it summarily affirmed two lower court decisions upholding sodomy convictions for homosexuals. *Doe v. Commonwealth's Attorney for City of Richmond*, 425 U.S. 901 (1976), affirming without opinion 403 F. Supp. 1199 (E.D. Va. 1975).

87. *Carey v. Population Services Int'l*, 431 U.S. 678 (1977).

88. *Eisenstadt v. Baird*, 405 U.S. 438 (1972).

89. *Carey v. Population Services Int'l*, 431 U.S. 678 (1977).

90. *Roe v. Wade*, 410 U.S. 113 (1973).

91. *Planned Parenthood v. Danforth*, 428 U.S. 52 (1976).

92. *Carey v. Population Services Int'l*, 431 U.S. at 684-685.

93. Louis Henkin, "Privacy and Autonomy," 74 *Colum.L.Rev.* 1410, 1420 (1974).

94. *Olmstead v. United States*, 277 U.S. 438, 478 (1928) (Brandeis, J., dissenting). Thomas M. Cooley used this phrase in *The Elements of Torts* (Chicago: Callaghan, 1895).

95. Ernest van den Haag, quoted in Gerety, "Redefining Privacy," at 262 n.106.

96. Comment, "A Taxonomy of Privacy: Repose, Sanctuary, and Intimate Decision," 64 *Cal.L.Rev.* 1447 (1976).

97. Ibid., at 1451.

98. *Welsh v. Pritchard*, 241 P. 2d 816 (1952).

99. Comment, "A Taxonomy . . . ," at 1482. The author concludes that the privacy of sanctuary is more likely to be recognized by courts when tangible goods are at stake than intangible things such as reputation.

100. See Prosser, "Privacy."

101. *Barber v. Time, Inc.*, 159 S.W. 2d 291 (1942).

102. Miles O. Price and Harry Bitner, *Effective Legal Research*, 3rd ed. (Boston: Little, Brown, 1969), p. 3.

103. Bernard F. Cataldo et al., *Introduction to Law and the Legal Process*, 2nd ed. (New York: John Wiley & Sons, 1973), p. 9.

104. The "common law does not consist of absolute, fixed and inflexible rules, but broad and comprehensive principles based on justice, reason, and common sense, and is of judicial origin and promulgation, and principles are susceptible of adaptation to new conditions, interest, relations, and usages as the progress of society may require" (Words and Phrases, "Common Law," 108).

105. Henry J. Friendly, *Federal Jurisdiction: A General View* (New York: Columbia University Press, 1973), pp. 16, 32, 48.

106. Henry J. Abraham, *The Judiciary*, 2nd ed. (Boston: Allyn and Bacon, 1969), p. 179.

107. Warren and Brandeis, "The Right to Privacy."

108. Timothy Atkeson, "Introduction," in Erica L. Dolgin and Thomas G. P. Guilbert, eds., *Environmental Law* (St. Paul, Minn.: West, 1974), p. 5.

109. *Sabbath v. United States,* 391 U.S. 585, 590 n.7 (1968), citing *Smith v. United States,* 257 F.2d 486, 488 n.1.

110. For example, *Roth v. United States,* 354 U.S. 476 (1957) relied in part on the definition of obscenity handed down in *United States v. One Book Called "Ulysses,"* 5 F.Supp. 182, 184 (1933). See Frederick F. Schauer, *The Law of Obscenity* (Washington, D.C.: Bureau of National Affairs, 1976), pp. 1-29.

111. *Bantam Books, Inc. v. Sullivan,* 372 U.S. 58 (1963).

112. 384 U.S. 436 (1966).

113. Examples are from Peter W. Lewis and Kenneth D. Peoples, *The Supreme Court and the Criminal Process* (Philadelphia: W. B. Saunders, 1978), p. 453.

114. *Stoner v. California,* 376 U.S. 483 (1964).

115. *United States ex rel. Combs v. La Vallee,* 417 F. 2d 523 (2d Cir. 1969), certiorari denied 397 U.S. 1102 (1970); *Maxwell v. Stephens,* 348 F. 2d 325 (8th Cir. 1965), certiorari denied, 382 U.S. 944 (1965); *State v. Kinderman,* 271 Minn. 405, certiorari denied 384 U.S. 909 (1965).

116. *United States v. Goodman,* 190 F.Supp. 847 (D.C. Ill., 1961); *United States v. Sferas,* 210 F. 2d 69 (7th Cir. 1954), certiorari denied, 374 U.S. 934; *In re Fried,* 161 F. 2d 453 (2d Cir. 1947), certiorari dismissed, 332 U.S. 807.

117. Note, "Evasion of Supreme Court Mandates in Cases Remanded to State Courts Since 1941," 67 *Harv. L.Rev.* 1251 (1964).

118. 347 U.S. 483 (1954).

119. Walter F. Murphy, "Lower Court Checks on Supreme Court Power," 53 *American Political Science Review* 1018 (1959).

120. *Commonwealth v. Romberger,* 347 A. 2d 460 (Pa. 1975).

121. *People v. Disbrow,* 545 P. 2d 272 (Calif. 1976), rejecting *Harris v. New York,* 401 U.S. 222 (1971).

122. The state has the duty to protect those who cannot protect themselves.

123. For example, the judge in *In re Quinlan* 355 A. 2d 647 (1976) said that *Griswold's* privacy right was broad enough to include the right of a person to refuse medical care. See Annotation, "Power of Court to Order or Authorize Discontinuation of Extraordinary Medical Means of Sustaining Human Life," 79 A.L.R. 3d 237, 242.

124. Concurring in *Doe v. Bolton,* 410 U.S. 179 (1973).

125. *Schmerber v. California,* 384 U.S., 757, 767 (1966).

126. Ibid.

127. *Breithaupt v. Abrams,* 352 U.S. 432 (1957).

128. *Rochin v. California,* 342 U.S. 165 (1952).

129. Not all agree that *Schmerber* and *Breithaupt* help define a right to bodily privacy. For example, dissenting in *Schmerber v. California,* 384 U.S. at 779, Justice Fortas opined that it is "an act of violence" for the state to obtain evidence from an unwilling suspect's body no matter what the procedure followed.

130. *Jacobsen v. Massachusetts,* 197 U.S. 11 (1905), as cited in *Roe v. Wade,* 410 U.S. 113 (1973).

131. *Jacobson v. Massachusetts,* 197 U.S. 11 (1905).

132. *Buck v. Bell,* 274 U.S. 200 (1927). It is doubtful whether this decision would stand today inasmuch as the subsequent case of *Skinner v. Oklahoma,* 316 U.S. 535 (1942) established the right to procreation as a fundamental right.

133. *Roe v. Wade,* 410 U.S. 113 (1973). The controls are permissible if they protect the safety of the mother.

134. *Moos v. United States,* 118 F.Supp. 275 (D. Minn. 1954). See Bruce Ennis and Loren Siegel, *The Rights of Mental Patients: The Basic ACLU Guide to a Mental Patient's Rights* (New York: Avon Books, 1978), p. 132.

135. *Schloendorff v. Society of New York Hospital,* 105 N.E.92 (N.Y. 1914).

136. *Jacobson v. Massachusetts,* 197 U.S. 11 (1905).

137. *Board of Education v. Maas,* 152 A. 2d 394 (1959), affirmed 158 A. 2d 330, certiorari denied, 363 U.S. 843; *Sadlock v. Board of Education,* 58 A. 2d 218 (1948); *State v. Drew,* 192 A. 629 (1937); *Stull v. Reber,* 64 A.419 (1906).

138. *Peterson v. Widule,* 147 N.W. 966 (1914).

139. *State ex rel. Holcomb v. Armstrong,* 239 P. 2d 545 (1952).

140. *Moore v. Draper,* 57 So. 2d 648 (1952).

141. *Matter of Quackenbush,* 383 A. 2d 785 (1978). But see *Long Island Jewish-Hillside Medical Center v. Levitt,* 342 N.Y.S. 2d 356 (Sup. Ct. 1973), in which the Court approved the appointment of a guardian for an eighty-four year old to compel a life-saving operation for gangrene. See also *United States v. George,* 239 F.Supp. 752 (D. Conn. 1965).

142. *In re Quinlan,* 355 A. 2d 647 (1976).

143. *Application of President and Directors of Georgetown College, Inc.,* 331 F. 2d 1000 (1964), rehearing denied, 331 F. 2d 1010, certiorari denied, 377 U.S. 978.

144. *United States v. George,* 239 F.Supp. 752 (D.C. Conn. 1965).

145. *John F. Kennedy Memorial Hospital v. Heston,* 279 A. 2d 670 (1971).

146. *Matter of Quackenbush,* 383 A. 2d 785 (1978).

147. *In re Quinlan,* 355 A. 2d 647 (1976).

148. *Matter of Quackenbush,* 383 A. 2d 785 (1978).

149. *Erickson v. Dilgard,* 252 N.Y.S. 2d 705 (1962).

150. *In re Brooks Estate,* 205 N.E. 2d 435 (1965).

151. *Prince v. Massachusetts,* 321 U.S. 158 (1944). See also Annotation, "Power of Courts or Other Public Agencies, in the Absence of Statutory Authority, to Order Compulsory Medical Care for Adult," 9 A.L.R. 3d 1391, 1392.

152. *Application of President and Directors of Georgetown College, Inc.,* 331 F. 2d 1000 (1964). See 9 A.L.R. 3d 1379.

153. *Mitchell v. Davis,* 205 S.W. 2d 812 (1947).

154. *In re Karwath,* 199 N.W. 2d 147 (1972).

155. *In re Sampson,* 278 N.E. 2d 918 (1972). But see *In re Green,* 292 A. 2d 387 (1972).

156. *Raleigh Fitkin-Paul Morgan Memorial Hospital v. Anderson,* 201 A. 2d 537 (1964), certiorari denied 377 U.S. 985.

157. *Jacobson v. Massachusetts,* 197 U.S. 11 (1905). See *Gamble v. State,* 333 S.W. 2d 816 (1960); *Anderson v. State,* 65 S.E. 2d 848 (1951); *State v. Drew,* 192 A. 629 (1937); *Commonwealth v. Green,* 168 N.E. 101 (1929).

158. See *Application of President and Directors of Georgetown College, Inc.,* 331 F. 2d 1000 (1964), rehearing denied 331 F. 2d 1010, certiorari denied 377 U.S. 978; *Hoener v. Bertinato,* 171 A. 2d 140 (1961); *People ex rel. Wallace v. Labrenz,* 104 N.E. 2d 769 (1952), certiorari denied 344 U.S. 824.

159. Annotation, "Power of public authorities to order medical care for a child over objection of parent or custodian," 30 A.L.R. 2d 1138, 1139 (1953).

160. *Re Tuttendario,* 21 Pa. Dist. 561 (1911).

161. *Re Frank,* 248 P. 2d 553 (1952).

162. *Re Vasko,* 263 N.Y.S. 552 (1933).

163. *Re Rotkowitz,* 25 N.Y.S. 2d 624 (1941).

164. Oliver Wendell Holmes, quoted in Bernard Schwartz, *Constitutional Law* (New York: Macmillan, 1972), p. viii.

CHAPTER SEVEN

Procedural Rights Under the Constitution

Court cases are either civil or criminal. In a civil case a party files suit, claiming that another party violated one or more of his or her legal rights. It results in a civil judgment, such as a financial settlement or an injunction. To illustrate, consider Illinois's law on adoption, which lets a resident adopt a child only if he or she has lived in the state at least six months.[1] Assume that a new resident wants to adopt a child. Forbidden to do so by statute, the resident files suit against the state, claiming the statute violates one of his or her rights, such as the constitutional freedom of interstate travel. The judicial holding will be civil; it may, for example, nullify the law on the grounds that it unreasonably interferes with the appellant's Fourteenth Amendment liberty.

A criminal law, in contrast, results in a criminal penalty such as imprisonment or a fine.[2] In a criminal case the government charges a person with violating a criminal law. A statute is part of the criminal law if it imposes criminal penalties. For example, one section of the federal criminal code says that "[w]hoever utters any obscene, indecent, or profane language by means of radio communication shall be fined not more than $10,000 or imprisoned not more than two years, or both."[3] The Illinois criminal code says that "[a] person commits an assault when,

221

without lawful authority, he engages in conduct which places another in reasonable apprehension of receiving a battery. . . . Assault is a Class C misdemeanor."[4]

Criminal laws become grist for civil lawsuits when they interfere with an individual's rights. People convicted of a crime might later challenge the *substance* of criminal laws. A convicted prostitute might claim the state's antiprostitution law violates her Fourteenth Amendment freedom of contract. A man convicted of willfully destroying a U.S. flag might claim the federal flag desecration law stifles his freedom of speech. Offenders also challenge the *methods* officials used to enforce the law they were convicted of violating. A prostitute might claim police pressured her to confess in violation of her Fifth Amendment privilege against self-incrimination. The flag destroyer might claim police illegally searched his home in violation of the Fourth Amendment ban on unreasonable searches and seizures.

The preceding chapters examine criminal and other laws for their substantive constitutionality. This chapter turns to the procedures by which the state enforces its criminal laws. In so doing it defines the constitutional rights of defendants who are brought within the criminal justice system. This system embraces individuals, such as police officers, prosecuting attorneys, judges, probation officers, prison personnel, and parole officers; and procedures, such as arrests, searches, arraignments, sentencing, and parole, which together form an apparatus for trying, convicting, and punishing criminal offenders.[5] The apparatus comprises

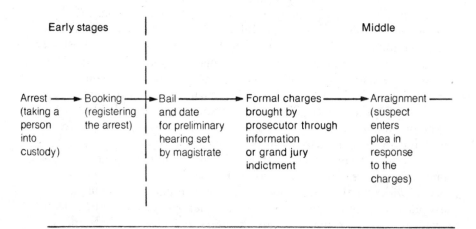

FIGURE 7.1
THE STAGES AND LENGTH OF THE CRIMINAL
JUSTICE SYSTEM

orderly steps the state follows as it prosecutes and tries suspected criminals. A distinguishing feature of the criminal justice system is, then, its length. Months and even years may elapse between the first step and the last (see Figure 7.1).

The system also has width in that it shunts some cases from the central corridor to adjunct hallways. It diverts misdemeanors early in the process and sends cases involving minors to special juvenile justice systems. Some jurisdictions settle minor disputes through arbitration.[6] Here they appoint an arbitrator to review the facts of the dispute informally with the parties. The arbitrator helps negotiate a solution and the dispute ends at that point. The suspect is not tried nor does he build a criminal record. Another source of diversion is plea bargaining; by pleading guilty in exchange for leniency, the defendant bypasses the trial and returns to the central apparatus for sentencing (see Figure 7.2).

A third feature of the criminal justice system is the range of case-by-case decisions for which it is responsible. All participants make discretionary decisions custom-fitted to the circumstances of individual cases. The seeming lack of structure of individual discretionary decisions contrasts to the formal apparatus of criminal procedure. "Discretionary justice," writes one observer, "suggests latitude of decision-making rather than formality or certainty."[7] Prosecutors use discretion to decide whether formally to charge a person with a crime, judges use discretion when they sentence a convicted offender, and parole officers use discretion when granting a prisoner parole. Each suggests that "idiosyncracy

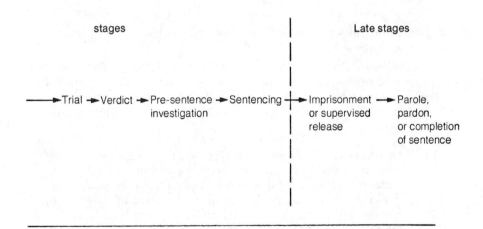

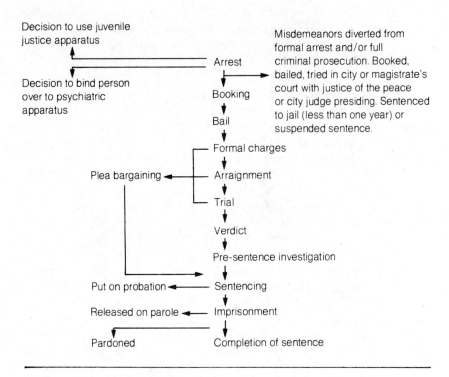

FIGURE 7.2
THE WIDTH OF THE CRIMINAL JUSTICE
SYSTEM

rather than rules may guide decision-making within the administration of criminal justice."[8]

Although the criminal justice system features a central series of formal steps, several diversionary outlets, and many discretionary decisions, the Constitution addresses only the formal steps, and only several of those. Its key procedural guarantees lie in the Fourth, Fifth, Sixth, and Eighth Amendments:

Amendment IV The right of the people to be secure in their persons, houses, papers, and effects, against unreasonable searches and seizures, shall not be violated, and no warrants shall issue, but upon probable cause, supported by oath or affirmation, and particularly describing the place to be searched, and the persons or things to be seized.

Amendment V No person shall be held to answer for a capital, or otherwise infamous crime, unless on a presentment or indictment of a Grand Jury . . . ; nor shall any person be subject for the same offence to be twice put in jeopardy of life or limb; nor shall be compelled in any criminal case to be a witness, against himself, nor be deprived of life, liberty, or property, without due process of law; nor shall private property be taken for public use, without just compensation.

Amendment VI In all criminal prosecutions, the accused shall enjoy the right to a speedy and public trial, by an impartial jury of the State and district wherein the crime shall have been committed, which district shall have been previously ascertained by law, and to be informed of the nature and cause of the accusation; to be confronted with the witnesses against him; to have compulsory process for obtaining witnesses in his favor, and to have the Assistance of Counsel for his defence.

Amendment VIII Excessive bail shall not be required, nor excessive fines imposed, nor cruel and unusual punishments inflicted.

The Constitution is silent on other parts of criminal procedure. However, this does not leave the defendant unprotected as he or she passes from each explicit constitutional guarantee nor does it leave the defendant wholly vulnerable at discretionary points, such as at plea bargaining or during sentencing.

As with substantive rights, procedural rights depend on judicial interpretation to give them life. Judges willing to interpret the Constitution have machinery for breathing life into the Constitution's terse procedural guarantees. First, each guarantee is elastic and judges may expand the coverage of each. The Supreme Court, for example, has eased the Sixth Amendment's right to counsel to cover stages in criminal procedure other than the trial itself. Second, judges may use the Constitution's "conscience," the due process clause, to demand fundamental fairness in all criminal procedures. Due process prevents the state from arbitrarily and capriciously intruding on the rights of defendants.[9] It is an overarching principle that controls state practices by its role in creating a fundamentally fair system of justice. For example, the Court holds that in the interest of fundamental fairness a parole board must hold a hearing before revoking an offender's parole.[10]

For decades judges shunned this machinery and allowed police, courts, and correctional personnel to make and enforce their own policy. Only in the last two decades have courts replaced their "hands-off" policy with an active review of criminal procedure. The change dates to the Warren Court's incorporation decisions in the 1960s, which signalled the Court's willingness to review state criminal procedure. The decisions unleashed many and varied appeals that forced the Court to review previously overlooked state procedures. Many of the Court's decisions snowballed; for example, *Mapp v. Ohio*[11] (making illegally seized evidence inadmissible in state courts) and *Miranda v. Arizona*[12] (requiring police to tell suspects of their right to silence and representation by counsel) prompted thousands of appeals that turned attention to early stages in criminal adjudication. Then, the Civil Rights Act of 1964 gave U.S. citizens the right to sue state agents for depriving them of constitutional "rights, privileges, or immunities."[13] The act allowed prisoners to sue prison officials for constitutional violations and turned judicial attention to post-trial practices. Finally, the civil rights movement of the 1960s sparked interest in the substantive rights of marginal groups, including prisoners and criminal defendants.

Today, after extending the scope of stated constitutional rights and giving a broad cast to due process, the Court has filled the spaces separating each constitutional guarantee so that most procedures fall within at least limited constitutional purview. The present chapter reviews early steps of arrest and search, middle stages of prosecution and adjudication, and later correctional stages. Each section answers the same question posed throughout the book: what guidelines has the Court handed down to put meaning on the terse words of the Constitution? Procedural guidelines are usually more straightforward than those governing substantive rights.

EARLY STAGES OF CRIMINAL PROCEDURE

In sheer volume of cases entertained, criminal law procedure handily outweighs other areas of constitutional law. It occupies thick chapters in constitutional law casebooks, long sections in legal encyclopedias and law reporters, and pages rather than columns in law review indices. Much of this bulk relates to the Fourth Amendment's ban on "unreasonable searches." The circumstances of arrests and their accompanying searches are more varied than those of other steps in criminal adjudication. Defying the imagination of dedicated novelists, the idiosyncrasies of each arrest and search pose a special challenge to judges who apply Fourth Amendment principles to the case at bar. Consider, for example, the arrest of one Steven Vance Scott.[14] When on a 2:00 A.M. patrol on New Year's Eve 1973, California police spotted Scott and this three-year-old son on a traffic island on Highway 101. Scott appeared to be urinating. As officers approached he muttered something to the effect of "Oh, Hell, we are going to be busted." He seemed to be drunk and officers volunteered to take him and his son home. For their "own protection" the officers patted down Scott for weapons. They asked him to raise his arms and as he did so the officers spotted "a clear plastic baggie containing green matter which appeared to . . . be marijuana." One of the officers "squeezed the outside of the baggie, and its contents felt pliant and crunchy." The police arrested Scott for possession of marijuana. They also arrested him for LSD possession after they saw a brown bag, looked inside, and found two cans of beer and tablets that appeared to be LSD. Thus, police stopped a man because he appeared to be *drunk*, searched him for *weapons*, and arrested him for *drug* possession. Scott's arrest raises questions about the conditions under which police may arrest and search a person. First, under what circumstances may police search a citizen? Recall that the police volunteered to drive Scott home. Inasmuch as they were not ordered to drive him, one wonders whether police had the authority to search Scott in the first place. Can police search a person "just in case" he or she is armed or do they need a reason to believe he is armed? Can they search a person who is not suspected of a crime? Can they search a person without a warrant? Second, what items may police seize in a search? May police search a person for one type of evidence and seize other evidence they come across? May they seize items, such as the bag containing the LSD, that are near but not on the person?

The Fourth Amendment governs two early steps in criminal procedure: arrests (the seizure of persons) and searches (the seizure of things). It has three key terms: "unreasonable," "warrant," and "probable cause." Before considering the constitutionality of Steven Scott's arrest and search, we will examine the law on arrest, the law on search and seizure, and the relation of each to reasonableness, warrants, and probable cause.

Arrest

When police arrest a person they take him "into custody that he may be held to answer for a crime."[15] Technically an arrest is nothing more; the person is a "suspect" not a criminal, the state presumes he is innocent, and no formal charges have been filed. Yet an arrest irreversibly affects a person. Acquaintances label him a criminal, expenses multiply, and the suspect unable to raise bail finds himself imprisoned pending trial. The depressed conditions of local jails in early English days made an arrest a "terrible calamity" that could cost a suspect his life.[16] Consequently, the English bequeathed to us a "very strict body of law" on arrest[17] as well as a tradition that the Constitution's framers codified in the Fourth Amendment.

The Fourth Amendment states that all arrests must be reasonable. It then states that warrants must be issued by a *court* ("supported by oath"), upon showing of *probable cause* (to believe a crime has been committed and the suspect committed it)[18] and particularly *describing* what is to be seized and where. It does not say what makes an arrest reasonable, but presumably an arrest made with a warrant meeting these three conditions is reasonable. This formula would be satisfactory were it not for the human urge to flee the scene of a crime and make oneself unavailable after hearing police are suspicious. Such was the reaction of two would-be burglars caught tiptoeing down an apartment hallway by an off-duty officer peering out of his keyhole.[19] When the officer went outside to investigate the culprits fled. The officer overtook one of the men, patted him down, found burglary tools, and arrested him. Had the officer excused himself to get an arrest warrant, he would have had proper documentation but no suspect to show for it. The realities of law enforcement often make it impossible for officers to obtain a warrant before arresting a suspect. The framers of the Fourth Amendment apparently appreciated this fact; the amendment does not say that a warrant *must* accompany an arrest. Instead it says an arrest must be reasonable and then goes on to describe a proper warrant.

Courts interpret the Fourth Amendment to say that an officer may make a warrantless arrest so long as he or she has probable cause to believe a crime has been committed and the suspect committed it.[20] This preserves probable cause as a precondition of an arrest but strikes the warrant as a go-between. It enriches the above formula to say:

1. An arrest must be reasonable.
2. A reasonable arrest is one made when an officer has probable cause to believe the suspect committed a crime, secures a warrant on that basis, and arrests the suspect.
3. It is often impossible to secure a warrant.
4. A reasonable arrest is one made when an officer has probable cause to believe the suspect has committed a crime and arrests without a warrant when it is impractical to obtain one.

The formula requires an understanding of probable cause and of the situations in which it is impractical to secure a warrant.

Courts give breathing space to probable cause. "In dealing with probable cause," the Supreme Court has written, "we deal with probabilities. These are not technical; they are the factual and practical considerations of everyday life on which reasonable and prudent men, not legal technicians, act."[21] Probable cause, writes another court, "defies precise definition. It is something less than proof needed to convict and something more than a raw, unsupported suspicion. It is a suspicion (or belief) of guilt that is 'well-grounded'."[22] To decide whether police have probable cause to arrest, courts examine all the facts of the case or the "totality of the circumstances."[23] Recall the case of the tiptoeing burglars. In deciding whether the officer had probable cause to arrest, the Court reviewed all the facts of the case, which started when the officer heard strange noises in the hallway.[24] He peered through the keyhole and saw two strangers behaving suspiciously (tiptoeing). He opened the door and the two fled (another suspicious act). He captured one of them, patted him down, and found burglars' tools. None of these facts taken alone amounted to probable cause; being a stranger did not establish probable cause nor did tiptoeing or running. But taken together, these facts gave the officer cause to believe a crime was in process, and the Supreme Court upheld the warrantless arrest.

In ruling on probable cause courts look through the eyes of police officers. "Conduct innocent in the eyes of the untrained," wrote one court, "may carry entirely different 'messages' to the experienced or trained observer."[25] Courts recognize that a narcotics officer, for example, spots clues pointing to a narcotics sale unseen by an untrained person. Courts also consider the crime itself.[26] In one case police arrested a man on a narcotics charge when they saw him carrying a large canvas bag to an apartment where a drug sale reportedly was to take place.[27] Although the appellate court later held the bag did not give police probable cause to arrest, the case illustrates crime-specific behavior: acts suspicious in one case may not be in another, depending on the crime in question. A large canvas bag contributes to probable cause in a drug operation but not in a prostitution stakeout.

Probable cause excuses police from securing a warrant some, but not all, of the time. Assume, for example, that an informant tells police a woman is running a drug-selling operation from her home. Police stake out the house, watch known drug offenders going and coming, and see at least one person injecting himself after leaving the house. After a week police decide they have probable cause to arrest and they take the woman into custody. Recall that a warrantless arrest is permissible when it is impractical for police to secure a warrant. Here, police had ample time to secure a warrant but did not. The arrest is thereby unreasonable. Courts hold it is impractical to obtain an arrest warrant in an "exigency" or emergency.[28] One exigency arises if the officer has reasonable grounds for believing the suspect will escape if not arrested at once[29] and a second occurs when a person flees the scene of a crime. A third arises when evidence is endangered. For example, the estranged husband of a murder victim voluntarily went to the police station after officers called him on the telephone.[30] Officers noted a dark spot, like blood, on the man's finger and asked to scrape his fingernails. He refused and then began rubbing his hands together behind his back. He also put his hands in his pocket and rattled something metallic. Police feared he was scraping evidence from his nails and arrested him on the spot. A court later upheld the arrest, saying that when police combined the scraping with other known facts,[31] they had probable cause to arrest in order to preserve evidence. A fourth exigency occurs when police come across an escaped prisoner,[32] and a fifth when they face a stop and frisk situation; that is, when they see a person acting suspiciously, have reasonable grounds for believing he is armed, and find weapons in a patdown.[33] Courts treat most arrests as automatic exigencies.[34] This means most arrests are warrantless. As a result the Fourth Amendment's warrant provision offers less protection to the suspect than its probable cause provision.

Search and Seizure

State police showed little concern about the reasonableness of their searches and seizures before the 1961 case of *Mapp v. Ohio*.[35] The exclusionary rule governed fewer than one-half of the states, and police saw the fruits of their searches in court even if illegally obtained. The Court reviewed searches on a case-by-case basis and only struck evidence seized in a shocking manner.[36] After *Mapp v. Ohio* held inadmissible evidence seized by state police in violation of the Fourth Amendment, however, police laxity changed abruptly. If police continued to seize evidence illegally, the state would end up with few successful prosecutions. *Mapp* thus bade the states to figure out what was and was not a reasonable search.

The Fourth Amendment sets up the same formula for searches as for arrests. A search and seizure must be reasonable but the Amendment does not say what makes a reasonable search. It does say that a search warrant must be based on probable cause, be particularly written, and be issued through a court. Presumably a search meeting these three conditions is reasonable. But, as with arrests, suspects do not cooperate enough to make this formula work. Just as police must make warrantless arrests in order to keep the suspect from disappearing, so must they make warrantless searches in order to keep the evidence from disappearing. Recall the case of the estranged husband busily scraping evidence from his fingernails. Had police arrested him, waited for a search warrant, and then searched him, they would have given him ample time to scrape and wash away the evidence.

Courts interpret the Fourth Amendment to say that police may make a warrantless search incident to a lawful arrest.[37] A lawful arrest, in turn, is based upon probable cause and is made with an arrest warrant in ordinary circumstances and without one in exigencies. From this search police may retrieve the fruits of a crime (such as money from a bank robbery), "mere evidence" (such as an item of clothing similar to that worn by the bank robber),[38] and weapons (to prevent the suspect from harming officers or anyone else). The search may cover the suspect's *body*. For example, the Court upheld the search of Willie Robinson.[39] Believing Robinson to be driving a car without an operator's license, police pulled Robinson over and arrested him when their suspicion proved true. Incident to the arrest they patted Robinson down and found fourteen heroin capsules in his shirt pocket. Following his conviction for heroin possession, Robinson filed suit, claiming police exceeded their authority by patting him down when they had no reason to believe he was armed. The Court upheld the search, saying police lawfully in a place doing something they are lawfully permitted to do, such as arresting a person under probable cause, may conduct a search and seize whatever incriminating evidence they find. Second, police may extend the search *into* the suspect's body if they follow reasonable procedures. Without a warrant, police may scrape an arrestee's fingernails, take a blood sample, obtain hair samples, conduct a breath analysis, and take voice recordings. They may not, however, force a suspect to vomit nor may they pump a suspect's stomach against his or her will.[40] Third, police may search the area within an arrestee's *immediate control* in order to prevent him or her from grabbing a weapon or destroying evidence.[41] Fourth, they may seize evidence lying in *plain view*.[42] "It has long been established," wrote the Court, "that objects falling in the plain view of an officer who has a right to be in the position to have that view are subject to seizures and may be introduced as evidence."[43] Police may not search beyond these four areas in a suspect's home or workplace[44] *except* when they are in hot pursuit and reasonably believe the suspect will destroy evidence if a thorough search is not made at once. For example, after chasing a man who fled the scene of a robbery into his home, police thoroughly searched the home for clothing similar to that worn by the man seen fleeing the crime.[45] They found the clothing in the clothes washer, a shotgun and pistol in the toilet top, and ammunition under the mattress. The Supreme Court later upheld the thorough search because it was made in hot pursuit. Fifth, police may search beyond these areas when arresting someone in an *automobile*. Because cars are mobile they "may be searched without a warrant upon facts not justifying a warrantless search of a residence or office."[46] Police may even search a car before arresting if they have probable cause to believe the car contains evidence of a crime[47] and may search it one week after impounding it, even though they had plenty of time to obtain a search warrant.[48] (See Table 7.1.)

The preceding discussion is about warrantless searches incidental to a lawful arrest. In two situations police may also conduct warrantless searches *not* incidental to an arrest.[49] First, they may search a person or place if the subject consents to it. But suppose three officers bang on a

TABLE 7.1
PRINCIPLES OF WARRANTLESS SEARCH AND
SEIZURE

WHAT may be seized

Weapons

Evidence of a crime

Fruits of a crime (contraband)

WHEN it may be seized

When police are lawfully in a place doing something they are lawfully permitted to do. This includes:

Making a custodial arrest

Conducting a stop and frisk

Conducting a search when the owner intelligently consents to it

---

WHERE it may be seized

On the suspect's body (e.g., in a pocket)

In the suspect's body if it is a limited intrusion done under sanitary medical conditions (e.g., taking a blood sample)

In the home or workplace:	In the automobile:
In the area within the suspect's immediate control (e.g., on a table)	In the area within the suspect's immediate control (e.g., on the front seat)
In plain view of the officer (e.g., on a table in the next room)	In plain view of the officer (e.g., on the back seat)
In out-of-the-way places *if* police chase the suspect into his or her home in hot pursuit	In out-of-the-way places

person's door in the middle of the night and ask to search the premises? Few people will resist when faced with such a show of authority. To decide whether a person gave knowing and intelligent consent, courts examine the "totality of the circumstances." They are likely to find the consent voluntary if the suspect gives written permission and if one or two officers arrived at a reasonable hour, act politely, and do not threaten the suspect.[50] If, however, several police arrive in the middle of the night with guns drawn, the circumstances point to involuntary consent. Second, police may make a warrantless search when a stop and frisk is in order. The Court allows police to stop and frisk someone, where there is no probable cause to arrest, *if* the person acts suspiciously and the police have probable cause to believe he or she is armed.[51] A stop and frisk is limited to a weapons' patdown. In one case police watched a suspect talk with known drug addicts in a restaurant. They then went up to him and asked him to leave the restaurant. As he began to reach into his pocket, the officer reached in and pulled out heroin. The Court later said the heroin was inadmissible as evidence.[52] The police did not have probable cause to believe the suspect was armed and dangerous and had no right to make a stop and frisk: "[t]he search was not reasonably limited in scope to the accomplishment of the only goal which might conceivably have justified its inception—the protection of the officer by disarming a potentially dangerous man."

In addition to deciding what may be seized and when,[53] courts examine how something may be seized. A search and seizure commonly evokes images of officers rummaging through drawers and poking under beds. But today's technology bids us to revamp this image. Competing with blunderbuss searches are sophisticated electronic techniques that allow the state to collect evidence without police presence. The pen register records the telephone numbers suspects dial, other devices record the telephone conversations themselves, and still others record conversations in homes and in streets. After holding a contrary position for thirty years, the Court now treats electronic surveillance as a "search" and the evidence secured (words) as a "seizure" within the meaning of the Fourth Amendment.[54] In electronic as well as traditional searches, then, officers must follow the Fourth Amendment's counsel to secure particularized search warrants based on probable cause before monitoring conversations. The Court pays special attention to the warrant in eavesdropping cases because the technique "involves an intrusion of privacy that is broad in scope."[55] The warrant must "particularly describ[e] the place to be searched and the person or things to be seized" and specify how long the monitoring will take place. It may not be a blanket, limitless warrant. The state must inform the suspect of the monitoring unless it can show "special facts" or an exigency. The exigency must "appear more important in eavesdropping, with its inherent dangers, than that required when conventional procedures of search and seizure are utilized."[56]

Eavesdropping protections are less exemplary in practice than theory, in part because of the 1968 Omnibus Crime Control and Safe Streets Act. Title III of the act contains a long list of crimes open to state eavesdropping that range from sabotage to conspiracy.[57] The state may secure a warrant for eavesdropping merely by telling the judge that "traditional methods have failed to solve the case, or [by explaining] why they are unlikely to succeed if they are used."[58] Of the 1,889 state and federal warrant applications made between 1968 and 1971, 1,887 were granted, thereby showing the ease with which judges issue warrants.[59]

We return now to Steven Vance Scott's claim that police finding him on a traffic island unreasonably searched and arrested him in violation of the Fourth Amendment. Police may make a warrantless arrest if they have probable cause to believe the suspect committed a crime. Scott's marijuana gave police probable cause to arrest, but the appellate court held the police did not have authority to search Scott in the first place. Police may make a warrantless search in an exigency, in a stop and frisk, or when making a lawful arrest. None of these conditions was present in Scott's case. No exigency existed, police had no cause to arrest Scott (the record made no mention of police intention to arrest Scott for public intoxication), and neither of the conditions of a stop and frisk (suspicious behavior and reasonable grounds for believing the suspect is armed) was present. The police actions essentially amounted to a stop and frisk and, without authority to make a stop and frisk, evidence seized was unreasonable and violated the Fourth Amendment. The exclusionary rule forbids the admission of illegally seized evidence in court, the evidence was useless, and the appellate court reversed Scott's conviction.

The Suspect as Informant

> . . . nor shall any person be . . . compelled in any criminal case to be a witness against himself. . . . (U.S. Constitution, Amend. V)

Much evidence comes not from searches and seizures but from the voice of the suspect himself or herself. Suspects often turn out to be surprisingly loquacious and give police detailed confessions. The case of *People v. Paton* is not atypical.[60] It involved one Betty Jane Paton, who stabbed (and killed) her common law husband after they had argued about her infidelity. Immediately after the stabbing she called the sheriff's office and said, "Get a deputy out here quick, and send an ambulance. It is Betty Paton. I just stabbed my husband." The deputy went to her house, said "Hello," walked to the couch where the victim was lying and Mrs. Paton was kneeling, said "Hello, Betty," and asked "What happened?" She replied, "The same thing as last time. I stabbed him again." After the ambulance arrived, the deputy informed Mrs. Paton of her rights and she gave a detailed account of the stabbing. At the stationhouse she made and signed a written confession. Other times suspects openly admit things they hope will help them, unaware the admissions are damaging. A suspect may, for example, rush to blame his or her partner and, in the process, solidly implicate himself or herself. Or a suspect may confess to behavior that links him or her to the crime. In one case a woman called police, claiming that her son-in-law had raped her.[61] The police, the woman, and her lover went to the suspect's house, where they found him and his wife. Police asked the suspect if he had raped his mother-in-law. He denied it but did admit having intercourse with her, a damaging admission, and police arrested him on the spot. Still other times suspects confess less as an inapposite blurt and more because of police coercion. Suspects often recant confessions made after prolonged interrogation or other duress.

To talk about the suspect as informant is to turn to the Fifth Amendment's privilege against self-incrimination. Popular lore about self-incrimination places it in the courtroom where the wily prosecutor cross-examines the defendant who staunchly refuses to answer on the grounds that he or she may incriminate himself or herself. But self-incrimination comes into play well before the trial and may even be more important in these early stages. Because most cases are disposed of in plea bargaining, not criminal trials, pre-trial events are critical to the defendant. The state improves its bargaining position as it builds up evidence. The suspect's early incriminations help the state: the stronger the state's case, the more likely is the defendant to plead guilty and waive his or her right to trial while a bargain can still be struck.

The suspect's Fifth Amendment right to silence starts when police stop inquiring and begin accusing. At this point the suspect is no longer free to leave and the formal criminal process has begun. Police must be able to recognize the point of accusation because, according to *Miranda v. Arizona*, they must then inform the suspect of his or her right to silence.[62] If they fail to warn the suspect, his or her incriminating statements are inadmissible in court. It is sometimes tricky to know when questioning turns from routine investigation to accusation. Not infrequently police will go to the scene of a crime, ask casually, "What happened?" and receive a full-fledged confession in turn. Such happened when Betty Jane Paton confessed to stabbing her husband. It also happened in Alabama when two officers went to the scene of a shooting.[63] One of the officers attended the victim, who was slumped in a car, and the other officer stayed in the squad car. Suddenly a man, Gene Robert Ison, walked out of the house carrying a pistol. One of the officers asked if he had done the shooting and he said that he had. Usually such general on-the-scene questions are not thought to be accusatory because they lack "the compelling atmosphere inherent in the process of in-custody interrogation." No one compelled Gene Robert Ison to admit he had just shot someone. Ison approached the police officer, who was sitting in his squad car; nothing suggested to Ison that he was not free to leave. Had both officers approached Ison with guns drawn and demanded to know whether he shot the victim, the situation might have been different in that it would have suggested a compelling atmosphere.

Miranda's rationale is twofold. First, a right is hollow if the victim is unaware of it. When faced with the trappings of law enforcement, few suspects unaware that they have the right to remain silent will in fact keep quiet; the Miranda warning is designed to let them know they have a constitutional right to silence. Second, Miranda guards against involuntary confessions. Before Miranda the Court tackled the problem of coerced confessions on a case-by-case basis, asking whether the "totality of the circumstances" pointed to a voluntary confession. It even accepted confessions the defendant later recanted if the circumstances indicated the confessions were "probably true."[64] The Court appreciated the weakness of this approach and noted that no "talismanic formula" indicated whether a confession was coerced.[65] Miranda introduced a new technique for dealing with involuntary confessions: it *presumed* that any confession made in an accusatory setting where the suspect was unaware of his or her right to silence was involuntary and thereby inadmissible in court.

Miranda was a pivotal decision in a series of decisions. Not the sudden, revolutionary holding many made it out to be, Miranda instead topped a series of cases in which the Court showed growing skepticism about recanted confessions.[66] Similarly, the early post-Miranda decisions continued the tradition. The Court's first two post-Miranda decisions expanded the right[67] but then, just as the Burger Court put the exclusionary rule on a plateau after the Warren Court groomed and built it, so did the Burger Court decline to extend Miranda's principle further. In 1971 it held that if the defendant makes incriminating statements without having been given the Miranda warnings and later takes the stand in his or her own defense, the state may use the illegally secured statements to point out inconsistencies in the defendant's testimony.[68] This, the so-called *Harris* rule, allows the state to use illegally secured confessions to impeach the defendant's testimony. While still supporting *Miranda* in principle, the Court held that those warnings must not "be construed to include the right to commit perjury."[69] The *Harris* ruling is illustrated by a case involving a shooting.[70] While quarreling with his neighbor over a dog, Robert Riddell shot his neighbor in the foot. The state charged Riddell with second degree assault. To convict, the state had to show that Riddell willfully pulled the trigger. When Riddell took the stand in his own defense, he claimed the gun accidentally went off when his wife hit his arm. The deputy prosecuting attorney asked, "And did you have it [the rifle] pulled back or cocked?" Riddell answered "No." At this point the attorney referred to an earlier statement Riddell had made without *Miranda* warnings: "I cocked the hammer and pulled the trigger. I thought the rifle was aimed towards the ground and only intended to scare Mr. Lewis." Using the *Harris* principle, the Court allowed the state to introduce illegally obtained evidence to show that Riddell was lying.

Booking and Bail

After a suspect is arrested and informed of his or her rights, police register the arrest (book him or her) at the stationhouse.[71] During booking police will question, fingerprint, photograph, search the suspect and perhaps put him or her in a lineup. Questioning is the only one of these procedures that amounts to a "critical" stage during which the suspect has a right to counsel.[72] Next the suspect appears before a magistrate, who will fix bail.[73] Bail must be set immediately in federal jurisdictions,[74] but most states specify only that it be done within a "reasonable" time.[75] It is important because a freed suspect can prepare a better defense than a confined suspect. Among other things, he or she may shop for a lawyer, find defense witnesses, and do independent legal research. Second, bail protects an innocent person from imprisonment and undeserved punishment. The framers might have had this in mind when they placed the constitutional ban on excessive bail in the Eighth Amendment next to the ban on cruel and unusual punishment, rather than in the Fourth or Fifth Amendment where it would have fitted more appropriately with the order of criminal procedure. Third, bail symbolically reaffirms the suspect's presumed innocence.[76] Recent studies suport these assumptions about bail's importance by showing that bailed defendants are more likely to receive suspended sentences and less likely to be sentenced to prison than nonbailed defendants.[77]

The Eighth Amendment governs bail. It warns that "[e]xcessive bail shall not be required. . . ." The Supreme Court calls bail "excessive" when it is "set at a figure higher than an amount reasonably calculated" to fulfill bail's intended purpose, which is to assure the defendant's presence at his or her trial.[78] The Court has not incorporated this right, but most state constitutions do forbid excessive bail.[79] On the other hand, some states deny bail altogether for felonies.[80]

MIDDLE STAGES OF CRIMINAL PROCEDURE

Prosecution

To this point the suspect has been arrested, booked, and probably released on bail. However, an arrest does not guarantee the suspect will be tried for that crime or, indeed, will be tried at all. The suspect next encounters three people having a say in the matter: the prosecuting attorney, trial judge, and his or her own lawyer.[81] Occurring first in the middle stages is the prosecutor's decision whether formally to charge the suspect and, if so, for what crime. To decide, the prosecutor or one of his or her assistants reviews a complaint filed by the victim or arresting officer as well as the available evidence.[82] The prosecutor's decision is affected by politics (he or she may have no choice but to bring charges in a highly publicized crime), economics (the state cannot file charges in all cases without overloading its resources), facts of the individual case (the arrest in itself may be sufficient punishment for a first offender, for example), and the suspect himself or herself (in plea bargaining the defendant cooperates with police in exchange for the prosecutor's promise to reduce or drop the charges that will be sought).[83] After deciding which charges to seek, the prosecutor undertakes formally to bring these charges by showing that he or she has probable cause to believe the suspect committed the crime and ought to be formally charged. The prosecutor proceeds either through the preliminary hearing or the grand jury.

In the preliminary hearing the prosecutor appears before a judge to show there is probable cause to believe the defendant committed the crime and ought to be formally charged.[84] The hearing resembles a trial in that it is open to the public and the suspect attends it, has the right to counsel, to cross-examine witnesses, and to speak briefly in his or her own behalf. It lets the suspect see what evidence the state has, which helps him or her prepare the defense and decide whether to plea bargain.[85] Its disadvantage to the suspect lies in the publicity it sparks. Because the state presents most of its evidence and the suspect has little opportunity to rebut it, the publicity is apt to be unfavorable. After hearing evidence, the judge decides whether the state has probable cause formally to charge the suspect. If probable cause exists, the prosecutor files a bill of information. One-half of the states use the preliminary hearing for some or all crimes.[86]

In some cases the prosecutor brings charges through a grand jury rather than the preliminary hearing (see Table 7.2). The Constitution calls for a grand jury indictment for serious federal crimes: "No person shall be held to answer for a capital, or otherwise infamous crime, unless on a presentment or indictment of a grand jury." In addition, one-half of the states use the grand jury.[87] The grand jury is a body of laymen. Twenty-three members sit in federal grand juries (only sixteen are needed for a quorum); state juries range from five to twenty-three members.[88] If the requisite number of jurors (twelve in federal courts) believe enough evidence exists to bring the suspect to trial, the prosecutor files an indictment. The grand jury little resembles a trial. No judge presides,[89] it sits in secrecy,[90] and the prosecutor enjoys the luxury of one-sided

TABLE 7.2
BRINGING FORMAL CHARGES AGAINST A
SUSPECT

	Preliminary hearing	Grand jury
The	prosecuting attorney	prosecuting attorney
tries to show to the	judge.	grand jury
in what is known as a	preliminary hearing	grand jury session
that he or she has probable cause to bring the suspect to trial.		
The proceedings are	public	secret
and the defendant	may appear, cross- . . . . . . examine witnesses, and offer an alibi.	may not appear.
If the	judge.	grand jury
finds probable cause to bring the defendant to trial, the prosecutor files a[n]	bill of information.	indictment.

argumentation. Typically, he or she will question a witness, dismiss him or her, ask the jurors for questions they would like to pose, reintroduce the witness, and then ask the new questions. No witnesses speak on the defendant's behalf; indeed, the defendant is not permitted to be present. Unlike a trial the prosecutor may introduce illegally seized[91] and hearsay[92] evidence. The Court holds that grand jury proceedings are not part of formal criminal prosecution.[93] As a result, the grand jury is almost entirely removed from due process requirements. The defendant has no right to counsel, to cross-examine witnesses, or call witnesses on his or her behalf. Even the witnesses enjoy few protections. A witness must testify even if testimony will criminally implicate him or her.[94] If granted immunity, the witness loses his or her Fifth Amendment right to silence. The witness has the right to counsel but because the attorney may not attend grand jury proceedings, the attorney and witness must consult in a separate room. At least one commentator has advocated a "bill of rights for witnesses" requiring, among other things, the right to counsel, decent notice before being called to appear, and the right to be informed of these protections.[95] If the Court were to extend due process protections to witnesses and suspects, this would not be inconsistent with other decisions extending minimum due process to steps outside the criminal adjudication core.[96]

After being formally charged, the suspect is arraigned. Here he or she appears before a judge who tells him or her of the formal charges and asks the suspect to enter a plea. Typically a suspect pleads not guilty, guilty by reason of insanity, guilty, or in some jurisdictons, no contest (the equivalent of a guilty plea).[97] Between 80 and 90 percent of suspects plead guilty at this point, having reached a bargain with the prosecutor in the days or hours preceding the arraignment. The defendant bargains for reduced charges, dismissed charges, or sentencing short of imprisonment.

The state bargains to get the defendant to cooperate with police or testify in later trials and to save the time and money of a full trial. Because the defendant usually waives his or her right to appeal as part of the bargain, the state benefits from seeing the case finally disposed.[98] The Supreme Court calls plea bargaining "an essential component of the administration of justice" and notes that plea bargaining quickens the disposition of cases, prevents long confinement for suspects unable to post bail, protects the public from guilty suspects who can post bail, and hastens whatever rehabilitation comes from sentencing.[99]

Plea bargaining is the vortex of criminal adjudication. "There is no doubt," writes one commentator, "that the guilty plea, *not* the trial, is the chief form of criminal adjudication in our society."[100] Yet the Constitution does not mention plea bargaining. It is a practice that lodges between the steps formally recognized in the Fourth, Fifth, Sixth, and Eighth Amendments. This is ironic, given the importance of plea bargaining for the defendant. "[A] plea of guilty is more than an admission of conduct," writes the Court, "it is a conviction."[101] The defendant who pleads guilty waives not only his or her right to trial by jury but also the right to confront accusors and sometimes the right to appeal. The consequences of a guilty plea may be enormous. Consider the case of Edward Boykin, a 27-year-old Alabaman indicted on five counts of common law robbery.[102] Boykin pleaded guilty to all counts at his arraignment. As required by Alabama law, a jury met to fix Boykin's sentence. Armed robbery was punishable by imprisonment or death in Alabama, and the jury sentenced Boykin to five concurrent death sentences. As one commentator put it, "A sentence of five times in the electric chair is possibly the worst bargain ever received by a defendant who has engaged in plea bargaining."[103]

The Court holds that the defendant has a right to counsel when making his or her guilty plea.[104] It also requires a showing that the defendant pleaded guilty knowingly and intelligently.[105] Thus, the Court reversed Boykin's conviction and multiple death penalty on the grounds that the judge erred by accepting Boykin's plea without a showing that Boykin made it intelligently and voluntarily. The record failed to show the judge questioned Boykin about his plea or that Boykin even appeared before the judge. To decide whether the suspect's plea was made voluntarily, the Court looks for signs of coercion and false promises.[106] Plea bargaining speeds up criminal justice but does not always lead to the conclusion expected by the defendant. Messages get mixed, attorneys and judges retire or are removed from a case, ill-founded promises are made, and the presiding judge may be unwilling to accept the bargain's conditions. Consider the case of Rudolph Santobello, who was indicted on two charges: promoting gambling in the first degree, and possession of gambling records in the first degree.[107] Santobello pleaded guilty to a lesser offense—possession of gambling records in the second degree—after being assured the prosecutor would make no recommendation on the sentence to be imposed. In the meantime, however, the judge originally scheduled to hear the case retired and a new prosecutor replaced the one who originally negotiated the plea. Contradicting the original bargain, the new prosecutor urged the judge to give Santobello the maximum sentence. Santobello appealed. The Supreme Court remanded the case, noting that a defendant lured by false promises cannot knowingly make a guilty plea. The Court held that "when a plea rests in any significant degree on a promise or agreement of the prosecutor, so that it can be said to be part of the indictment or consideration, such promise must be fulfilled." Other courts have noted, however, that if the attorney clearly tells the suspect leniency is probable but not absolutely certain, the defendant "takes a calculated risk in pleading guilty and cannot subsequently complain because his hope was not realized."[108] Finally, the Court asks whether the totality of the circumstances point to a voluntary plea.[109] In one case, for example, a man pleaded guilty to first degree burglary in North Carolina, knowing that he would be sentenced to no more than life imprisonment if he pleaded guilty but that a jury could sentence him to death if it found him guilty.[110] He later contended his plea was involuntary because the state law induced him to plead guilty in order to avoid a harsher sentence if convicted by a jury. The Supreme Court held that all circumstances pointed to a voluntary guilty plea and rejected his claim.

Adjudication

Early Englishmen decided a suspect's guilt or innocence by the "ordeal."[111] Differing in detail over time and place, the ordeal's common feature was its irrationality. One form, the ordeal of the morsel, had the suspect swallowing or at least trying to swallow an ounce of cheese or barley bread. A suspect who swallowed the piece whole and retained his normal skin color was pronounced innocent; a suspect who "choked and grew black in the face" was found guilty. Another form, the ordeal by hot iron, had the hapless suspect carrying a hot piece of iron, weighing one to three pounds depending on the seriousness of the offense, nine feet. Witnesses bandaged the hand and the suspect was exonerated if, after three days, the wound healed. If the wound festered, however, the suspect was proclaimed guilty. English law enveloped the ordeal with meticulous procedure, thereby pointing out the gap between procedure and substance. On the surface a practice may appear highly rational but in substance be highly subjective. Adjudication today, if not decided by plea bargaining, occurs in a criminal trial. It too is governed by ritualized, detailed procedure, some of it stipulated in the Constitution, others in statutes, rules of legal procedure, and common law. But unlike the ordeal, its substance comprehends greater rationality. The following section summarizes five procedural guarantees contributing to a "fair" trial.

Right to a Jury Trial

In all criminal prosecutions, the accused shall enjoy the right
to a speedy and public trial, by an impartial jury of the State
and district wherein the crime shall have been committed. . . .
(U.S. Constitution, Amend. VI)

The trial of all crimes, except in cases of impeachment,
shall be by jury, and such trial shall be held in the State where
the said crimes shall have been committed; but when not committed within any State, the trial shall be at such place or places
as the Congress may by law have directed. (U.S. Constitution,
Art. III, sec. 3)

Many defendants are tried by a judge rather than a jury. Wary of a
jury's vagaries and sensing a judge will be more lenient than a jury,
some defendants deliberately opt for a bench trial. Others have no
choice. According to the Court the Sixth Amendment guarantees a jury
trial only for crimes carrying a possible prison term of over six
months.[112] Some states grant a jury trial in cases involving fewer than six
months in jail but most do not. Thus the state must give a defendant on
trial for armed robbery a jury trial if robbery carries a possible prison
term of over six months and if the defendant wants one. If the defendant
does not want a jury trial he or she may waive the right in two-thirds of
the states.[113] Assume that a defendant has pleaded not guilty, is eligible
for a jury trial, and has chosen to have one. Even after opening all the
gates to a jury trial, more surprises may yet face the defendant. Although
the archetypal jury trial seats *twelve impartial peers* in the jury box who
either *unanimously* vote to convict or retire as a hung jury, these four
stipulations are relative rather than absolute. Consider, first, size.

The Court holds that the traditional twelve-member jury is "a historical accident" not essential to a fair trial.[114] The jury need only be
large enough "to promote group deliberation" and "to provide a fair possibility for obtaining a representative cross-section of the community."[115]
The federal rules of criminal procedure require a twelve-member jury in
federal trials,[116] but many states allow fewer jurors to sit and the Court
has upheld juries with as few as six members.[117] Although the twelve-
juror tradition may not have a rationally based origin, today's research
suggests that large juries are rational. One study showed that the
probability of convicting an innocent person grows when the jury drops
from twelve to six members. The investigator concluded that a six-
member jury "would commit 800 additional errors over a span of 10,000
jury trials."[118]

Unanimity is a second feature of the classic jury trial. Numerous fictional works pit a lone principled juror persuaded of the defendant's innocence against eleven jurors, at least one of whom is a villain who yearns to be free from the stalemated deliberations. In the end the holdout by now thoroughly despised by the other jurors, is vindicated when a surprise character confesses to the crime. A contemporary novelist or playwright tapping this archetypal plot must do some preparatory research, however, in that not all jurisdictions require unanimity. The Court holds that the Constitution requires unanimity in federal trials only when the defendant may be sent to prison for six or more months[119] and it requires only that a "substantial majority" vote for conviction in state courts. The Court decides "substantial majority" on a case-by-case basis. It has upheld convictions secured by 9–3, 10–2, and 11–1 jury votes.[120]

Third, the classic jury is one of peers. Yet only recently has the Court struck down long-standing practices that systematically excluded classes of people, notably racial minorities and women, from juries.[121] Even now the Court requires only that the jury loosely reflect a cross-section of the community. The jury "need not be a perfect mirror of the community or accurately reflect the proportionate strength of every identifiable group."[122] It may underrepresent groups by 10 percent or more and still be a jury of peers.[123]

Fourth, the jurors must be impartial. Peremptory challenges allow the defense to weed out some biased jurors, but pre-trial publicity may be so widespread that all prospective jurors are tainted. Typically the defense will move for a change of venue but more often than not the trial will go ahead in the same jurisdiction, in accordance with the Sixth Amendment's stipulation that the defendant has the right to trial in the "district wherein the crime shall have been committed." It is assumed a juror is able to "lay aside his impression or opinion and render a verdict based upon the evidence presented in court."[124] Sometimes the judge will sequester jurors or "gag" the press, the latter a move that endangers free press and conflicts with the defendant's right to a public trial. Courts will reverse a conviction for jury partiality only in unusual circumstances. For example, the Court reversed the conviction of Wilbert Rideau after a local television station aired a taped and filmed confession Rideau made in jail.[125] Officials estimated that most of the town's 150,000 residents saw the interview at least one of the three times it was aired. The Court stated the trial court should have granted Rideau's motion for a change in venue. "[T]o the tens of thousands of people who saw and heard it," wrote the Court, the interview "*was* Rideau's trial—at which he pleaded guilty to murder."

Right to a Speedy and Public Trial

> The accused shall enjoy the right to a speedy and public
> trial. . . . (U.S. Constitution, Amend. VI)

The Court nationalized the right to a speedy trial in 1967.[126] The right applies to criminal proceedings, detainers, and probably to probation revocation hearings.[127] It does not, however, apply to civil proceedings.[128] No court have decided whether it applies to deportation orders or parole violations.[129] The Court nationalized the right to a public trial in 1948,[130] but this too is a relative right. Commonly it is balanced against the defendant's right to an impartial jury, as discussed above.

Right to Counsel

> In all criminal prosecutions, the accused shall . . . have the
> Assistance of Counsel for his defense. (U.S. Constitution,
> Amend. VI)

A criminal trial is a ritualized event having intricate rules, expectations, and terminology. It comprehends assorted motions, objections, and rebuttals, the technicalities of which practitioners learn after prolonged legal training. Lawyers are middlemen who free defendants from representing themselves, just as legislators free constituents from direct rule. In the same way that lawmaking is only as good as the legislators elected to make the laws, so is legal representation only as good as the lawyers who contract to defend the client in court. A lawyer attuned to the law's many hues builds a defense calculated to withstand challenges from a variety of angles. A mediocre lawyer will conduct an adequate defense but miss possible strategies and weaken his or her client's defense as a result. A defendant not represented by counsel is decidedly at a disadvantage in the criminal trial. Added to the weight the state inherently enjoys in the criminal process is the suspect's lack of familiarity with the protections the law does offer. For example, some rules require defendants to raise claims of faulty procedure at the trial (called "timely objections") in order to raise these claims in later appeals. A person unrepresented by counsel and unaware of these rules will inadvertently forfeit his or her right to raise certain claims.[131]

The Sixth Amendment guarantees the suspect the right to retain counsel for his or her defense. At the very least it prevents the state from refusing to allow the suspect to consult with his or her lawyer when he or she asks to do so. The key right-to-counsel cases of the century have not revolved around this issue, however. Instead the landmark decisions have centered on the state's responsibility for providing counsel for indigent suspects. The Court holds that in certain steps of criminal adjudication the state has the affirmative duty to provide poor defendants with counsel. A suspect unrepresented at trial because he or she cannot afford representation is denied due process. Representation by counsel is a *right* (it requires the state to do something) as well as a *liberty* (it forbids the state from interfering with client–lawyer interaction).

The Supreme Court has greatly expanded the right to counsel since the 1930s. Four areas of this expansion are discussed in the following paragraphs. First, the right to counsel now covers stages prior to the trial itself (see Figure 7.3). This is important because the criminal justice apparatus rolls into gear well before the trial. The state begins accumulating evidence at or even before the point of arrest and the defendant's fate may be virtually sealed well before the trial. Even more significantly, plea bargaining means most defendants do not even have a day in court. A suspect without pre-trial counsel may already have lived through a number of events that irreversibly affect the disposition of his or her case. Suppose, for example, a witness to a bank robbery describes the robber as a young man with a dark complexion, possibly Mexican-American, wearing a black leather jacket. Suppose the state puts the suspect in a lineup along with four white men. The state loads the dice by making it likely the witness will identify the suspect as he is the only one with a dark complexion. Even if police place the suspect in a second lineup with dark-complexioned people, the witness will tend to stick by his or her original choice. As the Court has said, "once a witness has picked out the accused at the lineup, he is not likely to go back on his word later on, so that in practice the issue of identity may . . . be determined there and then, before the trial."[132] An actual example of dice-loading occurred in the case of a Mr. Foster, arrested for robbing a Western Union office.[133] The office's night manager, Joseph David, witnessed the crime. After Foster's companions implicated him, Foster was picked up by police and placed in a lineup with two other men. He differed from the other two because he was tall (six feet as opposed to their five feet, six inches) and wore a leather jacket (the witness had told police the robber wore a leather jacket). David tentatively picked Foster out as the culprit and then, to resolve his uncertainty, met with Foster face to face. He still was unsure, however, so ten days later police staged another lineup. This lineup contained five men. Foster was the only one to appear in both lineups, a fact surely not overlooked by the witness. This time David positively identified Foster. The Court found the procedure

EARLY STAGES

At the point of accusation; e.g., when one is in custody or is "otherwise deprived of his freedom of action in any significant way."
Miranda v. Arizona (1966)

During station house questioning
Escabedo v. Illinois (1964)

Not at pre-indictment lineup
Kirby v. Illinois (1972)

Not at mugshot session
U.S. v. Ash (1973)

Not at fingerprinting
Davis v. Mississippi (1969)

MIDDLE STAGES

Preliminary hearing
Coleman v. Alabama (1970)

Arraignment
Massiah v. U.S. (1964)

Post-indictment lineup
U.S. v. Wade (1967)

For capital crimes in extraordinary circumstances
Powell V. Alabama (1932)

For all federal felony trials
Johnson v. Zerbst (1938)

For all state felony trials
Gideon v. Wainwright (1963)

For all case in which a prison sentence is possible
Argersinger v. Hamlin (1972)

At sentencing

For first appellate felony conviction
Douglas v. California (1963)

Not for convictions in which defendant not actually sentenced to jail

LATE STAGES

Not for first appeal after misdemeanor

Not for second appeal after felony conviction
Ross v. Moffitt (1974)

In probation and parole revocation hearings on a case-by-case basis
Gagnon v. Scarpelli (1973)

Not at prison disciplinary hearings

FIGURE 7.3
PLACES WHERE THE STATE MUST PROVIDE
COUNSEL TO AN INDIGENT DEFENDANT

"unnecessarily suggestive," "conducive to irreparable mistaken identification," and a denial of due process. Foster "stood out" in each lineup so that "[i]n effect, the police repeatedly said to the witness, 'This is the man'."

Questionable procedures may also attend mugshot sessions in which witnesses identify suspects from photographs. Police violate a suspect's rights if they show the suspect's picture and hint to the witness that other evidence indicates the suspect is the culprit. Or police may show single pictures of each stooge but several of the suspect, again giving cues about the "correct" choice. In short, stationhouse questioning, lineups, and other pre-trial procedures are more than innocuous steps. They are key points at which the state gathers information it may later introduce in court or use as a bargaining chip in plea negotiations. Evidence gathered at any one of these stages may be enough to "clinch" the suspect's later loss of liberty. The Court, however, sees only some pre-trial procedures as "critical" stages endangering the suspect's constitutional rights and requiring the presence of counsel.[134] These include the custodial interrogation,[135] preliminary hearing,[136] and post-indictment lineup.[137] A lawyer's presence at these stages warns the police not to load the dice against the defendant and permits the lawyer to observe what is going on in order to prepare a better defense, see what evidence the state has against the defendant, raise procedural questions at the trial, and caution the suspect not to incriminate himself or herself. Other pre-trial stages are not "critical" and therefore are not covered by the right to counsel. They include the pre-indictment lineup,[138] mugshot sessions,[139] and sessions in which handwriting samples,[140] voice recordings,[141] and fingerprints are taken. Even though the Court does not require counsel at these stages, it will presumably reverse a conviction if police used "unnecessarily suggestive" techniques to obtain the evidence.

It is not always clear how the Court decides what is a critical and what is not a critical stage. One wonders, for example, how a pre-indictment differs from a post-indictment lineup when the two are equally vulnerable to the kind of manipulation occurring in Foster's case. Similarly, mugshot sessions yield incriminating evidence but are not thought by the Court to be critical. A partial explanation lies in the Court's changing composition. The Warren Court initiated pre-trial counsel but the Burger Court appears little inclined to extend it further. Thus, when faced with a new claim relating to the right to counsel at a lineup, the Burger Court avoided extending the right to counsel by creating a fine distinction between post- and pre-indictment lineups. The Warren Court's earlier decision involved post-indictment lineups; the case before the Burger Court involved a pre-indictment lineup. The Burger Court held the latter was not a critical stage.

Second, the Court has applied the right to counsel to selected post-trial stages. The offender has the right to counsel for the first appeal after a felony conviction,[143] although not for the second appeal after a felony conviction[144] nor to the first appeal after a misdemeanor conviction.[145] The Court has declined to extend a blanket right to counsel for probation or parole revocation hearings but it has agreed to a case-by-case appeal over the question.[146] The test is this: the parolee or probationer should be granted counsel when he or she asks for counsel on the grounds that the conditions of parole or probation were not violated, or that the conditions were "complex" and/or the parolee or probationer had "substantial reasons" for violating them. The prisoner does not have the right to counsel at hearings involving prison discipline. [147]

Third, the Court holds not only that the defendant has the right to counsel but that the state must inform him or her of this right. *Miranda v. Arizona* required police at the first critical stage—that of custodial interrogation—to tell the defendant that he or she has the right to remain silent and to the assistance of counsel, and that the state will provide counsel if the defendant cannot afford to retain his or her own lawyer. It is not clear whether the defendant must be informed of this right at other stages. Usually it varies by jurisdiction. Some, for example, require the judge who sentences a convicted offender to inform him or her of the right to appeal and the right to appointed counsel.[148]

Fourth, the Court has extended the right to counsel to different kinds of trials. Its first right-to-counsel case, *Powell v. Alabama*, provided only that the state must provide counsel in capital crimes in which the circumstances of the case were extraordinary.[149] That case involved nine indigent black youths accused of raping two white women. The townspeople were hostile, the suspects uneducated, and the likelihood of a fair trial dim. Later the Court required counsel in all federal felony cases[150] and then in all state felony cases.[151] Still later it extended the rights to all cases in which a jail sentence is possible.[152] The Burger Court recently contracted this ruling by holding that the right applied only when the defendant was actually sentenced to jail.[153] Thus, an indigent person on trial for a crime carrying a possible jail sentence but who was not sentenced to jail may not later claim the state violated his or her constitutional rights by failing to appoint counsel. The right to counsel applies only when the defendant loses his or her liberty through imprisonment.

In addition to broadening the right to counsel in these four ways, the Court has given the suspect the right to waive counsel. However, the defendant may represent himself or herself only if he or she does not deliberately disrupt the courtroom[154] and if the defendant waived his or her right to counsel knowingly and intelligently.[155] Consider, for example, the case of Charles L. Thomas, who was charged with murder, robbery, and criminal conspiracy.[156] Thomas elected to conduct his own defense even though he was charged with a capital offense. Relying on an earlier decision in which the Court held that self-representation was a personal right for which the defendant "will bear the personal consequences of a conviction" and which must be "honored out of 'that respect for the individual which is the lifeblood of the law',"[157] the court upheld Thomas's right to represent himself. In concluding that Thomas waived his right to counsel knowingly and intelligently, the court considered these things: the defendant's age (forty-two), education (eleventh grade), intelligence (he was "articulate" and "literate, competent and understanding"), familiarity with legal procedure (he had been arrested and arraigned twice before) and awareness of what he was doing ("he was aware of the seriousness of the crime and the possible consequences," was warned by the judge that his decision could mean the difference between life and death, and was warned he would have no grounds for later appealing his own competency). All of these facts indicated that Thomas knew what he was doing and made his choice "with eyes open."[158]

Courts also consider whether the defendant has a constitutional right to quality counsel. Indigent defendants are represented by court-appointed counsel, public defenders, or voluntary defenders.[159] For various reasons these attorneys may not be as careful as they would be with a privately contracted client. In one case, for example, an attorney failed to find out his client had been committed to mental institutions three times and had tried to commit suicide twice.[160] He also neglected to have his client examined by a psychiatrist and did not study the report issued by a state-appointed psychiatrist. Does such paltry representation violate the defendant's right to counsel? If so, how does one distinguish between incompetent and merely imperfect representation?

The Court has said that "defendants facing felony charges are entitled to the effective assistance of counsel."[161] The Court has not decided a quality-of-counsel case on its merits, however, so one must look to the lower courts for guidance. Most of the tests used by lower courts in the past favored the counsel. Under them defendants bore a heavy burden in showing they received ineffective counsel. These tests include the so-called "mockery of justice" test:

> a conviction will be held invalid on the basis of ineffective assistance of counsel only if the representation was a farce, a sham, or a mockery of justice.[162]

> The test is whether the representation is so adequate as to

amount to no counsel at all and to reduce the trial to a sham and a mockery of justice.[163]

One of the few defendants successfully to use this test was the one with the uninformed attorney referred to above. More recent tests include the following "reasonableness" tests:

The representation must be equal to that which the ordinarily prudent lawyer, skilled and versed in criminal law, would give to clients who had privately retained his services.[164]

A constitutional right to counsel is fulfilled when he is assigned counsel who is a qualified member of the Bar and acts diligently in the defendant's behalf.[165]

The assistance of counsel required under the Sixth Amendment is counsel reasonably likely to render and rendering reasonably effective assistance.[166]

An opinion expressed by one lower court captures today's sentiment about quality of counsel: "an accused is not entitled to the ideal, perfect defense or the best defense but only to one which under all the facts gives him reasonably effective representation."[167] Courts find counsel ineffective if the lawyer made repeated errors,[168] met with the client for only a few minutes,[169] or failed to seek out key information, such as an inquest report or the fact that the client had confessed.[170] They do not equate mere inexperience with ineffective representation,[171] however, nor tactical errors[172] such as the failure adequately to voir dire the jury[173] or make "certain objections and to pursue certain lines of investigation"[174] that hindsight shows would have been preferable.

The Right to Cross-Examine Witnesses

In all criminal prosecutions, the accused shall enjoy the
right . . . to be confronted with the witnesses against him. . . .
(U.S. Constitution, Amend. VI)

This right, part of a centuries-old tradition, guarantees the defendant the chance to confront and cross-examine people who testify against him or her. Were it not for this right, courts would accept false and damaging testimony as given. Cross-examination is the "greatest legal machine ever invented for the discovery of the truth."[175] It gives defense lawyers a chance to point out weaknesses, inconsistencies, and untruths in the witness's testimony; it gives the jury a chance to judge the witness's credibility; it discourages falsification by making witnesses testify under oath.[176]

To illustrate how the state may deprive a defendant of this right, consider the case of Robert Pointer.[177] The state charged Pointer with robbery after the victim, Kenneth Phillips, testified against him at a preliminary hearing. Pointer had no counsel at the hearing so no one cross-examined Phillips, who then moved to another state. The prosecution introduced a transcript of Phillips's testimony at Pointer's trial. On appeal Pointer claimed the state denied him his Sixth Amendment right to confront witnesses. The Supreme Court agreed; Phillips's testimony was never subject to cross-examination. Or, consider the trial of Joshaway Davis, indicted for stealing a safe.[178] The chief prosecution witness, Richard Green, was a minor on probation for burglary. The defense was prevented from impeaching Green's credibility by a state law forbidding the admission into court of evidence revealing a minor's criminal record. Weighing the suspect's right to cross-examine witnesses against the state's interest in preserving the confidentiality of a minor's criminal record, the Court balanced in favor of the suspect: "In this setting we conclude that the right of confrontation is paramount to the state's policy of protecting a juvenile offender."

The Court's confrontation-clause rulings follow a pattern similar to its rulings on other procedural rights. First, it nationalized the right.[179] Second, it allowed the defendant to waive the right if done knowingly and intelligently.[180] Third, it applied the right to stages in the criminal justice system before and after the trial: the right to cross-examine witnesses applies to juvenile proceedings[181] and to probation and parole revocation hearings.[182] It does not apply to the grand jury or other pre-trial hearings,[183] nor to prison disciplinary hearings.[184] Fourth, the Court rounded out the meaning of the right itself. The confrontation clause not only gives the suspect the right to question accusers, but it also gives the suspect the right to "presence," that is, to be "present at all stages of the proceedings where fundamental fairness might be thwarted by his absence."[185]

The Right to Secure Witnesses

> In all criminal prosecutions, the accused shall enjoy the
> right . . . to have compulsory process for obtaining witnesses
> in his favor. . . . (U.S. Constitution, Amend. VI)

Suppose a person charged with assault spent the evening of the crime with a business acquaintance who did not want the details of the transaction publicized and refused to testify on the defendant's behalf. The Sixth Amendment's compulsory-witness clause addresses the problem of the reluctant witness by giving the defendant the right to produce witness on his or her behalf. Through laws empowering the state to subpoena witnesses, the defendant may compel witnesses to appear.[186] The same clause protects the defendant from laws forbidding the testimony of witnesses, such as parts of the English common law that forbade a defendant accused of treason or a felony from producing any witnesses or that barred the defendant from testifying on his or her own behalf.[187] In one case, for example, the Court struck down a Texas law forbidding a co-defendant from testifying on behalf of his or her companion.[188] The Court held that Texas arbitrarily denied the defendant's right to produce a "capable" witness with "relevant" testimony. It opined that the state's rationale—to prevent perjury—bore no rational relation to the statute in that one may not presume a co-defendant will lie to save his or her accomplice. This is not to say that the defendant has an absolute right to secure witnesses, however. Most states by law exempt certain communications from introduction at trial. Among these privileged communications are those between lawyer–client, husband–wife, physician–patient, and accountant–client.[189] Normally the privilege extends only to communications and not to actions. One commentator gives this example:

> a wife may usually testify as to what her husband did but not what he said, i.e., she may reveal that when he came home his clothes were bloody and that he burned his clothes but she may not reveal that he said "I just killed a child with my hunting knife.[190]

The Court calls the right to secure witnesses one of the "minimum requirements of due process."[191] It has nationalized the right[192] and extended it to points other than the actual trial. The compulsory witness guarantee applies to juvenile proceedings[193] and to parole and probation revocation hearings.[194]

Sentencing

Sentencing follows convictions. The offender is sentenced in a separate court appearance that is a "critical" stage requiring the right to counsel. The judge imposes a sentence if the defendant pleaded guilty in plea bargaining; the judge or the jury, depending on the state, imposes a sentence after a jury conviction;[195] and the presiding judge passes sentence after a bench trial. The decision in each case is highly discretionary. The sentencing agent, normally a judge, decides what form the sentence will take and for how long it will be. With *probation*, defined as "a sentence to community supervision without incarceration,"[196] the offender goes free provided he or she follows certain rules, such as reporting all travel and work changes to the probation board.[197] The sentencing agent decides the length and conditions of probation, and the mechanics of imposing the probation in the first place. He or she may, for example, sentence the offender directly to probation, impose a prison term and then suspend its execution in lieu of probation, or may simply put the offender on probation.[198] With a *fine*, usually imposed only for misdemeanors,[199] the sentencing agent decides the amount and, if the offender is indigent, proposes a substitute way for the offender to compensate the state and/or victim.[200] With *imprisonment* the judge decides the maximum and minimum lengths, subject to the statutory limitations, and the prison to which the offender will be sent.

The presentence report, a document containing information about the defendant's criminal record, family life, and cooperation with police, enhances discretion, as does the defendant's statement before the judge.[201] Both the presentence report and the offender's statement allow the judge to tailor the sentence to the circumstances of the individual case. The still-extant hands-off policy followed by courts in sentencing also enhances the judge's discretion. Apellate courts normally uphold sentences,[202] and the Supreme Court indicates this may give the judge unreviewable discretion.[203]

The judge's discretion is limited by bargains earlier reached between the defendant and prosecutor. It is also limited by statutes and the Constitution. The state and federal governments have their own criminal codes defining the time offenders may be sent to prison. Among other things the legislature may, for a particular crime, impose a flat sentence and give the judge only limited discretion, a maximum and minimum sentence and let the judge impose his or her own lengths within the statutory boundaries, or set a minimum length and allow the judge to set the maximum length.[204] Two provisions of the Constitution govern sentencing. The Eighth Amendment bars "excessive" fines and forbids the imposition of "cruel and unusual punishment."

The meaning of cruel and unusual punishment has changed over time. Noting that "bodily pain is not the sole test of cruelty,"[205] the Court now recognizes that punishment need not be physical to amount to "cruel and unusual punishment." For example, the Court has held it is cruel and unusual to deprive a person of his or her citizenship[206] and to punish a person for being a drug addict, inasmuch as the addict cannot control his or her condition.[207] To decide whether punishment is cruel and unusual, the Court considers first the punishment itself, as it did in the expatriation case and in challenges to a public execution,[208] a more severe sentence on habitual criminals than on first-timers,[209] the spanking of school children,[210] and the death penalty.[211] Second, the Court considers the behaviors being punished. For example, it holds that legislators cannot make the mere status of drug addiction a crime. Third, the Court looks at the way officials enforce punishments, holding that a punishment permissible in itself may be unconstitutional because enforced arbitrarily.[212] In 1972, for example, the Court reversed the death sentence of William Henry Furman because his state, Georgia, imposed the death penalty arbitrarily, particularly because it executed a disproportionate number of blacks and very few whites.[213] The decision, *Furman v. Georgia*, prompted thirty-five states to change their death sentence laws so as to reduce discretion in sentencing. Twenty of these states imposed mandatory death sentences for crimes such as first-degree murder[214] but the Court struck down the mandatory death sentence on Eighth Amendment grounds.[215] Noting that the Eighth Amendment requires judges to review the circumstances of each case before imposing a penalty as serious as death, the Court struck down North Carolina's mandatory death penalty law because it treated all offenders as a class, "as members of a faceless undifferentiated mass to be subjected to the blind infliction of the penalty of death."[216] The Court also struck down Louisiana's law mandating death for first-degree murder of a police officer, saying that the state must take into account "particularized mitigating factors."[217] *Furman* and these later cases show that states must strike a delicate balance in sentencing. They must allow some discretion before imposing serious penalties but must not allow enforcement to fluctuate wildly.[218] Fourth, the Court looks at the relation between the crime and punishment, striking down "excessive" punishment. An excessive punishment "makes no measurable contribution to acceptable goals of punishment and hence is nothing more than the purposeless and needless imposition of pain and suffering."[219] This includes imprisoning of a man for three years for hiding a gallon of moonshine whiskey[220] and sentencing a man to thirty-six years in jail for writing bad checks worth $1,500.[221] An excessive punishment is also "grossly disproportionate to the severity of the crime."[222] This includes executing a man for rape.[223] Rape is violent, it injures the victim both psychologically and physically and, "short of homicide, it is the 'ultimate violation of self'." But it does not take away a life. To execute a person for raping another is grossly disproportionate to the crime and is therefore cruel and unusual.

LATER STAGES OF CRIMINAL PROCEDURE
Double Jeopardy

By this time the defendant has either been acquitted or convicted and sentenced. But he or she is not necessarily free from criminal procedure's early and middle stages. Consider the case of Alfonse Bartkus, who was acquitted of bank robbery by a *federal* district court.[224] Savoring his acquittal only briefly, Bartkus next found himself charged with the same crime under *state* law and convicted as a result of the second trial. Or consider the case of Rocco Tateo,[225] who pleaded guilty to four counts of bank robbery and one count of kidnapping. The state dropped the kidnapping charge and the judge sentenced Tateo to twenty-two and a half years in prison for the robberies. Tateo later claimed his guilty plea was involuntary. The appellate court agreed and reversed his conviction, whereupon the state indicted Tateo again, but this time of all five counts. Each case raises questions about the defendant's rights under the Fifth Amendment's double-jeopardy clause: "nor shall any person subject for the same offense to be twice put in jeopardy of life or limb."

Double jeopardy occurs when (1) the state prosecutes a person for the same offense after he or she was acquitted; (2) the state prosecutes for the same offense after the person was convicted; and (3) the state punishes a person more than once for the same offense. One problem involves the meaning of the "same offense." Suppose the state tries a suspect for aggravated assault but the jury acquits him or her. The state then uses the same evidence to try him or her for armed robbery. On the surface the state tries the defendant for a different offense and does not violate the Fifth Amendment. But the state bases each charge on the same evidence. Does this mean it is in fact trying the suspect for the same offense? Most courts say the same evidence is not equivalent to the same offense.[226] It is no more double jeopardy for the state to use the same evidence to bring new charges than for the state to use the same evidence to bring more than one charge in the first place. Defendants who plea bargain might profit from knowing this. By pleading guilty to one or more charges in exchange for the state's promise not to bring new charges later, defendants free themselves from the real possibility of ongoing prosecution.

Two principles limit double jeopardy's scope. First, it covers only certain jurisdictions. It protects a person from being twice jeopardized by the city or twice jeopardized by the state. It also protects a person from being tried first by the city and then the state or vice versa. Thus, Philadelphia cannot twice try a man for selling pornography on the basis of the same evidence, nor can Pennsylvania twice try the man. Moreover,

Philadelphia cannot try him for the same crime as did Pennsylvania nor can Pennsylvania try him for the same crime as did Philadelphia. Double jeopardy does not, however, bar duel state–federal prosecutions. Double jeopardy only limits governments in the same sovereignty and, here is the catch, the Court calls federal and state governments separate sovereignties.[227] Thus, Pennsylvania may try a man for selling pornography after the federal government tried him for the same offense and vice versa.[228] Second, the state may try a person for the same offense if an appellate court reverses his or her conviction on an appeal.[229] This point is often lost to citizens who react angrily to reports that a court reversed an offender's conviction. Reversal does not necessarily free the person; it still allows the state to try him or her again but this time without whatever deficiencies led to reversal the first time around. The state may not, however, charge the person with a greater offense.[230]

The Court nationalized the privilege against double jeopardy in 1969[231] and later made this protection retroactive.[232] The Court also holds that the doctrine of collateral estoppel is part of double jeopardy.[233] Collateral estoppel makes final the outcome of litigation between two parties. It bars the same parties from relitigating an issue. Consider a Washington State murder case in which someone mailed a bomb that killed two people.[234] The state tried a man on one count of murder but a court acquitted him. The state then indicted the man for killing the second victim. The Court said this disregarded collateral estoppel. The first trial established that the suspect had not mailed the bomb. It made the outcome final and barred relitigation.

The Right of Appeal

All states have laws establishing the right of appeal. It is not constitutionally required, however, nor is it absolute.[235] Plea bargainers often waive their right of appeal or at least lose many legal bases for appeal;[236] offenders convicted via a trial lose the opportunity to raise some questions on appeal if they failed to raise "timely objections" during the trial.[237] Most of the Court's decisions have made it easier for offenders to appeal. A number of decisions focus on the rights of indigent offenders and are designed to give poor and rich offenders equal opportunities to appeal their convictions. Holding that "there can be no equal justice where the kind of appeal a man enjoys 'depends on the amount of money he has',"[238] the Court has struck down state practices on equal protection grounds that discriminate against impoverished offenders. For example, a California rule gave state-appointed counsel to indigent offenders appealing their convictions only if an appellate court decided from the trial court record that counsel "would be helpful to the defendant or the court."[239] The Court invalidated this rule on equal protection grounds because it required an appellate court to examine (and possibly prejudge) the trial record of poor persons but not of wealthy persons before giving them the assistance of counsel. In another case the Court required the state to provide a trial court transcript to an indigent defendant for use in his appeal[240] and in a third case held that the state must do so even in misdemeanor convictions and even when the offender is not sentenced to prison.[241] Finally, it held that prisons must provide law materials to prisoners who cannot afford to get them on their own[242] and that prisoners have a "fundamental constitutional right of access to the courts."[243] To put the prisoner's right to access into effect, the prison must "assist inmates in the preparation and filing of meaningful legal papers by providing [them] with adequate law libraries or adequate assistance from persons trained in the law."

Probation and Its Revocation

Increasingly judges put convicted offenders on probation rather than sentencing them to prison. A judge may impose a sentence and then suspend it in favor of probation or may defer sentencing altogether and directly impose probation. Probation sets an offender free to live and work in the community provided he or she follows rules set down by the court. It eases the burden on prisons and bespeaks the suspicion that imprisonment fails to reform criminals and may even harden them.

Probation's conditions are detailed and restrictive. They include standard requirements that the offender report job changes, travel plans, and family developments to the probation officer and refrain from associating with known criminals, owning firearms, or consuming liquor.[244] They also include restrictions tailored to the case at hand. For example, the juvenile court of Bristol, Virginia, required two minors who had thrown stones at a woman's house to attend church as part of their probation. Specifically, the court ordered each to "attend Sunday School and church each Sunday hereafter for a period of one year, and present satisfactory evidence of such attendance at the conclusion of each month to the Probation Officer."[245] A California judge put one Mercedes Dominguez on probation after she was convicted of second-degree bank robbery.[246] As one of the conditions of probation the judge told Dominguez, "you are not to live with any man to whom you are not married and you are not to become pregnant until after you become married." In a third case a court dealt a three-time purse-snatcher this order: "Defendant is not to go out of his house unless he is wearing shoes with leather soles and metal taps on the soles and heels."[247]

Probation limits the offender's rights, just as incarceration limits a prisoner's rights. The probationer undeniably "is held to a higher standard of morality and is more restricted in his movements than citizens not under sentence."[248] Yet the probationer is not bereft of constitutional protection and courts are increasingly willing to review the substantive rights of probationers. Each of the examples above involved conditions that violated the probationer's rights. The church sentence violated the youths' religious freedoms as guaranteed by the state and federal constitutions; Mercedes Dominguez's antipregnancy condition violated due process because it had no rational relation to the crime for which she was convicted (robbery).[249] The purse-snatcher, arguing that the shoe taps were "tantamount of hanging a sign around [his] neck that says 'I am a thief'," claimed it was cruel and unusual to require him to wear taps on his shoes. The appellate court disagreed, but it did strike down the condition for ambiguity. The order did not make clear whether the probationer was to wear the shoes at all times (if so, he would be unable to participate in sports) or just when leaving the house, which would have no relation to purse-snatching.

Courts look closest at probation conditions that intrude on a probationer's constitutional rights. For example, one court struck down an order that the offender make no public speeches while on probation, inasmuch as the condition intruded on his freedom of speech.[250] Work is not a fundamental right, however, so courts usually uphold limits on the probationer's ability to change jobs. As a general rule courts will uphold conditions that do not intrude on the probationer's constitutional rights and that are rationally related to the crime committed. These include forbidding a person convicted of bookmaking by telephone from having a telephone in his home[251] and barring a doctor from practicing medicine after he had performed a lewd act on a ten-year-old patient.[252] One court suggested this test for reviewing the constitutionality of a probation condition: "A condition of probation which (1) has no relation to the crime of which the offender was convicted, (2) relates to conduct which is not in itself criminal, and (3) requires or forbids conduct which is not reasonably related to future criminality, does not serve the statutory ends of probation and is invalid."[253]

Recent decisions also extend limited procedural rights to offenders facing probation revocation. Consider the case of Gerald Scarpelli, put on probation for seven years for armed robbery.[254] One month after sentencing police caught Scarpelli robbing a house. He confessed but later recanted his confession. The probation board revoked his probation, reimposed his original fifteen-year prison sentence, and sent him to jail. On appeal he claimed the state violated his right to due process by depriving him of his liberty without a hearing. The Supreme Court agreed. In a significant decision the Court held that due process entitled a probationer to two hearings: one for the state to determine whether the probationer did in fact violate the probationary conditions and another to decide whether the board should revoke probation for the misdeed. Probation revocation is not formally a part of criminal prosecution said the Court, but it does deprive a person of his or her liberty and thus requires minimal due process.

Serving Time

Substantive rights of prisoners The state punishes an inmate by taking away his or her freedom to live, move, and work in society. As it turns out, however, prison life compounds this punishment in sometimes unexpected ways. Incarceration may lead to assaults and even murder by fellow inmates, the mental torment of solitary confinement, and health problems sparked by unsanitary living conditions. Prison reformers have traditionally directed their attention to brutal jail conditions that endanger inmates. Their efforts, when combined with the growing inclination of inmates to file suit for shoddy and degrading prison life, have led to more court rulings on internal prison conditions. Courts have found individual conditions cruel and unusual, such as shocking isolation cells[255] and "deliberate indifference" to prisoners' "serious needs,"[256] and have also found whole prisons so sordid as to amount to cruel and unusual punishment in themselves.[257]

Imprisonment deprives an offender of his or her liberty as part of a quid pro quo for the offender's having harmed society. Yet liberty is more than the freedom to move; it also is the freedom to think, believe, and make mundane decisions. The question then arises as to what extent a prisoner's other liberties survive incarceration. In theory prisoners share all rights enjoyed by free citizens except those withdrawn by law,[258] yet in practice prisoners find their constitutional rights shortchanged. Many of their grievances involve less visible privations of prison life. For example, a standard rule that inmates be shorn of facial hair disturbs the Orthodox Jewish prisoner whose religion forbids the cutting of body hair. Daily meals of pork or foods cooked in pork fat inconvenience Muslim prisoners whose religion proscribes pork.[259] Censorship and limits on reading materials and visitation also deprive prisoners of basic freedoms. Reformers have recently addressed these and other privations that cause mental rather than physical discomfort.

Prison life is one of the last bastions of criminal justice to break from the hands-off policy of courts. Believing themselves less competent than prison officials to oversee prison policy, judges traditionally avoided reviewing this policy. Without judicial oversight, officials overrode inmates' constitutional rights with impunity. A body of law defining prisoners' substantive rights is growing, however, and judicial review undeniably has helped improve prison conditions. Yet even with these changes prisoners are still a marginal group having only truncated constitutional rights. This is true because courts use tests for deciding when the state violates an inmate's constitutional rights that differ from those it uses to decide when the state violates a free person's rights. Consider, for example, state rules that forbid inmates from soliciting members for prison unions.[260] Such rules intrude on inmates' associational freedoms and arguably violate their First Amendment rights. The Supreme Court has upheld such rules, however, saying that officials may limit associational rights if they reasonably believe the forbidden activities will disrupt prison order. If an analogous law limited the associational rights of free citizens, the Court would use the clear and present danger test and require the state to show the forbidden activities imminently endanger public safety and order. Dissenting in the prison union case, Justice Marshall opined that this was the first First Amendment case in which the Court "deferred to the judgment of . . . officials simply because their judgment was 'rational.' "

At times courts do use the same tests on prisoners as on free citizens, but the outcome still differs because the ground rules differ. Consider the balancing of First Amendment rights against other social interests. Balancing recalls the bromide that "your right to swing your arm ends with my nose," that is, we enjoy freedoms only until they harm society. "Society" to free citizens is the community at large; "society" to inmates is the compact prison community. The different setting changes the probability of balancing's outcome in that it is easier to prove harm to the prison community than to the general community. For example, the government could not justifiably bar the distribution of racially inflammatory Black Muslim literature, but officials have successfully barred this literature in prisons on the ground that it endangers prison order.[261] Because it takes a smaller spark to ignite disorder in the compact prison community than in the society at large, courts have upheld prison rules that prevent a maximum security prisoner from going to religious services,[262] Muslims from receiving allegedly inflammatory publications,[263] and prisoners from wearing religious medals that could double as weapons.[264] The

Supreme Court has also upheld mail censorship when it promotes a substantial government purpose and is the least restrictive alternative,[265] and prison rules forbidding reporters from singling out a particular prisoner for interview.[266]

Procedural rights of prisoners   The inmate is subject to prison rules and to punishment for breaking them. Punishment takes several forms, including the revocation of privileges, solitary confinement, loss of good time, transfer to a less desirable (higher security) prison, and notice to the parole board of the prisoner's misdeed.[267] Each limits a prisoner's freedoms and raises the question whether it intrudes on the prisoner's Fourteenth Amendment liberty and ought to be governed by due process. Consider the case of Nicholas Palmigiano, sentenced to life imprisonment for murder.[268] After Palmigiano served some time in prison, officials accused him of "inciting a disturbance" and informed him they would hold a hearing to consider the charges. They told Palmigiano he had the right to remain silent but that his silence would be used against him. Palmigiano did remain silent, was found guilty of the charges, and was placed in solitary confinement for thirty days. In another case officials transferred one Arthur Fano to a less desirable prison after holding a disciplinary hearing in which they allowed witnesses to testify against Fano and allowed Fano's lawyer to be present, but did not allow the inmate himself to be present.[269] Palmigiano's and Fano's cases are typical because each disciplined a prisoner after holding a hearing that gave the inmate only abbreviated due process rights.[270] Palmigiano had no true right to silence; Fano had no right to cross-examine witnesses.

The hands-off policy still thrives in the area of prison discipline. The Supreme Court did not entertain the procedural merits of a prison disciplinary case until 1976.[271] In that and later decisions it set forth several assumptions. First, inasmuch as "there is no iron curtain drawn between the Constitution and the prisons of this country," prisoners do have some constitutional rights in disciplinary matters. Second, these rights are truncated because disciplinary hearings are not part of formal criminal procedure.[272] Third, the punishment at issue decides whether discipline deprives an inmate of Fourteenth Amendment liberty. Serious penalties, such as loss of time and solitary confinement, do intrude on liberty;[273] "lesser" penalties, such as transfer to another prison, do not.[274] Fourth, minimum due process protection does accompany serious penalties.[275] Before imposing such penalties, officials must notify the prisoner of the charges twenty four hours before the hearing, let him or her call witnesses when doing so will not jeopardize prison safety, provide an impartial hearing, and require the hearing body to state in writing its decision and the reasons for it.[276] The prisoner does not, however, have the right to cross-examine witnesses or to be represented by counsel. Fifth, the Court has not decided whether minimum due process must accompany lesser penalties.[277] Sixth, the Court believes the "better course" is to leave prison matters "to the sound discretion of state prisons," thereby reaffirming its hands-off principle in prison disciplinary matters. Seventh, the prison's unique environment puts different ground rules on procedural balancing. For example, outsiders have the right to confront witnesses but prisoners do not because confrontation "carries obvious potential for disruption" within the prison walls.

Parole and Its Revocation

The inmate either serves out his or her time or hopes for early release through executive clemency[278] or parole. Parole conditionally releases the prisoner.[279] It allows the prisoner to serve the term of sentence outside of the prison provided he or she follows the conditions set down by the parole board. The conditions recall those of probation: among other things they forbid an offender from consorting with known criminals, drinking alcohol, or changing jobs or leaving town without the parole officer's permission. Parole is a discretionary decision of the parole board. If an offender receives a minimum/maximum prison term, the board holds a hearing at the end of the minimum number of years to decide whether to grant parole. The board considers the offender's presentence investigation, behavior while in prison, and evidence suggesting whether he or she is sufficiently reformed to make further incarceration useless. Courts still treat parole as a hands-off matter and the board's decision is usually final. A prisoner who is denied parole must simply await the next hearing.[280]

The offender is free on parole only so long as he or she follows the conditions of parole. If the parole board has reason to think the parolee has violated these conditions, it will revoke parole, as it does in some 35 to 45 percent of cases. Revocation is serious in that it sends the offender back to jail. Moreover, some jurisdictions refuse to credit the offender for time spent on parole. Thus, if the offender serves one year of his or her three years in prison, is paroled for one year, and loses parole, the offender gets no credit for the year on parole and must serve two more years in prison.[281] By being paroled and then losing it, the offender's freedom is curtailed for a longer time than had he or she not been paroled at all. The Court treats parole revocation the same way it treats probation revocation. Each takes away liberty and warrants due process. Each is governed by modified due process, however, because neither is part of formal criminal procedure. Modified due process entitles a parolee to two hearings: a preliminary hearing to decide whether the conditions of parole were violated, and a second to decide whether parole should be revoked. The parolee has the right to appear at each hearing and question evidence brought against him or her. The parolee does not have a flat constitutional right to counsel but is entitled to counsel in certain circumstances.[282]

Rights of Convicted Felons

Assume that a person has moved through each step in the criminal justice system, starting with arrest and ending with conviction, incarceration, and release. He or she will never wipe out the effects of criminal adjudication, perhaps having lost a spouse, job, or reputation. To be convicted of a crime is to be a social miscreant and invite all the hostility people are capable of mustering. In addition to these expected reactions of friends and acquaintances, the offender faces other, perhaps unexpected, discrimination. A convicted felon is subject to legal disenfranchisement, forfeiture of property, exclusion from jury duty, and barriers to public office. Each of these practices is subject to attack under the equal protection clause but because courts usually review them under minimum scrutiny, prisoners have not fared well via the equal protection clause. Moreover, the Supreme Court has upheld disenfranchisement of felons on the basis of Section 2 of the Fourteenth Amendment, a little-known section basing representation on all twenty-one-year-old males except those participating "in rebellion, or other crime."[283] At present forty-six states limit the voting rights of criminals. One-half permanently disenfranchise the felon unless he or she is pardoned; the other half enfranchise felons after they serve their time.[284] Most states restore felons' civil rights after they serve their sentence or are paroled. These states usually require the offender to take the initiative, however; only one-quarter of the states restore a former convict's rights automatically.[285]

SUMMARY

Criminal adjudication is made up of a series of steps in which the state brings offenders to task for their acts. This chapter divides the steps into three stages: early (apprehension and arrest); middle (formal charges, trial, and sentencing); and late (corrections). These stages are shown in

Figure 7.1. Many secondary steps connect these primary stages and smooth out the juncture between each. Between booking and arraignment, for example, police do other things, such as questioning the suspect, preparing mugshots, collecting handwriting samples, and meeting with prosecuting and defense attorneys to set out the ground rules of plea bargaining.

Criminal adjudication is also affected by a series of rights granted the suspected offender. The Bill of Rights contains at least 17 guarantees that make up a "code of ethics" to guide the state as it moves from one adjudicatory step to the next (see Table 7.3). Yet just as secondary steps connect the primary stages, so do secondary protections connect the explicit constitutional guarantees of Table 7.3. The Court has interpreted the Constitution in such a way as to read implicit rights from it and to give each guarantee broader protections than its terse words indicate.

With hindsight we can see a pattern to the way the Court broadens each stated right. First, it nationalizes each right, bringing state as well as federal officials under its control. Second, it broadens the right to cover different steps in the length and width of the criminal justice system. Third, it broadens the meaning of the right itself, giving it new tones and hues. Fourth, it gives the defendant the power to waive the right. To illustrate, consider the Court's treatment of the Sixth Amendment right to counsel. First, it nationalized the right in 1932; second, it broadened the right lengthwise so that today the right to counsel starts well before the trial itself—when the police question the suspect at arrest—and continues well beyond the trial to the first appeal after conviction and, in

TABLE 7.3
EXPLICIT PROCEDURAL PROTECTIONS IN THE
BILL OF RIGHTS COVERING THE THREE STAGES
OF CRIMINAL ADJUDICATION

Early stages

   Reasonable search
   Reasonable arrest
   Reasonable bail

Middle stages

Grand jury indictment	Speedy trial	Arraignment
Double jeopardy	Public trial	Cross-examination
Self-incrimination	Impartial jury	Compulsory witness
Due process	Trial in same district	Counsel

Late stages

   No excessive fines
   No cruel and unusual punishment

limited circumstances, to probation and parole revocation hearings. The Court has also applied the right widthwise to juvenile proceedings. Third, the Court has enriched the meaning of right to counsel by requiring "effective" counsel, and, fourth, it allows the defendant to waive the right to counsel if done intelligently and knowingly. Through these modifications the Court has helped mold one constitutional guarantee to the realities of law enforcement.

To illustrate further how judicial interpretation helps bring the Constitution in line with the daily workings of criminal adjudication, consider the middle stages of criminal justice, which include the filing of formal charges, the trial, and sentencing. Figure 7.4 plots each step on a horizontal axis; it plots the number of explicit guarantees governing each step on the vertical axis. Clearly, most guarantees relate to the trial itself. Figure 7.4 would present little problem if the focal point in criminal procedure were the trial. But plea bargaining, not the trial, is the actual focus of criminal procedure and the prosecutor, not the judge and jury, the most important actor. Figure 7.5 depicts the actual importance of each step as defined by the number of cases disposed within each. When we superimpose Figure 7.5 on Figure 7.4, we see a discrepancy between the Constitution and the realities of adjudication.

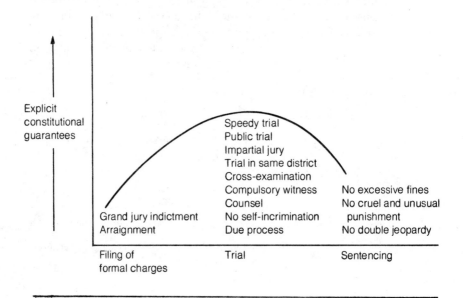

FIGURE 7.4
EXPLICIT CONSTITUTIONAL PROTECTION

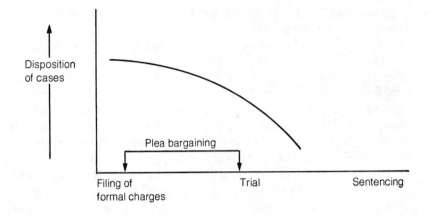

FIGURE 7.5
DISPOSITION OF CASES

At this point we must acknowledge that raw numbers do not adequately measure the Constitution's protection. Instead, judicial decisions determine the Constitution's potency. Figure 7.6 plots a curve depicting the Constitution's protection as defined by Supreme Court decisions. When we superimpose Figure 7.6 on Figure 7.5, we see a closer correspondence than when we pair Figure 7.5 with Figure 7.4. The closer the convergence the more does the Constitution keep pace with the realities

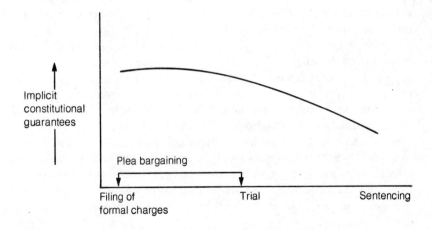

FIGURE 7.6
IMPLICIT CONSTITUTIONAL PROTECTION

of criminal procedure. To this extent the Court has groomed the Constitution as a living document.

To decide how far to extend each procedural right, the Court makes two presumptions. First, it presumes that some steps in criminal procedure deprive a person of liberty and some do not. Due process comes only with those steps that deprive a person of liberty. For example, the right to counsel applies at any trial that sends a defendant to prison. However, it does not apply to a prison disciplinary hearing that sends an inmate to another prison because this punishment does not deprive the inmate of his or her liberty. Second, the Court presumes that some steps are part of formal criminal procedure and some are not. Full due process comes only with steps formally a part of criminal proceedings. A criminal trial is part of criminal procedure. A grand jury session is not, thus explaining why suspects enjoy virtually no due process protection during the grand jury. In short, the reach of each procedural right depends on the step at issue. A step that falls within formal criminal proceedings *and* deprives a defendant of his or her liberty (for example, a trial carrying a possible prison term) brings full due process protection (the right to counsel, cross-examination of witnesses, privilege against self-incrimination and so on). A step that neither falls within formal criminal proceedings nor deprives a person of liberty (for example, grand jury proceedings) brings little if any due process protection. A "mixed" step—one that falls within formal proceedings but does not deprive a person of liberty (for example, a misdemeanor trial carrying no prison term) or that falls outside of formal proceedings but that deprives a person of liberty (for example, parole revocation)—brings some, but not total due process protection.

This chapter shows that the Court has broadened procedural rights more during the early and middle stages than the late stages of criminal justice. The Court tends not to see late steps as part of criminal procedure or as deprivations of liberty. Two things help explain this position. First, the participants in the late stages are nonjudicial personnel and courts traditionally hesitate to review policies framed outside the judicial branch. Second, the Court has changed composition. The more liberal Warren Court heard appeals rising in the early and middle stages; the more conservative Burger Court has heard grievances arising in the late stages of criminal justice. Had the Warren Court sat long enough to hear late-stage appeals, it may very well have expanded procedural rights to cover late stages.

Today's implicit constitutional protection is comprehensive when compared with earlier decades. It is spotty when compared with the size to which it is capable of stretching, however. The Burger Court's hesitance to expand the Constitution's protection leaves open the question whether it will leave today's protection as is or will compress it. The latter happened, for example, when in 1979 the Court drew back from its 1972 decision extending the right to counsel to all trials in which a prison term is possible to apply the right only when the defendant is actually sent to prison.

Questions for Thought

1. Procedural due process affects the rights of people other than criminal defendants because the Fifth and Fourteenth Amendments guarantee that a person will not be deprived of any type of liberty or property by the state without due process. Still, it is an ironic fact that courts have only recently and sketchily outlined the procedural guarantees enjoyed by nondefendants. Consider, for example, the incomplete due process rights accruing to mentally troubled people about to be institutionalized. Even though they may end up being hospitalized indefinitely, they are often institutionalized with fewer procedural protections than those offered the criminal defendant. What precisely are the judicially defined requirements of due process granted to involuntarily institutionalized mental patients? How do they lag behind those granted criminal defendants? Use *American Jurisprudence* and *American Law Reports.* See also *O'Connor v. Donaldson,* 422 U.S. 563 (1975), and Bruce Ennis and Loren Siegel, *The Rights of Mental Patients: The Basic ACLU Guide to a Mental Patient's Rights* (New York: Avon Books, 1978).

2. Lawyers once exercised their power to challenge potential jurors through face-to-face questioning but today they increasingly rely on data produced by social scientists who have used correlational analysis to show the kind of people most likely to vote to convict, acquit, and so on. This has led to what some call the "science" of jury selection. See Jay Schulman et al., "Recipe for a Jury," *Psychology Today,* May, 1973, p. 37; and Edward Tivnan, "Jury by Trial," *The New York Times Magazine,* November 16, 1975, p. 30. In the past judges have looked to such things as sex, race, and age to determine if a jury is truly representative. The science of jury selection raises the possibility that a jury will look representative on its face but be systematically biased in its attitudes. Do new techniques of jury selection warrant changes in what judges look for in an impartial jury?

3. Under the "*Frye* doctrine" the results of scientific tests such as lie detectors and fingerprinting will be admitted in court only if the test is "sufficiently established to have gained general acceptance in the particular field to which it belongs." *Frye v. United States,* 293 F. 2d 1013 (D.C. Cir. 1923); see Peter W. Lewis and Kenneth D. Peoples, *The Supreme Court and the Criminal Process* (Philadelphia: W. B. Saunders Company, 1978), p. 496. New research

has created new methods of gathering evidence, including toothmark identification and voice analysis. Look through *American Jurisprudence* and *American Law Reports* under "Evidence" to find information on these and other new
techniques. How closely do they live up to the *Frye* doctrine?

4. From the crude wiretapping devices of the 1920s and 1930s have come
sophisticated monitoring devices such as the legendary cocktail-pick
recorder. Investigate some of the newest James Bond-like devices (use books
on wiretapping and Congressional hearings on proposed electronic surveillance laws). Do any stand out as particularly ominous? Can you suggest a test
for deciding when electronic devices are so repugnant that they should not be
used in spite of society's strong interest in bringing criminals to justice? Or are
you more concerned about the *procedures* governing the use of the devices?
What are these procedures? See *Berger v. New York,* 388 U.S. 41 (1967), and
the cases cited therein. See also *United States v. United States District Court,*
407 U.S. 297 (1972), in which the Court interpreted Title III of the Omnibus
Crime Control and Safe Streets Act of 1968. A good summary of Court cases
relating to electronic surveillance is contained in Lewis and Peoples, pp.
363-372 (cited in question 3 above).

5. A recurring issue in criminal justice involves entrapment, which is the
"inducement or encouragement of an individual to engage in illegal activity in
which he would otherwise not be disposed to engage" (excerpted from Justice
Department guidelines on FBI undercover operations as reported in *The New
York Times,* January 6, 1981, p. 11). Entrapment got new attention during the
1980 Abscam scandal, in which agents posing as Arab businessmen set up a
"sting" operation that led to the convictions of several U.S. Congressmen.
Read excerpts from the taped conversations between the agents and Congressmen. Do you think the operation amounted to entrapment? This question,
along with the two above, relates to the reasonableness of searches and seizures. In the early part of this century reasonableness tended to center on the
absence of heavy-handed police tactics. Many of today's cases deal with
more subtle methods of gathering evidence such as electronic monitoring and
entrapment. Should what judges look for today in defining a reasonable search
differ from what they looked for yesterday? If so, in what ways?

6. Most courts have done away with the traditional hands-off policy on prison
matters and now actively oversee prison conditions. Today judges recognize
that prisoners do not "leave their constitutional rights at the jailhouse door"
and that they enjoy at least limited versions of the rights of free people. Using
criminal law books, *American Jurisprudence,* and the ACLU's handbook *The
Rights of Prisoners* as guides, describe the First Amendment rights of
prisoners. Do the cases suggest that judges think some First Amendment
rights are *inherently* more dangerous than others when exercised within the
prison community? Does the Supreme Court think some First Amendment
rights are more dangerous than others when exercised in the community at
large? Is there a correspondence between the two rankings? What does your
answer tell you about the values our society places on First Amendment
rights? On the nature of balancing?

NOTES

1. Ill. Rev. Stat. 1977, ch. 40, § 1502. The law does permit a resident of fewer than six months to adopt a child related to him or her or one placed by an agency.

2. Criminal laws usually control acts posing more serious danger to the public. See Vernon Rich, *Law and the Administration of Justice* (New York: John Wiley & Sons, 1975), p. 79.

3. 18 U.S.C. § 1464 (1976).

4. Ill. Rev. Stat. 1977, ch. 38, § 12-1.

5. See Rich, p. 11.

6. Milton Heumann, *Plea Bargaining* (Chicago: The University of Chicago Press, 1978), p. 167.

7. Burton Atkins and Mark Pogrebin, eds., *Discretionary Decision-Making in the Administration of Justice* (Cincinnati, Ohio: Anderson Publishing Co., 1978), p. 1.

8. Ibid.

9. Donald J. Newman, *Introduction to Criminal Justice,* 2nd ed. (New York: Lippincott, 1978), p. 36.

10. *Gagnon v. Scarpelli,* 411 U.S. 778 (1973).

11. 367 U.S. 643 (1961).

12. 384 U.S. 436 (1966).

13. 42 U.S.C. § 1983 (1976).

14. *People v. Scott,* 546 P. 2d 327 (Cal. 1976).

15. David Fellman, *The Defendant's Rights Today* (Madison: The University of Wisconsin Press, 1976), p. 29.

16. Ibid., p. 28.

17. Ibid.

18. Ibid., p. 30.

19. *Sibron v. New York,* 392 U.S. 40 (1968).

20. Rich, p. 16.

21. Quoted in Arnold Markle, *The Law of Arrest and Search and Seizure* (Springfield, Ill.: Charles C Thomas, 1974), p. 51.

22. *State v. Davis,* 231 A. 2d 793 (1967), certiorari denied 389 U.S. 1054.

23. *Davis v. United States,* 409 F. 2d 458, 459-460 (1969), certiorari denied, 359 U.S. 949.

24. *Sibron v. New York,* 392 U.S. 40 (1968). The case is examined carefully in Markle.

25. *Davis v. United States,* 409 F. 2d 458, 459-460 (1969).

26. Ibid.

27. *United States v. Branch,* 545 F. 2d 177 (D.C. Cir. 1976).

28. *Draper v. United States,* 358 U.S. 307, 312-313 (1959). In *Payton v. New York,* 63 L.Ed. 2d 639 (1980) the Court held that police must have a warrant to make any felony arrest in a private home when no emergency existed. In 1976 the Court had held that police could make a warrantless felony arrest in a public place even if no emergency existed, however. *United States v. Watson,* 423 U.S. 411 (1976). Then, in the same year the Court heard an appeal based on the case of a woman who was standing in the doorway of her home and went inside when she saw the officers coming. They caught her and found heroin in a bag she was carrying. Was the heroin

admissible as evidence in court? Yes, said the Court; the woman was in a public place when she stood at the threshold of her home so the police were within the bounds of the Fourth Amendment when they started to make a warrantless arrest. When the woman started into her house an emergency situation existed so the police were again correct in entering without a warrant. *United States v. Santana,* 427 U.S. 38 (1976).

29. Fellman, p. 30.

30. *Cupp v. Murphy,* 412 U.S. 291 (1973).

31. Police also knew the killer did not force entry into the home, leading them to suspect the killer knew the victim. They knew the husband and wife did not get along, the husband had been at the home that night, and that the other person in the house—a son—did not have fingernails capable of making deep gashes on the victim's neck.

32. Fellman, p. 30.

33. Markle, p. 51. For the principles of stop and frisk see *Terry v. Ohio,* 392 U.S. 1 (1968).

34. Jacob W. Landynski, "Search and Seizure," in Stuart S. Nagel, ed., *The Rights of the Accused in Law and Action* (Beverly Hills: Sage Publications, 1972), p. 35.

35. 367 U.S. 643 (1961).

36. See, for example, *Rochin v. California,* 342 U.S. 165 (1952).

37. *United States v. Robinson,* 414 U.S. 218 (1973). "[I]n the case of a lawful custodial arrest a full search of the person is not only an exception to the warrant requirement of the Fourth Amendment, but is also a 'reasonable' search under that Amendment."

38. *Warden v. Hayden,* 387 U.S. 294 (1967).

39. *United States v. Robinson,* 414 U.S. 218 (1973).

40. *Rochin v. California,* 342 U.S. 165 (1952).

41. *Chimel v. California,* 395 U.S. 752 (1969).

42. Ibid.

43. *Harris v. United States,* 390 U.S. 234 (1968).

44. *Chimel v. California,* 395 U.S. 752 (1969).

45. *Warden v. Hayden,* 387 U.S. 294 (1967).

46. *Dyke v. Taylor Implement Manufacturing Co.,* 391 U.S. 216, 221 (1968).

47. *Husty v. United States,* 282 U.S. 694 (1931). The Court struck down the search of a car in *Dyke v. Taylor Manufacturing Co.,* 391 U.S. 216 (1968), however, because the officers lacked probable cause for the search.

48. *Cooper v. California,* 386 U.S. 58 (1969).

49. See Markle, pp. 51-52. See also *Coolidge v. New Hampshire,* 403 U.S. 443 (1971).

50. See Markle, p. 263.

51. *Terry v. Ohio,* 392 U.S. 1 (1968).

52. *Sibron v. New York,* 392 U.S. 40 (1968).

53. Another search and seizure issue concerns the administrative search, in which officials inspect businesses or homes for conformity with fire codes, the Occupational Health and Safety Act, and other laws passed as part of the state's police power. Because inspections will lead to penalties if they uncover noncompliance, many argue that the Fourth Amendment's warrant requirement ought to govern these inspections. The Court now holds that administrative searches do fall within the Fourth Amendment, but it does not require a particularized warrant for every search. Instead, it allows

officials to get an area warrant to inspect blocks of buildings. *Camara v. Municipal Court*, 387 U.S. 523 (1967). The Court held that the Fourth Amendment is activated whenever a person's privacy is threatened by "arbitrary invasions by government officials." *Camara* reversed *Frank v. Maryland*, 359 U.S. 360 (1959), in which the Court held that the Fourth Amendment was activated only when state searches were designed to secure evidence for criminal prosecution. *Camara* is significant not only for its position on administrative searches but also for its more liberal interpretation of the purpose of the Fourth Amendment. It means, says Landynski, pp. 44-45, that the Fourth Amendment protects ordinary citizens as well as suspected criminals.

The Court still declines to treat trips by welfare caseworkers as searches, however. In *Wyman v. James*, 400 U.S. 309 (1971), it rejected the argument that a caseworker must obtain a warrant before visiting the home of a welfare recipient. One Ms. James had claimed that because a visit might lead to the loss of welfare, it was a search within the meaning of the Fourth Amendment. The Court said the recipient could refuse to let the caseworker in but must be prepared to lose payments as a result.

54. *Katz v. United States*, 389 U.S. 347 (1967). The decision reversed *Olmstead v. United States*, 277 U.S. 438 (1928), the Court's first wiretap case, in which the Justices read the Fourth Amendment literally to mean that a "search" had to involve an actual trespass on a person's premises and a "seizure" had to be of tangible items. Between *Olmstead* and *Katz*, the Court held that eavesdropping by way of a spike mike was a search and seizure (*Silverman v. United States*, 365 U.S. 505 [1961]) as was a detectaphone that picked up sound waves and hence conversations in a room (*Goldman v. United States*, 316 U.S. 129 [1942]).

55. *Berger v. New York*, 388 U.S. 41 (1967).

56. Ibid. See also *Katz v. United States*, 389 U.S. 347 (1967).

57. See Landynski, p. 42.

58. Ibid.

59. Ibid., p. 44.

60. *People v. Paton*, 62 Cal. Rptr. 865 (1967).

61. *People v. Allen*, 272 N.Y.S. 2d 249 (1966), reversed 281 N.Y.S. 2d 602 (1967).

62. The suspect "must be warned prior to any questioning that he has the right to remain silent, that anything he says can be used against him in a court of law, that he has the right to the presence of an attorney, and that if he cannot afford an attorney one will be appointed for him prior to any questioning if he so desires." *Miranda v. Arizona*, 384 U.S. 436, 478-479 (1966).

63. *In re Gene Robert Ison v. State*, 200 So. 2d 511 (1967). See also *Rhode Island v. Inis*, 64 L.Ed. 2d 297 (1980), a case in which officers informed a murder suspect of his *Miranda* rights and then drove him to the police station after he informed them he wanted to see a lawyer. As the police drove, they discussed the possibility that a handicapped child would find the murder weapon. The suspect overheard and directed the police to a place where the weapon was hidden, apparently fearing a child would hurt himself with the gun. The Court held that this was not a violation of the suspect's rights because the police hadn't secured the incriminating confession through "interrogation" and had no way of knowing their conversation would appeal to the man's conscience.

64. Peter W. Lewis and Kenneth D. Peoples, *The Supreme Court and the Criminal Process* (Philadelphia: W. B. Saunders, 1978), p. 419.

65. *Kingsley International Pictures Corp. v. Board of Regents,* 360 U.S. 684, 696 (1959) (Frankfurter, J., concurring). See also *Carter v. Kentucky* No. 80—5060 (decided by the Supreme Court March 10, 1981). In this case the Court held that the Fifth Amendment requires a trial judge to instruct the jury that it may not infer guilt from a defendant's failure to testify on his or her behalf *if* the defendant makes a "timely request" to the judge to so advise the jury. In *Griffin v. California,* 380 U.S. 609 (1965), the Court had held that the judge could not comment adversely on the defendant's failure to testify; the *Carter v. Kentucky* decision requires the judge to make a positive comment in order to "limit the jurors' speculation on the meaning of" the defendant's silence.

66. For a review of these decisions see O. John Rogge, "Confessions and Self-Incrimination," in Nagel, p. 67.

67. *Mathis v. United States,* 391 U.S. 1 (1968), held that Internal Revenue Service officials must give *Miranda* warnings to suspected tax offenders and *Orozco v. Texas,* 394 U.S. 324 (1969) made clear that custodial interrogation occurs at the point of arrest, even if the arrest is made at the suspect's home rather than the station house.

68. *Harris v. New York,* 401 U.S. 222 (1971). See also *United States v. Havens,* 446 U.S. 620 (1980).

69. *Michigan v. Tucker,* 417 U.S. 433, 467 (1974).

70. *Riddell v. Rhay,* 484 P. 2d 907 (1971). 404 U.S. 974.

71. Newman, p. 162. If the suspect has committed a minor offense, police will give him or her a citation ("an order to appear at a later date") instead. Ibid.

72. *Miranda v. Arizona,* 384 U.S. 436 (1966). Counsel is not required during fingerprinting (*Davis v. Mississippi,* 394 U.S. 721 [1969], dictum) or the pre-indictment lineup (*Kirby v. Illinois,* 406 U.S 682 [1972]).

73. If the suspect is arrested with an arrest warrant, this stage may be omitted because the warrant will have specified the bail. Lewis and Peoples, p. 76.

74. *Mallory v. United States,* 354 U.S. 449 (1957).

75. See Newman, p. 167.

76. These three reasons are from *Stack v. Boyle,* 342 U.S. 1 (1951).

77. See Lewis and Peoples, p. 965. Of course, this presumes that all other factors are equal.

78. *Stack v. Boyle,* 342 U.S. 1 (1951).

79. Newman, p. 167.

80. Ibid.

81. Ibid., pp. 205-206.

82. Ibid., p. 207.

83. See Fred E. Inbau et al., *Cases and Comments on Criminal Procedure* (Mineola, N.Y.: The Foundation Press, 1974), pp. 487-490, for things the prosecutor takes into account in deciding whether to prosecute. See also Newman, p. 209.

84. This description of the preliminary hearing is based on Newman, pp. 213-221.

85. Lewis and Peoples, p. 773. For example, it gives the defendant the testimony of prosecution witnesses so he or she may point out any inconsistencies between their early testimony and their testimony at the trial.

86. Ibid., p. 73.

87. Newman, p. 213.

88. For example, Virginia requires five, Indiana and South Dakota six, and Tennessee twelve.

89. The only people present are the jurors, prosecutor, stenographer, and witnesses. The jury foreperson carries out tasks such as swearing in witnesses. For a description of grand jury proceedings see Marvin E. Frankel and Gary P. Naftalis, *The Grand Jury: An Institution on Trial* (New York: Hill and Wang, 1977), pp. 43-51.

90. Secrecy is designed, among other things, to encourage witnesses to speak freely (the Court has said that the grand jury's investigative power must be broad if its public responsibility is adequately to be discharged) and to protect the person who is not, in the end, indicted. See *United States v. Proctor and Gamble Co.,* 356 U.S. 677, 681 n.6 (1958).

91. *United States v. Calandra,* 414 U.S. 338 (1974).

92. See Robert O. Dawson, "The Sentencing and Correctional Process," in Nagel, p. 263.

93. *United States v. Mandujano,* 425 U.S. 564, 581 (1976).

94. Ibid.

95. See, for example, Frankel and Naftalis, pp. 123-128.

96. See *Gagnon v. Scarpelli,* 411 U.S. 778 (1973), extending minimum due process rights to parolees and probationers for hearings concerning revocation of parole or probation.

97. Newman, p. 221.

98. For a discussion of plea bargaining's benefits for both state and defendant, see Lewis and Peoples, pp. 974-975.

99. *Santobello v. New York,* 404 U.S. 257 (1971).

100. Newman, p. 223.

101. *Boykin v. Alabama,* 395 U.S. 238 (1969).

102. Ibid.

103. Lewis and Peoples, p. 982.

104. *Pennsylvania v. Claudy,* 350 U.S. 116 (1956). See also *Williams v. Kaiser,* 323 U.S. 471 (1945).

105. Neither federal (*McCarthy v. United States,* 394 U.S. 459 [1969]) nor state (*Boykin v. Alabama,* 395 U.S. 238 [1969]) courts will accept a guilty plea if it does not appear to have been made knowingly or intelligently.

106. *Brady v. United States,* 397 U.S. 742 (1970).

107. *Santobello v. New York,* 404 U.S. 257 (1971).

108. Joel Jay Finer, "Ineffective Assistance of Counsel," 58 *Cornell L.Rev.* 1077, 1083 (1973). See, for example, *Davidson v. State,* 437 P. 2d 620 (1968).

109. *Brady v. United States,* 397 U.S. 742 (1970).

110. *Parker v. North Carolina,* 397 U.S. 790 (1970).

111. For a description of these and other forms of ordeal, see Frankel and Naftalis, p. 8.

112. *Baldwin v. New York,* 399 U.S. 66 (1970).

113. Only one-third of the states *require* a jury trial for all felonies; the other states allow a defendant to waive that right. Newman, p. 236.

114. *Williams v. Florida,* 399 U.S. 78 (1970). The Court said the 12-member jury was just "a historical accident, unnecessary to effect the purposes of the jury system and wholly without significance 'except to mystics.'" The last refers to Lord Coke's

explanation of the 12-person jury as being connected with the sanctity of the number 12. "The *number of twelve*," he wrote, "is much respected *in holy writ*, as 12 *apostles*, 12 *stones*, 12 *tribes*, *etc.*"

115. *Williams v. Florida*, 399 U.S. 78 (1970).

116. Federal Rules of Criminal Procedure, Rule 23(b).

117. *Williams v. Florida*, 399 U.S. 78 (1970).

118. This research is reported by Lewis and Peoples, pp. 604-605.

119. *Apodaca v. Oregon*, 406 U.S. 404 (1972). Congress requires the same thing. Federal Rules of Criminal Procedure, Rule 31(a).

120. *Johnson v. Louisiana*, 406 U.S. 356 (1972), approved a vote of 9–3; *Apodaca v. Oregon*, 406 U.S. 404 (1972), approved votes of 10–2 and 11 – 1.

121. *Taylor v. Louisiana*, 419 U.S. 522 (1975), overturning *Hoyt v. Florida*, 368 U.S. 57 (1961). The state may not automatically exclude women as potential jurors.

122. *Swain v. Alabama*, 380 U.S. 202 (1965). See also *State v. Taylor*, 508 P. 2d 731, 736 (1973): "A defendant is not entitled to a jury which is composed of, with mathematical precision, the exact proportion of his race as exists in the general population. All that is required is a jury selected by a process where the members of his race are not systematically excluded."

123. *Swain v. Alabama*, 380 U.S. 202 (1965).

124. *Irvin v. Dowd*, 366 U.S. 717, 722-723 (1961).

125. *Rideau v. Louisiana*, 373 U.S. 723 (1963).

126. *Klopfer v. North Carolina*, 386 U.S. 213 (1967).

127. At least one lower court has so ruled. See *Fariss v. Tipps*, 463 S.W. 2d 176 (Tex. Sup. Ct. 1971).

128. See, for example, *Levine v. United States*, 362 U.S. 610 (1960). See also Lewis v. Peoples, p. 672.

129. Dawson, "The Sentencing and Correctional Process," p. 275.

130. *In re Oliver*, 330 U.S. 257 (1948).

131. See Lewis and Peoples, p. 1041.

132. *United States v. Wade*, 388 U.S. 218 (1967).

133. *Foster v. California*, 394 U.S. 440 (1969).

134. *Mempa v. Rhay*, 389 U.S. 128 (1967).

135. *Miranda v. Arizona*, 384 U.S. 436 (1966).

136. *Coleman v. Alabama*, 399 U.S. 1 (1970).

137. *United States v. Wade*, 388 U.S. 218 (1967).

138. *Kirby v. Illinois*, 406 U.S. 682 (1972).

139. *United States v. Ash*, 413 U.S. 300 (1973).

140. *Gilbert v. California*, 388 U.S. 263 (1967).

141. Ibid.

142. *Davis v. Mississippi*, 394 U.S. 721 (1969), dictum.

143. *Douglas v. California*, 372 U.S. 353 (1963).

144. *Ross v. Moffit*, 417 U.S. 600 (1974).

145. Lewis and Peoples, p. 584.

146. *Gagnon v. Scarpelli*, 411 U.S. 778 (1973).

147. Lewis and Peoples, p. 539.

148. See Inbau, et al., p. 1480.

149. 287 U.S. 45 (1932).

150. *Johnson v. Zerbst,* 304 U.S. 458 (1938).

151. *Gideon v. Wainwright,* 372 U.S. 335 (1963).

152. *Argersinger v. Hamlin,* 407 U.S. 25 (1972).

153. *Scott v. Illinois,* 59 L.Ed. 2d 383 (1979).

154. *Illinois v. Allen,* 397 U.S. 337 (1970).

155. See *Faretta v. California,* 442 U.S. 806 (1975). The Judiciary Act of 1789 gives the parties in a dispute the right to "plead and conduct their own cases personally or by counsel." See Fellman, p. 226.

156. *Thomas v. Santa Clara,* 126 Cal. Rptr. 830 (CA Cal. 1976).

157. *Faretta v. California,* 422 U.S. 806, 834 (1975), citing *Illinois v. Allen,* 397 U.S. 337, 350-351 (1970) (Brennan, J., concurring).

158. Ibid., at 1058, citing *Adams v. United States ex rel. McCann,* 317 U.S. 269, 279. Not all judges favor the right to self-representation. They argue that it harms the defendant and contradicts the Court's progression of cases granting counsel to all defendants. See *Thomas v. Santa Clara,* 126 Cal. Rptr. 830 (Cal. 1976) (Kane, Assoc. J., concurring): self-representation goes "contrary to a steady trend of the United States Supreme Court to advocate the assistance of counsel at every critical stage of the criminal process." They also argue that self-representation endangers the criminal justice system itself. The bungling self-made lawyer reduces respect for the legal process. Associate Judge Kane, ibid., also notes that self-representation leads to a "veritable breeding ground for interruptions, disruptions and endless admonitions to the jury to disregard improper questions or statements by the defendant. . . ." In addition, self-representation puts the prosecutor in an "untenable position" for it gives him or her no one with whom to bargain and consult prior to trial.

159. Inbau et al., p. 1349.

160. *Brooks v. Texas,* 381 F. 2d 619 (5th Cir. 1967). See Finer, "Ineffective Assistance of Counsel," at 1086.

161. *McMann v. Richardson,* 397 U.S. 759, 771 (1970). See Lewis and Peoples, p. 586.

162. *State v. Watson,* 559 P. 2d 121 (SC Ariz. 1976), referring to *State v. Tellez,* 523 P. 2d 62 (1974). See also *United States v. Jones,* 512 F. 2d 347 (9th Cir. 1975).

163. *Flowers v. State,* 168 N.W. 2d 843, 850 (1969).

164. *State v. Harper,* 205 N.W. 2d 1 (1973).

165. *State v. Meredith,* 469 P. 2d 820, 821 (1970).

166. *Beasley v. United States,* 491 F. 2d 687, 696 (6th Cir. 1974).

167. *State v. Harper,* 205 N.W. 2d 1 (1973).

168. See, for example, *State v. Anderson,* 285 A. 2d 234 (App. Div. 1971).

169. *United States v. Helwig,* 159 F. 2d 616 (1947). Among other things the counsel had no chance to obtain witnesses to testify on behalf of the defendant. The court held that counsel "must be appointed by the court sufficiently far in advance of trial to enable counsel adequately to prepare the defense."

170. *Smotherman v. Beto,* 276 F.Supp. 579 (N.D. Tex. 1967).

171. *United States v. Helwig,* 159 F. 2d 616 (3rd Cir. 1947).

172. *State v. Farni*, 539 P. 2d 889 (1975).

173. *State v. Watson*, 559 P. 2d 121 (1976).

174. *Watkins v. State of Nevada*, 560 P. 2d 921 (1977).

175. *California v. Green*, 399 U.S. 157 (1970).

176. Ibid.

177. *Pointer v. Texas*, 380 U.S. 400 (1965).

178. *Davis v. Alaska*, 415 U.S. 308 (1974).

179. *Pointer v. Texas*, 380 U.S. 400 (1965).

180. *Brookhart v. Janis*, 384 U.S 1 (1966).

181. *In re Gault*, 378 U.S. 1 (1967).

182. *Gagnon v. Scarpelli*, 411 U.S. 778 (1973); *Morrissey v. Brewer*, 408 U.S. 471 (1972).

183. *Pointer v. Texas*, 380 U.S. 400 (1965).

184. *Wolff v. McDonnell*, 418 U.S. 539 (1974).

185. *Faretta v. California*, 422 U.S. 806 (1975), referring to *Snyder v. Massachusetts*, 291 U.S. 97 (1934).

186. See Fellman, p. 98. The Sixth Amendment also gives the defendant the right to testify in his or her own behalf.

187. See *Washington v. Texas*, 388 U.S. 14 (1967) for a short history of the confrontation clause. These restrictions were designed to prevent witnesses with an interest in a case from lying under oath.

188. *Washington v. Texas*, 388 U.S. 14 (1967).

189. See Inbau et al., pp. 1016-17.

190. Ibid., p. 1017.

191. *Morrissey v. Brewer*, 408 U.S. 471 (1972).

192. *Washington v. Texas*, 388 U.S. 14 (1967).

193. *In re Gault*, 378 U.S. 1 (1967).

194. *Morrissey v. Brewer*, 408 U.S. 471 (1972); *Gagnon v. Scarpelli*, 411 U.S. 778 (1973).

195. Newman, p. 254. Some states allow councils of judges to do the sentencing.

196. Ibid., p. 281.

197. See Dawson, "The Sentencing and Corrections Process," p. 268, for examples.

198. See Newman, p. 281.

199. Lewis and Peoples, p. 1009.

200. Courts may not imprison an indigent person in lieu of paying a fine. Such violates the Fourteenth Amendment equal protection clause. *Tate v. Short*, 401 U.S. 395 (1971).

201. The defendant is normally given this opportunity, but it is not constitutionally required. *Hill v. California*, 368 U.S. 424 (1962).

202. Newman, pp. 300-301.

203. *McGautha v. California*, 402 U.S. 193 (1971).

204. For a detailed description of the different statutory formulas governing sentencing, see Newman, p. 256.

205. *Weems v. United States*, 217 U.S. 349, 372 (1910).

206. *Trop v. Dulles,* 356 U.S. 86 (1958). Trop's penalty, expatriation, was "more primitive than torture." Ibid.

207. *Robinson v. California,* 370 U.S. 660 (1962).

208. *Wilkerson v. Utah,* 99 U.S. 130 (1878).

209. *McDonald v. Massachusetts,* 180 U.S. 311 (1901).

210. *Ingraham v. Wright,* 430 U.S. 651 (1977).

211. *In re Kemmler,* 136 U.S. 436 (1890); *Gregg v. Georgia,* 428 U.S. 153 (1976); *Proffitt v. Florida,* 428 U.S. 242 (1976); *Jurek v. Texas,* 428 U.S. 262 (1976); *Woodson v. North Carolina,* 428 U.S. 280 (1976).

212. *Furman v. Georgia,* 408 U.S. 238 (1972).

213. Ibid. The case was decided with two others.

214. Fellman, p. 419.

215. *Woodson v. North Carolina,* 428 U.S. 280 (1976).

216. Ibid.

217. *Harry Roberts v. Louisiana,* 431 U.S. 633 (1977).

218. See *Gregg v. Georgia,* 428 U.S. 153 (1976); *Proffitt v. Florida,* 428 U.S. 242 (1976); and *Jurek v. Texas,* 428 U.S. 262 (1976).

219. *Coker v. Georgia,* 433 U.S. 584 (1977).

220. *Nowling v. State,* 10 So. 2d 130 (1942), described in Fellman, p. 105.

221. *Faulkner v. State,* 445 P. 2d 815 (Ala. 1968), described in Fellman, p. 406.

222. *Weems v. United States,* 217 U.S. 349 (1910).

223. *Coker v. Georgia,* 433 U.S. 584 (1977).

224. *Bartkus v. Illinois,* 359 U.S. 121 (1959).

225. *Tateo v. United States,* 377 U.S. 463 (1964).

226. Jay A. Sigler, "The New Broom: The Federalization of Double Jeopardy," in Nagel, p. 291.

227. *Waller v. Florida,* 397 U.S. 387 (1970). See Sigler, p. 387.

228. *United States v. Lanza,* 260 U.S. 377 (1922). Sigler, p. 293, thinks this rule will eventually fall. Lewis and Peoples, p. 387, think its validity is questionable in light of *Benton v. Maryland,* 395 U.S. 784 (1969), which nationalized double jeopardy.

229. Lewis and Peoples, p. 386.

230. *Price v. Georgia,* 398 U.S. 323 (1970). See Lewis and Peoples, p. 389.

231. *Benton v. Maryland,* 395 U.S. 784 (1969).

232. *Ashe v. Swenson,* 397 U.S. 436 (1970).

233. Ibid. Previously courts treated collateral estoppel as part of due process.

234. *Harris v. Washington,* 404 U.S. 55 (1971), described in Lewis and Peoples, p. 404.

235. Lewis and Peoples, p. 1040. The Court has not directly addressed the question, but it has indicated in dictum that the state need not provide for appeal. See *Ross v. Moffitt,* 417 U.S. 600, 606 (1974).

236. Lewis and Peoples, p. 1040.

237. Ibid., p. 1041.

238. *Douglas v. California,* 312 U.S. 353 (1963).

239. Ibid.

240. *Griffin v. Illinois,* 351 U.S. 12 (1956). A transcript may cost over $300. The state may, said the Court, substitute information making up a "record of sufficient completeness" for a full transcript.

241. *Mayer v. City of Chicago,* 404 U.S. 189 (1971).

242. *Younger v. Gilmore,* 404 U.S. 15 (1971).

243. *Bounds v. Smith,* 430 U.S. 817 (1977). Presumably this right rests upon due process, although the Court did not specify its source.

244. For a description of common conditions of probation, see Lewis and Peoples, p. 1009, and Newman, pp. 313-319.

245. *Jones v. Commonwealth,* 38 S.E. 2d 444, 445 (1946).

246. *People v. Dominguez,* 64 Cal. Rptr. 290 (1967).

247. *People v. McDowell,* 130 Cal. Rptr. 839 (1976).

248. Lewis and Peoples, p. 1009.

249. Nor did the condition bear a reasonable relation to the likelihood of future criminality. As the court remarked, "It is certainly not pragmatically demonstrable that unmarried, pregnant women are disposed to commit crimes."

250. *Hyland v. Procunier,* 311 F.Supp. 747 (N.D. Cal. 1970).

251. *People v. Stanley,* 327 P. 2d 973 (1958).

252. *People v. Frank,* 211 P. 2d 350 (1949).

253. *People v. Dominguez,* 64 Cal. Rptr. 290 (1967).

254. *Gagnon v. Scarpelli,* 411 U.S. 778 (1973).

255. See, for example, *Jordan v. Fitzharris,* 257 F.Supp. 674 (N.D. Cal. 1966). The inmate was confined for eleven days to a six foot by eight foot, four inch "strip cell" in which "he was not adequately protected from the wet weather, he was deprived of all items by which he might maintain bodily cleanliness; he was forced to eat the meager prison fare in the stench and filth caused by his own vomit and body wastes; he could wash his hands only once every five days; and he was required to sleep naked on a stiff canvas mat placed directly on the cold concrete floor." Ibid., at 680.

256. *Estelle v. Gamble,* 429 U.S. 97 (1976).

257. See *Holt v. Sarver,* 300 F. Supp. 825 (1969); *Holt v. Sarver* II, 309 F. Supp. 362 (1970). The Court said in *Holt v. Sarver* I that "[f]or the ordinary convict a sentence to the Arkansas Penitentiary today amounts to a banishment from civilized society to a dark and evil world completely alien to the free world. . . ." The court referred to the prison's trustee system, unsanitary conditions, racism, and lack of rehabilitation program.

258. *Procunier v. Martinez,* 416 U.S. 396, 422 (1974), (Marshall, J., concurring), quoting *Coffin v. Reichard,* 143 F. 2d 443, 445 (6th Cir. 1944). "A prisoner retains all the rights of an ordinary citizen except those expressly, or by necessary implication, taken from him by law."

259. *Finney v. Hutto,* 410 F.Supp. 251 (1976).

260. *Jones v. North Carolina Prisoners' Labor Union, Inc.* 433 U.S. 119 (1977).

261. See, for example, *Pierce v. La Vallee,* 212 F. Supp. 865 (1962), affirmed 319 F.2d 844, certiorari denied 376 U.S. 918.

262. *Graham v. Willingham,* 265 F.Supp. 763 (1967), affirmed 384 F. 2d 367.

263. *Knuckles v. Prasse,* 302 F.Supp. 1036 (1969).

264. *Rowland v. Jones,* 452 F. 2d 1005 (8th Cir. 1971).

265. It holds, however, that prison officials must notify the prisoner of censorship and allow him or her to protest. *Procunier v. Martinez*, 416 U.S. 396 (1974).

266. *Pell v. Procunier*, 417 U.S. 817 (1974); *Saxbe v. Washington Post*, 417 U.S. 843 (1974). The Court said this made the press equal to everyone else. The decision was directed to the press more than prisoners but interfered with the rights of prisoners in the process.

267. David Rudovsky, et al., *The Rights of Prisoners*, rev. ed. (New York: Avon Books, 1977), pp. 19-20. The last will affect the prisoner's chances of parole.

268. *Baxter v. Palmigiano*, 425 U.S. 308 (1976).

269. *Meachum v. Fano*, 427 U.S. 215 (1976).

270. Often no hearings are held at all. See Rudovsky, p. 19.

271. *Wolff v. McDonnell*, 418 U.S. 539 (1974).

272. See *Baxter v. Palmigiano*, 425 U.S. 308 (1976).

273. *Wolff v. McDonnell*, 418 U.S. 539 (1974).

274. *Baxter v. Palmigiano*, 425 U.S. 308 (1976). It said in *Meachum v. Fano*, 427 U.S. 215 (1976), that because "life in one prison is much more disagreeable than in another does not in itself signify that a Fourteenth Amendment liberty interest is implicated when a prisoner is transferred to the institution with the more severe rules."

275. *Baxter v. Palmigiano*, 425 U.S. 308 (1976).

276. *Wolff v. McDonnell*, 418 U.S. 539 (1974).

277. *Baxter v. Palmigiano*, 425 U.S. 308 (1976).

278. A prisoner who is pardoned enjoys permanent freedom inasmuch as the pardon is final and free from judicial review. Lewis and Peoples, p. 903. A person who accepts a pardon implicitly admits his or her guilt—*Burdick v. United States*, 236 U.S. 79 (1915)—a fact giving some balm to those angry with Gerald Ford's pardon of Richard Nixon.

279. Dawson, "The Sentencing and Correctional Process," p. 276.

280. Ibid.

281. *Morrissey v. Brewer*, 408 U.S. 471 (1972).

282. Ibid.

283. *Richardson v. Ramirez*, 418 U.S. 24 (1974).

284. Lewis and Peoples, p. 799.

285. Ibid., p. 804.

‖ Conclusion

This book started off with three litigants—a young man "sentenced" to wear tap shoes, a member of a religious sect who refused to have his picture on his driver's license, and a young man who had to wait three years longer than his female friends to buy beer in the state of Oklahoma. Each ran headway into a state practice and each claimed the government violated one of his constitutional rights—the first his Eighth Amendment right to be free from cruel and unusual punishment, the second his First Amendment right freely to exercise his religion, and the third his Fourteenth Amendment entitlement to the equal protection of the laws. These cases illustrate the variety of claims entertained in the courts each year. They also point out the dilemma at the base of constitutional interpretation. The Bill of Rights grants us liberties but, as one jurist has said, "Your right to swing your arm ends where my nose begins." No one said our rights and liberties are absolute. But neither does the state have free clearance to regulate whenever and wherever it thinks necessary. The true status of our constitutional rights comes from the meaning judges put into the Constitution's skeletal words as they balance social right against social right in the progression of cases that come before them each year.

Judges approach these cases with a cushion built by generations of preceding case law. Far from sitting on the bench with untainted naiveté, judges have at their disposal the values and principles handed down by their precedessors as they too balanced social right against social right. Chief Justice Earl Warren once said that we live in a sea of ethics, but we must not carry the sea metaphor too far because it suggests untamed elements that thwart human efforts of understanding while in fact the empiricism of the Western mind shuns romanticism in order to identify, understand, and control natural phenomena. Thus, just as the scientist studies the sea empirically, so can the student of the legal process analyze the ethical foundation of our law in order to make it more fathomable. It is hoped that this book's discussion of the gradations the Supreme Court has given our constitutional rights will help readers understand our sea of judicial ethics and approach the legal dilemmas coming before the courts each year with an appreciation of the values with which judges see the cases.

A principal theme of this book is that the Court has created gradations *among* liberties in the Bill of Rights that show its preference for some liberties over others. The void-for-vagueness and overbreadth tests, for example, show a special Court concern for the First Amendment; the strict scrutiny test shows the Court's distrust of racial classifications and its willingness to use the Fourteenth Amendment to purge statute books of these laws. But once this theme is expressed, one may properly ask "So what?" Of what significance is the fact that some liberties are more protected than others? What do these gradations tell us about the nature of our legal values? Our social and political values? Might the reader prefer a different ranking? If so, what does this say about his or her values?

A second theme is that the Court has created gradations *within* each guarantee in the Bill of Rights. Thus, free speech is complex and prismatic, not monolithic, as is free press, the right to a fair trial, the right to privacy, and other guarantees. Again we ask "So what?" What do these gradations tell us about the nature of our social, political, and legal values? Should more gradations be created? Or should the Court move back toward monolithic guarantees? To illustrate, is it better to have slightly different case law for each of the media that make up the press or is it better to treat all media the same? Is it preferable to treat some speech as more useful than others or should all speech be equally valued? Should procedural due process be the same in the early, middle, and late stages of criminal adjudication or should lesser protections be afforded in the early and late stages?

These questions presuppose a rationality in constitutional interpretation. It is important to keep in mind, however, that each gradation is not necessarily a carefully planned, inductively reached cog in a larger legal framework. Instead, some gradations may well be sired by idiosyncratic quirks in judicial reasoning. Our law is the product of miscellaneous, sometimes indecipherable, influences. Thus, to the above questions may be added these: Which gradations have the strongest *legal* foundation? Which are less well grounded in precedent and based instead on quixotic, less easily identifiable influences? And most importantly, is a doctrine any less respectable if not squarely grounded on precedent?

A third theme emerges in the questions posed at the end of each chapter. Chapter 3 asks about the effects that nonscarce cable television are likely to have on free press law. Chapter 5 considers a legal quandary that arose after a man was surgically transformed into a woman; Chapter 6 looks at the dilemmas caused by sophisticated fetal experimentation and the availability of artificial life-support machines; and Chapter 7 poses questions about voice analysis, toothmark identification, and electronic surveillance. Each question revolves around technological changes in our society and each points to the need to keep the Constitution alive and in tune with rapidly accelerating technological advances. No end is in sight for more scientific wizardry in the coming decades. Among the envisioned changes will be in-the-home computer systems, test-tube conception and gestation, and genetic manipulation. Each promises new grist for the evolution of our rights and liberties, particularly for the right to privacy. Keeping in mind that the right to privacy is not explicitly stated in the Constitution, we are justified in asking about the adequacy of the document in the twentieth-century world. It is fitting that the Constitution "live" through interpretation, but one wonders if there is a danger when an unstated right receives so much attention that people lose sight of the fact that it was not included in the document as originally framed. Thus, we may ask about expected changes in the contours of the Constitution in the next twenty to thirty years. Will technology relate to some guarantees more than others? Will public attention shift to one or more rights in particular? Might others become anachronistic in the twentieth and twenty-first centuries?

Related to technological changes are the sometimes overwhelming social changes afoot in our society. These, too, suggest a continued shift in the evolution of rights and liberties. Consider, for example, the effects a growing divorce rate will have on the nature of the family. The right to privacy gives the family power to make intimate decisions. But what is the "family?" What if there are two sets of parents and four or more sets of grandparents? Are blood ties always stronger than marital ties? Should a blood-linked grandparent have greater authority than a step-parent to make decisions about a child's welfare? Or consider the aging of the U.S. population. Policy-makers are increasingly concerned about the financial burden an aging population will put on the shrinking "younger" base of people. Might the aged mount the next human rights movement as did blacks and women in the 1950s through 1970s? Another development comes from problems in the American economic system that create such maladies as inflation and that gnaw away at the government's ability to pay for expected services. This forewarns of a change in the way we do things; for example, rising prison costs may force us to revamp our ideas about what to do with convicted criminals and to consider alternative ways of penalizing them. Finally, we can foresee great changes coming from shortages of natural resources. Traditionally we approve government intrusions into our private lives if the government's interest in imposing them is compelling. We usually think that *compelling* means the survival of the state through the control of violence and war. But does survival now go beyond the preservation of peace? How far can the government reach into our rights and liberties to ration and regulate natural resources? How will paucity where there was once abundance affect the values that go into the balancing of rights and liberties?

"There is no such thing as an achieved liberty," Justice Jackson wrote, "[and] like electricity, there can be no substantial storage and it must be generated as it is enjoyed or the lights go out." This book outlines the status of our liberties today and alludes to the frustrating and delicate processes that went into the evolution of these liberties. The questions this conclusion poses point to the tenuousness of the liberties and warn that the study of civil liberties must not impart an air of finality. The Justices will continue to interpret, perhaps adding to our liberties and perhaps subtracting from them. Yet the principles covered in this book will still be pertinent because they feed the sea of ethics that is the foundation of our system of jurisprudence. The predisposition to use precedent ensures that judges will tap this foundation as they interpret the Constitution in yet unknown ways.

Appendix ‖

SELECTED AMENDMENTS TO THE CONSTITUTION

AMENDMENT I

Congress shall make no law respecting an establishment of religion, or prohibiting the free exercise thereof; or abridging the freedom of speech, or of the press; or the right of the people peaceably to assemble, and to petition the Government for a redress of grievances.

AMENDMENT II

A well regulated Militia, being necessary to the security of a free State, the right of the people to keep and bear Arms, shall not be infringed.

AMENDMENT III

No Soldier shall, in time of peace be quartered in any house, without the consent of the Owner, nor in time of war, but in a manner to be prescribed by law.

AMENDMENT IV

The right of the people to be secure in their persons, houses, papers, and effects, against unreasonable searches and seizures, shall not be violated, and no Warrants shall issue, but upon probable cause, supported by Oath or affirmation, and particularly describing the place to be searched, and the persons or things to be seized.

AMENDMENT V

No person shall be held to answer for a capital, or otherwise infamous crime, unless on a presentment or indictment of a Grand Jury, except in cases arising in the land or naval forces, or in the Militia, when in actual service in time of War or public danger; nor shall any person be subject for the same offence to be twice put in jeopardy of life or limb; nor shall be compelled in any criminal case to be a witness, against himself, nor be deprived of life, liberty, or property, without due process of law; nor shall private property be taken for public use, without just compensation.

AMENDMENT VI

In all criminal prosecutions, the accused shall enjoy the right to a speedy and public trial, by an impartial jury of the State and district wherein the crime shall have been committed, which district shall have been previously ascertained by law, and to be informed of the nature and cause of the accusation; to be confronted with the witnesses against him; to have compulsory process for obtaining witnesses in his favor, and to have the Assistance of Counsel for his defense.

AMENDMENT VII

In suits at common law, where the value in controversy shall exceed twenty dollars, the right of trial by jury shall be preserved, and no fact tried by a jury, shall be otherwise re-examined in any Court of the United States, than according to the rules of the common law.

AMENDMENT VIII

Excessive bail shall not be required, nor excessive fines imposed, nor cruel and unusual punishments inflicted.

AMENDMENT IX

The enumeration in the Constitution, of certain rights, shall not be construed to deny or disparage others retained by the people.

AMENDMENT X

The powers not delegated to the United States by the Constitution, nor prohibited by it to the States, are reserved to the States, respectively, or to the people.

AMENDMENT XIII

Section 1 Neither slavery nor involuntary servitude, except as a punishment for crime whereof the party shall have been duly convicted, shall exist within the United States, or any place subject to their jurisdiction.

Section 2 Congress shall have power to enforce this article by appropriate legislation. [Adopted in 1865.]

AMENDMENT XIV

Section 1 All persons born or naturalized in the United States, and subject to the jurisdiction thereof, are citizens of the United States and of the State wherein they reside. No State shall make or enforce any law which shall abridge the privileges or immunities of citizens of the United States; nor shall any State deprive any person of life, liberty, or property, without due process of law; nor deny to any person within its jurisdiction the equal protection of the laws. [Adopted in 1868.]

AMENDMENT XV

Section 1 The right of citizens of the United States to vote shall not be denied or abridged by the United States or by any State on account of race, color, or previous condition of servitude.

Section 2 The Congress shall have power to enforce this article by appropriate legislation. [Adopted in 1870.]

Case Index   ∥

291

Subject Index

303